# Fallen Astronauts

# Fallen Astronauts

## Heroes Who Died Reaching for the Moon

### Colin Burgess and Kate Doolan, with Bert Vis

WITH A FOREWORD BY
Captain Eugene A. Cernan, U.S. Navy (Ret.), Commander, Apollo 17

UNIVERSITY OF NEBRASKA PRESS  •  LINCOLN AND LONDON

© 2003
by the Board of Regents
of the University of Nebraska
All rights reserved
Manufactured in the United States of America
⊗
Library of Congress Cataloging-in-Publication Data
Burgess, Colin, 1947–
Fallen astronauts ;
heroes who died reaching for the moon /
Colin Burgess and
Kate Doolan, with
Bert Vis ;
with a foreword by Eugene A. Cernan.
p.   cm.
Includes
bibliographical references
and index.
ISBN 0-8032-1332-8
(cloth : alk. paper)
ISBN 0-8032-6212-4
(pbk : alk. paper)
1. Astronauts—United States—Biography.
2. Astronauts—Soviet Union—Biography.
3. Space flight to the moon—History.
4. Astronauts—Death.
I. Doolan, Kate 1962–
II. Vis, Bert.
III. Title.
TL789.85.A1B85 2003
629.45'0092'2—dc21
[B]
2003042662

In memory of Dr. Patricia ("Patty") Hilliard Robertson, 1963–2001
NASA Astronaut Class XVII, 1998

*She touched our lives only briefly,*
*and her dreams died in a mere instant of time,*
*yet the authors wish to dedicate this book*
*to the extraordinary and prodigious life of a person*
*whose dedication, spirit, and tenacity*
*went hand in hand with a gentle and capricious amiability*
*that endeared her to all those who knew her or knew of her.*

*Now it is time to take longer strides—time for a great new American enterprise—time for this nation to take a clearly leading role in space achievement, which in many ways may hold the key to our future on Earth. . . . First, I believe that this nation should commit itself to achieving the goal, before this decade is out, of landing a man on the Moon and returning him safely to the Earth. No single space project in this period will be more impressive to mankind, or more important for the long-range exploration of space; and none will be so difficult or expensive to accomplish.*

From U.S. President John F. Kennedy's
Special Address to Congress on Urgent National Needs,
the Capitol, Washington DC, 25 May 1961

*We choose to go to the Moon. We choose to go to the Moon in this decade and do the other things not because they are easy, but because they are hard; because that goal will serve to organize and measure the best of our energies and skills; because that challenge is one that we are willing to accept, one we are unwilling to postpone, and one which we intend to win, and the others, too.*

From U.S. President John F. Kennedy's
address at Rice University, Houston,
12 September 1962

Fleeting Shadows
(For the Eight)

*These noble few, whose names recall*
*A time of loss, a hero's fall.*
*When shrieking rockets pierced the sky*
*And soaring upwards lit my eye*
*To wondrous things, to frontiers new,*
*But there was pause, and silence too.*
*Who knows what ventures yet to see,*
*But suddenly, so suddenly,*
*Dark headlines brought your names afore,*
*Explorers gone, their dreams no more.*
*Oh noble few, whose starry light*
*Fell like a moonbeam o'er the night,*
*Fly once together into space,*
*Dreams unfulfilled you might embrace.*
*In bold formation contrails signed*
*Dancing daggers far behind.*
*As to the darkest night of all*
*Each lifted in their spirit's call.*
*A playful sunlight flayed their wings*
*And sparkled spoke of earthly things.*
*Up they flew, beyond the blue,*
*Where star-kissed heavens soft imbue.*
*All outward flew, and yet too soon*
*Cast fleeting shadows on the Moon.*

Colin Burgess

# Contents

# Illustrations

# Foreword

Over the past three decades, hardly a day has gone by when I am not asked about some aspect of being the last man to stand on the moon. Millions upon millions of words have been written about this amazing adventure, and yet people are still curious to know what it was like. I even wrote my own book, not just to help answer many of these questions but also so my own grandchildren would know through my words what it was like to live out my dreams. I did not think there could possibly be another book about the Apollo program that would reveal something new or some avenue that had not been explored. But I was wrong.

This is a book about some extraordinary men I worked with in accomplishing that lunar triumph. Most were my good friends as well as colleagues but tragically they fell short of their dreams. In eight years we went from blasting a man into space on a quick ballistic flight to that incredible day in July 1969 when Neil Armstrong first set foot on another world. For each of those eight years we lost an astronaut, but the tremendous pain of this loss could not be sustained for long in our nation's race to the moon. Mission followed hard on the heels of mission, and our training took place at breakneck speed as engineers and planners worked with diligence and inspiration to achieve our goal of a manned lunar landing.

This wonderful book brings back many profound and even long-forgotten memories of the men behind those eight names—not just as NASA astronauts training to go into space (and these stories are told) but as loving sons, husbands, fathers, and brothers whose loss still sits deep in the hearts of those they left behind.

It is quite rightly pointed out that these men would have accomplished much in Apollo and post-Apollo programs. Several of them would have gone to the moon, and some undoubtedly would have walked across its powdery surface. The history of human spaceflight altered significantly because of their deaths, and many of us realize we got our chances only because they were no longer in the queue in front of us.

In these pages the authors recall a day in 1991 when the Astronaut Memorial Mirror was unveiled at the Kennedy Space Center, and it was a day I remember well. The families of all fifteen astronauts named on the Mirror had been invited, and I was up on stage representing the astronaut corps. It was an incredibly moving experience for me as I looked out on this sea of many familiar faces—the families of those men I'd known so well so long ago. They were the ones who truly knew the meaning of the sacrifices involved in such a major undertaking. Some were openly weeping as they made their way up on stage, and some were smiling. Many told me how intensely proud they were that day and of the enormous love they still felt for those whose names are forever engraved into this wonderful memorial. The epilogue's reflective words of the children moved me a great deal, as they spoke of fleeting recollections or even in some cases a father they had never known.

Yes, I found out a lot about these men, and I am astonished by the thoroughness and respectful sincerity of the research carried out by the authors. I am impressed that they turned up so many new facts and fresh anecdotes after the passage of more than three decades and that this could be accomplished by three people living around the world. It means a lot to me that the authors derived most of the information from the families of these men rather than reiterating tired and often incorrect profiles from old newspapers and magazines. Every chapter was meticulously checked and edited by at least one member of each family to ensure complete authenticity, and I know the loved ones appreciated this opportunity. That the authors managed to capture the spirit of each of the men in these stories, at the same time intertwining the fascinating story of our race to the moon, is a credit to them and their spirit of perseverance.

This book means a lot to me, because Ted, Elliot, Charlie, Gus, Roger, both Eds, and C.C. meant a lot to me. I now know a great deal more about them and admire them still, even though there were passages in this book in which I had to relive the anguish and trauma of their passing.

The publication of *Fallen Astronauts* provides a fitting closure to the story of Apollo, and I know as I write these words that it is one book I will always accord a prominent place on my bookshelf and in my heart.

*Captain Eugene A. Cernan, U.S. Navy (ret.)*
     Pilot, Gemini IX
     Lunar module pilot, Apollo 10
     Commander, Apollo 17

# Introduction

In the final phases of the last moon walk by the Apollo 15 astronauts on 2 August 1971, a small but unsanctioned ceremony was carried out amid the deep lunar valleys at Hadley Rille.

Mission commander Dave Scott had recently conducted his "Galileo Experiment" in front of the lunar module *Falcon,* simultaneously dropping a falcon's feather and a geology hammer, with both hitting the lunar surface at the same instant. Soon after, Scott disappeared behind the Lunar Rover, which he and Jim Irwin had driven across the moon's surface. Back in Houston, CapCom (Capsule Communicator) and fellow astronaut Joe Allen, anxious to record every activity, asked what was taking place up there at Hadley Base. "Oh, just cleaning up the back of the Rover here a little, Joe," was the noncommittal response. In fact Dave Scott and fellow moon walker Jim Irwin were conducting a small, unofficial commemoration of the eight astronauts and six cosmonauts known (at that time) to have died prior to their lunar mission.

Meanwhile the third member of the Apollo 15 crew, Al Worden, was orbiting the moon in *Endeavour,* the command module. As his part of the tribute he had organized a small tin figurine by noted sculptor Paul Van Hoeydonck called *The Fallen Astronaut.* Jim Irwin's responsibility had been to place the fourteen names alphabetically on a small metal plaque. In these few stolen moments, and without NASA's knowledge or consent, Dave Scott stuck the plaque into the lunar soil and placed the deliberately toppled figurine in front of it. He then moved back and photographed the small memorial.

All was later revealed at the postflight press conference, and years after Dave Scott would recall the crew's tribute to the fourteen men. "We made a plaque for all the astronauts and cosmonauts that had been killed. And a little figurine, a Fallen Astronaut, and we put it right by the Rover. You can see it in the picture [NASA photo 88–11894]. That was just a little memorial, in alphabetical order. In relative terms, we had lost a lot and, interestingly enough, we didn't lose any more after that until *Challenger.* That's what I was doing when I said I was clearing up behind the Rover. Jim knew what I was doing. We just thought we'd recognize the guys that made the ultimate contribution. We felt satisfied in doing it. Several good guys didn't get to go."

This book is a further manifestation of that commemoration to a handful of men who died reaching for their ultimate goal—the moon. Four astronauts died in aircraft accidents, three suffered a horrifying death in a launch pad fire, and another was killed in an automobile crash.

These eight men were all superb pilots, and each undoubtedly would have had a profound participation in NASA's Apollo program. The composition of several Apollo crews would doubtless have been different had they lived, and it might even have been an astronaut called Gus who placed the first human footprint in the lunar soil, rather than a colleague named Neil.

Ted Freeman, killed in a T-38 crash in October 1964, was on the verge of being appointed to backup duties on a Gemini crew and would definitely have flown on an Apollo moon mission. Elliot See and Charlie Bassett were also killed in a T-38, which, ironically, hit the McDonnell Aircraft Corporation building in which their capsule was undergoing final assembly and checks. Following their Gemini mission they most likely would have rotated onto later Apollo crews, with See already penciled in as backup commander for the Gemini 12 flight. Chief astronaut at that time, Donald "Deke" Slayton, is already quoted as saying that Charlie Bassett would have moved on to the position of command module pilot for Frank Borman's crew, which eventually flew on the history-making Apollo 8 mission in December 1968. In doing so, he would have become one of the first three men to fly to the moon.

Slayton also had big plans for astronaut C.C. Williams, yet another to die in a T-38 crash, this time in October 1967. Williams had already been selected as the fourth man to walk on the moon alongside Charles "Pete" Conrad. Alan Bean was assigned to fill that role after Williams's jet unaccountably plummeted into a Florida forest.

Then there was Mercury astronaut Virgil "Gus" Grissom, whose bravery and competence were unfairly questioned in the otherwise excellent book and film *The Right Stuff*. According to Betty Grissom, Deke Slayton had already informed her husband that, on the completion of his Apollo 1 earth-orbiting mission, he would do what he could to get him The Big One—the first Apollo lunar landing. This effectively put Grissom first in line to set foot on the moon. That decision alone makes a mockery of Tom Wolfe's onerous innuendoes concerning the moral fiber of Gus Grissom. Only the best of the best could be the first person on the moon. Sadly Grissom and his crewmates Ed White and Roger Chaffee perished when an oxygen-fed fire engulfed the interior of their Apollo capsule during a launch pad simulation.

Ed Givens, so cruelly killed in an automobile accident, was well on his way to becoming one of NASA's brightest stars in the astronaut corps. He was training as a command module pilot before he met his fate on a rain-slicked Texas road in June 1967—a year that claimed the lives of five of NASA's finest. It is highly probable that the hardworking Givens would have journeyed to the moon.

Of course speculation cannot displace the ultimate course of history, but all eight men lost their opportunity to reach for the moon as the result of accidents. In the fatal blink of an eye they also lost their chance for spaceflight immortality. Their families, too, suffered deeply, not only through the traumatic loss of a loved son, husband, sibling, or father, but also through subsequently losing their own familiar role as the wife, child, or other loved one of an astronaut. Most of the widows, no longer feeling like part of the astronaut community, soon sold up and moved away.

In many ways this has not been an easy book to write, and not just because of the disadvantage of conducting research from Australia. Dozens of friends and families of the eight astronauts were contacted as well as many educators and colleagues whose lives crossed those of the fallen men. Fortunately many recognized the worth of this venture and responded, despite the necessity for them to recall many sorrowful events, and their participation is greatly appreciated.

Beyond supplying photographs, NASA could offer only brief, stock biographies of the eight men, but we also understand the need for the agency to maintain codes of privacy and integrity concerning its astronauts.

The passage of more than three decades presented an almost insurmountable challenge, but one that we mostly and steadily overcame. Several Apollo-era astronauts who were friends of the eight men were contacted, but many, mistrustful because of an odious commercial market in astronaut signatures, initially chose to ignore our letters and messages. Happily, once family members assured them of our good intentions, a few came around, supplying information and anecdotal material on their former colleagues. Also, fortunately, many others had discussed the deceased astronauts in a proliferation of post-Apollo astronaut biographies, and the authors have gratefully drawn upon these memories and words to present a more balanced account of the men's lives.

There is a great iniquity in the stories of these eight astronauts—and it is a major reason for compiling this book. With the obvious exception of the Apollo 1 crew, precious little has ever been written about these remarkable men, their shortened lives, their ambitions, and their hard-won place as one of their nation's revered astronauts. Searching recent authoritative chronologies for their names has shown that in many instances they are missing.

Colin Burgess undertook to research and tell the stories of Ted Freeman, Elliot See, Charlie Bassett, C.C. Williams, and Ed Givens, while Kate Doolan had the task of compiling the stories of Gus Grissom, Ed White, and Roger Chaffee, who died while trapped in their Apollo 1 spacecraft. The two authors assisted each other with research, proofreading, and writing in order to present a seamless narrative.

For his welcome and prodigious assistance, the authors are thankful to longtime friend and dedicated spaceflight researcher Bert Vis from the Netherlands. His knowledge of Soviet-CIS spaceflight matters is extraordinary, and his strong friendships with many former, current, and future cosmonauts have been the result of numerous self-funded trips to Zvezdny Gorodok (Star City), home of the Yuri Gagarin Cosmonaut Training Center, just outside of Moscow. This made him an ideal and willing choice to assist in the book by writing authentic biographies of the deceased cosmonauts, unblemished by years of half-truths and propaganda.

The eight cosmonauts whose lives are recounted in this book deserve their own volume, but even for a thorough and stubborn researcher such as Bert Vis, gathering reliable facts on them from official records and their peers is a complex and often delicate operation. Their true stories are substantially marred by years of untruths and a state-manufactured glorification. The life of Yuri Gagarin has been featured in several books, but one feels it might be an easier task to separate the Red Sea than to divine the full, factual story of the world's first spaceman. Sadly, Gagarin's real story will probably never be told, although many have tried. The facts have become blemished by decades of propaganda and an entrenched mistrust by those who knew him best of open debate about his life and death.

This book also pays tribute to the short but dynamic life of Valentin Bondarenko, who died in the most appalling manner while training for spaceflight. Though his name was unknown to westerners for more than three decades, it is almost certain he would have become one of his nation's most outstanding cosmonauts. His participation in the Soviet space program was carefully shielded from everyone, and those few who knew of his death were warned to keep their silence.

We attempt to rebut exaggerated stories of the Soviet space program regarded as fact. Vladimir Komarov, for example, should be remembered as a brave and tenacious man who flew on two of the most dangerous Soviet spaceflights and died as his out-of-control spacecraft slammed into Earth. Yet, because of a wall of silence that immediately surrounded his death, he is mistakenly remembered as a man who childishly screamed abuse at the Soviet premier and cowardly accepted his impending death.

The young cosmonauts knew they were involved in a juggernaut—a race between two superpowers, with the moon as the ultimate trophy. Even though many expressed serious concerns about the dangers of unreliable hardware and last-minute changes to their flights, they were resolute in their dreams of flying in the cosmos and stepped up to the launch pad. Given the same circumstances of hastily prepared missions, dangerous shortcuts, and ill-prepared equipment, America's astronauts would have openly rebelled, and rightly so. Although one could argue that any dissension would quickly see cosmonauts shown the door in disgrace, the fact that they performed their flights, and performed them extraordinarily well, is a lasting tribute to their integrity and determination.

It is the sincere wish of the authors that this book helps to fill a capacious void in astronaut, spaceflight, and indeed American and Soviet history. We should never forget the brave and remarkable men of both the United States and the Soviet Union who gave their lives in their countries' unquenchable search for knowledge and understanding.

# Acknowledgments

We owe our sincere thanks to many. The mere listing of names can in no way suggest our tremendous feelings of gratitude toward the individuals who willingly helped in the research and compilation of this book. We are greatly indebted to all of them. Without their interest and cooperation it would have been literally impossible to collect, transcribe, organize, or publish the information and stories in this book.

We thank Debbie Dodds and Jody Russell at the Johnson Space Center's Media Resource Center, Margaret Persinger and Kay Grinter at the Kennedy Space Center, fellow Aussie Lucy Lytwynsky at NASA's Astronaut Office in Houston, Dr. Roger Launius at the History Office at NASA headquarters in Washington DC, Mary Hardin at the Jet Propulsion Laboratory in Pasadena, and Dill Hunley at Dryden Flight Research Center. Also former NASA Director of Public Affairs Paul Haney, Bob Stevenson, Gratia Lousma, Dee O'Hara, Tracy Lempke, Bill Dana, David Harland, David Shayler of *Astro Info Service,* Rex Hall, Andy Turnage, J. L. Pickering, Jurgen Esders, Bob Tower, Charles Temple, Jim Winter, Dan Coleman, Jim Kelly, Jim Lee, Dr. John Duckworth, Paul and Rollin Becker, Fred Becker, the late James Schefter, Larry Turoski, Tome Neal, Glenn Fleming, Ed Hengeveld, Shane Stezelberger, Dr. Sam Puma, Laura Puma, Reverend Monseigneur Eugene Cargill, Lewis Morrisey, and Professor Emeritus Harm Buning at the University of Michigan. Ernestine Edwards, Hazel Brittingham, Joe Hudson, Barbara Watkins, Bill Hall, Fred Koch, Joe Algranti, John White of KIXC Radio and Carolyn Eggleston, both from Quanah, Texas, and Alice Creighton and Gary LaValley at the Department of the Navy's Special Collections and Archives Department, U.S. Naval Academy, Annapolis, were all of considerable help in tracking down photos and information. Kate would like to thank the staff, officers, and alumni of the United States Military Academy at West Point, New York, who have assisted her above and beyond the call of duty. The Association of Graduates, the Public Affairs Office, Major Chris Garrett, USA, who located the records of Cadet Edward White, Colonel Bill McWilliams, USAF (ret.), Colonel Morris Herbert, USA (ret.), Major General Jim ("Bulldog") Drummond, USA (ret.), Major General Dick Larkin, USA (ret.), Colonel Charlie Roades, USAF (ret.), Colonel Hank West, USAF (ret.), Jeff Madsen, Colonel Woody Spring, USA (ret.), Colonel John Witherell, USA (ret.), Colonel Marcus Oliphant, USA (ret.), and the late Colonel John ("J.D.") Smith, USA (ret.). A special thanks to the alumni from many classes, especially the Class of 1952, for sharing their treasured memories of Ed White with me. A very big thank you to the staff of the USMA Archives—Sheila Biles, Suzanne Christoff, and Judy Sibley—who have encouraged my research since 1994— Go Army, Beat Navy! Thanks also to Kathleen Markee of the Purdue University Library Archives, Kate Cooper of the Apollo 1 Memorial Foundation, Ray Puffer of the Edwards Air Force Base History Office, the staff at the Victorian State Library, and

Iris Coopersmith and the entire Class of 1948 at Western High School. Thank you to my mother, Phyl Doolan, a senior registered nurse, and John MacDougall, M.D., for explaining medical terminology to a biology blockhead. Heartfelt thanks to my friends Geoff Allshorn, Judy Brewer-Fischer, Nigel Denning, Mark Hillyer, Helen Hodgman, Therese Power RSM, Ian Whalley, and the remarkable Sister Gerardine Cooney for their ongoing assistance, friendship, and encouragement.

Further sincere thanks go to Apollo-era astronauts Neil Armstrong, David Scott, Tom Stafford, Michael Collins, Wally Schirra, Scott Carpenter, Gordon Cooper, Edgar Mitchell, Vance Brand, Jerry Carr, Don Lind, and Gene Cernan, and to an astronaut friend from today's shuttle program, Timothy ("T.J.") Creamer, for his special insights into flight procedures. We must also thank noted spaceflight author Michael Cassutt, Simon Vaughan, Francis French, and fellow Australian space enthusiasts Justin Wigg and David Sander for their perusal of the draft manuscript and their incisive, helpful comments and corrections.

Finally, to the families of the deceased astronauts who helped make this book a reality, very special thanks and appreciation go to Jeannie Bassett, Karen Bassett, Peter Bassett, Bill Bassett, Sally See Kneuven, Sally See Llewellyn, Beth Williams, Gertrude Williams, Catherine Williams, Jane Dee Williams, Faith Freeman Herschap, Anna Mae Freeman Thompson, Perry McGinnis, Morgan and Cathrine Doyle, Ed Givens III, Martha Chaffee, Sheryl Chaffee Marshall, Jeanne Whatley, Bonnie Baer, Ed White III, and Betty and Scott Grissom.

It is incredibly satisfying to know that in this new millennium, the names and deeds of the sixteen men listed here will live on. We feel deeply honored to be entrusted with their stories, and we present with considerable pride the stories of these indomitable men, whose one golden dream was to take those first bold steps into our universe and to walk on another world.

Major Charles Arthur Bassett II, USAF

Colonel Pavel Ivanovich Belyayev

Senior Lieutenant Valentin Vasilyevich Bondarenko

Lieutenant Conmander Roger Bruce Chaffee, USN

Lieutenant Colonel Georgy Timofeyevich Dobrovolsky

Captain Theodore Cordy Freeman, USAF

Colonel Yuri Alexeyevich Gagarin

Colonel-Engineer Vladimir Mikhailovich Komarov

Major Edward Galen Givens Jr., USAF

Lieutenant Colonel Virgil Ivan Grissom, USAF

Captain Grigory Grigoryevich Nelyubov

Viktor Ivanovich Patsayev

Elliot McKay See Jr.

Vladislav Nikolayevich Volkov

Lieutenant Colonel Edward Higgins White II, USAF

Major Clifton Curtis Williams Jr., USMC

# 1  A Routine Training Flight
## Captain Theodore Cordy Freeman, USAF

*When the original seven Mercury astronauts were selected back in 1958, the ten-tative question sometimes put to them was "What if . . . ?" What would happen when the first astronaut died in a fiery launch pad explosion? Suffocated in an explosive decompression in space? Was incinerated in a reentry mishap? These were always the questions most difficult to answer, but the Mercury astronauts were collectively stoic in their responses: "The space program can, and must, go on."*

*Ted Freeman was the first of America's astronaut corps to fall. When he was killed during a routine flight in a NASA training aircraft, it was totally unexpected, and his death caused a sad, uncomfortable disquiet to descend on the normally strong astronaut community. The Space Race saw the transition from dangerous one-man flights, with astronauts flung into space atop unreliable booster rockets, to the end of the Gemini program fatality-free during actual missions. NASA performed with magnificence, although there had been some very close calls. The astronauts themselves had lost several good friends and colleagues engaged in test-flying high performance, supersonic aircraft—a particularly hazardous business. Realistically, they also expected to lose some astronaut buddies along the way, but they felt this was most likely to occur in a spaceflight mishap. With every successive manned launch they felt they were defying the odds, but those odds were acceptable to them in such a worthy undertaking.*

It was Saturday morning, 31 October 1964. After a frustrating delay caused by a thick morning fog that had finally lifted, the operations people at Ellington Air Force Base finally gave astronaut Ted Freeman permission to stroll out to his waiting NASA T-38A Talon aircraft and ready himself for takeoff.

Ellington AFB was located just four miles from the astronauts' workplace—what was then called the Manned Spacecraft Center, or MSC (nowadays the Johnson Space Center, or JSC)—and eighteen miles southeast of Houston's sprawling downtown. Freeman, wearing his orange flight suit, was glad to be on the move at last. He gathered up his helmet and parachute, and then collected the aircraft's log books from the maintenance people.

Some low-hanging clouds still lingered over Ellington, but they caused Freeman little concern as he made his way out of the NASA hangar and walked toward the sleek, waiting aircraft. As usual, the slate-gray pillows of Gulf clouds that could pile up unexpectedly and produce sudden torrents of rain never really paused but drifted quickly by on the southerly breezes passing over the airfield. This pattern generally meant clear skies by midmorning.

Of more concern were reports that flocks of geese had been seen close to the ground that day, due to the low-hanging fog. In fact other pilots in the area had reported seeing these geese with increasing frequency over the past three weeks. But the skies now appeared to be clear of these and any other potentially hazardous bird life.

Slender and brown eyed, with a receding hairline, thirty-four-year-old Ted Freeman had a reputation as a friendly, soft-spoken man with a wry sense of humor who usually chose to ride a bicycle the three blocks from his home to the space center. But this outward appearance belied a man who was described by many of his peers as an outstanding pilot, perhaps one of the best in the astronaut corps.

Just two weeks earlier, on 18 October, he and his wife, Faith, had celebrated the first anniversary of his official selection to NASA's astronaut corps, and he was already piling up the credits at MSC as he looked to his first mission assignment.

Flying was something that had never become wearisome for Freeman, and he looked forward to his first hop that day with mounting anticipation. Those who knew they belonged above the clouds loved nothing better than streaking solo across the skies in a high-performance aircraft, soaring and swooping, at one with the heavens. This would be the first of two proficiency flights scheduled for Freeman that day; he planned to carry out the second later that afternoon.

According to the maintenance team, the T-38 he would fly that day was a good, clean bird. Fellow astronauts Dave Scott and Dick Gordon had flown it back to Ellington on Friday evening and had not logged any problems. They had been in New Mexico on a geology field trip near the Los Alamos atomic installation. Freeman was also scheduled to take part in one of these field trips later that week, during which he and another astronaut or two would undertake similar geology training in Bend, Oregon.

As Freeman neared the T-38, his mind was running over the events of the coming evening. It was Halloween, and his ten-year-old daughter, also named Faith but known to the family as "Faithie," was ready to go out dressed and made up like the other local kids. His new job as an astronaut kept him away from his wife and daughter a lot—too much—so he was pleased he could be home to share this special evening with his family. He always kept them up to date with his astronaut activities in what he called his "kitchen seminars," but tonight he and his wife would simply curl up in their lounge chairs, sipping steaming cups of coffee and talking in between answering the doorbell many times over. The game for them would be trying to guess the identity of the other astronauts' kids standing on the doorstep in their Halloween outfits, holding out chubby hands, demanding treats.

There was some preliminary work to be done before Freeman flew that day, and his attention reverted to the job at hand—checking out his aircraft. In his usual meticulous way he carried out his preflight inspection of the gleaming jet trainer, moving slowly around the fuselage, looking for any potential problems such as hydraulic fuel leaks or anything that looked to be out of the ordinary.

The aircraft seemed to be in perfect shape and ready to go. One more glance at the skies, but they were fine. Over the past couple of weeks thunderstorms more reminiscent of spring than fall had subdued the steely heat of a wrathful summer, and Houston had enjoyed clear, cool, clean days. Recently, however, gray, damp days had begun descending in a mantle of fog and charcoal clouds, and downpours of rain were an ever-present possibility.

Having checked that everything was in order, Freeman clambered up the small ladder to the dual cockpit and eased himself into the forward seat of the two. As he buckled in he slowly ran his eyes over the familiar instruments, and then made sure he had all the necessary paperwork for his flight. Satisfied, he pulled on his helmet and checked the oxygen connectors.

When he reported to NASA in January 1964, eight outdated T-33s and four of the newer F-102s comprised the space agency's fleet of jet trainers. However, the agency had been evaluating other jet aircraft that might prove suitable for astronaut training. Eventually the Flight Operations Division settled on the dual-seat T-38A Talon, a lively and reliable aircraft manufactured by Northrop. That May, NASA accepted the first of thirty T-38s intended to serve the space agency in a number of roles, but principally to maintain the flight proficiency of astronauts. Many of these men had already flown the T-38 as part of their military training and were pleased with the choice.

The craft boasted a remarkably good high-altitude cruise speed and was capable of flying at a top speed of Mach 1.35. When light on fuel the T-38 could rocket from the runway at an impressive angle of attack and reach 40,000 feet in just under two minutes. When the craft was employed as a jet trainer, the instructor and student would sit in tandem, one behind the other, on rocket-powered ejection seats in a pressurized, air-conditioned cockpit. Students would learn aerobatics, formation flying, supersonic techniques, and cross-country navigation as well as night and instrument flying.

Freeman was already more than proficient in the T-38, having conducted much of the aircraft's final test work while stationed at Edwards AFB in California. He knew better than most that NASA had made a wise decision in its selection.

Following procedures, Freeman checked his rudder trim and readied his radio and navigation instruments before switching on the battery and preparing to start the right engine. As the J85 engine whined into life he called in, "Ellington Ground, NASA 188."

The controller came back with an acknowledgment, and Freeman continued, "Ellington Ground, NASA 188 . . . good morning, Sir. Clearance requested."

Moments later the tower responded. "NASA 188, you are cleared as filed. Climb and maintain 2,000 feet, expect 14,000 feet ten minutes after departure. Departure frequencies are standard." He then received his transponder squawk code— a transmitted signal by which his aircraft would be identified to ground controllers.

Freeman repeated the clearance as he started up the left engine and completed his cockpit checks. Both engines were running smoothly, and all the indicator lights

1. Prior to joining NASA as an astronaut, Ted Freeman was a test pilot at Edwards Air Force Base, California. (Courtesy Faith Freeman Herschap)

glowed green. The tower confirmed the read back was correct, and he verified he was ready to taxi out to the runway.

"Roger, NASA 188," came the call. "Taxi to runway 14L and hold short." Freeman released the brakes and poured on some power. His T-38 responded beautifully, and as he began to taxi he completed some further cockpit checks. He took in the surrounding hazy skies again. No problems there.

Suddenly a funny little thought tweaked at his memory and made him smile. Tomorrow would be the first of November, and he recalled something Faith had said four weeks earlier. Unlike her husband she was laden with superstitions, and on the first morning of October she had startled him by leaping out of bed and yelling "Rabbit!" It was a new superstition, she explained; if you said the word "rabbit" first thing on the first day of a new month it would bring good luck. Lord only knew where she got this stuff from, and he wondered if Faith would remember this new tradition in the morning, after what would probably be a late evening.

Once Freeman reached the hold short position he swept this and other distracting thoughts from his mind as he gently pulled up and once again called the tower. He was instructed to taxi into position for takeoff, and at 10:01 A.M. he lined up on the runway, ready to go. He moved the throttles to the military power setting, made sure that the engine nozzles closed down to the proper setting, and checked the engine exhaust gas temperatures (EGT).

Moments later the tower controller gave further instructions. "NASA 188: upon departure turn 090, climb to 2,000, contact Departure. Cleared for takeoff!"

Freeman repeated the clearance, checked that the hydraulic pressures were okay, and kicked in the power. He moved the throttle to full afterburners and watched the EGT to ensure the engine nozzles were open to their full setting. All appeared normal, so he let off the brakes and the gleaming jet trainer accelerated smoothly along the runway.

Around 2,500 feet down the strip Freeman reached takeoff speed and eased the nose of the T-38 into the air. The jet howled upward into the waiting skies, flying southwest over the Gulf Freeway. Soon after, another turn to the left put his aircraft on a flight path right over the top of the MSC.

Once the astronaut had reached a convenient altitude, he made two more standard calls. "NASA 188, frequency change." This was on the tower's frequency, and then he twirled the dial to change frequencies to departures and called, "Departure Control, NASA 188 . . . 1,000 for 2,000."

Alone in the sky. It was an exhilarating feeling, one he knew well. He belonged here and was perfectly comfortable. He knew that soon he would take an even longer stride into the heavens—one that would take him out into the perilous, raw blackness of space.

§

Theodore Cordy Freeman was born in Broomall, Pennsylvania, on 18 February 1930. He was the son of local woman Catherine (née Wilson) and John Freeman, and a baby brother to Anne, Betty, and Jack.

Originally from Lewes, Delaware, the family had moved to Philadelphia in 1924 at the onset of the Depression. There John Freeman, hailing from Newfoundland, New Jersey, was able to find work as a carpenter. Later the family moved to Broomall, a suburb on the west side of Philadelphia, where John built a nice home in which Ted was born. He was named Theodore after the man who had raised his father, and who would always be regarded as his grandfather, Theodore Cullen Donovan, and Cordy after Thomas Cordy Wilson, his maternal grandfather. He was only fifteen months old when the family was able to return to Delaware in 1931 and move into a neat little house his father had built on a five-acre farm near Five Points, a crossroads west of Lewes. John Freeman now happily tended crops of sweet corn and other vegetables, berries, and flowers.

Founded in 1631, Lewes was situated where Delaware Bay and the Atlantic Ocean meet at Cape Henlopen. Young Ted grew up in a place where the sun, sand, and sea were a great distraction for any young boy, especially one living on a farm. He would often make the trip to nearby Rehoboth Beach, where he and his friends would spend the day swimming in the cool waters and playing on the hot sands. Any trip to the beach would almost certainly include a visit to Dolle's on the boardwalk, where the boys would empty out their pockets and load up with caramel popcorn and saltwater taffy. The state park in Lewes was a breathtakingly beautiful place, with miles of golden beaches, nature trails, and bird sanctuaries. Curiously enough, Freeman would say that as he grew up he considered Delaware to be a rather dismal place.

"Ugly; flat," he told an interviewer. "So as a child I looked at all that ugliness and said who knows if it mightn't look a bit less ugly if you saw it from above? Then one day when I was six I said to my father, 'Will you take me up in an airplane?' So then my father saved some money and took me up in an airplane and I realized that Delaware wasn't ugly but beautiful when you looked down on it from high above."

Ted, who seemed destined to follow in his father's and brother Jack's footsteps and become a farmer or carpenter, entered first grade at Lewes Elementary School in September 1936 and completed his early schooling in June 1944.

"Until I was fifteen I was just a farm boy," Freeman said. "Like my father I had spent very little time at school, but when I was fifteen I realized that you didn't learn much about things being a farmhand and I said so to my father, and my father said you learn about things by reading. So I began to read a great deal and my father took me out of the fields and sent me to school where I did very well."

Catherine Freeman recalled that while he was attending high school, flying proved to be a very important part of her son's life: "I remember when he was a little boy, he and his brother, Jack, would save their money. They didn't save their pennies for movies or candy. They saved for plane rides at the Rehoboth airport." "I sort of grew up at the airport," Freeman once said.

Part-time work at Rehoboth Airport entailed working as a grease monkey and gassing up aircraft, but Freeman did not mind a bit—he simply adored being around airplanes and tinkering with their engines. A former school friend, Joe Hudson, worked with him at the airport under the supervision of Dan Cochran from Aircrafters, Inc. "We both started working at the airport when we were fifteen," Hudson said. The two boys also worked alongside Cochran after school and on weekends. During this time they also took flying lessons, often with Freeman's older brother, but along the way Jack seemed to lose interest and went on to other pursuits.

Most of the money Freeman earned at the airport went into his flying lessons, and on his sixteenth birthday he achieved his pilot's license, with 450 flying hours already to his credit. Thereafter, while most of his friends were still trying to get their automobile driver's license, Freeman was out there at the stick of a Piper Cub, learning to do barrel rolls and other basic aerobatics, spending his early Sunday afternoons happily engaged in hedge hopping about the outskirts of Lewes. After he had landed, he would clean himself up and rush over to the local Midway Presbyterian Church for afternoon service.

He may have been a quiet, slight youth, but he was not afraid to stick up for what was right. His older sister Anne recalled an occasion in high school when a classmate made an unnecessarily rude comment to a part-time teacher. Young Freeman took offense on behalf of the startled teacher, stood up, and punched the offender in the mouth. Both would end up in the local hospital that day with minor injuries from the skirmish. In later years, as these things sometimes go, Freeman and the other man both joined the air force and became firm friends.

Catherine Freeman once spoke about the time when her son got his pilot's license. "The first time he flew it scared me. He was just a youngster, and came home one day, and said, 'Mama, I saw you in the backyard.' 'When?' I asked. My heart skipped a beat when he told me he had been in a plane that had flown over our house. But from then on, I've looked on it as just the same as driving an automobile." Not long after, young Freeman took his mother up for a ride. "He was turned around talking to me and I said, 'Oh, honey, turn around and look where you're going," she pleaded. But her son just laughed. "He said, 'Mum, for goodness sakes, you can't run into anything up here.'" His words were sadly prophetic.

At this time, and while Freeman was undergoing his high school education, Delaware Senator John Williams somehow got to hear of the young man's desire to better himself and go into aviation. He arranged a meeting with John Freeman and promised that if his son applied himself and continued to get good marks, he would nominate him to attend the Naval Academy without any need to pay fees. He went on to explain that the navy had aircraft carriers and was always on the lookout for promising young pilots.

By now Freeman knew his future was in flying, so after his father broke the news to him he knuckled down to the task. Joe Hudson recalled that his friend "liked to study and was real good in all subjects which would lead to a career in aviation." He was popular in school, serving as president of the Lewes High School Student Council in his senior year. But he did not date many girls at the time according to another friend, Emory Brittingham. "We didn't see him in town much," she said. "He was at the airport or his home."

Freeman played right field on the school's baseball team, and though he was slight of figure he also played football with the first team. In the Rehoboth football game of 1947—the last in his senior year—he went into a heavy tackle and had his teeth knocked well out of alignment, giving him a severe cross-bite.

In June 1948 he was ranked third in a class of twenty-five and graduated as an honors student and president of the local chapter of the National Honor Society. In his final year at high school he completed his application for the U.S. Naval Academy in Annapolis, which was countersigned as promised by Senator Williams. He passed the scholarship examination with little difficulty, but to his acute disappointment he failed the medical exam because of his crooked teeth. However, he was told that if he had them straightened he would be accepted the following year.

Eager to further his education while waiting for his appointment to Annapolis, Freeman enrolled as a freshman at the University of Delaware in Newark. He continued to work at Rehoboth airport, and in his free time he earned a few extra dollars by flying small aircraft over the Atlantic off the coast of New Jersey, spotting and reporting on schools of fish for the local fishing fleet. Most of this money went straight back into purchasing aviation fuel.

Meanwhile, determined to let nothing prevent him from entering the Naval Academy, he sought his father's assistance to pay for an operation to correct his cross-bite. This operation went well, and then, after having some teeth ground down to even things up, he was fitted with braces that he had to wear for several months. He knew that one day it would all be worth the effort.

His persistence paid off, and he was admitted into the academy's Class of 1953 (each class is known by its year of graduation) on 17 June 1949.

Ted Freeman's first sight of Annapolis came with an abruptness and startling totality. As his parents' car approached the Naval Academy from Baltimore on the Governor Ritchie Highway, the road, cresting a slight rise, dropped suddenly down to the glistening water of the Severn River. On the opposite shore, with the neat perfection of a panoramic painting, sat the well-ordered buildings, the tree-shaded walks, the close-cropped parade grounds, and the trim geometric fringe of docks and basins belonging to the greatest naval institution in the world.

The magnificence of the place took his breath away, and he was suddenly filled with misgivings. Would he really fit in here? He could make out the massive bulk of Bancroft Hall, the great brooding dome of the chapel, the historic gun mounts, the moored ships and little sailboats in the boat basin. The place was drenched in history, and he was excited to be there, but he also knew through reading the brochures that a quarter of the eager young men now filing through the gates to take their Oath of Allegiance would not make it past the first year.

Founded as the Naval School in 1845, the academy achieved a rich history of preparing students morally, mentally, and physically to be professional officers in the United States Navy and Marine Corps. It imbued them, as it does today, with the highest ideals of duty, honor, and loyalty. While at the academy the students, known as midshipmen—a rank between chief warrant officer and ensign—would be on active duty in the U.S. Navy. In 1933 Congress authorized the academy to begin awarding bachelor of science degrees, giving it an even greater attraction.

The many impressive sights greeting Freeman inside the gates included lush green lawns sweeping gently toward the broad, slow-flowing river beyond the whispering sea wall. The chapel, facing the Severn, dominated the entire academy, and Freeman knew it was the final resting place of the first and most famous of American naval heroes, John Paul Jones.

The postcard-picturesque campus was known simply as the Yard. The meticulously maintained lawns abounded in tree-shaded monuments that commemorated the bravery and heroism that was (and remains) an integral part of the academy's heritage.

New students would report for induction in early July of each year and begin what is known as Plebe Summer with their new classmates. On their first day at Annapolis, these midshipmen had to learn a new vocabulary of nautical and Naval Academy terms. Floors no longer existed—now they were decks. Walls became bulkheads, kitchens were now galleys, and restrooms became heads.

At Annapolis there are four midshipmen phases. First they are freshmen, fourth class (or plebes); then sophomores, third class (or youngsters); juniors, second class (or segundo), and finally seniors, first class (or firsties). They all reside in Bancroft Hall, a vast dormitory complex that boasts forty acres of floor space and three miles of corridors. They are assigned to a room with one or more midshipmen, and by alternating weeks of housekeeping duties must keep their room immaculately clean and shipshape, ready for a full military inspection at any time. They must also keep their uniforms in regulation condition. Demerits are issued for a uniform or room that is not in proper order.

Daily routines include a rigid inspection held during a daily noon muster in which the new plebes are inspected by company officers before they are marched off to the mess hall. Newcomers are placed on report if their shoes are not properly shined, their trousers uncreased, or any part of their uniform soiled. At the time Freeman was at Annapolis, around twenty-two hundred midshipmen took their noon meal in a huge mess hall in the basement of Bancroft Hall.

The new midshipmen eat, sleep, drill, play, and compete as teams with their company mates during Plebe Summer, which is no gentle easing into the military routine. During the first few weeks, days start at dawn with an hour of rigorous exercises and end long after sunset. In this time they learn customs and regulations and memorize things they can and cannot do. These are drilled into the men until they just about find themselves repeating regulations in their sleep. They learn to shoot on the rifle range, sail, row, tie knots, and practice the semaphore and blinker. Later, basic fundamentals of seamanship are taught through sailing exercises.

Midshipmen are required to learn seamanship in small sailing boats and cutters, but they earn the privilege of using them for private recreation with their families or sweethearts after they pass certain requirements. They can also compete with the nation's outstanding yachtsmen in ocean races such as the Bermuda Classic.

Traditionally the upperclassmen brigade returns from summer training in late August, and then the academic year begins. Every year students assume ever more important roles in running their company, battalion, and brigade.

After Freeman and the other wide-eyed appointees passed through the gate on this particular induction day, they were escorted to the second deck of Bancroft Hall, where each of them took the Oath of Allegiance below the flag flown by Oliver Hazard Perry at the Battle of Lake Erie. On the flag Freeman could read the stirring, roughly drawn inscription, "Don't give up the ship." Each man received a close haircut and was put into uniform, after which first-class midshipmen and officers who led the indoctrination program taught them the correct way to salute. Then followed a mad scramble for the uniform accompaniments. Next, under the watchful supervision of an officer, they used a machine to cut name stencils with which they would mark their clothing. They were then assigned a roommate and quarters in Bancroft Hall.

As a humble fourth classman, Freeman had to quickly memorize a bewildering number of rules and regulations. He should walk only down the center of corridors, turn square at each corner, and stand with a ramrod-stiff posture. He had to address all upperclassmen as "Sir," and before entering a room he was required to remove his cap, stand to attention, and sound off, "Midshipman Freeman, fourth class, Sir!" Although many of these customs and disciplines initially seemed nonsensical, Freeman came to learn that this process was simply a part of the long path to obedience, self-discipline, and regimentation that was an integral part of learning leadership.

Freeman found the studies at Annapolis relatively easy, and with so many activities to attend the months and years slipped away. He especially enjoyed the midshipman cruises. The first of these took him down to the Panama Canal Zone in 1950, and a later cruise to England and France in 1952.

By now, Freeman knew he did not want to stay in the navy, and in this he was very fortunate. In 1947, two years before he entered Annapolis, the U.S. Air Force was created, and he heard its officers were on the lookout for talented recruits. The navy allowed the air force to take 20 percent of any future graduating Annapolis class, with volunteers selected by a lottery. Once again Freeman's luck held out, and he was free to join his nation's air force on graduation.

In another piece of good fortune he had also met his future wife, Faith Dudley Clark, the daughter of Walter and Jennifer Clark from Orange, Connecticut. They had been introduced at a party in Pennsylvania that Freeman attended with friends. Faith, pretty and laden with personality, had graduated from the Knox School in Cooperstown, New York, and when they met she was on vacation from the Katherine Gibbs secretarial school in Boston. Though she was outgoing and loved parties—definitely the opposite of the shy young midshipman—she and Freeman were quickly attracted to each other. Later, while they were courting, Faith took on a position as a radio script and continuity writer for a station in New Haven, Connecticut. Freeman did not own a car, so he borrowed his brother Jack's to drive up to Connecticut while he was courting Faith.

Freeman and Faith eventually made plans to get married but were well aware of the academy regulation forbidding midshipmen to marry before their graduation. As a result, the academy's chapel was always busy on graduation day, with weddings scheduled every thirty minutes. They decided to become one of those happy couples, and Freeman made all the necessary arrangements. Meanwhile he wrote to Faith every day to keep her up to date with his activities.

On 5 June 1953, four years after first walking through the Induction Gate at Annapolis, Freeman graduated with a bachelor of science degree and an athletic track award for the year 1951–52. In a class originally of 1,300 (925 remained at graduation) he came in at position 238. He scored higher grades than another cadet who would spring to prominence many years later—presidential hopeful Ross Perot, who graduated in position 453. The student graduating first in the Class of 1953 was Carlisle Trost—later to become chief of Naval Operations.

The graduation ceremony, held in Dahlgren Hall, closed with a time-honored tradition as the former midshipmen whooped and tossed their caps high into the air. The caps, no longer needed, generally contained the names and addresses of the former owners and would be eagerly swept up as souvenirs by the young ladies and family members in attendance.

After the graduation ceremony came another proud moment. On the campus, and near the Japanese Bell as decreed by tradition, Faith and Freeman's mother placed on his shoulders the new insignia of his rank. A single gold stripe on his shoulder boards now identified him as Ensign Theodore Freeman. Afterward Freeman and Faith were married in the academy's Presbyterian chapel. The wedding reception was held that evening in a Baltimore hotel with family and friends.

Following his graduation from Annapolis, Freeman announced to his family that he was electing to take up his commission as a second lieutenant with the USAF rather than continue in the navy. He subsequently began his two years of air force flight training in a little yellow T-6 Texan at the newly reactivated Hondo Air Base in Texas, together with a mixed group of Annapolis and West Point graduates.

The North American T-6 was undoubtedly the most versatile single-engine aircraft ever built and was considered docile enough for any novice flier to begin his military flying career. As an adaptable and rugged training aircraft it spawned generations of young pilots, many of whom went on to become astronauts. The T-6 featured an enclosed canopy over a tandem cockpit, and from a control panel in the rear cockpit instructors could temporarily upset instruments in the trainee's front cockpit to simulate emergencies. Most aspiring pilots would need around twenty hours of dual control flying in the T-6 before they were proficient enough to go solo. Following this they would graduate to the Lockheed T-33 jet trainer, which began entering service in 1947.

The instructors at Hondo were civilians under contract to teach the new guys flight basics, and Freeman's proficiency blossomed under their guidance. He set an all-time academic record at Hondo and completed his primary pilot training on 25 March 1954. Six days later he was assigned to nearby Bryan Field, where he received his wings, finishing fourth in the overall class standing.

On 18 July 1954 the Freemans became parents to a beautiful baby girl they named Faith Huntington Freeman, who quickly became known to them as "Faithie."

In September that year Freeman attended the USAF Advanced Flying School, learning to fly the F-86 Sabre fighter jet at Nellis AFB, ten miles from Las Vegas,

2. At home Ted Freeman relaxes with his two Faiths. (Courtesy Faith Freeman Herschap)

Nevada. As usual his family went with him. Then, for thirty months from 27 January 1955, he underwent foreign service as a Tactical Air Command fighter pilot and maintenance officer with the 18th Fighter Bomber Wing, an F-86 outfit stationed in Okinawa, Japan. His wife and daughter sailed over to see Freeman once he was settled. He laughed when Faith told him that little Faithie had learned to walk while on the way across, and he was fully expecting her to grow up with a sailor's gait. His family managed to spend six months with him in Japan before returning home.

On his own return to the States, and by now a first lieutenant, Freeman was posted for a year at George AFB in Victorville, California, with the 1st Fighter-Day Squadron, whose commander was the legendary Colonel Chuck Yeager. Freeman arrived at the base on 4 August 1957. George AFB was located some fifty miles from Edwards AFB, and just like at Edwards the wives had to constantly battle against the omnipresent dust, which blew into their air force houses and settled everywhere. All the crockery and utensils would have to be rinsed before use. Faith bore up stoically and had soon formed friendships with other air force wives, many of whom also had young children.

The outfit Freeman had joined was the first daylight air defense squadron in the Tactical Air Command and flew the supersonic F-100 Super Sabres. They were given the first Sidewinder missiles and practiced firing them at unpiloted tow drones. The pilots at George were good—very good. They had to be, when each Sidewinder they fired off cost fifteen thousand dollars. There was a lot of pressure on them to be accurate.

Flying beneath four-engine tankers holding nearly thirty thousand gallons of fuel, the pilots also practiced airborne refueling techniques under all kinds of weather conditions. Chuck Yeager later reflected, "Commanding an elite group eager to bust their tails to please me was a wonderful position to be in . . . it was a pleasure watching a squadron of really proficient fighter pilots flying crisp and precise."

By now the air force had recognized in Freeman a rising, promising young officer, and in 1958 his superiors sent him to the University of Michigan in Ann Arbor for some graduate work in aeronautical engineering. There he studied under Professor Wilbur Nelson, chairman of the aeronautical and astronautical engineering department, who recalled Freeman as being "a good student." Other future astronauts who passed through Professor Nelson's department were Jim McDivitt and Ed White. These two men would later fly together on the history-making Gemini 4 mission, during which White would become the first American to conduct a space walk, or extravehicular activity (EVA).

Freeman eventually graduated from the University of Michigan with a master of science degree in aeronautical engineering; he also completed some graduate studies with the U.S. Air Force Institute of Technology (AFIT) at Wright-Patterson AFB in Ohio.

As the next step in his career path, Captain Freeman (he had been promoted in June 1960) was assigned to the Directorate of Flight Test at the U.S. Air Force Flight Test Center at Edwards AFB as a flight test engineer. There he underwent test-flying experience over the next two years with the 6512 Test group, flying advanced and high-performance jet aircraft such as the F-106A, T-37B, and F-104D. As project engineer, and with Captain Albert Crews as his project pilot, in June 1961 Freeman helped to test a high-density fuel and the addition of two wingtip tanks to increase the range of the F-104D.

With his mind now set on becoming a test pilot, and with his theory and practical flying experience to back him up, Freeman lodged an application for the U.S. Air Force Flight Test Pilot School (known as TPS) at Edwards AFB in California.

The TPS had an academic curriculum virtually equivalent to the final two years of aeronautical engineering at college level. As the air force began to look at the future, and projects beyond the atmosphere, additional courses were introduced. These were aimed at qualifying TPS graduates for potential spaceflight duties. The latest jet aircraft began arriving at Edwards, while advanced computer systems were installed. A T-27 spaceflight simulator was now an integral feature of the new curriculum. It could replicate many of the sights, sounds, and other sensations a pilot might encounter during spaceflight. Three F-104 Starfighters appeared on the flight line, converted to NF-104s by the installation of a rocket engine in the tail to permit zoom climbs above 100,000 feet.

From 12 October 1961 the new ARPS curriculum Freeman had applied for was separated into two distinct phases: the Experimental Test Pilot Course and the Aerospace Research Pilot Course. As a minimum, applicants now had to be no more than thirty-two years of age, be serving on active duty as a pilot with a grade of major or below, and have at least five hundred hours as a pilot or instructor pilot. Most important, they had to possess a bachelor of science degree in engineering, physical science, or mathematics.

To his joy Freeman's application was accepted, and he was assigned as an aerospace engineer at Edwards AFB prior to commencing Experimental Test Pilot School. One of his instructors at the Edwards school was Tom Stafford, later to join NASA as a member of the second astronaut group.

Edwards AFB is a three hundred thousand-acre military base situated on the western edge of the Mojave Desert, a hundred miles northeast of Los Angeles. The first military use of its forty-four-square-mile dry lake, often cited as the world's best natural landing field, dated back to the early 1930s. The lakebed was used as a bombing range until it became a training field early in the Second World War. After the war, the famed x-series of rocket-powered aircraft was tested at Edwards. It was here on 14 October 1947 that a brash but highly skilled pilot named Chuck Yeager became the first person to fly faster than the speed of sound in level flight, when his Bell x-1 *Glamorous Glennis* went supersonic over the Mojave Desert. Five years later Yeager flew a more powerful Bell x-1A to 1,650 miles per hour—this time more than twice the speed of sound.

On 2 January 1962 Freeman began his eight-month stint as a student in the Experimental Test Pilot Course, graduated on 17 August, and was looking to move on to the next phase, if accepted. Meanwhile he took on duties as an instructor.

It was during this period that Freeman experienced his first serious crash, aboard a Martin B-57 Intruder, a twin-engine, straight-wing bomber. On 12 March, as a Performance Branch instructor, he was aboard the B-57 piloted by Captain John Morrison, another instructor in the Stability Branch of the ARPS. While Morrison was attempting to land the aircraft in a severe crosswind at Sheppard AFB in Texas, the left tire blew, causing the B-57 to skid off the runway, shear its nose gear, and damage its underside. The two men were shaken but escaped uninjured. An investigation later pointed to a defective left brake cylinder as the primary cause of the accident.

Just over two weeks later, on 31 March 1963, it was announced that Freeman had been chosen to go on to the second phase and become a USAF spaceflight trainee at the ARPS. He would be joining the school's fourth course, which began on 13 May 1963. Fourteen other pilots were in this trainee course, including two who were also destined to become NASA astronauts, Dave Scott and Jim Irwin.

Another in Freeman's group was Captain Mike Adams, who would later fly the experimental x-15. Sadly, on the flight in which Adams qualified for his USAF astronaut rating by exceeding fifty statute miles, his x-15 went into a spin and broke up, killing the pilot.

One truly controversial member of Class IV was Captain Edward Dwight, who had entered the air force in 1953, eventually logging more than two thousand hours in jet fighters while also carrying out a two-year tour as a b-57 pilot. Dwight, who had a degree in aeronautical engineering, found himself the focus of much unwanted media attention when he joined the aerospace school. He was African American, and there was extreme pressure on the arps to qualify him as an astronaut. It was tantamount to an order, and it came directly from General Curtis LeMay, the air force chief of staff. He was responding in turn to a demand from Attorney General Bobby Kennedy to qualify a black officer as an astronaut, whatever it took, so the administration could assert there was no discrimination in the air force or in the nation's space agency.

Dwight had originally been part of a reserve list to join Class IV, but the orders from above saw his name included in the list of fifteen. This only served to outrage the head of the arps, Chuck Yeager, who checked out Dwight and rated him as "an average pilot with an average academic background. He wasn't a bad pilot, but he wasn't exceptionally talented either. Flying with a good bunch in a squadron, he would probably get by. But he just couldn't compete in the space course against the best of the crop of experienced military test pilots." Dwight eventually graduated, but Yeager had made sure his name was placed at the very bottom of the list of graduates, knowing full well that nasa would only ever consider the top eight in each class for the civilian space program.

Freeman's class—the last pure aerospace research pilot course—graduated on 20 December 1963. By this time, with his graduation near the top of his group just a formality, he had already been accepted by nasa to join its next group of astronauts. His shift to nasa would not take place until January, so he continued to patiently serve out his last air force assignment at Edwards as flight test aeronautical engineer and experimental flight test instructor for the arps. He was involved for the most part in performance flight and stability testing.

On 17 October 1963 the names of the nation's fourteen newest astronauts were announced, raising the number of active astronauts to twenty-eight. Those selected in the third group were Air Force Major Edwin ("Buzz") Aldrin Jr., Air Force Captain William Anders, Air Force Captain Charles Bassett II, Navy Lieutenant Alan Bean, Navy Lieutenant Eugene Cernan, Navy Lieutenant Roger Chaffee, Air Force Captain Michael Collins, civilian Walter Cunningham, Air Force Captain Donn Eisele, Air Force Captain Theodore Freeman, Navy Lieutenant Commander Richard Gordon Jr., civilian Russell Schweickart, Air Force Captain David Scott, and Marine Captain Clifton Williams Jr.

nasa arranged a press conference on 18 October to officially announce the names. Freeman's instructions were to proceed to Houston a day or two earlier and check in to the Rice Hotel on Main Street. To his puzzlement he was told not to use his real name when he checked in, but to register under the alias Max Peck. He duly gave that name at the hotel desk and wondered why the clerks kept smiling at him throughout the check-in process. Before long he started bumping into pilots he knew from Edwards and elsewhere who had also gained selection. They soon discovered they had all checked in under the same name and would laugh when they later found out that Max Peck was actually the general manager of the hotel. It was a delightful subterfuge and the source of many jokes as the pilots mentally prepared themselves to face the media onslaught the next day.

As well as congratulating each other and meeting any new faces, the men discussed another potentially large change in their lives, which would come about with a rumored financial windfall from the Time-Life astronaut contract. It had already been a source of great debate in the press.

In 1959 the seven Mercury astronauts, through a Washington lawyer named Leo De Orsay, had put up for sale to the highest bidder the book and magazine rights to their stories. De Orsay, who accepted no fee for his part in this deal, had convinced the astronauts that an exclusive contract would shield them against unwanted and intrusive media interest in their flights, training, and even their family lives.

Initially strongly opposed to the idea, NASA finally granted approval after John Glenn personally explained its unseen benefits to President Kennedy. Glenn maintained it would prevent unwanted media pressure during their training, and a lid could be kept on what was being written about the astronauts. Kennedy saw the sense in this and recommended to James Webb that he permit the deal to proceed. Once NASA had relented, De Orsay quickly signed a contract with *Life* magazine— the highest bidder. This effectively gave the magazine exclusive rights to the stories of the astronauts, and each man shared in the half-million-dollar deal to the tune of twenty-four thousand dollars per man per year for three years.

With the selection of the second group of astronauts, a fresh contract was drawn up, and this time it amounted to $16,250 annually per man for four years. Field Enterprises World Book Science Service was a co-signatory this time, and the company contributed $10,000 per man, with $6,250 from Time-Life. As with the original Mercury group these rights would cover *Life* magazine articles, books, television programs, and film rights. The publishing contract was worth half a million dollars over the four-year period, to be shared equally by the sixteen astronauts, with an option for another four years. As well there was the added inducement of a $100,000 life insurance policy for each astronaut, provided without cost by both publishers.

The money enabled the new astronauts to purchase homes near the space center and to gain insurance contracts, which, because of their new occupation, would have ordinarily meant extortionately hefty premiums. They were still on regular military wages, and while the deal did not make them financially well off, it did greatly ease the financial burden on them and their wives. The new astronauts were basically happy to go along with this contract, despite public and media mutterings about them becoming rich while still employed by the taxpayers. It was thought the same amount of money could be automatically thrust at the newest group of astronauts, and that would eventually prove to be the case.

However, the thought of signing on the dotted line made Ted Freeman a little circumspect. NASA's director of public affairs at this time was the ebullient Paul Haney. He first met Freeman and the other astronaut appointees the night before their big press conference, and he still recalls his first impression:

> Ted Freeman had dark, dank holes for eye sockets. He was skinny to the point of being skeletal. I met him and other members of the third group of fourteen at a mixer-social in a suite at the Rice Hotel in downtown Houston. So it was rather festive. Freeman approached me with an interesting proposition. He introduced himself and then asked me about the Life contract. How it worked. How the stories were put together and the timing. I gave him the rundown. Then he said he wasn't interested in being part of the Life deal. He said he'd thought it over and he realized the money would be helpful—it was down to a bit over sixteen thousand dollars per man every year with the third group coming aboard. He didn't get into a big raving scene about it. He just wanted me to know that he didn't think that would be appropriate for him. I don't know to this day if he signed up.
>
> The thing about Freeman that stuck to me was his wholesome down-home quality. He came from a little farming community in Delaware. Of the ten summers I lived in Washington—from '54 to '63—I spent every August at the beach in Rehoboth. Freeman grew up nearby. He told me once I was the only NASA guy he'd met who even knew where Delaware was!

Shortly after Christmas of 1963 the Freemans packed their bags and took their leave of Edwards, driving down to their newly built home in Nassau Bay, nestled on Clear Lake, and very close to the space center. This was accomplished using two cars; Ted was in one vehicle along with the family's pet German shepherd collie mix, Poopsie J. Sputnik III. The two Faiths made the long journey in another car, with their fretful tomcat Kitty Cat and a favorite philodendron plant taking up any vacant space.

When Freeman began his career as an astronaut, construction of the new MSC was nearing completion, so the space agency had some offices in the new center and others scattered around Ellington AFB. The new astronauts were given small, temporary offices in a hangar at Ellington.

While they were learning the ropes, they sat through Monday morning group briefing sessions at the MSC Astronaut Office, generally presided over by Deke Slayton. He would bring them up to speed on what was expected of them, not only as astronauts in training, but in the performance of other duties associated with their new careers. Slayton told the new group that as things stood at that time, he expected each of them to get a couple of flights.

The new astronauts had also begun a daunting 240-hour instruction course that concentrated on relevant subjects such as geology, flight mechanics, digital computers, guidance and navigation, rocket propulsion, upper atmosphere physics, space medicine, astronomy, and aerodynamics.

By far the largest course was geology, encompassing fifty-eight hours, a source of great debate. But the men soon realized they were being trained for lunar exploration and would have to know what they were looking for once they got to the moon. Combined with their classroom studies were field trips with trained geologists, and the first of these took the new astronauts into the Grand Canyon. It was interesting stuff, and Freeman was getting a good feeling for his life as a potential moonwalker.

As another facet of their astronaut training, Alan Shepard asked the men to decide individually which responsibilities they were best qualified to handle. The first two groups of astronauts had assumed areas of responsibilities, and this method had worked well enough to continue the process. Others from Group 3 eventually went into such specialties as spacecraft communications, recovery systems, guidance and navigation, and mission planning. After consideration, Freeman decided he would like to concentrate on launch vehicles, or boosters, and this specialty area was assigned to him.

The astronauts were also given a much-anticipated treat—flights aboard NASA's KC-135 aircraft. Virtually a Boeing 707, the aircraft had been specially modified by the removal of interior seating and fixtures, while the walls had been padded. These changes had to be made for weightless training. By flying a series of parabolic arcs, those in the cabin could experience bursts of simulated zero G for up to thirty seconds at a time. On one such exercise, Freeman was teamed with classmates Buzz Aldrin and Charlie Bassett. *Life* photographer Ralph Morse was also on board, and he recorded a series of pictures in which the three astronauts tumbled and rolled about in simulated weightlessness, obviously enjoying the experience to the hilt.

One thing was certain—Freeman was quietly going about the business of becoming a proficient astronaut, and it was not going unnoticed. Deke Slayton had formed a good opinion of the soft-spoken pilot and would later say that he had his eye on Freeman to fly in Gemini. The first assignment he seemed to have under consideration was that of pilot to Tom Stafford on the backup crew of Gemini 9. Based on the rotational crew selection formula then in operation, this would have placed them as prime crew on the final Gemini flight, GT-12. Whatever Slayton's plans, it all became moot after the last Saturday in October.

On Friday, 30 October, Ted Freeman and Buzz Aldrin were engaged in a little public affairs activity for NASA, demonstrating their spacesuits and a mock-up of the Gemini spacecraft for a few members of the press. After Aldrin had answered some questions, Freeman took his turn and stated that he had trained for a year as an astronaut with the air force before joining NASA the previous October. "We all specialize in one particular part of the project," he said of his current training. "My line is boosters."

When asked how his wife felt about him being an astronaut, he replied, "She understands. She knows this is what I love doing. Astronauts' wives have to be pretty understanding, or we couldn't do the job at all."

After giving standard responses to a few more standard questions, the two men clambered into their space suits. Then they walked with the press down to where a fully functional mock-up of the Gemini spacecraft sat waiting for them. Along the way a photographer took a shot of two serious young men who looked to be dressed and ready to go into space. On reaching the mock-up both men carefully squeezed in and settled down into their respective couches. Flashbulbs popped as Freeman pointed out the various instruments and controls and explained how he would operate them while orbiting the earth.

"Sometimes when you are doing trials," he said, "they ask whether you want a certain switch to be automatic or manual. You say 'manual' and that's what they work on. It makes you feel pretty good." He then pointed to tiny flashlights on the fingertips of Aldrin's gloves. "See that? That was one of Colonel Glenn's suggestions after he made his trip."

The reporters were lapping it up, but all too soon it was time for final questions. One asked Freeman whether he thought about the risks involved in spaceflights. He grinned—it was a question he had been asked scores of time, and the answer came automatically: "We don't look on this as dangerous work. It's about the most fascinating job I could imagine." Pencils flew over notepads as the reporters scribbled down these pearls of wisdom. Then came another question, about flying jets from one training area to another. "It's convenient for getting around," Freeman replied. "And it keeps us in practice. We have to keep in flying trim."

It was with undisguised relief that the two men bade goodbye to the press and stripped off their suits. Later that evening, someone who knew Freeman's routine on Saturday mornings jokingly asked him if he was going to see his beloved geese the next day. He replied that he was getting a bit behind in his flight time and had already decided to take out a T-38 in the morning and clock up a few more hours.

It was certainly unusual for Freeman to be flying on a Saturday. Generally it was something he tried to avoid so he could be with his family. On Saturdays, even if his wife and daughter did not feel like going out on their bicycles, he would convince them that they would feel better for getting out of the house and getting in a little exercise. One thing they would do on these family outings was cycle to Nassau Bay to watch the snow geese landing and drinking. In fact a lot of people who knew Freeman well used to kid him about his regular Saturday outings to watch the geese. Most evenings the family would also be seen cycling around Nassau Bay, although

Friday night was out of the question. That was when Freeman would catch the only show he bothered watching on television—*The Danny Kaye Show.*

He once told Italian journalist Oriana Fallaci, "The other evenings I take my bicycle and go for a ride. I take Faith and little Faith with me, and maybe they grumble, 'I don't want to Daddy,' [or] 'I don't want to Theodore,' but I say 'Come on, it does you good to go out on the bicycle.' And then I go out on my bicycle in the morning at half past six or seven o'clock when it's cool and the sky is still clean; later it gets dirty. I go for five miles to Nassau Bay where there are geese. I love geese so much."

As things turned out, it was the one day of his life when he should have stuck to his regular routine.

§

As Freeman swept around over Harris County ready to line up for a landing on runway 4, an Ellington tower controller transmitted a request that he go around again, as other traffic had been noticed in the area. It was a fairly common and routine safety precaution, so he simply poured on the power once again and began climbing. Soon after he decelerated enough to begin banking gently to the right, flying in a big looping circle that would bring him around for a second attempt at landing from the southwest. At the same time he descended to 2,100 feet, then to 1,800.

Just as Freeman was completing his turn he suddenly encountered a flock of snow geese flying right across his path. They filled his windscreen and must have presented a terrifying sight. He probably ducked instinctively as one of the birds slammed violently into the left side of his canopy. The Plexiglas windscreen exploded into fragments, which were immediately ingested into the air-breathing intakes of both engines. Meanwhile the goose had impacted heavily with the rear cockpit seat, splattering blood and feathers everywhere before its shattered body spun out and away from the aircraft. Choked with Plexiglas splinters, the T-38's two engines began to flame out, and they eventually quit. In the few moments of power he had left in his aircraft, Freeman attempted to swing it around toward the nearby runway.

He had been involved in a tense landing situation once before, in Okinawa. On that occasion an engine had caught fire, and despite being advised to bail out he managed to land successfully and pull up before leaping out and running away from the aircraft in case it blew up. Firemen were quickly on the scene and managed to quell the flames before they became too intense. All they had to do afterward was replace the faulty engine and repair part of a wing.

With that experience behind him he probably felt he could do it again, despite the damage to his cockpit. Like any well-trained pilot familiar with his aircraft, he was loath to punch out of it too soon. He knew that the nitroglycerine-charged ejection could also prove fatal; he was aware of several instances in which pilots had bailed out procedurally but had died when they hit part of the aircraft. The extent

3. The Northrop T-38A Talon. (Courtesy Northrop Aircraft Company)

of the damage must have also given Freeman cause for grave concerns about the integrity of his canopy's release mechanism. If this failed to work he would almost certainly be killed during the ejection process, his seat passing straight through the jammed canopy. In preparation, however, he attached his low-altitude lanyard, which would automatically pull the ripcord on his backpack chute once he had separated from his ejection seat. Then he lowered the jet's wheels and tried hard to hold it on course.

He was rapidly losing height but still attempting to dead-stick the T-38 onto the runway approach. At around 1,500 feet and in a dead, silent glide, he must have finally realized he could not possibly clear a small cluster of military houses on the Ellington base, which was right in his approach path. Some of them were the homes of his fellow astronauts. He desperately banked again, away from the houses, but this unselfish act would prove to be a fatal decision. Those few moments may have kept him away from a lightly populated area, but they cost Freeman his life. He was now dropping toward a field, but without power the T-38 rapidly arced and fell into a nose-down dive.

There was no choice left; Freeman had to get out. He jammed his body, head, and feet hard back into his seat and raised the handgrips located on either side of his seat. This exposed the ejection triggers, which he squeezed. The canopy was fired out into the slipstream, followed milliseconds later by the rocket motor firing.

Shocked motorists on the busy Gulf Freeway were beginning to pull over and scramble out of their cars. Many had witnessed the aircraft desperately writhing through the sky, obviously in serious trouble. They would later testify that as they watched, the forward canopy popped in a small explosive cloud and flew away from the plunging jet around 110 to 180 yards from the ground. They could only watch in horror as the pilot was flung outward a heartbeat later.

It was all to no avail. As Freeman took his hands from the controls to initiate the ejection process, the airplane had nosed down even more. As a consequence he blasted out almost horizontally, hurtling away from his doomed jet before it crashed into the soggy oilfield between the Gulf Freeway and the Old Galveston Road, about a mile east of the Ellington Field cutoff. Freeman's parachute began to deploy, but he was too late, going too fast, and now headed straight for the ground. His body slammed into the field at high speed 110 yards from the downed aircraft, killing him on impact.

Sam Puma was a bright young air force flight surgeon on loan to NASA, and that morning he was working in the hangar at Ellington AFB when he heard the crash alarms and knew a pilot was in trouble. Shortly after, a helicopter landed nearby and a crew member ran over. He spotted Puma and yelled, "Hey, aren't you a NASA doc?" When Puma indicated that he was, the man shouted, "Come on, jump in—one of our birds is down!" Both men scrambled aboard, and moments later they were airborne.

Within minutes the helicopter was hovering above the crash scene. The weed-covered field was home to several oil wells, pipelines, and storage tanks, but the men could see the downed jet and crash debris scattered amid the long grass. Once they had touched down, Dr. Puma ran over to a patch of grass where a couple of men were standing over an orange-clad body strapped in an ejection seat. A partially deployed parachute was trailing away from the scene.

One look told the young surgeon all he really needed to know. The ejecting pilot had smashed into the ground at high speed, and from the appearance of the body he had obviously been killed at the moment of impact. Although shocked, he made a brief examination and officially pronounced the pilot to be dead. It was a tragedy of monumental proportions for Puma when he recognized the body as that of Ted Freeman. He and his wife had been good friends with the Freemans, and he knew the loss would hit Faith very hard. He briefly wondered who had the miserable task of telling her she was now a widow.

Soon after other officials from MSC, including NASA's chief pilot Joe Algranti, began arriving at the scene. Flight surgeon Dr. Fred Kelly, who worked with Puma, had also responded to an urgent call. "When I arrived at the crash scene," he recalled, "Sam looked up at me and told me what we both knew. 'Ted Freeman . . . ejected too late.'"

AERIAL PHOTO OF WRECKAGE  PHOTO NO. 1
1. Flight path heading approximately 285°
2. Forward canopy.
3. Forward canopy impact.
4. Nose gear impact.
5. Main gear impact
6. Aft section of aircraft.
7. Nose section of aircraft.
8. Ejection seat impact.
9. Pilot impact.
10. Position of pilot.
11. Position of seat.
12. Impact area.

604' aircraft to seat impact distance

NASA AIRCRAFT ACCIDENT
T38A S/N 638188
31 OCTOBER 1964

4. An aerial photograph showing the accident scene following the crash of Ted Freeman's T-38A Talon. Descriptive captions on the photograph added by NASA investigators. (NASA)

Deke Slayton was relaxing at his home in Friendswood when the phone rang. It was Ellington tower advising him that a T-38 had crashed, the pilot had been killed, and though the man's name was not immediately known, it was one of his astronauts. Dazed, Slayton leapt into his silver Corvette and quickly covered the five-mile drive from his house to the crash site, arriving around the same time as Dr. Puma. As he walked over to the pilot's body with deep trepidation, he took one look and recognized Freeman. His shoulders slumped, and he shook his head in sadness. One of his boys was dead.

By now another NASA physician, Dr. Charles Berry, had arrived, and the two men discussed the tragedy for several minutes. Deeply shocked, Slayton then drove back to his office to set the necessary procedures in operation. He knew one of his first

5. The wings of the snow goose that struck Ted Freeman's jet are displayed together with shattered Plexiglas from the front cockpit. (NASA)

duties would be to personally inform the unsuspecting widow, and he had already agreed with Berry that they would meet at the Freeman home.

Astronaut Jim Lovell, who would make the first of his four space flights the following year, unintentionally became involved in the tragedy. As he tells it in his book *Lost Moon*, he was returning from a day spent, coincidentally, goose hunting with fellow astronaut Pete Conrad. As they drove past Ellington Field, Conrad noticed a group of people milling around what turned out to be the remains of a T-38 jet. Lovell immediately pulled over, and the two men ran through the weed field to the scene of the accident. He asked a shaken bystander what had happened, and the man told him he had seen the aircraft zooming toward the ground, the pilot ejecting far too late. The men knew by the number of the tailfin that it was one of NASA's jets, so Lovell hesitatingly asked if anyone knew who the pilot was. "Yeah," the man said. "A fellow called Ted Freeman."

Lovell and Conrad then moved over to the aircraft, which, apart from severe damage to the nose, was surprisingly intact. Some minor wreckage was strewn west to east. Lovell, who had studied aviation safety and had been a navy squadron safety officer, took in all the details. The front canopy was missing, consistent with an ejection. He would later learn it had been found a few hundred feet behind the crash site. Lovell could also see that most of the Plexiglas windscreen was missing. The Plexiglas on the rear canopy, still attached to the jet, was similarly shattered, and the seat was spattered with what looked like blood and the remnants of feathers.

Afterward, the two astronauts gave statements on their trained observations to NASA officials. Deke Slayton later contacted Jim Lovell to thank him for the thoroughness of his report, and placed him in charge of the subsequent investigation.

By now Dr. Berry, the MSC's medical officer and chief physician to the astronauts, had consulted with Dr. Puma and confirmed his opinion that Freeman's death was caused by multiple injuries. After a while he ordered the astronaut be cut from the parachute risers and placed into a crash bag.

Freeman's body was later removed to the morgue at Ben Taub Hospital, where Dr. Donald Thursh of the aviation division of the Armed Forces Institute of Pathology in Washington DC performed an autopsy. He had been flown to Houston to conduct the autopsy and was assisted in the grim task by Dr. Berry and Harris County Medical Examiner Joseph Jachimczyk. It was determined that Freeman had died of a skull fracture and severe chest injuries, either of which would have been instantly fatal.

For some hours after the fatal crash the actual cause was still a mystery to Jim Lovell and his investigation team, although a bird strike was logically suspected. He knew the missing Plexiglas from the front windscreen had a lot to do with it. Pete Conrad, keen to help out, decided to backtrack from the crash site and flew a helicopter to a field pinpointed by Lovell as the probable site where something had crippled the jet.

Based on eyewitness accounts, Lovell knew the aircraft's generator power had been lost, freezing the navigation instruments. He thus calculated the field as the area where Freeman's engines had cut out. Conrad set down his helicopter and began a systematic search by foot. Before long he began to find shards of broken Plexiglas in the tall grass, and then he suddenly came across the shattered body of a Canadian snow goose, surrounded by bloodied fragments of the windscreen. It was just what they had speculated to be the likely cause of the crash.

With these physical facts the sequence of the accident became abundantly clear. The goose had impacted with the front canopy, shattering the Plexiglas. Its body had then slammed into the rear seat, splattering blood and feathers everywhere before spinning away from the aircraft. The splinters of Plexiglas had then hurtled into the jet's intakes, choking them and causing a double flameout.

Freeman had probably noticed the snow goose a split second before impact and had apparently ducked instinctively as the large bird hit. His cockpit would then have been a maelstrom of gushing air, broken Plexiglas and other debris, and for a few moments the frightening, hideously loud shrieking of engines in trouble.

Sadly, Faith Freeman would learn of her husband's death in the most galling of circumstances. As chief astronaut, Deke Slayton knew it was his responsibility to break the tragic news, but just as he was about to leave his office and drive to the Freemans, his phone rang. It was the city editor of the *Houston Chronicle,* and he not only knew about the crash but also had somehow found out that an astronaut was involved—he just did not know which one. Slayton, in a quandary, asked the editor not to break the news that an astronaut had died until he had spoken to the man's wife. In exchange, he would reveal to him the astronaut's name and allow himself time for a brief interview with a reporter at the astronaut's home immediately following the notification, just to ensure the newspaper got the facts right.

The editor was then given Freeman's name, and he got his best people straight onto preparing a biographical obituary for the astronaut. He then called in a young but talented reporter named Jim Schefter, gave him the bare facts, and told him he had been given permission to interview Slayton at the Freemans' house after the notification.

Although not a senior newsman, Schefter was well known to many of the astronauts, including Freeman, as someone well versed in space matters and one who generally wrote positive things about the space program. He was deeply shocked by the loss of a man he both knew well and admired. He also knew that Faith Freeman was recovering from a recent minor surgery, and he was concerned about the effect the devastating news might have on her.

Pensively, Schefter drove over to the Freeman house at 18214 Blanchmont in Nassau Bay, and he noticed a silver 1964 Corvette parked in front. He knew Slayton owned this type of car, so he assumed this was the chief astronaut's car. He sat and watched the front door, waiting for Slayton to make an appearance from within.

After some time had passed he opened his car door and slowly made his way to the front door, paused, and rang the bell. He had met Faith several times in the past and did not feel his presence would be unwelcome despite the circumstances. The door swung open, and beyond was not a grim-faced Slayton, but Faith standing there with a pleasant, faintly surprised smile.

Jim Schefter realized something was terribly wrong with his timing, and the shock must have shown on his face. Faith frowned with uncertainty and asked what it was he wanted, as Ted was out flying and was not home at that time. Schefter, caught off guard, did not know what to say, so he blurted out that he had expected Deke Slayton to be there. Faith began to respond, about to ask why he thought Slayton might be in her house, when a terrible realization suddenly struck home. Anguish and understanding swept her face, and her eyes demanded more of the young reporter.

"There's . . . been an accident," he finally blurted out, his words cloying the air, the tension almost unbearable. "Deke's supposed to be here."

Trying desperately to regain her composure, Faith mumbled something about calling to find out what had happened, and she closed the door in Schefter's face. A short time passed, then the door was torn open again, this time by a large, red-faced neighbor of the Freemans who demanded to know what the hell a damned reporter was doing there at a time like this.

Just as Schefter was trying to explain things, an identical silver 1964 Corvette pulled up behind the first car, and Slayton clambered out. He took in the scene, muttered darkly, and stormed past the two men into the house.

Dr. Berry was already there. Unable to locate Slayton, he had gone into the next-door neighbor's house to tell them and make hasty arrangements. The shocked neighbor's wife had made some coffee for Dr. Berry while her husband went next door, ostensibly just dropping in for a neighborly chat, to be supportive of Faith once Slayton arrived.

Later, Slayton launched a blistering attack on the young reporter through the *Chronicle*'s editor, but the editor argued that Schefter was simply following instructions from Slayton himself. As time passed and tempers cooled a little, Slayton actually assumed some of the blame for the appalling incident, as he had not gone directly to the Freeman house after driving to the crash scene. Instead, he had returned to his office to set things in motion. He had then taken his time driving to the house in Nassau Bay, obviously dreading the task before him. Had he gone straight there from the accident scene, things might have been a whole lot different.

Soon after, and in order to prevent a similar breakdown in communications, strict procedures were laid down. These required that other astronauts and their wives, friends of the deceased, were to inform and console the astronaut's wife as soon as possible. Never again would a newly widowed wife find out about the death of her husband through a reporter standing on the front doorstep.

Several years later, after Slayton clarified his role in the Faith Freeman incident, her former neighbor rang Jim Schefter and apologized for his understandably explosive behavior on the day. They met for coffee and shook hands after agreeing that the whole episode had been an unfortunate occurrence on what was a truly terrible day for everyone concerned. It was never established who owned the silver Corvette Schefter said he saw outside the Freemans'—he had always assumed it belonged to Charles Berry, but Berry insists that he has never owned a Corvette, let alone a silver one. Schefter passed away on 21 January 2001 with many questions still unresolved.

At the time of the accident Paul Haney was MSC's director of public affairs. He and his staff rushed to the space center and Ellington to handle requests for information that had begun pouring in from all around the country. First of all, his office immediately notified the White House, the Department of Defense, and several high-ranking NASA officials.

MSC Director Dr. Robert Gilruth was holding talks at a contractor's plant when Haney's office informed him of the accident. He later issued a statement saying, "I am terribly sorry to hear of this. All of us are naturally shocked at this loss. Our deepest sympathies go out to Mrs. Freeman, their daughter, and astronaut Freeman's parents. We will do all we can to help them through this tragic period."

On Tuesday, 3 November, a funeral service for Freeman was held at the Seabrook Methodist Church, some three miles from the space center. The entire astronaut team was in attendance as well as newly retired astronaut John Glenn. Pallbearers for the service included five of Freeman's astronaut colleagues—Charlie Bassett, Frank Borman, Dave Scott, Bill Anders, and Mike Collins as well as Dr. Clifford Duncan, the chief of MSC's guidance and control division. The altar of the church was bedecked with hundreds of red roses, hastily organized by Faith.

The Reverend Conrad Winborn conducted the twenty-minute service, and said in part, "No eulogy is necessary in this service. Ted Freeman's life speaks for itself. This is the way it should be with every man. Thanks be to God for the quality of life known in Ted Freeman. May it be so among the sons of all men, that having run our race, having ended our brief pilgrimage, we may return to the Father our Lord, Jesus Christ."

The following day Freeman's body was flown to Washington for burial at Arlington National Cemetery with full military honors. The funeral was not widely reported in the next day's newspapers—the headlines were reserved for the overwhelming result of the 1964 presidential election. The outcome had never really been in significant doubt, as the memory of John Kennedy's assassination was still fresh in people's minds. Most voters also seemed to think Lyndon Johnson deserved an opportunity to carry on the tasks he had begun as the slain president's successor, and he swept in with a massive 61 percent of the votes. It was also a momentous win for NASA, as Johnson was a true champion of its activities. But on that day, despite the euphoria surrounding Johnson's win, the space community in Houston was still in mourning for one of its own.

On the morning of 4 November a funeral procession of slow-moving vehicles slowly wound through Arlington before arriving at Freeman's gravesite near a large tree. Faith, wearing a simple white dress with a black hat and veil, stood holding little Faith's hand. Dressed in a pale blue coat with a red ribbon tied in her blonde hair, little Faithie was crying for her father. Standing with them, silently mourning, were his parents and siblings.

Behind the family stood all twenty-eight astronauts as well as John Glenn, who had attended wearing his full dress marine uniform. Some time later, it was realized that this would be the last occasion in history when every one of NASA's astronauts was gathered in the same place at the same time.

There, on a high hillside that Wednesday afternoon, all eyes were on Freeman's flag-draped coffin as it rested on the grass and the minister said his prayers. Then a military guard fired a rifle salute, and taps was sounded.

Tom Stafford, Frank Borman, Alan Bean, and Ed White slowly approached the coffin, reverently removed the flag, folded it five times, and presented it to Faith. Later, when most of the mourners had gone, the coffin was slowly lowered into the ground.

The NASA community and the country at large honored Freeman's contributions for years to come. The Captain Theodore C. Freeman Memorial Library in Houston was dedicated on 6 February 1966, and fellow astronaut Charlie Bassett spoke with obvious affection about a man who was not only his late air force and astronaut colleague, but also a good friend. He said, in part:

> I am privileged to represent the Manned Spacecraft Center in this dedica-tion of the Theodore C. Freeman Memorial Library. Ted Freeman was a very good friend to me, but he was a very good friend to many people. His forthrightness, honesty and integrity made him easy to know and easy to admire.
>
> Now time has dulled the sharp pain of his passing, and the void that remained has somehow been filled. It is uniquely proper that we are gathered to dedicate a library to his memory. In his life he influenced many people through his easy friendliness and his concern for his fellow man. With this dedication he will reach out to us still more, but through a different medium—books. And how fitting, for no one knew the value of books more than Ted.
>
> Just as Ted was a shining example of American manhood, this library is a shining example of American determination and dedication. It is the product of a group of people with enough self-reliance and confidence to undertake a tremendous task without government aid and without profit motive, only for the good of the community. One of these people I'm speaking of is Betty Ulrich, the librarian.
>
> Ted Freeman accepted his challenge as an astronaut. Betty Ulrich and her volunteer group have accepted the challenge to provide our community with the very best library possible. As we each face our challenge, let the Theodore C. Freeman Library aid us in our search for fulfillment and happiness.

The city of Lewes, Delaware, commemorated the life and loss of Freeman by naming a highway in his honor in 1966. The Theodore C. Freeman Highway is the Lewes approach road from Kings Highway to the Lewes-Cape May Ferry.

In 1967 another tribute was paid to Freeman when four islands off the California coast were officially named after him and the three astronauts who died in the Apollo 1 fire. The islands, all man-made and about a third of a mile long, lie just off Long Beach in San Pedro Bay. City of Long Beach officials decided to name them Island Chaffee, Island Freeman, Island Grissom, and Island White, and the names became official upon recognition by the office of Geological Survey in the Department of the Interior.

Freeman's name was given to a lunar crater as a special tribute for his role in enabling the successful flight of Apollo 8 in December 1968. Freeman Crater, fifty-four miles in diameter, was marked as such by the three astronauts during their flight around the moon.

Following the death of her husband, Faith Freeman received a modest service pension and around one hundred thousand dollars in insurance payouts, but nothing could compensate her for the loss of her husband. According to the younger Faith, her mother was devastated for a long time. "After my father died my mother hardly ever left the house. She was just so lonely, so sad. She would just sit in the dark in the living room and cry."

Charlie and Jeannie Bassett gave great emotional support to the two Faiths at this time, and Charlie took care of most of their finances. His death in another T-38 accident just sixteen months after her husband sent Faith on another downward spiral of grief and uncertainty.

The insurance payout she received after her husband's death was something of a mixed blessing, as Faith told a *Life* reporter in 1968. "When Ted was killed, one of the first things my mother said to me was, 'Well, thank goodness you don't have to pull up and go look for a job.' I'm not sure this is right. Perhaps if we had to go out and look for a job, we get well faster. Your first urge is to keep moving. And never look back." This bravely spoken statement contradicts the impression her daughter still retains of a lonely, sad woman who shut herself off in a darkened house and cried herself to sleep most nights, hardly venturing out for a long time after the accident.

Faith, the first astronaut widow, was also the first to remarry when she later wed Victor Ettredge. He was with NASA, though he was an engineer, not an astronaut. He was a widower, having lost his first wife about the same time Ted died. He had three daughters and a son, so the couple had an "instant" family of five children. Although he lived in a large house in Nassau Bay they decided to live in the Freeman's smaller home, as they felt it was architecturally more interesting.

The marriage lasted only six years but ended without bitterness. Faith would later marry again, this time Bill Alexander. She sold the house in Nassau Bay and moved up to Falls Creek, Virginia, with her new husband.

Sadly, this marriage fell apart after just a year, and Faith returned to the place and people she loved best, near the space center. She tried to repurchase her old home but was not successful, so she bought a small condominium nearby. For a time things seemed to improve for Faith; she went out fishing and boating and would spend hours swimming at a friend's pool. She also became involved in fundraising for the Captain Theodore C. Freeman Memorial Library.

Just when a lot of her former vivacity seemed to have returned, Faith received another blow when it was revealed that she had contracted cancer of the mouth and lungs—the sad legacy of her long smoking habit. She fought the disease bravely over the next six years, but she ultimately lost the battle at the age of fifty-three.

Meanwhile little Faith had gone on to the University of Texas and graduated. She later married and moved to Tulsa, Oklahoma, where her three children, Tyler, Lydia, and Mara, were born. Now living in Austin, Texas, she is currently working in the software business.

Following the loss of her son, Freeman's mother, Catherine Freeman, made several trips to the Houston area as the guest of NASA and families of Ted's fellow astronauts. She also brought to many school groups and community organizations a very human face of the nation's man-in-space program, giving a short film-clip presentation on the life and training of her son. She was subsequently named Delaware's 1965 Mother of the Year.

It is difficult to speculate on what Ted Freeman might have achieved had he not flown into that flock of geese. What is known is that he was highly regarded by those at NASA who determined future projects and flight crewing, and it is believed he was on the verge of being appointed to the backup crew of Gemini 9 at the time of his death. By extrapolation of the crewing system then in place, he would have rotated onto the prime crew of Gemini 12, likely into the EVA role carried out so successfully by Buzz Aldrin, which won him a seat on the first lunar-landing mission.

Given the esteem in which he was already held, it seems virtually certain that Captain Ted Freeman would have flown to, and probably one day walked on, the moon. A simple accident on a routine flight robbed him of that chance and a far more illustrious place in spaceflight history.

# 2 Gemini Twins

## Elliot McKay See Jr.
## Captain Charles Arthur Bassett II, USAF

*In the months following the announcement of their assignment to the Gemini-
Titan 9 (GT-9) mission, astronauts Elliot See and Charlie Bassett had become
regular commuters between Houston and St. Louis in NASA's fleet of T-38 jet
aircraft. Stationed at what was then called the Manned Spacecraft Center (MSC) in
Houston, they frequently flew the ninety-minute "hop" from nearby Ellington
airfield to Lambert Field in St. Louis. Adjoining Lambert was the McDonnell
Aircraft Corporation plant where, by February 1966, their Gemini capsule was in
the final stages of assembly and testing. For See and Bassett, flying was a fairly
routine part of their business; the greater risks would come the following May, they
thought, when they were scheduled to fly into space.*

*At 7:41 A.M. (CST) on a clear winter Monday morning, 28 February 1966,
See and Bassett took off from Ellington Air Force Base (AFB). Together with their
backup crew of Tom Stafford and Gene Cernan, they had been directed to carry out
ten days of rigorous rendezvous training on a Gemini simulator at the McDonnell
plant. The principal goal of their spaceflight would be a complex docking maneuver
with an Agena target rocket, so they needed all the time they could get on the
engineering simulator. The four men were also going to inspect their spacecraft as
it neared completion. But See and Bassett never stepped safely from their plane
onto Missouri soil.*

The routine journey to Lambert, though bad weather was predicted along the way,
probably posed no worries for See and Bassett. Up to the time of what would be his
last flight, See had a total of 3,969 flight hours, of which 124 were in the T-38. He had
previously flown to St. Louis a total of twenty-five times. Bassett had accumulated
3,545 flight hours, which included 226 in the T-38. He had flown to St. Louis seven
times in the previous six months.

The day before, a Sunday, See and his family had attended a religious service
in downtown Houston and then enjoyed a matinee rodeo performance in the As-
trodome. The next day he arose at 5:00 A.M. and quietly prepared a breakfast of
cereal, juice, and toast. When he left home he was in good humor, eager to begin his
training exercise in St. Louis.

The Bassett family had also attended the Sunday rodeo. Before retiring that night,
Charlie Bassett had completed his usual 5BX program, which he followed religiously.
He also clambered out of bed at 5:00 A.M. and went for a short run before enjoying
a hot breakfast followed by coffee. He too was in high spirits when Gene Cernan
picked him up and the two friends departed for Ellington. On arrival at the base

Bassett proceeded to the flight line and performed routine preflight inspections on both aircraft to be flown to St. Louis that day, NASA 901 and 907. When he had completed his checks he remained with the aircraft and discussed the upcoming Gemini 9 flight with the crew chief.

Meanwhile, during his preflight briefing, and with his usual diligence, See called air traffic controllers in St. Louis to discuss the current weather situation, the types of approaches available, and the approach minima at Lambert Field. He informed the tower that his aircraft and that of the backup crew, Stafford and Cernan, would be landing there in a couple of hours. Next, he discussed the different runways at Lambert Field with Cernan and filed their flight plan with the FAA through facilities available at Ellington AFB. No approach plate for the Localizer Runway 12R approach to Lambert Field was available to the pilots at the early hour of their scheduled takeoff. Rather than delay the flight until this document could be obtained, the pilots elected to diagram the approach on the back of a flight data card. Only one such diagram was made and was carried in the aircraft piloted by Stafford, not the lead aircraft. Crucial information, including the missed approach procedure, was missing from the diagram drawn by Cernan. Next, See made his way out to T-38 No. 901 with copilot Bassett.

The two men walked around their aircraft and checked the exterior baggage pod, which held all four men's personal effects, including their clothing and NASA identification badges. These pods, actually fuel tanks specially converted for the purpose, had been known to tear loose in flight. This, and the fact that they created a little extra drag, did not sit well with the hard-flying, competitive astronauts, but at least their clothing arrived without being crushed, which happened when it was crammed into the back seat stowage.

Their walk around completed, See clambered into the front seat, while Charlie climbed into the rear to act as copilot. Stafford and Cernan did likewise in T-38 907, ready to fly wing position to St. Louis.

The two aircraft took off, with Stafford bringing up the rear, and then climbed to 41,000 feet, getting into formation. The skies above the light cloud cover were bright blue after the grayness below, and as Stafford eased up into position on See's wing, he and Cernan could easily make out the other two pilots with their white helmets.

The flight proceeded normally, with instrument flight clearances and procedures used. An en route radio check of the weather over St. Louis was carried out at 8:18 A.M. with the Little Rock Air Force Base Meteorological Office. Little Rock issued a forecast indicating an overcast ceiling of 600 feet, visibility of two miles, rain, fog, and a broken ceiling, with little change expected for the men's arrival in St. Louis.

The pilots contacted Kansas City Center by voice and radar seventeen minutes later, and the center gave the Lambert Field forecast, posted at 8:25 A.M. The men noted that there was still partial obscuration, with a measured ceiling of broken clouds at 800 feet, and overcast ceiling at 1,500 feet, while visibility over the field had diminished to one and a half miles. At 8:39 a radar letdown was initiated under the control of Kansas City before the flight was passed over to St. Louis Approach Control nine minutes later for radar vectors to an Instrument Landing System (ILS) approach to the southeast runway 12R at Lambert Field. The pilots received another weather forecast, but it was the same one given earlier at 8:25. At this time they were well within safety limits for the type of approach they were using. Other pilots flying into and out of Lambert Field around this time later stated that the weather was far worse than reported and was deteriorating rapidly. The two pilots had no way of knowing this.

As the two aircraft approached Lambert Field's runway 12R, rain and fog made visibility poor, and the jets jarred and shuddered as they descended into the murkiness below. Incredibly, Approach Control employees later stated that they were unaware the flight consisted of two aircraft, and they gave a vector to the localizer that required a tighter than desirable turn of about seventy degrees, causing the two aircraft to fly through the localizer two or three times before intercepting the final approach course. At this time both pilots would have been watching their instruments for signs of reception of the glide slope signal while in the vicinity of the outer marker. As See was maneuvering on the localizer course, either he or Bassett was answering radio transmissions from Approach Control and Tower, and the pilots passed over the outer marker—apparently unawares. It wasn't until they were well past the marker beacon that they realized the glide slope transmitter was not functioning. They finally broke through the cloud cover at 8:55 A.M., and both pilots realized they had overshot the runway for a straight-in landing. Stafford contacted See's aircraft immediately. "Hey, we missed the runway!" he called out.

See apparently decided to stay below the cloud cover and keep the field in sight, which was no problem as far as obstacle clearance was concerned, as they were over the runway and still in protected airspace. The conditions had deteriorated markedly from what the team had expected, with decreased visibility and a light snow flurry causing further obscuration. A jagged shelf of clouds hung along the line of sight above the ground, but lower than the present altitude of the aircraft. See threw the aircraft into a steep left turn to avoid a fog bank that shrouded the hills on that side of the field, and transmitted his intention of lining up for another approach, this time on southwest runway 24.

While delaying his own turn momentarily for adequate landing spacing, Stafford stuck behind See and continued to circle through 240 degrees of left turn before an underhanging section of cloud caused him to briefly lose visual contact with See's aircraft. At this time Stafford decided it was prudent to initiate a missed-approach procedure, rolled his wings level, and informed Approach Control of his heading and intentions. They caught another glimpse of 901 as it continued to turn smoothly, crossing over the approach end of 12R. "Goddamn!" Stafford cried. "Where the hell's he going?" The lead aircraft then disappeared from view as Stafford climbed into the murk, ready to make another instrument approach.

The Accident Investigation Board later stated, "Several more transmissions were made between 907 and Approach Control in the next several seconds, which tended to mislead personnel on the ground in Approach Control and in the Tower as to what both aircraft were doing at that time."

As See continued his turn, he reported, "Ah . . . this is 901. I'll turn over and come on in . . . I think it's runway two four." He then transmitted, "Final ils 24." The controller responded, "NASA 901 and 907, this is approach control. Climb and maintain 3,000 on a heading of 360." But there was no acknowledgement or response from 901, perhaps due to the confusion caused by having two aircraft in close proximity suddenly initiating different abort procedures. The tower then asked, "Do you have the airfield in sight 01?"

The T-38 with See and Bassett aboard continued to lose altitude slowly, but conditions at the northeastern boundary of Lambert Field were in a chaotic state of flux and had deteriorated even more since their first pass over the field. In all probability, both pilots on board would have been keeping a sharp lookout for the runway 24 approach lights. Bassett, observing strict regulations, would not have been engaged in any backseat flying, but would have been aiding See and reducing the pilot's workload in every way possible. Apparently See suddenly noticed the high intensity approach lights to 24 and sent the aircraft into an abrupt, steep left turn, with the gear down and full flaps. This move induced a rapid sink rate from which a quick recovery would have been difficult to accomplish. It is probable, given the prevailing weather conditions, that the aircraft experienced heavier than normal airframe buffeting, causing the left wing to drop to a near-vertical bank as it passed over a guardhouse near the northeast corner of the McDonnell plant. Flying just 100 feet above the ground, See must have realized their sink rate was excessive and kicked in the afterburners. He threw the T-38 into a steep right turn to avoid the buildings suddenly looming before them. But he performed the maneuver too late.

At 8:58 A.M. the T-38's left wingtip hit the metal roof of McDonnell's three-story Building 101, a vast corrugated iron structure enclosing engineering and administration areas called Gemini Space Operations. The building also housed the Gemini 9 capsule that the astronauts planned to inspect. The right wing then cut into the roof like a can opener and was ripped from its mounts, slowing sufficiently to stay on the roof. Moments later the wing's fuel tank exploded in a ball of flame as the fuselage continued on its path. The left and right horizontal stabilizer, both main landing gear, the equipment pod, and the nose wheel were also stripped from the aircraft near the initial contact point. The plane, still nose-up, then bounced and slammed into the roof again, tearing support structures.

Sometime between the initial strike and the fuselage hitting a corner girder anchoring the roof, many of the ballistic devices in both ejection seats fired on their own. Neither seat received any upward thrust from its rocket catapult since the components were rapidly breaking up at this time, but as the forward fuselage area began to disintegrate, the two pilots and their seats were propelled forward from the aircraft. Bassett, thrown clear upside down, hit a sharp metal stanchion on the roof and was instantly decapitated.

At a distance of 112 feet from the initial impact point, the airframe of the T-38 rose above the roof and then, having bounced twice and almost out of energy, rolled over the edge of the roof before cartwheeling to the ground. The main fuselage, with the left wing and engine still intact, came to rest in a construction site a little over 100 feet from the west wall in the plant's courtyard parking area, which was littered with building material, construction sheds, and trailers. Both bodies, in their ejection seats, also fell into the courtyard.

§

A gentle but dedicated man who went about his work with a calm efficiency, Elliot See was born in Dallas, Texas, on 23 July 1927, becoming part of a family committed to the study and practice of Christian Science. His father, also named Elliot, was a highly skilled electrical engineer who worked almost twenty years with the General Electric Company. His services had been required in such diverse areas as dam construction and working on ships, and he was a recognized expert in engine corrections. At one time he had also worked in Chile for Bessemer Steel, which was involved in recovering ore for steel production in Chuquicamarta, also home to the biggest open pit copper mine in the world. When this work was completed he made his way back to the United States, arriving on Armistice Day of 1918. He then settled in Dallas, Texas.

Elliot See would later marry Mamie Drummond, an attractive and determined young woman. As her first job out of college she had taken work in the advertising department of Neiman-Marcus, a high-end Dallas retailer, and in 1922 was one of the first two graduates of the new department of journalism at the University of Texas in Austin. Mamie, engaged in many local and church activities, was a woman much admired for her strength of will and compassion—qualities she would one day pass on to her children. In her later years she took on work in the real estate and insurance businesses but would also continue writing on a freelance basis.

Elliot and Mamie's first child, born in 1927, was a cherubic son they decided to name after his father. Later on, a baby sister named Sally would complete their family. As Sally grew older she idolized her big brother and would tag along with him whenever she could. An artistic woman later in life, she would enjoy a career as an interior designer in Dallas.

As he grew up, young Elliot attended elementary and high school in Dallas's Highland Park School District. During those formative years, and among other interests, he enjoyed five years as a Boy and Eagle Scout. He took three years of Latin at school, was involved in Greek fraternities, and joined the Reserve Officer Training Corps (ROTC) Rifle Team. While never one to attract undue attention to himself, he was nevertheless involved in several varsity sports, including boxing.

Graduation came in the winter of his senior year of high school, but America had been thrust into the Second World War after the bombing of Pearl Harbor, and he began to contemplate going into service for his country. To See, it just seemed the natural and right thing to do, but through his parents he also knew the intrinsic value of a good education. He later revealed that he was in a bit of a quandary when it came time to make the shift from high school, "where you have to go, and college, where you don't."

The thought of flying airplanes had always held a great fascination for See, so while he was trying to decide what he should do next he applied for aviation cadet training but was unable to pass an overly rigorous physical. "Then, suddenly, going to college became the most important thing to me," he said in a later interview. "It was the key to everything that has happened since."

Within a few months of entering the University of Texas, See was enjoying his studies so much that thoughts of military training receded, and once he fully settled in he pledged to the Phi Kappa Psi fraternity. Although he was on a strict budget he somehow managed to set a little money aside each week for flying lessons, eventually receiving his private pilot's license. It was a defining moment in his life. He now felt that in aviation and engineering he had a definite focus for his future, and he often talked over his plans and hopes with his parents, who proved highly supportive. He decided to apply for military officer training, and in 1945, while living in Grand Prairie, Texas, he was thrilled to receive an appointment to the United States Merchant Marine Academy at Kings Point on Long Island.

The U.S. Merchant Marine Cadet Corps was officially founded on 15 March 1938 under the auspices of the U.S. Maritime Commission, then chaired by Joseph P. Kennedy, father of the future president. Initially the training of cadets was carried out aboard government-subsidized ships, but in February 1942 the Coast Guard took over administration of the program. Cadet appointees had to meet certain criteria: the applicant had to be between eighteen and twenty-five years of age; of good moral character and unmarried; meet Navy physical requirements; have sound teeth, feet, and posture; and possess good eyesight, color perception, speech, and hearing. The height requirements were quite flexible and covered most applicants, but academically they had to have accumulated at least fifteen high school credits.

Early on, after eight weeks of preliminary shore training, cadets would go to sea under an arrangement between a shipping company and the U.S. Maritime Service. But the need for a permanent shore facility prompted Congress in 1942 to fund the purchase of a former Chrysler estate on Long Island, New York, which became home to the Merchant Marine Academy. At the same time, cadet schools were established at Pass Christian, Mississippi, and San Mateo, California.

The Merchant Marine Academy's campus was dedicated on 30 September 1943. In opening the facility, President Franklin D. Roosevelt proudly affirmed, "the Academy serves the Merchant Marine as West Point serves the Army and Annapolis serves the Navy." The academy became privileged among the nation's five federal academies as the only institution authorized to carry a battle standard as part of its color guard. The standard would perpetuate the memory of the 142 academy cadets and midshipmen who were casualties of World War II.

As World War II drew to an end plans were initiated to convert the academy's wartime curriculum to a four-year, college-level program able to meet the peacetime requirements of the merchant marine. That course was instituted in August 1945—the year See signed on.

Prior to this, See and other applicants had to undertake competitive examinations for appointment as cadet or midshipman, which were held four times annually. Admission was based on examination scores and state quotas. The physical requirements were basically those for the Navy, and the age spread was from sixteen years and six months to less than twenty-three years of age. On graduation, a midshipman would receive a bachelor of science degree in marine transportation or marine engineering, a Coast Guard license to sail as a third mate or third-assistant engineer, and a commission in the U.S. Naval Reserve.

Life with the Merchant Marine Academy was all that See had hoped it would be and more, and he happily served his plebe year at Pass Christian in Mississippi. Then, during his midshipman days at the academy, he commanded the Third Company as cadet officer, joined the Propeller Club, was a varsity boxer, ran with the mile relay team, played softball, and was even head cheerleader. Notable among other distinctions he achieved at the academy were his appointment as cocaptain of the rifle team in December 1948 and being awarded the prestigious Captain Tomb Trophy for rifle and pistol marksmanship. That same month he also earned the coveted Scholastic Star and wore the accompanying epaulets with pride.

One of See's close friends at the academy was Jim Lee, whom he had met in the summer of 1945 at Pass Christian School. Lee recalls that they were also "room mates, team mates in sports, and travel mates during 'liberty' off the academy grounds, and at Pass Christian. So we were living together for three years out of the four in the Merchant Marine schooling. While room mates at Kings Point, Elliot was always statistician on our intramural softball team, keeping good records on runs, hits, and errors. He and I usually made runs and hits, but no errors that I can remember."

Lee also says that he and See would often march together in parades as part of the rifle team: "Once at a Presidential inauguration in Washington, several Armistice Day parades in New York City, and home and away football games for Kings Point."

Midshipmen always mustered in the hallway outside of their rooms for morning calisthenics, and one day Lee recalls opening their door to find a large and fancy sign hung there (in complete violation of the rules) that said *See & Lee Chinese Laundry—No Tickee, No Laundry!* It cracked them right up. In company with Lee, as well as Don Seth, Jim Kelly, Ralph Rogers (who would later be best man at his wedding), and others, See would check out sailboats most Sundays. For long, lazy hours, he and his friends would enjoy the simple pleasures of each other's company, talking of desultory things as they sailed on Long Island Sound.

There was also some excitement to recount: one time, during a Christmas leave, Lee and See were involved in an incident that could very easily have ended in disaster, as Lee recalls:

*Being in the U.S. Naval Reserve as Midshipmen, we were allowed to hitch passage on military aircraft when on leave for holidays. Elliot was as adventurous as I was in those years, and he and I hitched a ride on a Navy TBM torpedo bomber out of Floyd Bennett field in Brooklyn to Norfolk, Virginia. The three of us—the Navy pilot, Elliot in the gunner's station, and myself in the bomber's station, took off from the field in fine style, both of us Midshipmen in dress blue uniforms crammed into this TBM. Upon arriving in Norfolk the pilot discovered the wing flaps would not operate to slow the plane for landing. And then, after touchdown on the runway, the wheel brakes wouldn't work. There was an awful racket from the warning horn in the plane, but at the time Elliot and I didn't know what this meant. The pilot used up the runway, and then took off again. He came on the intercom and told us what was wrong, and that we would try again to land. On the second attempt he used up the runway, then took off again. On the third try he landed as close as possible on the field approaches, used the entire runway, and ran off the far end into deep sand. The sand bogged the wheels down and flipped the plane up on its nose, destroying the propeller and probably the engine. A Navy truck took us into the hangar, where Elliot and I bade the pilot farewell and thanks, and we 'lucked' into another Navy plane bound for Jacksonville, Florida. That trip was uneventful. From there we flew on to Panama City, then he went over to Pensacola and caught another Navy plane bound for Dallas.*

See first experienced the wonders of overseas travel in his third year at the academy, and it was a period of his life he would always remember with fondness. "One year we sailed to five countries in Africa and Japan," he later recalled for an interviewer. "We went all over the world."

Still wishing to pursue a career in aviation, and knowing there were hordes of ex-GIs searching for full-time civilian work, See decided to apply for a position with his father's former employer, the General Electric Company. He set down his credentials and aspirations in a letter, drafted several times until he was fully satisfied, and sent it off. Some time later he was overjoyed to receive a job offer from the company, although in a letter he wrote to his parents in May 1949 he mentioned that "it is difficult to determine at this time what my initial assignment will be."

The following week See and his classmates sat for their marine engineer's licenses. The exams would last a full week and were traditionally tough. "Many of us feel we have done more studying in the last week than in all the rest of our time at Kings Point," See revealed to his parents in another letter home. "I feel saturated with knowledge and am practically a walking encyclopedia of facts about Steam, Diesel, and Electricity, with Refrigeration thrown in for good measure. I truly feel prepared though, mentally and spiritually." It was therefore a huge relief when he was told he had passed. The license, issued by the Coast Guard, was not only a requirement for all seagoing engineers, but also necessary if he was to graduate from the academy. A commission in the United States Naval Reserve would follow.

Soon after his graduation See took on temporary summer work with the Lykes Brothers Steamship Company, sailing out of New Orleans, and on 1 September began his fledgling career with General Electric in the company's Aircraft Gas Turbine Division in Boston. He never looked back; with his education, background, and experience to assist him, he steadfastly applied himself to any tasks he was given, and he would eventually realize his hope of becoming a flight test engineer with the company.

When General Electric moved its Aircraft Gas Turbine Division to Cincinnati, See made the move, too, and together with three male friends he rented a country house. Not long after he met and began courting an attractive young secretary with the company, Marilyn Jane Denahy from Georgetown, Ohio. After they had known each other for a short while she found herself falling for the soft-spoken, up-and-coming young engineer.

By now he and housemate Ray Haney had combined forces and incomes to purchase an all-aluminum 8-series Luscombe Silvaire. The two friends looked after the high-wing, two-seater aircraft with a shared pride and enjoyment, and both would spend many happy hours tinkering away on its 65-horsepower fuel-injected Continental engine. They took the Luscombe up as often as possible, and the silvery airplane became a familiar sight in the skies around Cincinnati. In friendly rivalry with each other they would perform basic aerobatics within the capability of the small airplane—quite often to the chagrin of their neighbors on the ground, who were grudgingly familiar with these two young men and their aerial antics. Among other increasingly competitive benchmarks, See and Haney would see who could touch down closest to a white handkerchief positioned on the local airstrip. More often than not it was See who walked away wearing the victor's grin.

As their flying and navigation skills grew, the two pilots would often make cross-country trips. One of their favorite destinations drew them south to the beaches of Tallahassee, where they would laze around and soak up the sun for a few hours before packing up and flying back to Ohio.

Although he knew the aviator's maxim about there being old pilots and bold pilots, but no old, bold pilots, See had so much confidence in his own flying ability that one day on a hop over to Michigan, he decided that conditions were right to see how well he could navigate without using his instruments. He had spotted a massive cumulus cloud ahead of him, so he pointed the Luscombe's nose directly at the billowing whiteness and plunged into its seemingly benign folds. Almost immediately he became disoriented and realized just how quickly the loss of visibility could affect one's equilibrium and sense of direction. When he finally emerged from the cloud he was alarmed to find himself in a spiral dive, from which he quickly corrected. It was a sobering experience, and he knew then he still had a lot to learn about the serious business of flying.

In November 1952 See was involved in an aircraft accident, but it would not cause him to lose his interest in aviation nor diminish his confidence. He had taken Marilyn up for a flight in the Luscombe when its engine began to sputter badly, and he knew he had to find somewhere to set down as quickly as possible. While attempting to land on an unimproved short field the airplane's tail wheel failed to clear a power line in its path. It snagged, and the Luscombe slammed into the ground. Fortunately Marilyn was not seriously injured, but See sustained some deep cuts to his face. Later, in the hospital, he would have to undergo some remedial plastic surgery, but his major concern as always was for Marilyn. He carried a facial scar from that time on as a legacy of the incident.

Fortunately, just as the crash did not deter See from flying, Marilyn's interest in the dashing young pilot had not wavered. Despite the mishap, they continued to date and soon became a devoted couple. They fell deeply in love and eventually began making plans to marry.

By now See was working as a flight test engineer at General Electric's Evandale plant in Ohio, but the following year he was called to active service as a naval reservist—quite a common occurrence at the end of the Korean War, when most of the pilots who had been assigned to active duties were finally allowed to return to civilian life. He would later be based at the Miramar Naval Base in San Diego.

On 30 September 1954 See and Marilyn tied the knot, and the happy newlyweds took up residence in the base's married quarters. A month later Naval Reserve Lieutenant Elliot See was involved in a sixteen-month tour of duty as a member of Fighter Squadron VF-144, known as "The Bitterbirds," attached to Air Group 14.

The first few months of this tour life were dedicated to orientation and familiarization. Initially this entailed formation and tactics flying, followed by long hours of debriefing, in which the pilots would be told what they had done, or should have done, in the air. The aviators and crews also had to acquaint themselves with the idiosyncrasies of pressurization, hydraulic leaks, gun sights, and ejection seats.

As time wore on and things became more familiar to the men, operations were stepped up accordingly. Now they were taught combat proficiency and readiness, and this training caused the first long separation for the newlyweds. To have the best possible training conditions available to them, the men temporarily said goodbye to San Diego and their families in November and were shipped to El Centro to begin four weeks of training. This period was hard for See and his wife, but they knew such things were now part of a life they would face as a service couple.

El Centro lies east of San Diego between the Laguna and Chocolate Mountains. Situated just north of the Mexican border, it was ideal for naval aviation purposes because almost every day of the year flying conditions were close to perfect. Back then the base was surrounded by nearly uninhabited desert, which allowed the

6. Marilyn and Elliot See. (Courtesy Sally See Kneuven)

pilots to practice bombing, rocketing, and strafing techniques. Sortie after sortie was flown over the sand dunes just a few miles from the naval station. A second month of these activities would take place during February 1955.

It was hard work for the budding fighter pilots—up before five and shivering through takeoff preparations in the thin, cold desert air. It was not unusual for each of them to undergo three or four of these combat training flights every day.

Next on See's service agenda as part of his tour of duty was a Mediterranean cruise aboard the USS *Boxer*, beginning in October 1955. For most of their time at sea the pilots became a part of, and operated with, Task Force 77 of the Seventh Fleet. The *Boxer* was a veteran of ten years of continuous commissioned service and had been constructed after the Japanese attack on Pearl Harbor in December 1941. High performance combat aircraft operated from her 863-foot deck, and See's squadron would fly the F9F-5 Panther. His principal responsibility on the cruise was line maintenance, but he also became proficient at landing on the carrier under all conditions.

See's reserve unit subsequently visited Hawaii; Japan; the Philippine Islands ports of Subic Bay, Cupi Point, and Manila; and then Hong Kong, before returning to San Diego. During this time See qualified as an operational jet aviator and attained the rank of lieutenant commander. It was a tough and demanding time, but it had proved to be an experience beyond his expectations. Somewhere in the middle of all this he was even talked into becoming editor of his squadron's cruise book, a

7. Astronauts' nurse Dee O'Hara and Jim McDivitt share a joke about a drink cup while Elliot See, Ed White, and Tom Stafford look on. (NASA)

diary covering the period from October 1954 to February 1956. In a subsequent letter to his mother he bemoaned his lack of writing experience, telling her he was "fervently wishing more of your journalistic talents had rubbed off on me." He was also writing constantly to Marilyn, now pregnant with their first child. She kept herself busy with a vast array of courses, including classes in cooking, sewing, stenography, and shorthand, and also took up a correspondence course in business writing. See managed to just make it home for the birth of his first child on 22 February 1956, a baby girl named Sally.

Resuming his career with General Electric that year as a flight test engineer, See became a group leader and experimental test pilot based in Lancaster in southern California. His work at the nearby Edwards Air Force Base involved flying aircraft such as the F-86, XF4D, F-104, F11F-1F, RB-66, F4H, and T-38A Talon. His last job with GE prior to joining NASA was serving as project pilot of the J79–8 jet engine evaluation program in connection with the F4H Phantom aircraft. In this capacity he assisted the project engineer and flew most of the F4H missions. He was also conducting power plant test flights on the J-47, J-73, J-79, and CJ805 aft-fan engines. On the home front, his family continued to grow when baby Carolyn was born on 16 November 1957.

During this second period with GE, See undertook studies for his master's degree in aeronautical engineering, which meant driving a hundred miles each way from Lancaster to the University of California one night a week to attend classes. These classes were in addition to his flying with the Los Angeles Naval Reserve Unit, also about 120 miles each way. All that time away was hard with a wife and young family at home—"one of the toughest things I've done," he later described it. But his determination paid off, for he had his master's degree in two years. One of the professors who proved a great influence on him during his time at UCLA was the eminent science fiction writer Isaac Asimov.

Early in 1962 See heard that NASA was in the process of recruiting a second group of astronauts, and he worked out that he met all the qualifications. After talking it over with Marilyn he drew up an application and sent it in. It was duly acknowledged, and he was asked to undergo a preliminary evaluation and some medical tests. However, he did not allow this exciting prospect to stop him from making alternate plans, as he mentioned in a letter on 2 July to his parents. "I'm afraid this summer is going to slip by very fast," he wrote, "but that suits Marilyn fine this year. My Navy cruise starts next week and we'll be having it at our home base, Los Alamitos, since we're checking out in new aircraft this year. There always seems to be something coming along to keep the Reserve activity interesting. Since I was able to keep it up during school for the last two years, it would seem that I should be able to continue it now."

See also mentioned to his father that General Electric was "in a position of leadership on a broad technical front. There is still plenty of competition around though, and we have to strive all the time. For our part in Flight Test, we are trying to become more space oriented in our work, such as in ground testing of rocket engines, and control system development for a lunar landing simulator."

That same month NASA contacted See once again, and he allowed himself to become a little more excited. This time he underwent a far more daunting and exhausting barrage of interviews and medical examinations.

On 12 August 1962, the See family was rounded out with the birth of their son David. It would prove to be a momentous time for the Sees on many fronts—within a month of David's birth, his father was named as one of his nation's second group of astronauts. At thirty-five he was the oldest of the group, but he felt no disadvantage in this—he had just witnessed John Glenn flying into space at the age of forty, so he reasoned he had several good years as an astronaut ahead of him.

At the time of his selection by NASA, See had logged more than thirty-nine hundred hours of flying time, including thirty-three hundred in jet aircraft. He was an officer of the Society of Experimental Test Pilots and a member of the American Institute of Aeronautics and Astronautics. When asked how it felt to be chosen as one of his nation's space pioneers, he replied, "Overwhelmed isn't the right word. I was amazed and certainly pleased. It's a very great honor."

When it came time to report to NASA in Houston, See drove down from Edwards in company with another civilian test pilot who had also been selected in the second astronaut group. This clean-cut young man had flown the x-15 research aircraft, and the two spent many happy hours discussing this and other high performance aircraft. See did not know it at the time, but his traveling companion would one day become the first man to walk on the moon—Neil Armstrong.

"I don't remember whether the car was his or mine," Armstrong reflected. "If it were his, it would have been a convertible; he loved convertibles. He was enjoyable company; we enjoyed being together and wondering what our future would be."

The simple fact that See had become an astronaut immediately thrust him into an unfamiliar role in the media spotlight. Uncomfortable at first with all this hype and adulation, See's penchant for not attracting attention to himself seemed to give the impression that he was reticent in his dealings with the press. To them, although he was obliging and courteous, See always appeared as if he would rather be elsewhere.

This reluctance to talk about himself, whether real or imagined, underwent a substantial change during the two-week period in which he and fellow astronaut Charlie Bassett were CapComs during the history-making rendezvous flight of Gemini 6 and 7. See and other MSC officials met with newsmen to discuss the progress of the joint flight, and he not only seemed relaxed and comfortable, but would sometimes display a previously unsuspected and wry sense of humor. Often he stayed after the regular news conferences to discuss in broader terms any points of interest with reporters. Characteristically, his answers were generally well thought out and concise.

Typically enough, See was the last of the Group 2 astronauts to select a plot of land and build in Houston. Nothing he did was marked by extremes, and everything was carried out both methodically and without haste. This tendency extended to viewing dozens of potential building sites before selecting the lot at Timber Cove and personally designing a comfortable house for his family. In his free time he loved nothing better than the simple pleasures of swimming, playing golf, and horseback riding with his family.

On 8 February 1965 Deke Slayton announced the crew for the Gemini 5 (GT-5) flight. Veteran Mercury astronaut Gordon Cooper, together with the talented and amiable Charles "Pete" Conrad, would fly the long-duration mission. Neil Armstrong and Elliot See, the only two civilians in NASA's astronaut corps, were named as the backup crew.

"This was to be the first long duration flight," Armstrong recalled. "From the spring to fall of '65 we were together constantly; flying to the Cape, to North Carolina (for astronomy experiment development), to McDonnell Aircraft (to test the spacecraft), sitting in the simulator for endless hours developing rendezvous techniques and entry profiles, and learning the spacecraft systems."

The four men trained as a team over the next six months, until Cooper and Conrad flew into orbit on 21 August. Soon after the Titan-2 rocket carrying Cooper and Conrad lifted off from Cape Kennedy, a heater for their Gemini spacecraft's fuel cells failed to function properly, causing a crippling shortage of electrical power. By the sixth orbit the problem was serious enough for controllers to consider a curtailment of the flight and ordering the crew to make an early splashdown in the Pacific. The fuel cell was an essential device being used for the first time and was necessary because Gemini spacecraft could not carry the bulky, heavy load of standard batteries that would be needed for an eight-day flight.

Flight Director Chris Kraft ordered the implementation of an emergency rescue drill in the event NASA had to bring the spacemen back home prematurely, while stations tracking and analyzing reports from the spacecraft frantically tried to find a reason for the power loss. See had been closely involved in the development of the fuel cells, and he felt certain he and his General Electric engineers could solve the problem by devising procedures to repair the faulty cells in orbit. Kraft talked it over with See and finally agreed that he and his team could have twenty-four hours in which to come up with a solution to save the mission from an early end. The men worked through the night to find some answers and talked through numerous procedures with Pete Conrad. The fault was eventually traced to a thin, insulated copper wire that conveyed heat to a tank of supercooled liquid oxygen, keeping it in a state between liquid and gas. Now that they knew what the problem was, they were able to initiate repairs.

Twenty-seven hours after launch the two astronauts reported with undisguised relief in their voices that the problem had been rectified. Jubilant officials in Houston quickly announced that the flight would now complete its eight-day mission, as well as a raft of vital experiments. At the time, such an in-house repair aboard an orbiting spacecraft was considered a huge advance for the program, and much of its success was attributed to See.

Armstrong remembers a happy aftermath to the mission: "After each flight there was a 'pin party.' After a crewman made his first flight, he was given a gold lapel pin at this party. Usually there were 'comments' by various attendees about the conduct of the flight. As the backup crew [Elliot] and I assumed responsibility for the entertainment at the Gemini V pin party. We constructed a 'better than any previous production' satirical skit about what really happened on Gemini V using my tape recorder playing background music from the contemporary western comedy film 'Cat Ballou.' But the movie wasn't as funny as our skit. I've never seen anyone have so much fun as [Elliott] while he was creating the one-liners and situation comedy for that skit."

Given the crew rotational policy favored by Slayton, Armstrong and See should then have skipped the next two flights and flown together on the GT-8 mission. But after considering the makeup of this and later Gemini flights, Slayton eventually replaced See with Dave Scott and gave See his own command.

Something See always took very seriously was attention to his astronaut duties. In one instance, just a few days before the GT-5 mission, a few astronauts had gathered on nearby Cocoa Beach for a relaxed social evening and barbecue picnic. They had all turned up ready to eat the succulent hamburgers cooked at dusk, but See arrived with a paper bag tucked under his arm. When asked how he would like his hamburger cooked, he smiled and replied, "I have my supper here," then produced some bite-size chunks of a generally tasteless dehydrated food that NASA wanted tested for upcoming missions. That was See all over—he just wanted to do his best.

Though he preferred to keep out of the limelight, and privately denounced the lucrative promotional deals many of his colleagues had set up, See was nevertheless one of those who had staunchly defended the controversial Time-Life contracts. He did this despite dark grumbling from certain quarters that the astronauts had been selling themselves out to commercial interests. He recalled that on the day he was named as an astronaut, "nine radio, TV, and newspaper reporters came to my house and interviewed my wife. It was strenuous, and she was glad to do it. But not on a regular basis. We all know that the public has a genuine enthusiasm for the [astronauts] and has a right to know about them[, but] the men and their families also have to have some privacy. The contracts are just a way to limit the number of requests made on our private life."

As part of the publishing contract, See was asked to participate in an article for *Life* magazine. Each of the nine Group 2 astronauts was given the chance to talk about his particular specialty as part of the astronaut corps, and he gave this response:

> *My wife Marilyn says I use the word "interesting" more than any other word in the dictionary. Well, that's the way I feel about the space program and our part in it. Like all the others in our group, I want to make space flights as soon and as often as I can. But all of us realize that only a small—but important—part of this program will involve flying. The major contribution right now is made on the ground.*
>
> *I have two areas of responsibility; the electrical systems in the Gemini and Apollo craft . . . and mission planning. In Gemini we'll be using fuel cells as a power source for the first time—tiny batteries which combine oxygen and hydrogen to generate electricity. Regular storage batteries would weigh too much. Mission planning gives me a chance to look at the overall program. In Apollo, especially, we are facing questions that have never been answered before—or possibly even asked.*

One interesting problem he became involved in was determining the kind of lighting astronauts would need to land on the moon. Would it be best to make the landing in sunlight, or would earthshine—the light reflected from the Earth—be good enough? And if earthshine would do, how much was needed? This was an important decision, for several design areas of the craft built to land on the moon depended on the lighting conditions chosen. For instance, if astronauts landed in sunlight they would need more protection against the sun's radiation. Also, temperatures in the lunar daytime exceed 200 degrees above zero and plummet by night to 238 degrees below. The decisions See and the other engineers made would affect how the first men on the moon would dress.

To help solve the lighting problem he began making flights in airplanes and a helicopter wearing special welders' goggles, which would simulate various lunar conditions by letting in just the right amount of light. In trying to ascertain what could be viewed under those conditions, See would look at mountains to determine if they could be seen well enough to avoid them, would try to spot obstacles that might hinder a safe landing, and would try to define a specific landing area. In these tests the obstacles were trees or rocks; on the moon they might be huge craters or ridges. See wrote the following about his experiments: "I find that as I work on details like this—literally working out the problems of a lunar expedition—the whole mission becomes more real to me and less of an adventure into the unknown. Here we are rehearsing it, living it every day. Now, when I look at the moon at night, it seems more familiar to me. And sometimes I find myself thinking about the lunar surface and picture it just as though I were about to land there."

Prior to his command assignment to GT-9, See had not only carried out backup duties for the GT-5 flight of Gordon Cooper and Charles Conrad but also had served as a CapCom during the dramatic rendezvous mission involving Gemini 6 and 7. Paul Haney was the head of NASA's Public Affairs Office during the Gemini days, and he recalls See as being the "most quiet" in the Group 2 astronauts:

> *Of all the nine members of the second group, Elliot was the smallest—exactly as tall as [Gus] Grissom next to whom he's standing in an informal one-of-a-kind picture I have of the seven and the nine standing in the street in a long line. You got to know pilots by working mission shifts with them or going on geology hikes or doing a week or so of jungle training on site in Panama. He didn't drink or chase girls. See worked the CapCom position during Gemini 5, which was a long, dull flight. He worked his position conscientiously, always the quiet one but helpful to me in trying to figure out what Pete or Gordo meant when they said such and such. For instance, Pete responded to one call: "Sorry, Gordo can't come to the phone right now. He's busy." Translation: "Gordo has diarrhea and is trying to wipe himself up." Gemini, you recall, was the size of a front seat of a Volkswagen.*

Shortly after this particular flight See was asked which space mission, given his choice, he would most like to have flown. "I would probably have liked to have flown Gemini 5" was his considered response, "because it had a little bit of everything—long duration (eight days) and rendezvous. It was really a step forward."

When asked by the same reporter if he wanted to walk on the lunar surface one day, he smiled and replied without hesitation, "Sure I do. But my main interest in going to the moon is in doing the experimental test flying to get me there. I don't think my personal desires are of any consequence at all. The important thing is the development of the space program. I want very much to participate in it, and contribute to it. Being an astronaut is really engineering experiment test flying. To be a good test pilot requires a basic knowledge in extending the known engineering capabilities. In other words, instead of just being satisfied with what we know, we try to use that and then work to improve our knowledge."

Although being an astronaut took him away from his home and family much of the time, See was circumspect about the separation. "My wife is just as much for the program as I am," he said. "When I told her I had been selected for Gemini 9, she just gave a great big smile and exclaimed: 'Oh, really?' Needless to say she was pretty thrilled. The kids were too."

On 22 May 1965, in Maritime Day ceremonies at the United States Merchant Marine Academy, See received an Outstanding Achievement award from the Kings Point Maritime Association. His old Third Company of Midshipmen now carried a crescent moon on its company flag in his honor, and it flew proudly over the academy's Wiley Hall, signifying the hope of a lunar flight by a former and much-liked commander.

§

Major Charles Arthur Bassett II, by comparison, was patently outgoing. Born in Dayton, Ohio, on 30 December 1931 to Belle (née James) and Charles ("Pete") Bassett, he had served as a fighter pilot in Korea and as a test pilot at Edwards Air Force Base before joining the space program as one of the fourteen-strong Group 3 in 1963. An outstanding pilot, Bassett had already caught the eye of the astronaut hierarchy and seemed assured of a bright future.

His forebears William and Elizabeth Bassett had been among the thirty-five passengers who sailed for America on the *Fortune*. In November 1621 it became the second ship after the *Mayflower* to arrive at Plymouth in Massachusetts. Had Bassett been on the first or second moon landing, it would have made for an interesting analogy.

Realizing early on the importance of a solid education, he forged a steady path on his road to the stars. He received his secondary schooling at Berea, Ohio, before attending Ohio State University from 1950 to 1952. He then enrolled in the air force ROTC program at Ohio State and entered the air force as an aviation cadet in October 1952.

His initial training took place at Stallings Air Force Base in North Carolina and Bryan Air Force Base in Texas. He was commissioned upon his graduation from Bryan in December 1953, and then went to Nellis AFB in Nevada as a second lieutenant, flying aircraft such as the T-6, T-28, and T-33. He completed advanced work in the F-86 jet fighter in April 1954 and then went to Korea with the 8th Fighter-Bomber Group, where he also flew the F-86. Eventually returning for pilot duties at Suffolk County AFB in New York, he was promoted to first lieutenant in May 1955. Here he flew the F-86-D (which had a radar cone in the nose), the F-102, and just about anything else with wings, including the C-119. In August 1958 Bassett was assigned an electrical engineering course of study through the U.S. Air Force Institute of Technology (AFIT) at Wright-Patterson AFB in Ohio. Students did not have to physically attend the campus at Wright-Patterson; the program was also available through contracted universities and colleges. He found himself assigned to Texas Technological College in Lubbock and graduated with high honors in electrical engineering, gaining his bachelor of engineering degree in 1960. He subsequently did graduate work at the University of Southern California. That same year he was promoted to captain and spent a short period doing engineering work at Edwards AFB.

In January 1961 Bassett received a three-month assignment to attend Squadron Officer School at Maxwell AFB. Returning to Edwards, he continued as an engineer at the static rocket test facility and then entered the Air Force Experimental Test Pilot School. Following his graduation he was selected to the Aerospace Research Pilots School. Prior to his selection by NASA he had logged more than twenty-eight hundred hours flying time, with more than twenty-one hundred of those in jet aircraft.

He was often quoted as saying that as far back as he could recall he yearned to be an aviator. In November 1965, shortly after he and See were named as prime crew for the Gemini 9 mission, Bassett told Associated Press aerospace writer Ronald Thompson that he considered himself very fortunate to be an astronaut. "I'd always wanted to fly and wanted to fly jets, then I wanted to be a test pilot," he said. "So I was just lucky enough to follow it right along into the space program.

"I guess I was one of those few lucky people who knew right from the day he was born, practically, what he wanted to do, and then was able to do it. I remember when I was a kid five years old; I used to draw pictures of airplanes as they were taking off at Wright Field near Dayton, Ohio. I'd look out the window and draw pictures."

During his high school days Bassett was an avid model plane builder, according to his kid brother, Bill: "He belonged to the high school 'Model Bugs,' a club that built and flew U-control gasoline engine-powered airplanes in the school gymnasium. Charlie's planes were always built with tender loving care that reflected his attempts to replicate the airplanes that flew in the Thompson trophy races. One week he was flying his plane in the gym and one of the control wires broke and it slammed into the wall. He took it all home in a paper bag but several weeks later he had totally rebuilt it and it was just like new."

With an eye to the future Bassett made his first solo flight in a private airplane on his sixteenth birthday and took on jobs at Cleveland's airport. "I worked greasing, fuelling and polishing airplanes to pay for flying lessons, and finally got my license when I was seventeen," he said.

Shortly after, he worked out an arrangement with a man who would have a tremendous impact on his future, Earle ("Robbie") Robinson. A noncommissioned pilot during the war, Robinson ferried aircraft from place to place and gained a great deal of flying experience. Postwar he was a licensed aircraft and engine mechanic who loved buying, restoring, and selling old aircraft. He and Bassett got along well, and the latter would often lend a hand in restoring the old planes. By way of exchange, Robinson would allow his young friend to fly any restored airplane he owned at that time, as long as Bassett paid for the gasoline. It was a tremendous arrangement, and the young pilot ran up many hours flying a variety of wonderful old planes.

When the Korean War broke out Bassett entered the air force as part of his aviation cadet program. He had kept up a correspondence with Edythe Maxim, with whom he had learned to fly in Cleveland, and in a letter from Stallings AFB in Kinston, North Carolina, dated 17 November 1952, told her something of what flying meant to him: "October 6th finally came and now I'm at flight school, just like a dream come true. I've had a little over four hours in a T-6 now. Boy, that's really a wonderful airplane. I've never gotten such a bang out of flying an airplane. You know, there's nothing like flying; I think if anything should ever keep me down I'd be completely useless. The second that airplane breaks away from this dirty ole earth, I feel relieved of something, just like bein' let through the Pearly Gates. I think that someone that can go up and enjoy a good ride when he feels like it gets a helluva lot more out of life than someone who's strapped to the earth."

Bassett next went to Bryan AFB in Texas, where he was taught about instruments and formation flying on T-28 aircraft, before moving on to the T-33. He would later attend gunnery school and in 1954 was posted to Korea. Asked in a press interview some years later if he had wanted to go to war, Bassett stated quite emphatically that he was sorry he did not get a chance to fly combat missions over Korea. "I went over to Korea immediately after the war—I was really trying to get over there for the war," he said. "Gosh, yeah—I wanted combat time. That's the make of a pilot. You find out how good you are in combat. If you don't have any challenge, you never know how good you are. I always thought I was good, you see, and that's really what a fighter pilot is. His job is to fly combat. If you don't really want it, then I don't think you're a good fighter pilot."

In another press interview, Bassett also revealed the origin of his test pilot ambitions. "After a year in Korea I wanted to be a test pilot, and asked Pete Everest, one of the old-time greats in the business how to go about it. Pete said, 'Forget it until you get a degree.' So it was back to school. Through the Air Force I earned a B.S. in electrical engineering at Texas Tech. I applied for test pilot school while there, but did not make it until about a year and a half after graduation."

The first time Bassett really thought about a spaceflight career came soon after the Soviet Union launched Sputnik 1 into orbit in October 1957. By sending the world's first artificial satellite to circle the globe, Russia had thrown down the gauntlet, and what would become known as the Space Race had begun. He was twenty-five and knew that one day soon people would be flying into space, and he wanted to be one them. "I thought it was really, really neat," he said, reflecting on the pioneering days of spaceflight. "And I felt it was pretty inevitable that man would get up there.

"I can remember asking Colonel Chuck Yeager for advice about getting into the astronaut program. He is one of the finest pilots in the world and I pass on his answer to you: 'Shoot for getting as high as you can go.'"

Jeannie Marion Martin of North Hollywood, California, did not know it at the time, but she would first meet her future husband in 1936, when she was three months old. Young Charlie Bassett was visiting his Aunt Evelyn, a talented sculptor who lived just across the road from Jeannie. His aunt was married to Wade Boteler—a respected character actor in the movies during the thirties and forties. At the time he and Jeannie first met, Bassett was just four years old.

His father, known to everyone as Pete, was a career army engineering officer. During the First World War he had served as a young soldier in the Army Signal Corps. After the war he returned to civilian life for several years before joining the Army Air Corps, where he went to flight school and was subsequently commissioned in 1925. His flying license, issued on 16 November 1925, is signed by Orville Wright. He took his flight training at Stinson Field in San Antonio, Texas, a small field that still exists today. In those days it was common for the young cadets to land on the adjacent James property and even take the seven children up for a ride. Belle was the youngest of the James girls, and she soon formed a fondness for one of the dashing young pilots, Pete Bassett. They were eventually married in September 1927.

Charlie and his younger brother, Bill, were born while their father was stationed at Wright-Patterson Field in Dayton, Ohio. Bill, who would become affectionately known as "Buzz," was born on 6 December 1933. Their sister, Sharon, entered the world two years later while their father was attending the University of Michigan in Ann Arbor. Prior to the start of the Second World War, he had become involved in research and development engineering at airfields such as Wright-Patterson, McDill, and March. As a result, his family moved around a lot, as often as once a year.

When America became involved in the war the Bassett family was living in Tampa, Florida, until Pete was assigned the position of commanding officer at Shemya base in the Aleutian Islands. Belle and the children then moved to Houston, where they stayed for two years with her older brother Hugh James and his wife, Frances. The Jameses had an older daughter and two boys the same age as Charlie and Bill, and all the children got along tremendously well. It was a simple life they led; Uncle Hugh had his home and a small soap factory just outside of Houston, where the children all helped out. Their chores were mostly enjoyable activities, such as helping to raise and feed the chickens and cultivating a victory garden. In their free time they played in a nearby creek in the woods.

Then Wade Boteler passed away in North Hollywood, so Belle weighed her options. After discussing matters with her newly widowed sister, it was decided that Belle would take her children to California and live with Evelyn for a while. In this way, Jeannie and young Charlie met for the second time. North Hollywood, back then, was a great place to live, as Bill Bassett recently recalled, "There were citrus groves, horses, open land, and it was a fun place for a kid to grow up. Jean Martin (Charlie's wife to be) lived across the street and I vividly recall her home, the horse barn, and the trees overhanging the house. We had a great old time in the old rambling house that we lived in while there. Toward the end of the war Dad returned, and I can still remember sitting on the curbside anxiously awaiting his arrival after perhaps four years away."

When the Bassetts arrived in North Hollywood, Jeannie was eight years old and Charlie twelve. As Jeannie recalls, there was little to bring them together:

> *His sister and I were fast friends, and he was mostly interested in airplanes. We lived under the flight path for Lockheed Aviation so we saw many planes overhead during World War Two. I believe I could recognize a P-38 by ear even today, if there were any around to hear. Because Charlie was four years older than I, our paths didn't really converge. After all, think of the difference between a twelve-year-old boy and an eight-year-old girl. I thought he was pretty snobbish, and he in turn thought I was a pest.*
>
> *However, when he was attending gunnery training at Nellis Air Force Base in Las Vegas, Nevada, in 1954, he came to visit his aunt and the family. He was a handsome fighter pilot, I was eighteen, getting ready to go away to college for the year, and we just fell in love. We went dancing at the Hollywood Palladium, we went to the beach at Malibu, and we sat at the end of the runway at both Burbank and Los Angeles airports, watching planes. He talked about how he loved flying, and how important it was to him. He also longed to become a test pilot because they went faster and higher than other fliers, and they had to be the best. He'd excelled throughout all of his pilot training.*

After completing gunnery school Charlie Bassett was assigned to Far East duty in Korea. Prior to leaving he returned briefly to his Ohio hometown of Berea, where his parents had finally settled after his father retired from his military career. Later, on his way to the embarkation point at Parks AFB in northern California, Bassett made a purposeful stopover in North Hollywood to see Jeannie. She recalls he had something important to ask her. "We were swimming in the neighbors' pool when he proposed," she said. "He'd bought an engagement ring in Berea, not knowing what my response might be. Well, obviously I did say yes. Our courtship began rather backwards, you could say, with the engagement ring first followed by a long-distance, airmail romance."

While in Korea, Bassett continued to share his flying experiences with his old friend Edythe Maxim in Cleveland, with whom he had learned to fly. On 16 March 1954 he wrote about a significant event in his aviation career:

> Well, the F-86 and I finally got together. After a slow, fast month they finally let me fly it. It was a fast month because I was pretty busy, but it was slow because I was sure that it would never pass and I was doomed to look at F-86's the rest of my life. I've got to admit that I was just a little nervous walking out to the airplane but after we got started, I was too busy—not because I was inventing things. This plane is ridiculously easy to fly and still it is comfortable as an easy chair and powerful as a steamroller. The speed is its biggest drawing—it's supersonic in a dive. A week ago today she took me to 50,000 feet and in a terminal velocity dive (this airplane has no speed restrictions above 15,000 feet) she took me to Mach 1.1.

Bassett was stationed at K-13 near Suwon in Korea, a pleasant and well-equipped air base with three squadrons of F-86 jet aircraft. He was part of the 80th Fighter Bomber Squadron of the Eighth Fighter Bomber Wing. The squadron would later move to K-2 at Taego and become the 310th Fighter Bomber Squadron, which became known as the Top Hatter's Squadron.

Just before his assignment in Korea was completed, Bassett wrote and asked Jeannie to come up to Berkeley after her spring vacation and bring the engagement ring with her, which she did. When he returned to the United States on leave he spent two weeks in Berkeley, staying at his fraternity's chapter house. He and Jeannie then carried out the ritual "pinning" and engagement traditions at her sorority.

All too soon he had to resume pilot duties and traveled to Suffolk County AFB at Westhampton Beach, New York, as part of the air defense command. Here the pilots were prepared for combat duties if any unidentified and potentially hostile aircraft were spotted on radar. The training entailed many hours in the air on instruments and seemingly endless sessions in simulators. The pilots flew in all kinds of weather at any hour of the day, regardless of the conditions. One of the greatest hazards out at Eastern Long Island was the summer haze, which had the potential to seriously disorient even the best of pilots. It was an exhausting yet fulfilling time for Bassett, but after a month had gone by he called Jeannie, told her he was totally miserable without her, and was taking two weeks of leave. "Let's get married!" he added.

Jeannie suddenly had a wedding to plan:

> This was just as final exams began. Needless to say my academic career suffered greatly! I called my mother Mary and, bless her heart, she put together a small wedding. A neighbor was an incredible seamstress who

*had just completed a gorgeous wedding dress for the actress Ann Blythe. I'd seen the dress and loved it, so Helene made a near copy for me. Charlie's family always loved to entertain, so they had multiple parties for us. The cake and champagne were ordered and all was in good order with one exception—my father Wiley, a cameraman for Technicolor, was on location in Salina, Kansas, where they were wrapping up the filming of the movie "Picnic," with William Holden and Kim Novak. He told me his return to North Hollywood in time for the wedding would be a real touch-and-go thing. All of my pre-bridal jitters emerged at the thought of him not escorting me down the aisle, but the day before the wedding he arrived home. So now we had a wedding party!*

The happy couple exchanged vows in the North Hollywood Presbyterian Church on 22 June 1955. Jack Olson, the husband of Bassett's cousin Betty Boteler, was his best man, and their daughter Randi stole everyone's heart as the flower girl.

On Saturday, 21 December 1957, Bassett and his very pregnant wife decided they could risk attending a squadron Christmas party on Long Island. Their baby was not due for another week, and Jeannie felt they should go out rather than sitting at home and missing all the fun. In the midst of the festivities Jeannie took her husband aside and whispered that the baby was anxious to make an appearance, and he should take her straight to the hospital. A strict, unyielding nurse met them at the entrance of the Southampton Hospital and promptly turned Bassett around and shuffled him out the door, instructing him to go home and wait. Their daughter Karen was born at two o'clock in the morning. He was thrilled to have a daughter, especially since the old saw was that true fighter pilots always had girls!

On 7 April 1959 Bassett had some heart-stopping moments when he was involved in a night crash landing. He had taken off from Reese AFB, ten miles west of Lubbock, Texas, in a T-28A Trojan, a single-engine trainer and transport utility aircraft. Seated behind him was Jerome Witty, who was flying on instruments until Amarillo control was reached. As planned, permission was then received to conduct "touch and go" landings. In this basic training procedure, the pilot lands and then immediately revs his engine and takes off again without stopping, repeating the process as many times as needed. The flight down to Amarillo AFB went as planned, as did the first touch and go. After touching down a second time Bassett advanced the throttles to takeoff power. The piston engine accelerated smoothly and the T-28 became airborne at about 70 knots. After crossing the end of the runway and flying at about 50 feet with full flaps, the engine began to sputter and then cut out. Bassett coolly managed to start it again but only momentarily. Then it quit entirely. Due to the low altitude and airspeed a crash landing was unavoidable. Fortunately the two pilots escaped unharmed, but there was substantial damage to the Trojan. The fault was later traced to broken teeth in the intermediate impeller drive gear pinion and the accessory drive gear. Bassett suffered a compression fracture but did not realize this until he developed lower back pains a few months later.

He experienced yet another accident on 9 March 1960, when he was landing in a two-seat T-33. The report stated that "one or both pilots inadvertently retracted the gear following a routine landing." Neither of these experiences dampened his enthusiasm for flying duty.

On a far happier note the Bassetts' second child, Peter Martin, was born on 6 April 1961, while Bassett was completing Squadron Officer's School at Maxwell AFB in Alabama. This birth also provided Jeannie with a few anxious moments:

> Once again the baby was in a hurry. My parents lived about an hour away from Edwards AFB, so after calling Charlie to tell him the delivery was in progress, I contacted my parents who broke all land speed records to get there. My father took me to the hospital, sat in the waiting room with all of those young fathers-to-be, but didn't have to wait too long. Peter was born at two that afternoon. Charlie managed to get dispensation and made a quick trip home, scaring me because the only men allowed on the maternity floor aside from visiting hours were the chaplains. When the nurse told me a man was waiting to see me I had a huge moment of panic, for all Air Force wives know what the chaplain's visit means!

Less than a week after Peter's birth, on 12 April, Bassett was stunned to hear that a cosmonaut named Yuri Gagarin had successfully completed the first manned space flight—an event that would significantly alter the course of Bassett's life.

He graduated from the USAF Experimental Flight Test Pilot School at Edwards AFB on 17 August 1962. There were sixteen students in his Class 62-A, including Captain Ted Freeman. At ceremonies to mark their graduation, General Branch presented the diplomas and awards. Bassett received the A. B. Honts Award, "given to the student achieving overall first standing in the class, and the Empire Test Pilot School Award for the top student in academics."

Bassett then became an experimental test pilot at Edwards, attached to their Fighter Projects Office while he waited to hear if he had been selected to the Phase II program, the Aerospace Research Pilots School. With about three hundred applications per year, there was no lack of qualified candidates, all with extensive flight experience and many with advanced degrees under their belt. He made it through; on 22 October 1962 it was announced that he was one of ten officers handpicked for the third course at the advanced test pilot school. Among other future NASA astronauts in his Class III were Mike Collins (they would become close friends), Ed Givens, and Joe Engle.

Continuing his correspondence with old flying friend Edythe Maxim, Bassett wrote in a letter dated 23 November 1962, "I went to Mach 2 the other day for the first time. I was right above a cloud deck and wow, what a sensation of speed!"

The traditional performance and flying techniques Bassett had studied at the TPS would prove to be little more than a prelude to a highly rigorous program of space-related subjects, such as thermodynamics, bioastronautics, and Newtonian mechanics. The curriculum now included out-of-atmosphere training in maneuvering and reentry problems, carried out in the newly modified NF-104s. The converted Starfighter was fitted with a rocket engine in its tail, which flew students to altitudes where conventional control surfaces were ineffective, and reaction control jets were required to maintain stability and alter height and direction. It would prove to be an exhausting and time-consuming eight months, but he successfully graduated from the school on 31 May 1963.

When he applied to NASA for its third intake of astronauts, Bassett was nearly through the ARPS. He knew that on completion, if successful, he would be eligible to take part in any air force space program as an astronaut-designee. But he was looking beyond this—he had already set his sights on the civilian space agency and knew the top eight graduates would be recommended to NASA for possible selection.

Prior to submitting his application to NASA, Bassett was tapped to work with Colonel Bob "Silver Fox" Stephens on the then highly classified SR-71 strategic reconnaissance jet aircraft program. The "Blackbird," as it came to be known, was an advanced all-weather interceptor aircraft capable of flying at Mach 3 and altitudes exceeding 80,000 feet. The magnificent, sleek titanium SR-71 and its sister ship, the YF-12A (virtually identical in appearance and construction), would provide America with its next generation of supersonic spy aircraft, replacing the much-maligned U2.

The thought of being involved in either program—NASA or the SR-71—presented Bassett with a delicious conundrum. However, he was not sure that NASA would accept him, as he knew many qualified people who had been rejected on previous applications. It was also an uncertain time for him, since both agencies were now running all manner of security and personal background checks to confirm his suitability. In 1963, while this situation was being resolved, he was sent to Sapporo in Japan as part of the flight acceptance team for the F-104s to be received by the Japan Air Self-Defense Force (JASDF). Bassett was concerned with the Category III testing of the F-104J, mainly suitability and weapons testing. He was delighted that his cousin Doug Boteler was also part of that air force team, and despite the ten-year age difference they got on well, enjoying each other's company. It was while he was in Japan that Bassett received the news of his life—almost!

He knew that a call from Houston to advise him about his astronaut application was imminent, and he was on tenterhooks. When the call finally came in mid-October he picked up the telephone receiver as if it were lead, and gave his name. Deke Slayton was on the other end of the line. It was a very scratchy connection, but Bassett could hear Slayton's laconic voice at the other end. "Hi Charlie, umm, this is Deke Slayton . . ." And then the trans-Pacific cable connection was lost, and the line went dead! Bassett, now on pins and needles, had to sit it out for another thirty-six hours until a fresh connection could be made, and then he got the news he had been hoping to hear—he was going to report to Houston for astronaut training.

Once some quick arrangements had been made, Bassett was flown back home under top-secret travel orders. The shroud of secrecy surrounding the selection of NASA's newest group of astronauts and their names was intense, although they had been able to tell their wives on the strict understanding they were to keep it to themselves. Any breach could actually jeopardize their husband's pending appointment.

Although bursting to tell her family and friends, Jeannie kept the exciting news to herself. Meanwhile Bassett and the other candidates had been arriving in Houston and were put up at the Rice Hotel, with a press conference to announce the new astronauts scheduled for 18 October. Bassett registered at the hotel under the name of Max Peck, as he was instructed, and found himself sharing a room with a very excited navy Lieutenant Alan Bean, who later became a near neighbor, and who would go on to become the fourth man to walk on the moon. The two men quickly realized that they had both been told to register under the name Max Peck, and they later discovered, much to their bemusement, that all fourteen candidates had checked in under that name. The new astronauts, NASA's third group, were introduced to the waiting media at the press conference the following day.

Meanwhile back at Edwards AFB, and following the press conference announcement of her husband's selection, Jeannie Bassett called everyone she knew. She then joined Pat Collins and Faith Freeman at the Freemans' house on Rickenbacker Drive, where the three wives held a news conference. Their husbands were all stationed at Edwards AFB, so they had grouped together for mutual support in handling the press onslaught they knew would come once the names were known.

When it came time for Jeannie to field questions about her husband, she confirmed the biographical information given in the NASA press release, which to her surprise even disclosed that her family lived at 4848 Lindbergh Drive at Edwards. Privacy, it now seemed, was a thing of the past. One reporter, looking for an angle, asked at the end of the interview if Bassett had ever promised her the moon. She smiled and said, "No . . . but I'm going to have a serious talk about that with him."

It was difficult to leave their homes and friends behind at Edwards, but after a round of farewell and Godspeed parties the Bassetts prepared to make their way down to Houston. Before they left, and to mark the ascension of Charlie Bassett and Mike Collins into the hallowed astronaut corps, their friends in Flight Operations at Edwards made a little presentation to the two men. It was a garbage can, painted flat black, with a couple of windows cut into it, representing a Gemini capsule. Bearing the name *Ashcan 7* proudly on its side, the present was the source of much hilarity.

Once in Houston the Bassetts rented a house, and after looking around for a while they settled on a nice lot in a newly opened subdivision in Nassau Bay.

8. Jeannie Bassett described this as her favorite
photo of Charlie, seen during his desert training. (NASA)

On 4 January 1964 Bassett officially reported to MSC for his astronaut assignment. He was looking forward to settling into life at the Manned Spacecraft Center. As soon as they were able, he and Jeannie hired architect Clovis Heimsath to draw up plans for their new home. The house would be innovative, but Heimsath assured the Bassetts they would love it. He and his wife, Maryann, soon became close friends with the new astronaut and his family.

In July Bassett and several other astronauts were flown down to Panama for some hands-on lessons in jungle survival training, and the following month another group was transported to the Nevada Desert for the same reason. The men had to pair up for the exercise, so he and his friend from Edwards, Mike Collins, elected to form a team. NASA wanted its astronauts to be ready in case they landed in hostile terrain, but mostly the men just enjoyed the trips as a break from their daunting classroom routine.

Construction of the Bassetts' new home began in late 1964 with the digging of the foundation trenches, and it was eventually completed in September 1965. The house was open and airy, and the family loved it. Clay and Anne Fulcher were their next-door neighbors, while fellow Group 3 astronaut Buzz Aldrin and his wife,

9. C.C. Williams, Charlie Bassett, and Elliot See at the Mission Control Center, Houston, on 12 December 1965. They are in deep discussion following the scrubbed launch of Gemini 6. All three would die in T-38 accidents. (NASA)

Joan, owned the house behind them and shared their yard gate. Another of the new astronauts, Al Bean, lived two doors down with his wife, Sue.

As months of training rolled by, Bassett confided in Jeannie that he was a little downhearted. He felt he was being overlooked for a mission, as several of his group had already been given flight assignments. He need not have worried; he was called into Deke Slayton's office one day in October and walked out with a plum assignment—pilot on the GT-9 mission, which would include a space walk. He was told to keep it under his hat until the official announcement was made on 8 November, but he could tell his wife. He was tremendously excited when he got home, and hugged Jeannie so hard she knew he had heard some welcome news.

As things stood at that time, the GT-9 mission would carry at least five major scientific experiments, including a planned attempt by Bassett to retrieve a radiation measurement device mounted on the exterior of the Gemini capsule. He would remain tethered outside for at least one complete orbit around the earth. It was essentially the same type of space walk then planned for Dave Scott on the Gemini 8 mission the following year, but the first using a new backpack called the Astronaut Maneuvering Unit (AMU). See and Bassett would also try to maneuver up to and link with an unmanned Agena target satellite sent into orbit ahead of them. This was part of NASA's rendezvous and docking technique, so vital to future plans. Officially the two- to three-day voyage was scheduled for some time after 1 July 1966, but Bassett had been told it could begin as early as May, if all went well.

10. The prime and backup crew for Gemini 9. Seated at front are Elliot See and Charlie Bassett, while backup crew members Tom Stafford and Gene Cernan stand at rear. (NASA)

He did not know too much about the man assigned as mission commander, Elliot See, but quickly realized that he was a person not given to extroversion or bustle; he was there to do a job, and he would do it diligently and to the best of his ability. This suited Bassett, and they soon forged a good working relationship. Their backups were Tom Stafford and Gene Cernan, the latter also from Group 3.

Where the Bassett family now lived in Nassau Bay, they were only three blocks from the home of Bassett's backup pilot, Gene Cernan, and his wife, Barbara. The two men were understandably serious about the training for the mission extravehicular activity (EVA) to be conducted by Bassett (and later on Gemini 12 by Cernan) and knew that it would require a good deal of physical strength and dexterity. As a result they spent time in the gym, lifting weights and generally trying to strengthen the muscles in their forearms. According to Cernan:

> *Since Charlie and I were the ones who would perform the spacewalks, we also found ourselves in a lot of airplanes and sharing a beer or two in hotel bars, hammering at the mission, always the mission. The two of us became a team, helping the [Ling-Temco-Vought] Aerospace engineers in Dallas cobble up an AMU that would fit all our needs. After work, we would occasionally click our glasses in congratulations, for we realized*

*the rocket pack was a significant challenge that would be a headliner for*
*the space program, and it was all ours. The spacecraft commanders, our*
*seniors in experience, might do a wonderful job with rendezvous or save*
*a lot of fuel on reentry, but the big newspaper ink would belong to the*
*spacewalkers. As rookies, we got a couple of good laughs out of that, and*
*felt confident that if anybody could tame this backpack, we could.*

The risks associated with being an astronaut were never far from the minds of the men and their families, and these risks were realized with the death of Ted Freeman in October 1964. Bassett was one of the pallbearers at his friend's funeral service.

Freeman's death was a great shock to Jeannie and Charlie Bassett, and they sought comfort in their religion. Every Sunday they attended the Webster Presbyterian Church, and though Bassett was not a student of the Bible, he had a strong belief in God. This belief sustained him in his sorrow over a lost companion and carried him through life's rigors. According to Jeannie, there was "a great deal of talk about him being the All-American Boy and, although he did all things with incredible gusto and intensity—be it fishing, playing golf, going to church, dancing—he kept it on balance."

One of Bassett's chief passions in Houston was collecting and restoring old Model A Fords. His first such car was a two-door sedan he purchased while in high school. At the same time he was helping Robbie Robinson to restore old piston-engine aircraft, he was also lavishing a great deal of attention and work on his Ford. At Edwards AFB he and Jeannie owned another Model A, one that had a tradition of being handed along from one test pilot to another as they came and went. It also bore the nickname "Action," and pilots would laughingly tell friends it was always nice to spring into Action. In observance of the tradition associated with the car, Bassett sold it to another test pilot when he and Jeannie made the move to Houston.

One day while Jeannie was driving to Bassett's uncle's home, she happened to spot a Model A for sale in a Houston car lot. It was a coupe with a rumble seat, and she just knew her husband would love to own it. The car was up for grabs at $258, so she bought it, and he was as thrilled as when he had bought his first car. They had no idea who owned it previously, but it seemed to have belonged to a Roaring Twenties party, as they found part of a feather boa and an elegant cigarette holder tucked behind the seat. As a nod to the car he had owned up at Edwards, Bassett promptly nicknamed this Model A "Action." Although it had already been nicely restored, it needed a lot of work. It proved to be great therapy during Bassett's time away from his work at NASA.

As he worked to restore the coupe, a friend named Toke Kobiyashi told Bassett about a Model A he had for sale—a 1930 sedan, and a real beauty. Kobiyashi ran a small gas station on the main road to MSC, where a lot of the astronauts had their cars serviced. Bassett dropped by, and the car was virtually sold at first sight. This car was dutifully christened "Reaction." According to Jeannie, a lot of time and love went into both cars: "His favorite time to work on the cars, and usually the only time since he was in training out of town most of the weekdays, was Sunday mornings before church. The problem with Model A Fords is that they backfire—a lot, and very loudly. Here then was Charlie starting one of them up in the stillness of a Sunday morning—*kablam, kaboom!* Certainly the neighbors couldn't have appreciated this, but they never complained."

Bassett took great pride in keeping his Model As in good condition, and most days he drove one of the old Fords to the MSC. On other days he would ride a bicycle to work for a bit of exercise. When asked about his fondness for the vintage cars, he responded, "I'll take my speed in the air."

Back at the space center, training for the Gemini mission with Elliot See intensified. Bassett threw himself into the task with typical enthusiasm and vigor. Fellow astronaut Walt Cunningham once wrote of him: "What impressed me most about Charlie was his self-discipline. On field trips he seldom packed a lunch, taking the position that it was good discipline to do without. While the rest of us were feeding our faces, he would use the time to take notes. He was wound tight, dedicated, had fine mechanical skills, and undoubtedly would have made an excellent space pilot."

From early to mid-December 1965, Bassett worked as a shift CapCom for the Gemini 7/6 mission, together with Elliot See and Gene Cernan. He drew the "graveyard shift" of 11 P.M. to 7 A.M. but did not seem to mind. He also attended the launches of both Gemini missions at the cape, along with Al Bean, returning afterward to his CapCom duties. It was invigorating stuff.

Bassett never seemed to grasp the high regard in which his peers and superiors at the space center held him. But this esteem became evident when Deke Slayton unofficially told him that following GT-9 he was in line for one of the early lunar landing missions—probably as a command module pilot, or CMP. Slayton felt that Bassett would work well with Frank Borman and Bill Anders (both of whom would eventually fly on the Apollo 8 mission). If he performed well on that flight, there was a high probability he would later command his own lunar landing mission and become one of a handful of men to walk on the moon. When he confided this in Jeannie, she could see that he was thrilled, almost beyond words. Charlie Bassett, it seemed, was definitely on his way to the moon.

§

Kenneth Stovall from Ferguson, Missouri, was employed as a company linesman by Union Electric. He was walking through a substation parking lot near the McDonnell Plant when he heard the T-38 approaching from the east. He remembered it descending at "a fairly sharp angle." As he watched, the pilot cut in the afterburners, desperately throwing on extra power. Moments later the aircraft disappeared from view behind some stationary boxcars on the elevated railroad tracks skirting the northern side of the airfield. A split second later, according to Stovall, "I heard a roar and saw a ball of fire. I knew the pilots would be killed."

11. The foam-covered wreckage of Elliot See and Charlie Bassett's T-38. Behind
the tailfin, an arrow indicates where the jet struck Building 101 for the final
time before plummeting to the ground. (Courtesy *St. Louis Post-Dispatch*)

Adjacent to the building where the crash occurred, truck driver Cliff Bradley
from the local suburb of Arnold was delivering oil to Building 102 when he suddenly
heard the shrieking sound of an aircraft in distress. As he looked up he saw the T-38
slam into the roof of 101, bounce, and explode "like a gasoline bomb." He leapt out
of his truck and instinctively ran to the crash site to see if he could help, but there
was nothing he could do. Soon after, plant and field fire equipment from nearby
communities converged on the scene. In case of fire, the fuselage was covered in a
mass of foam. At this point, according to Bradley, the police also arrived and "chased
everyone away" before sealing off the crash site.

The bodies were covered with blankets to await the arrival of the coroner. Two
Catholic priests, the Reverend Joe Shocklee and the Reverend Al Lippert, were at
the nearby St. Ferdinand Catholic Church when they received an urgent telephone
call to come to the crash site. They administered last rites over the bodies.

Meanwhile Stafford and Cernan, totally unaware of the tragedy, touched down
safely minutes later. Their only real concern was in knowing if See and Bassett's
aircraft with the baggage pod dangling beneath it had diverted to another field. If
this were the case, they would not have a change of clothes or NASA tags. As they
taxied in, someone in the tower gave their call sign of NASA 907 and calmly asked that
they identify themselves by name. It was certainly unusual, but Cernan responded,
giving his and Tom's surnames. "In that obtuse way," he later stated, "Charlie and
Elliot were identified." When Cernan asked if aircraft 901 had diverted, he was told
to check with the Operations Office at McDonnell. It was not until they came to

a halt and clambered down that the faces on the ground crew told Cernan and Stafford that something was terribly wrong.

By now navy and air force personnel stationed at the plant, assisted by local police and plant security guards, had reinforced a cordon thrown around the scene of the tragedy. The press had also begun to descend on the plant and ask questions.

John Bickers was McDonnell's manager of advertising and worked in the Public Relations Office at the time of the crash. His phone rang just after nine o'clock, and he listened in stunned silence as Diane Riggs in another part of the plant told him a NASA aircraft had just crashed into Building 101. He immediately tried to contact Paul Haney from NASA's Public Affairs office in Houston but was unable to reach him for some time. Meanwhile he passed the grim news to Howard Gibbons of McDonnell's Public Affairs Office, who asked that he be informed of any further developments.

Bickers said that it was a morning he would never forget. Apart from the company of a work colleague, Charles Menees, he was alone in the Public Relations Office, acting as an official go-between for NASA, McDonnell Aircraft, the navy, the police, and the press. Here is his recollection:

> All of the members of the Public Relations Office, except Charles Menees, were at the accident site. Mr. Menees was handling all calls from the press, and as I understand it, he was advising everyone that an accident had occurred, that it had occurred on our property, and that was all he knew.
>
> I then learned from our flight visitors' office that the accident involved a T-38 aircraft. When [McDonnell's Ed] Regan returned from the scene to confirm that, I called Mr. Gibbons and so advised him. By this time he had acquired the tail numbers of the aircraft enroute to St. Louis. Soon after this, I was advised by the flight visitors' center that the airplane in question was tail number 701 [sic] and that the other aircraft had landed safely. This was passed along to Mr. Gibbons and he confirmed the names of the occupants of the aircraft, which by now was well established since Stafford and Cernan were in our facilities. This was not yet released.
>
> As time passed, a concern rose that the local press was not being permitted to take photographs, and permission for this was requested through Howard Gibbons[, who] responded that we should contact him after we had completed the making of official photographs. There was some confusion as to what constituted an official photograph, and since our company photographers had made numerous pictures by this time, we advised him that our official photography had been completed, and the Navy Office and ourselves believed it was time to permit photography and he agreed to this release. He also released a statement that the flight crew was from NASA and that they were probably astronauts, followed by another statement, "Upon direct query, they were astronauts." About two hours after the

*accident the names of the personnel involved, both in the accident and in*
*the other aircraft, were released by Howard Gibbons.*

Meanwhile, sixteen employees of the McDonnell Aircraft Corporation and one contract worker had been injured as a result of the crash. The employees were working at a Phantom jet fighter assembly line and suffered shock or wounds caused by falling beams and large chunks of debris. The most badly hurt was nineteen-year-old production worker Clyde Ethridge from Pine Lawn, who was taken to Deaconess Hospital with a serious back injury sustained when a heavy object fell and struck him. Another nineteen-year-old employee, Warren Ward of Columbia, suffered a fractured left ankle.

Around 150 employees had been at work on the building's mezzanine level that day, immediately below the roof where the T-38 hit. Several later said they heard noises similar to nearby thunder or sonic booms at the time of the accident. After a horrendous crashing noise and a sudden flash of fire, the assembly area quickly filled with dusty clouds of smoke and fumes, while sparks and debris showered the workers.

Plant engineer Richard Medved later told reporters that he heard the uncommonly loud sound of a jet approaching above Building 101. Suddenly there was a massive tearing crash on the roof above the mezzanine level where he was standing. "A hole was knocked in the roof," he said, "and the plane struck again, tearing a second hole about ten feet from my station!" The right wing, wrenched from the aircraft, was later discovered on the roof of the building and removed by firemen.

Shocked, and with no idea about what had caused the noise or devastation, the workers immediately grabbed extinguishers and fire hoses and attacked several small fires that had broken out in the building. Others rushed out to telephone an alert to the corporation's in-house fire department.

Within eight minutes the building was evacuated, the last to leave being supervisors who had conducted a careful search for any injured workers. Incredibly, workers at the opposite end of the massive building were not even aware of the tragedy until some colleagues who had rushed to the windows shouted news of the accident. "All we heard in this end of the building were two *ka-thumps*," one worker recalled for reporters. "Some thought it was a heater exploding in another building. Others said they heard something in the laboratory blew up."

Supervisor Rollin Becker worked on the Mercury and Gemini spacecraft construction programs in St. Louis, and thirty-three years after the event he still has vivid recollections of the tragedy, which occurred on his birthday:

> *It was foggy that morning, and I was doing some work in building 102.*
> *I was a supervisor in the machine shop—part of the model shop, in an*
> *annex in the corner of the building. Just to my left was a doorway through*
> *which I could see Building 101, about 250–300 feet away. It sat a little*
> *higher than 102. Anyway, I was working and all of a sudden there was a*

*big noise, kind of like a whummp, and then a little bit later I heard a loud thud. There was only a brief moment between the sounds.*

*I knew something was wrong. My first thought was that an airliner had crashed, and since the noises came from the direction of Building 101, I looked over that way. It was foggy, but I could see a pillar of smoke, and then I knew something had crashed. As much as I possibly could I kept people on their machines, since you can't just leave them abruptly. Everyone was distracted from their work. We didn't seem to be in any immediate danger, so I kept people working so the jobs wouldn't get ruined. Later, on my own time, I went over to Building 101 and they had the area cordoned off. There was visible damage to the roof from the inside, but you couldn't really get close to it for safety and investigation reasons. I don't think the [Gemini] capsule was damaged.*

Rumors and telephone calls swept the plant until finally the awful news filtered through. Then a simple announcement stating there had been a fatal jet crash was made over the intercom system, but without many details. Later the workers learned it had involved two visiting astronauts, and there was a general feeling of disbelief.

When James S. McDonnell viewed the wreckage and factory damage later that day he was a shaken man, but he still managed to express profound relief that, despite the horrific circumstances of the crash, none of his employees had been killed.

The telephone began ringing in the Timber Cove home of astronaut Jim Lovell and his wife, Marilyn. When Marilyn answered she immediately recognized the voice of John Young, who had been selected in the second astronaut group with her husband. But this time she sensed an uncomfortable flatness in his voice.

Young told Marilyn there had been an accident—not involving Jim, he was quick to point out—but Charlie Bassett and Elliot See had been killed. Marilyn suddenly felt light-headed with shock, and she sat down as he explained what had happened. She and Marilyn See were great friends, and then it struck her—she realized what John Young was going to ask of her.

"Has anyone talked to Marilyn yet?" she asked, already knowing the answer. There was a pause at the other end. "No," came the slow response. "Actually, that's what I wanted you to do." Young went on to explain that he did not want her to break the news to her friend; he just needed a loved one to be by her side when the bad news was given.

It was tough, but Marilyn Lovell managed to brighten up a little for her friend's sake as she walked the short distance to the See house, where Marilyn invited her in. They chatted about small things that had happened to them since they had last spoken.

At one point Marilyn See asked her friend if she was feeling all right. "You seem distracted," she remarked, her voice full of concern. Before Marilyn Lovell could make an appropriate response, the women heard a car pulling up in the driveway. Marilyn See cast a puzzled look at her watch and then peered out through the kitchen window. In the next few moments a terrible truth began to dawn on her as she saw John Young slowly climbing out of the car, together with a NASA official. Both were grim faced. Marilyn See shot a quick look of despair at her friend, and then sat down as Marilyn Lovell went to the front door.

After the two men had confirmed the awful news, Marilyn Lovell saw them out, then went back and sat with her friend, the two crying and embracing as reality set in. A short while later some other anxious wives turned up at the house to offer their support. It was a time each of them had dreaded through her husband's flying and astronaut duties—the day her spouse did not come home. With the house slowly filling, Marilyn Lovell left to pick up Sally and Carolyn See from school, before someone accidentally revealed the news to them.

Meanwhile, around ten o'clock that day, Buzz Aldrin heard the news and quickly phoned his wife, Joan. He told her about the accident and asked her to see Jeannie right away. He would be there as soon as he had told someone at NASA about his arrangements. As it turned out, Jeannie was away from the house doing some shopping, so Joan called the minister of the local Presbyterian Church and then let the minister and Buzz into the Bassett's kitchen. They made some coffee and anxiously waited for the arrival of Jeannie, hoping that she had not heard the news on the radio. The memory of Faith Freeman having her husband's death revealed to her by a reporter was still vivid in their minds.

Eventually Jeannie arrived home, but her friendly smile froze when she saw the three visitors standing awkwardly in her kitchen. This was the moment she had prayed would never come, but one look at Joan Aldrin and the minister told her more than any words could say. She shuddered, and her hands went to her mouth as she swallowed hard, trying to muster some words to say. "Thank you all for coming," she finally said in a wavering whisper, and then ran to embrace Joan, the tears coming hot and fast. Eventually Jeannie calmed down enough to sit with the minister, but his words could not help with her unbearable heartache and loneliness.

Meanwhile the space agency wasted no time in assembling a seven-man Accident Investigation Board, headed by Alan Shepard, who was at the cape when he heard about the crash. Other members of his inquiry board were astronaut Alan Bean; Joe Algranti, chief of aircraft operations at the Manned Spacecraft Center, and his divisional assistant Bud Ream; John Kanak, MSC's safety officer; Dick Lucas from aircraft operations; and Dr. John Zieglschmid, assistant chief of Medical Operations Division at MSC.

Together with other NASA personnel, the investigation team flew into Lambert Field at 2:45 that afternoon. Deke Slayton also flew in to relieve a distraught and emotionally drained Tom Stafford. Despite the trauma of losing two close friends,

12. Paul Haney from NASA's Public Affairs Office demonstrates
how the fatal crash occurred. (Courtesy *St. Louis Post-Dispatch*)

Stafford had assumed interim responsibility for all contact with the press. Paul
Haney, who accompanied Slayton, recounts this sudden call to duty:

> Deke called me in Washington and thirty minutes later I was on an
> Air Force jet out of Andrews bound for St. Louis. I recall never seeing
> the ground until we bumped it landing at St. Louis, the weather had
> deteriorated that badly. As I recall they closed the field after our plane
> landed. This would have been four or five hours after the crash.
>     Tom Stafford and Gene Cernan, See's backups, [had] landed success-
> fully minutes after the crash. The tower told them what had happened
> once they were on the ground. Cernan told me he went off ramp to throw
> up while Tom got the information together and called Deke Slayton. Later
> that evening, I bought a bottle of vodka, which got us through the night
> at a nearby motel.

At a press conference held late on the fatal day, Haney announced the formation
of the accident investigation team, which he emphasized could take up to six or
seven weeks to finalize its report, although Shepard would take time out to attend the
funeral services. The men would work out of Building 101. Haney also announced
that plans for the upcoming GT-9 flight would continue despite the tragedy, and the
backup crew of Tom Stafford and Gene Cernan would now likely fly the mission. It
would be the first time a backup crew had moved into the prime position.

Paul Haney's voice began to break with emotion as he told the press that he had attended Houston's Livestock Show and Rodeo the previous evening with Charlie and Jeannie Bassett. On the way home from the rodeo Charlie had dropped Haney at Hobby Airport so he could catch a midnight flight to Washington for what was then a monthly meeting of NASA public affairs officers.

That evening the coroner's pathologist, Dr. Eugene Tucker from the St. Louis County Hospital, performed autopsies on the bodies of the two astronauts. He confirmed that Bassett had died after being decapitated, while See died of injuries sustained when he was thrown through the shattered forward section of the fuselage. Tucker described the injuries as being similar to those suffered by motorists involved in a head-on collision.

Meanwhile, back at the space center, Bob Gilruth issued a formal statement in which he expressed his profound regrets. "It is with a deep sense of personal loss," he wrote, "that I learned of the deaths of astronauts Charles A. Bassett II and Elliot M. See, Jr. in an accident in St. Louis this morning. My deepest sympathies go out to their families. Both of these men were fine persons and excellent, professional test pilots. We will miss them more than I can say."

Despite the tragedy the Gemini flight timetable continued on schedule. On 2 March, just two days after the crash, Spacecraft No. 9 was moved out of Building 101 on its way to the flight dock for shipment to Cape Kennedy. As it slowly made its way out of the McDonnell plant it rolled by an American flag fluttering at half-mast, a potent reminder of the many risks involved in sending men into space. Flags at MSC also flew at half-mast as the numbed employees continued the day-to-day work of space exploration.

The lives of Charlie Bassett and Elliot See and their hopes of going to the moon were eulogized at memorial services carried out in small churches near their homes two days after the accident. See's memorial was held Wednesday morning at the Seabrook Methodist Church, while the Bassett service took place that afternoon in the Webster Presbyterian Church. Both services were brief and simple, with most of NASA's astronauts attending. They sat grim-faced and pensive during the eulogies. All of them had known flying buddies who had perished in accidents and were understandably uncomfortable with funerals. None of them appreciated getting so up close and personal with death.

On Friday, 4 March, separate services with full military honors were held at Arlington National Cemetery. Light rain had begun falling that morning, adding an even more somber tone to the occasion. At ten o'clock, six magnificent black horses pulled a caisson bearing the flag-draped coffin of Elliot See as it wound a path from the Fort Major chapel to the gravesite in Section 4 of the cemetery. An honor guard of two naval platoons and a color guard preceded the cortege. Some fifty cars formed a slow procession behind the caisson, one of them carrying Marilyn See and her three children. Others carried twelve astronauts, representing NASA as honorary pallbearers.

Once the caisson had pulled up beside a small hillside, six navy enlisted men unloaded the coffin, which was covered in a plastic rain sheet to protect the American flag. Solemnly they carried it up the muddy slope to the gravesite, where six Merchant Marine Academy midshipmen, together with the academy's superintendent, Rear Admiral Gordon McLintock, had formed another honor guard.

As Christian Science teacher and practitioner Peter Vanderhoef read the twenty-third Psalm, Marilyn See could no longer hold back her tears. Daughters Sally and Carolyn had been weeping from the time they were seated under a brown canopy, erected to shelter the gravesite from the misty rain. At one time nine-year-old Sally buried her face in the black overcoat of astronaut Ed White, a close family friend. David See, then just three years old and not truly comprehending what was going on, sat quietly throughout the short oration.

By two o'clock that afternoon the rain had eased, but the skies were still slate gray and overcast as a black hearse delivered Charles Bassett's flag-draped casket to his gravesite at Arlington. This was an air force ceremony and did not include a caisson as with See's funeral. His grave was situated just a few yards from See's, and Jeannie Bassett, wearing dark glasses, could not help but gaze at the freshly formed grave of the man who had died with her husband. It was a short but dignified service, lasting just ten minutes, and conducted by the Presbyterian minister from Webster, the Reverend Ernest Dimaline. Throughout the ceremony a pale-faced Jean Bassett clutched the white-gloved hand of her daughter, Karen. When the service was over they stood slowly, took four-year-old Peter by the hands, and slowly walked away.

Mike Collins, a close friend of the Bassetts, wrote the following about his colleague for this book:

> Charlie Bassett had it all: brains, personality, looks. Even in our hard-driving world, his dedication and work habits were in a class by themselves. While the rest of us grabbed a quick lunch, Charlie flew some overtime in the simulator. Academics came easy to him, but he never lorded it over the dunces like me. Instead he was always there, big smile on his face, ready to make it look easy.
>
> I have had a lot of close friends die in airplanes, but Charlie's death seemed to have an extra dimension—devastating not only to those who knew him, but a loss to the whole country as well. Charlie could easily have been the first man on the Moon. He deserved to be, and would have been a superb choice.

On 7 March the canvas-covered wreckage of the T-38 and associated debris was finally loaded onto a large trailer vehicle and hauled by truck to the Scott Air Force Base in Illinois for scrapping.

The Gemini 9 mission with replacement crewmembers Stafford and Cernan was scheduled for liftoff on 17 May, but the failure of an Atlas rocket carrying the Agena target satellite caused a postponement until 3 June, and a mission redesignation to Gemini 9-A.

Earlier, on 27 May, NASA Headquarters released the findings of the Accident Investigation Board. The members had listened to the testimonies of dozens of witnesses and people who had any information to offer. They had sifted through the wreckage of the T-38 and had slowly built up a list of conclusions. They completed their report by including findings on the pilots' medical histories and flying experience as well as the condition and maintenance of their aircraft. They discounted any mechanical problems with the T-38; it had functioned normally up to the time of the crash. Furthermore the two pilots were deemed to be in excellent physical and mental shape.

In its report the board disclosed that pilot Elliot See had spent the final three seconds of his life desperately trying to regain speed and climb away from danger. Foul weather that prompted low altitude maneuvering was also a contributing factor. Investigators determined that the flight began quite normally, and all instrument flight clearances and procedures were carried out as required. At 08:37 A.M. the weather observation at Lambert Field was forwarded to pilots Stafford and See, indicating "a partial obscuration, measured ceiling of broken clouds at 800 feet, an overcast ceiling at 1,500 feet, visibility one and a half miles with light rain, light snow and fog." The flight was then passed to St. Louis approach Control at 08:48 for radar vectors to an ILS (Instrument Landing System) approach to the southeast runway at Lambert.

The FAA landing minimum for aircraft similar to the T-38 and its particular approach was 400 feet ceiling and one mile visibility, allowing for a straight-in approach and landing, and 500 feet with one and a half miles visibility for a visual circling approach. The radar controller continued to give heading and altitude information, to which Stafford and See responded.

The board concluded, "the primary cause of the accident was the inability of [See] to maintain visual reference for a landing during local weather conditions that were irregular and deteriorating rapidly. The weather throughout the approach was characterized by low ceiling, obscured sky, limited visibility, light rain, light snow and fog." It determined that, at the time of impact, the landing gear and flaps were fully down and all components and systems functioning normally. As See and Bassett's T-38 was approaching for a second attempt at landing, See "remained below the clouds, in a left turn, attempting to maintain visual contact with the runway." Because of the adverse weather conditions he "was forced to maneuver at low altitude and inadvertently developed a rate of descent from which recovery was impossible." About three seconds before the crash, "the bank angle was reduced and afterburner operation was selected. The right afterburner was in full thrust at impact, and the left was lighted and building up to full thrust."

The accompanying medical officer's report gave an analysis of the human factors involved in the fatal accident. In part, it concluded that See "was a highly motivated, stable, well-integrated individual with high intellectual resources. [His] flying reflected his personality; namely, he was known to be cautious and conservative." The report also stated that Charlie Bassett was "a highly motivated, intelligent, emotionally stable individual who was known for his friendly, outgoing personality. He was furthermore recognized as a highly skilled aviator whose flying was above reproach."

The deaths of Elliot See and Charles Bassett caused a significant reshuffling of assignments at the tail end of the Gemini program and would lead Deke Slayton to later write that the accident wound up having a lot to do with who ended up landing on the moon.

A chain reaction occurred among the rest of the mission backups. John Young and Mike Collins were already in training for GT-10, so Slayton had no hesitation in shuffling the Gemini 11 and 12 backup team of Alan Bean and C.C. Williams to the same role for the Gemini 10 mission. Jim Lovell and Buzz Aldrin moved into the backup role for Gemini 9, while Charles Conrad and Richard Gordon of Gemini 11 now had Neil Armstrong and Bill Anders as their backups. According to the way the crew rotation system worked, Stafford and Cernan—originally backups for Gemini 9—would then have been in line for the job of prime crew on Gemini 12. This assignment now fell to Jim Lovell and Buzz Aldrin, with Gene Cernan and Mercury astronaut Gordon Cooper backing them up.

According to Slayton, "The GT-12 backup crew was a real dead end. There was no point in training somebody new. Elliot was going to be backup commander for GT-12. I figured I could rotate Gene Cernan back to this and still move him on to Apollo as originally planned. 'Gordo' Cooper, who was basically marking time, stepped in as backup commander. Without flying GT-12, it was very unlikely that Buzz would have been in any position to be lunar module pilot on the first lunar landing attempt."

In 1965 *Life* magazine's Ralph Morse had an interview with Neil Armstrong. Morse, among other spaceflight observers, was curious to know why rookie Elliot See was not on the GT-8 mission with Armstrong, when the two men had formed the backup team for GT-5. It was the first occasion on which a Gemini backup crew had been split instead of going on to form a prime crew. Armstrong had brusquely responded, "Elliot's too good a pilot not to have a command of his own."

In his honor, the U.S. Merchant Marine Academy at Kings Point, which See had attended from 1945 to 1949, and where he had won an award as one of the academy's three outstanding graduates, named its Command Board Conference Room in Wiley Hall after him. The academy's superintendent at the time See passed through was Rear Admiral Gordon McLintock. He wrote the following about the astronaut's cadet days:

*We had all looked forward to Gemini 9 when [See] was to be the Command Pilot. We were very proud of his accomplishments and gave him our highest honor, the honor of being our Reviewing Officer on May 22, 1965. He was a credit to his Academy and to his country.*

*Elliot was a quiet Cadet, studious and capable. He was Third Company Commander, carrying out his responsibilities with care and competence but always without bombast. His slow cheerful smile, and his readiness to perform his duties, at once characterized him as a kind and earnest man who was well-knit and well oriented to life. He was a church-goer and a believer and he was kind enough to tell me—though he did not talk much—that throughout his graduate years he remembered my talks to the Regiment and took many of my words to heart.*

*When I asked him what made him go into the space program he said it was because air navigation seemed to him to be an extension of surface navigation, and he said he thought President Kennedy summed this up when he said, "Space is the new ocean and we intend to sail upon it."*

In recent years, several Apollo-era astronauts have analyzed the accident and its repercussions in their autobiographies, and chief astronaut Deke Slayton in particular was pointedly critical of See's reactions to the flying conditions over St. Louis. NASA's former Public Affairs spokesman Paul Haney, who was heavily involved in the immediate and long-term aftermath of the crash, recently gave these comments on what he believed had happened that tragic day: "The scuttlebutt I picked up from various pilots was that See, who was driving, was a fair-weather southern California (Edwards) type pilot. Even though he was well-checked out on instruments, he was what the pilots called a fair-weather flyer. Always relying on a look out the window instead of what the dials were telling him. The window became a non-factor as he circled to land. And apparently he didn't read all the dials right. Bassett said and did nothing as good pilots in the rear seat are trained to do. The landing was certainly doable because Stafford landed perfectly soon after."

Neil Armstrong not only vigorously contends that See was a good pilot, but also still recalls his friend and fellow backup crewmember with great clarity and sincerity: "He was contemplative and thought carefully and effectively while facing the problems we were dealing with at that time. But he had a smile on his face more often than not, and was genuinely good natured and funny. He was my crewmate and my friend and I remember him with great affection."

A year after the crash in St. Louis, Marilyn See took an Easter trip to Mexico with her three children and a niece. "It's the first time we'd ever done anything like that," she later said in an interview. "Always before there seemed to be a hundred more hours of flying time to get in, or one more year of school." Although she had been very hesitant about going on the holiday, it seemed to do her some good. Six months later she went on her first visit to Europe, having persuaded Betty Grissom, widowed earlier that year, to accompany her. They enjoyed the trip immensely, and it helped both women to overcome their profound loss.

Marilyn stayed in Houston and worked as a court reporter in criminal and civil courtrooms for twenty-five years. She still lives there today, just a few miles from the space center, but ever since her husband's death she has been loath to involve herself in matters relating to his life as an astronaut. However, Sally, the Sees' older daughter, reflected back on the very few years she had with a father she adored:

> I knew him as a child knows her father. He was fun-loving, smiled a lot, rode horses with his children on Saturday mornings, built a tree house for his kids, loved a television show called "Bonanza," and was very principled. I wished for his smiling eyes, and I got them. I remember little things about him, but I didn't have the opportunity to grow into a larger understanding of the man.
>
> The men who were closest to my family after my dad's death were Ed White, Neil Armstrong, Jim Lovell, and John Glenn. Ed White came over to our home on several occasions that I remember distinctly—extending himself in compassion. Once he climbed up the huge pine tree in back of our house to hang a rope swing for Carrie, Dave and I. It was something a father would do for his children, if he were there to do it. Ed White's daughter, Bonnie, was my age. I think he well understood what it would be like for a child to lose a father. I hope someone did the same for his family when he was killed in the spacecraft fire.

Jeannie Bassett remained in Houston for a year after she lost Charlie. About a month after his death she was advised of his promotion to the rank of major on 1 March, the notification stating "for all purposes but pay." He was buried under this rank at Arlington, but Jeannie insists the husband she lost was Captain Charlie Bassett. She had a close circle of good, supportive friends who helped her come to grips with her grief, but when the first Christmas came around she traveled with Karen and Peter to her parents' home. She simply could not bear the thought of being in her own house at that time. After Christmas she and the children flew to San Francisco to spend New Year's Eve with a college friend. There she renewed her love for the enchanting city by the bay, and her children shared this appreciation. When the family finally returned to Houston, Jeannie began to feel that the whole area had lost its attraction for her, and that she would always be uncomfortably regarded as the widow of an astronaut. It was time to make a fresh start, so on a later trip to San Francisco she purchased a home, and then told Chief Astronaut Alan Shepard of her decision to leave Houston.

That same evening a fire broke out on Launch Pad 34, within a capsule being tested for the first manned Apollo mission. Astronauts Gus Grissom, Ed White, and Roger Chaffee died before they could be evacuated from their burning spacecraft.

Two weeks later, Jeannie took her family to live in San Francisco and stayed there for seven years, working for most of that time with a publishing company. The family moved back to Texas, and Jeannie returned to Charlie's alma mater, Texas Tech University, and earned bachelor's and master's degrees in history and historic preservation.

On 3 July 1979 she married Will Robinson, a professor of architecture at Texas Tech. During their marriage she worked closely with him in the research and writing of several scholarly works on the architectural history of Texas. Following his death in 1991, she worked in archives and libraries in Galveston, Texas, and Santa Fe, New Mexico. Now living in San Antonio, she is actively involved with the Institute of Texan Cultures and continues her deep interest in the varied aspects of architectural preservation programs.

In November 1996 Texas Tech University honored Charlie Bassett for his contributions to space technology when it dedicated an electrical engineering research laboratory to his memory. By that time the research annex bearing his name had been used by faculty and graduate students for more than fifteen years. NASA astronaut Rick Husband, also a Texas Tech engineering graduate, spoke at the dedication ceremony and passed on the words of NASA Administrator Dan Goldin: "This is a fitting tribute to a man who dedicated his life to pursuing the dream of space flight. It is gratifying to know that the laboratory bearing his name will help encourage today's students to achieve their own personal goals."

Bill ("Buzz") Bassett still entertains fond memories of his big brother, and he recently recalled an important incident stretching back over three and a half decades:

> *Back in the years when Charlie was training to be an astronaut I was a young engineer living near Philadelphia. The U.S. Navy had a facility at Johnsville Naval Air Station and there was a centrifuge that all of the astronauts trained on. On several occasions Charlie stayed with us when he trained there. In late 1965, Charlie came to Johnsville and I took two of my sons and we went over there. My oldest son Steve was at school at the time and the principal became aware of the fact that Charlie was in town and called to ask if there was any chance that he could drop by for an impromptu talk to the school. Charlie agreed, and when he became available we showed up at the school. As dear old Miss Rockefeller the principal said, she was so in awe of astronauts that she would have been more comfortable if it had been the president. Miss Rockefeller called the entire school together and he spoke to them. If there was ever a time when I was proud of my brother, that was it. He was a true ambassador for the space program to this young generation. He spoke at a level they could comprehend and was humble and gracious in every way. When at his funeral I had some people tell me that he would have been another John Glenn, I could have believed it.*

The day the crew of Apollo 11 splashed down in the Pacific after the historic mission in July 1969, exultation erupted in the home of Buzz Aldrin. As helicopters plucked moon astronauts Armstrong, Aldrin, and Collins from their life raft and carried them to the USS *Hornet,* champagne corks were popping as family and friends cheered the safe return of the astronauts. Jeannie Bassett was there, having flown down from San Francisco, and had been there most of the time since before the launch to offer support to her good friend Joan Aldrin. They had watched the launch together and shared the agonies and triumphs of the first manned lunar landing.

One minute Jeannie was sharing the joy of the men's safe return and drinking a champagne toast; the next she suddenly broke down and began to cry. Within moments she was sobbing uncontrollably and had to flee into the Aldrin's living room. She needed to be by herself for a while. Everyone was a little stunned and not quite sure what to do. Eventually Enid Farmer, covering the story for *Life* magazine, ventured into the room and comforted Jeannie, who was just beginning to calm down. The tears had been for her beloved husband, who should have been beside her, sharing in the excitement of this historic day. As she dried her eyes Jeannie whispered, "If only he could be watching from somewhere, . . ." to which Enid sympathetically responded, "How do you know he isn't?"

Soon after, Jeannie had regained her composure sufficiently to rejoin the festivities and finish her glass of champagne. But for the rest of that day fond images of Charlie found their way into her thoughts; he was sometimes laughing, sometimes incredibly serious. She vividly recalled one softly moonlit evening when she happened to look out into their backyard and saw Charlie standing there with his hands thrust deep into his trousers pockets, alone and pensive, looking up. The moon was so bright it threw shadows under the trees, and so large it could not for a moment be forgotten. His eyes were turned to the heavens, his jaw was jutting out, and he was just staring at the faraway moon with a profound look of curiosity and longing etched on his face.

# 3  Countdown to Disaster
## Lieutenant Colonel Virgil Ivan Grissom, USAF
## Lieutenant Colonel Edward Higgins White II, USAF
## Lieutenant Commander Roger Bruce Chaffee, USN

*Inevitably, there are times in a nation's history when its hopes, fears, and confidence in its own destiny seem to hinge on a single, unforgettable event. One of the more significant moments for the United States occurred at 9:07 A.M. Moscow time on 12 April 1961, when Soviet Air Force Lieutenant Yuri Gagarin was launched into the skies aboard a Vostok spacecraft, becoming the first person in history to leave the Earth's atmosphere and venture into space.*

*On the sunny spring morning of 5 May 1961, just three weeks after Gagarin's flight, thirty-seven-year-old naval test pilot Commander Alan Shepard also blazed a solo trail into space, and America soon entered into a well-documented Space Race with the Soviet Union. Just twenty days later President Kennedy made the trip across Washington DC from the White House to Capitol Hill to announce a monumental undertaking before a joint session of Congress. Tired of finishing second to the Soviets in spaceflight achievements, he was literally ready to shoot for the moon. Ignoring his closest advisers, he had decided a bold promise of action was required, and in one of his most passionate speeches the young president declared that the nation would commit itself to landing a man on the moon before the end of the decade.*

*In January 1967 three men stood ready to take the first manned Apollo mission into space. It was to be a crucial Earth-orbiting test flight of a spacecraft that, with modifications, would one day carry a crew to the moon, and the astronauts were well aware of the dangers they faced. The twice-flown commander was Virgil ("Gus") Grissom, and during a 1966 address to the Associated Press he had openly discussed those dangers. "If we die," he said, "we want people to accept it. We are in a risky business and we hope that if anything happens to us, it will not delay the program. The conquest of space is worth the risk of life." His words would be recalled as sadly prophetic following the catastrophic events of 27 January 1967—known as the Day of the Fire in the NASA corridors.*

During the 1960s the English-speaking world became inured to a phenomenon known widely as "NASAspeak." Acronyms such as EVA (extravehicular activity) and LEM (lunar excursion module) began to creep into the language. But there was another acronym in popular use back in the midsixties, and it did not derive from the space agency. It was TGIF, or Thank God it's Friday: a time to slow down, kick back, and get ready for the weekend and whatever fun it brings before reluctantly returning to work on Monday.

By 1967 it was becoming harder for Americans to relax. Students were in open rebellion throughout many universities and college campuses. The once peaceful Civil Rights movement was becoming increasingly violent, and there was the despised, escalating war that America was fighting in far-off Vietnam. More and more of America's young men were dying in a conflict that did not appear to have a purpose to an increasing number of people. A grieving nation watched in horror as the seemingly unending casualties of this grim war came home in a gut-wrenching procession of flag-draped coffins.

In January 1967, there was one organization in America for which the counting of days, at least to the end of each week, was not a great priority. There was no TGIF for NASA—the space agency had only one serious date on its agenda: 31 December 1969. This was the date by which the late president John Fitzgerald Kennedy had declared America would land a man on the moon and return him safely to Earth. That declaration had driven NASA and its employees and contractors since the day that immortal speech was delivered on 25 May 1961.

In the Cold War era of the 1960s the astronauts saw themselves as the purest form of Cold Warriors, defending the cause of freedom every time they were launched into space. The program that would get these American astronauts to the moon was called Apollo, after the Greek god of the sun. The name would prove to be an ironic choice. By January 1967, plans were being made for the first manned flight of the Apollo spacecraft the following month.

However, all was not well with Project Apollo, in spite of the optimistic opinions of NASA and main Apollo contractor North American Aviation (NAA). Unknown to the astronauts, the public, and the media, a team led by the Apollo program manager, General Sam Phillips, USAF, had visited the NAA factory in Downey, California, at various times during 1965. The team was appalled by what it found. The members wrote a scathing confidential report on the NAA and its deficiencies for Phillips's boss, Dr. George Mueller. Included in the "Phillips Report" was the unpalatable revelation that budget costs for the spacecraft had increased dramatically. Serious technical deficiencies were found in the welding and insulation of the Saturn 1B second stage, as well as stress corrosion in the Block 1 model of the command/service module.

At one point the question of using flammable materials such as Raschel netting attached with Velcro in the 100 percent oxygen environment was raised, and NAA was instructed to keep potentially flammable items at least four inches from anything that could create a spark.

Many of the problems were not of NAA's making, as some of the subcontractors were late in making hardware deliveries. AiResearch, manufacturers of the environmental control system, or ECS, was singled out for an especially poor performance. The ECS was a sophisticated complex of pumps, boilers, high-pressure tanks, and radiators designed to supply the astronauts with drinking water and oxygen and keep them warm during flight. It had eleven subsystems with eighty major components.

13. Johnson Space Center Director Dr. Robert Gilruth (*right*) announces the prime crew for the Apollo 1 mission. *Left to right:* Roger Chaffee, Ed White, and Gus Grissom (NASA)

During its development some, if not all, of these components had failed, requiring costly, ongoing redesign work.

The report also stressed that NAA's inability to meet deadlines on both the CSM and Saturn 1B was having a pronounced impact on NASA's ambitious launch schedule and had caused an unwanted rescheduling of the entire Apollo program. With regard to the CSM, Phillips wrote: "My people and I have completely lost confidence in the ability of NAA's competence as an organization . . . and I seriously question whether there is any sincere intent and determination by NAA to do its job properly . . . there is little confidence that NAA will meet its performance and commitments." General Phillips visited the NAA factory again in April 1966; he did not amend his conclusions to the original report, but told various NAA managers that he felt they were finally moving in the right direction.

Originally it was hoped that the first manned Apollo flight would coincide with the last two-man Gemini mission to give NASA a unique space spectacular, with both spacecraft in orbit at the same time. But continuing technical delays with Apollo preparations saw that option finally ruled out in early 1966.

On 21 March 1966 NASA named the prime crew for the first Apollo flight. Commanding the mission would be Virgil Grissom, a veteran Mercury astronaut better known as "Gus," who had already made two space flights, including the first Gemini mission. The senior pilot was Ed White, who had enthralled the world the previous year when he became the first American to walk in space. The pilot was Roger Chaffee, a thirty-one-year-old space rookie who had been an astronaut since 1963.

Also announced on that day was the designation of the flight as AS (Apollo Saturn)-204. The numbering system meant that AS-204 would be the fourth flight of the Saturn 1B launch vehicle. Saturn 1 flights were numbered in the two hundreds, while those involving Saturn 5 launch vehicles would be numbered in the five hundreds. Unofficially, Grissom and his crew referred to themselves as the Apollo 1 crew, and they had that designation incorporated into their crew patch.

NASA had given Grissom the option of an open-ended mission, and while the flight was expected to last somewhere between fourteen and sixteen days, it could be extended to eighteen days if necessary. The principal goals of the first manned Apollo mission were to check out launch operations, ground tracking, and control facilities and to carry out a thorough evaluation of the launch vehicle and Apollo spacecraft during launch and in Earth orbit.

During July and August 1966 NASA officials conducted a Customer Acceptance Readiness Review at the NAA factory in Downey, later issuing a Certificate of Worthiness and authorizing shipment of the hardware. However, the certificate listed instances of incomplete work, identifying 113 significant engineering orders at the time of delivery.

There was pressure, though few at NASA would admit it, to push Spacecraft 012 to a satisfactory completion for the scheduled delivery date. The haste was intensified by a worrying silence emanating from the Soviet Union. The superpower had not flown a manned mission throughout the entire Gemini program, and intelligence reports coming back suggested (correctly, as history would later reveal) that the Soviets were planning their own manned landing ahead of the Americans. When ship-out time came for the spacecraft, it still had many technical problems not resolved to Grissom's satisfaction. He even sounded off at his two fellow crew members; he felt they were not sharing the responsibility for ensuring their own safety.

In spite of the spacecraft problems, the astronauts and others involved in the program had come down with a malady widely known as "go fever." The astronauts determined that they were going to fly regardless of any consequences, even if their own safety was on the line. In their later memoirs, astronauts Alan Shepard, Wally Schirra, Frank Borman, and Gene Cernan concurred that the spacecraft itself was substandard and not truly fit to be flown. But despite their misgivings, the astronauts realized that if they backed off, if they chose not to fly, their colleagues would immediately volunteer to take their place. The unstated realization was that such coyness would virtually mean an end to their astronaut career.

Sections of the 204 spacecraft (number 012) began arriving at Florida's Kennedy Space Center during August 1966. On 26 August the command module also arrived from the NAA factory, and by early September the CM had been attached to the service module.

NASA released a checkout schedule in early September. It pointed out that while the Saturn 1B launch vehicle checkout was moving along on schedule, a similar schedule for the Apollo CSM lagged four days behind. On the same day, a combined systems check began. A total of 80 discrepancy reports were listed on 16 September, and this figure rose to 152 within just six days. One of the major problems was a short in the radio command system.

In her 1974 book *Starfall*, Betty Grissom wrote of her husband's increasing concerns about the safety of the spacecraft, and his impatience with the people involved in its design and systems: "Part of the pattern as Gus saw it was a diffusion of responsibility in NASA as well as among the thousands of subcontractors caught up in the Apollo program, which was several orders of magnitude more complex than either of the two preceding manned space programs. Several times he criticized his own colleagues for accepting inferior work instead of holding out for a better solution to a technical problem. He became such a gadfly, finally, in trying to enforce his standards of excellence that some contractor personnel tried to work paths around him."

During October 1966 the Apollo 1 crew participated in the first checkout of the spacecraft in an altitude chamber. Concerns were raised when the spacecraft reached a simulated altitude of 13,000 feet and a transistor failed in one of the inverters. The crew repeated the sixteen-hour test the following day and this time reported a major problem in the environmental control system, which was traced to a leak in the oxygen regulator. The unit had to be returned to California for some remedial work. Further checkout tests were postponed indefinitely when it became clear that the spacecraft required an entirely new environmental control system.

Early in January 1967 the CSM was finally removed from the altitude chamber and taken to Launch Pad 34, where it was carefully installed atop an unfueled Saturn 1B launch vehicle, and checks of the systems continued.

Gus Grissom had returned to his home in Houston for two days during a short break, and then left for what would be the final time. On his way out through the courtyard he reached out and plucked a lemon from a tree. He was so disgusted with the constant problems and failures of the spacecraft's systems that he hung the lemon on the simulator as a sign of his annoyance. The CM was in a perpetual state of breakdown, leading to pent-up frustration and consternation for the professional but outspoken astronaut. In the eyes of many he was once again living up to his nickname of "Gruff Gus."

Things truly were not going smoothly for the crew, and Grissom was becoming increasingly vocal about the lax state of preparedness and safety concerns by NAA. In the days of Mercury and Gemini he could take any problem directly to the president of McDonnell for rectification, but things worked differently with North American. Grissom perceived the company as having too many bosses, with too little, or inept, decision making going on. The North American employees were impatient with astronaut suggestions and dreaded listening to what they called "Mercury or Gemini war stories."

On 17 January the three crew members were flying to the Downey plant to check out an updated Apollo simulator when one of their T-38 jets suffered a minor technical problem and they had to divert to Nellis Air Force Base outside of Las

Vegas. While the jet was being fixed Grissom thought it might be an idea for the three of them to relax for the night and take in a live show. Frank Sinatra happened to be in town, and when he heard that the Apollo 1 crew was in the auditorium for his show he immediately had the men placed at a front table and introduced them with pride to his audience. All three were still wearing their NASA flight jackets, complete with name tags and mission badges, and when Sinatra mentioned that he would love to have one just like it, Grissom whipped his off and handed it over to thunderous applause. Sinatra was so moved he actually had tears in his eyes.

Everyone knew that the three men were involved in a highly dangerous undertaking, and late in 1966 the media asked them if the chance of a severe accident might be a consideration for them during their training. The subject came up during an interview conducted by CBS correspondent Nelson Benton. First off Benton asked Grissom if, having flown on both Mercury and Gemini, the law of averages so far as the possibility of a catastrophic failure bothered him at all. "No," Grissom responded. "You sort of have to put that out of your mind. There's always a possibility that you can have a catastrophic failure, of course, this can happen on any flight. It can happen on the last one as well as the first one. You just plan as best you can to take care of all these eventualities and get a well-trained crew, and you go fly."

Benton asked White whether he had any apprehension in taking part in the shakedown flight of the Apollo spacecraft. "No," was his considered reply, "I don't think so. I think you have to understand the feeling that a pilot has, that a test pilot has, that I look forward to a flight with a great deal of anticipation."

Benton then asked Chaffee if he had any major concerns as he trained for his first spaceflight. "Oh, I don't like to say anything scary about it," Chaffee responded. "There's a lot of unknowns of course, and a lot of problems that could develop or might develop and they'll have to be solved, and that's what we're here for. This is our business, to find out if this thing will work for us."

As the three men battled technical problems with their spacecraft and dealt with preflight anxiety, they stayed focused but maintained their sense of humor. Grissom and Chaffee joked that they would have to padlock their food lockers shut to stop White from snacking on their rations in space. During the final photographic session in front of the launch pad, Grissom mischievously pulled at White's space suit, causing his Mae West rescue vest to balloon.

Three important objectives were to be met before the revised launch date of 21 February 1967. They were a "Plugs Out" test, the Flight Readiness Test, and the Countdown Demonstration Test.

The "Plugs Out" test was scheduled for Friday, 27 January, and was planned as a rehearsal of everything that was to occur during the final countdown on the morning of launch. The day before this test the backup crew of Wally Schirra, Walt Cunningham, and Donn Eisele completed a full-up systems test of AS-204. This systems test meant that the spacecraft was fully powered, although the cabin was

14. Ed White, Gus Grissom, and Roger Chaffee. (NASA)

not being pressurized with 100 percent pure oxygen. Instead, Schirra's crew was breathing normal air.

Following the test Joe Shea, the Manned Spacecraft Center's Apollo program manager in Houston, held a short but intense debriefing with Wally Schirra and Gus Grissom. Schirra was blunt about the many shortcomings he and his crew had pinpointed in the spacecraft, and he directed his conclusions to Grissom. "Frankly, Gus, I don't like it," he said. "You're going to be in there with full oxygen tomorrow, and if you have the same feeling that I do, I suggest you get out."

Schirra also told Deke Slayton, director of Flight Operations, about numerous chronic problems with the Apollo spacecraft and suggested that Slayton squeeze into the spacecraft with the crew during the "Plugs Out" test to see what it was like from an insider's perspective. The idea was further discussed at breakfast the following morning, but it was found to be technically unfeasible for Slayton to communicate with either the crew or Mission Control in such an exercise. For the rest of his life, Slayton would wonder if he had done the right thing by monitoring the test in the launch blockhouse that day instead of being locked inside the spacecraft. He felt he may have been able to snuff out the fire at its source.

On the morning of 27 January, technicians at the Kennedy Space Center and Manned Spacecraft Center began to check systems for the "Plugs Out" test. By this time the spacecraft had undergone twenty weeks of tests and checkout at the Downey plant and a further twenty-one weeks of tests and modifications at the cape. All electrical, environmental, and ground checkout cables would now be disconnected to verify that the spacecraft and launch vehicle could function on internal power only after the umbilical lines had been disconnected at an appropriate phase of the countdown. At the end of the flight simulation the crew members were also scheduled to simulate an emergency egress through the spacecraft hatch. It was not considered a dangerous test of the spacecraft and its systems, as the Saturn 1 rocket was not loaded with fuel. A fueled test would occur only at the final "wet" mock test immediately preceding the scheduled launch the following month.

At 7:42 A.M. NASA technicians powered up the Apollo 1 spacecraft, sending electric current surging through nearly thirty miles of wiring coiled in thick bundles around the floor and through enclosed recesses above and below the three contoured couches where the astronauts would sit.

Following an early lunch the crewmates had biomedical sensors attached to their bodies and were then fitted into their space suits. They were driven to the launch pad, and installed into the spacecraft's couches, where they plugged themselves in to their respective communications and oxygen systems. Grissom, as commander, sat in the left-hand couch, White was in the middle, and Chaffee sat on the right. After the astronauts had been strapped in, technicians sealed the spacecraft's pressure vessel inner hatch, secured the heavy and cumbersome outer crew access hatch, and finally locked the booster cap in place. The crew now began to purge its spacesuits and spacecraft of all gases except pure oxygen, pressurized to sixteen and a half pounds per square inch to ensure no contamination could intrude from the normal outside atmosphere. The three astronauts slowly worked their way through the tedious series of checklists, becoming impatient as the checkout sequence was continually interrupted by a series of minor problems.

Soon after, Grissom detected an odor in the space suit loop, which he reported as "a sour smell somewhat like buttermilk." His two colleagues stopped to take a sample of the suit loop and after discussions with Grissom decided to continue the test. The next problem they encountered was a high oxygen flow indicator, which periodically set off the spacecraft's master alarm. The crew discussed this problem with the environmental control systems specialists, who felt that the problem simply stemmed from crew movements within the spacecraft, but the issue was not resolved to Grissom's satisfaction.

Undoubtedly the most serious problem at this stage of the test was in the important area of communications. At first this seemed to be one confined to Grissom and the control center, and the crew made some adjustments. Later, however, these difficulties extended to include communications between the Operations and Checkout Building and the blockhouse at Pad 34.

At one stage Grissom, who had managed to hold his temper in check throughout the afternoon, reached the boiling point. He growled, "How the hell can you expect us to get to the Moon if you people can't hook us up with a ground station? Get

15. Gus Grissom's exemplary work on the first Gemini mission with John Young (right) was later rewarded with the command of Apollo 1. (NASA)

with it out there!" To further complicate matters, no one person controlled the troubleshooting aspect of any communications problems. This failure caused yet another hold in the countdown at 5:40 P.M.

The countdown resumed after an exasperating delay of several minutes. Then, at 6:30:55 P.M., something happened inside the command module. Somewhere in those thirty miles of wiring, one segment arced across another with a spark of flame, and the greatest catastrophe to that time in the United States's space program began.

The first inkling of a problem for spacecraft technicians appeared when ground instruments recorded a two-and-a-half-second interruption of power on an alternating current bus, and other monitors showed an inexplicable rise in the oxygen flow into the crew's space suits. An acrid smell developed inside the spacecraft, and White's heart and respiration rates noticeably increased.

Mounted on the inner wall of the spacecraft beside Grissom was a small compartment for lithium hydroxide known as the Environmental Control Unit (ECU), which removed carbon dioxide from the oxygen the crew was breathing. Access to this compartment was through a small metal door—which had a very sharp edge. This door had been opened and closed several times, and the bottom of the door had apparently been abrading against two tiny sections of wire in the thick cable. In the opinion of those who later tried to determine the ignition point of the fire, this was "the most probable cause" of the conflagration that followed. Although the full facts and circumstances may never be known, it seems Grissom may have opened this door one last time and something inevitable had finally happened: a brief electrical arc flashed between the two bare segments of wire.

Some flammable Raschel netting was situated adjacent to the area of the arc—dangerously closer than it should have been. With the heat of the arc the netting instantly developed a hot spot, which sparked and grew longer, feeding greedily in the pure oxygen environment and probably causing the peculiar smell. The spark in the netting smoldered for nearly ten seconds in the left forward corner of the spacecraft, out of sight beneath Grissom's feet and the couch.

At 6:31:04 P.M. the first tongue of flame became apparent. Grissom yelled what sounded like "Hey!" (this may have been "Fire!"). Clear flames suddenly spread up the inside wall of the spacecraft. Chaffee's voice came through on the intercom, "Fire—I smell fire." Curiously enough there seemed to be no true concern in his tone. Two seconds later White's voice was heard—this time far more insistent. "Fire in the cockpit!" he cried.

In the blockhouse located near the pad, and at the various control centers, surprised engineers and technicians looked up from their consoles to television monitors showing the interior of the command module. To their horror they were witnesses to an unbelievable scene—intense flames were raging inside the spacecraft, and dense smoke was rapidly blurring the picture. John Tribe, an engineer from NAA, was one of those in a control room at the cape monitoring the crew and spacecraft systems by means of television receivers and recording instruments. What he heard through his headphones brought him instantly alert. He turned to the man beside him, bewildered. "Did he say 'fire'?" he asked. The man nodded, suddenly very serious and intent.

§

"I remember how happy he was when they told him he would be in that first crew to go to the Moon," Betty Grissom said, reflecting on the time her husband was apparently told by Deke Slayton that he would command the first lunar landing flight. "I thought to myself, 'How's that going to change our lives if he's the first on the Moon?' But I put that out of my mind. It was too far in the future, and I guess it's just as well I did."

Grissom never seemed to quite fit the archetypal American hero mold. A stocky, stubby man just five feet seven inches tall, Grissom always looked more like a mild-mannered motor mechanic or television repairman than an astronaut. But had fate not lent a final, tragic twist to his life, he might now be remembered as the first man to set foot on the moon's surface. If the Apollo 1 and subsequent missions had gone ahead as scheduled, his name would have become immortal. According to those close to Deke Slayton, who wielded immense power with regard to crew assignments, he had already informed Grissom that as far as he was concerned his

Mercury colleague and friend was at the head of the line to command the first lunar landing and would therefore be the first man to walk on the moon.

Virgil Ivan Grissom was born on 3 April 1926 in the small midwestern town of Mitchell, in southern Indiana. Mitchell, with a population of around three thousand, was well known as the place where rows upon rows of yellow school buses were manufactured and assembled at the Carpenter Body Works. It was an unpretentious Hoosier town just off State Road 37, where Lawrence County cornfields and quarries meet about ten miles south of Bedford. He grew up as the eldest of four children of Dennis David and Cecile Grissom. He had two brothers, Norman and Lowell, and a sister named Wilma. His father worked as a signalman for the Baltimore and Ohio Railroad, putting in wearisome six-day workweeks for a wage of just fifty cents an hour. While the family was far from rich, it nevertheless enjoyed a warm, comfortable life in a simple white-frame house at 715 Baker Street. Some years later the road was renamed to honor the memory of Mitchell's favorite son.

Young Grissom attended Riley grade school on the corner of Sixth and Vine, and it was there that he first developed a moderate interest in flying. Although he possessed an IQ said to have been around 145, he would later confess that he was far from a genius in school. "I guess it was a case of drifting and not knowing what I wanted to make of myself," he said. "I suppose I built my share of model aeroplanes, but I can't remember that I was a flying fanatic."

Younger brother Norman was emphatic that his sibling was never a starry-eyed dreamer as a youth. "He went out and did things," he recalled. "All the neighborhood boys wanted to fly, but he pursued it." Young Grissom also had a mischievous side, and it was not unheard of for him to participate in tipping over outhouses on Halloween, or taking forbidden swims at deep water holes in abandoned quarries— typical Hoosier horseplay according to Norman.

The nickname he would happily carry through the rest of his life came about during a game of cards when a young friend read "Gris" upside down on a scorecard and translated it as Gus. This caused much hilarity at the time, but the name just stuck, and Grissom liked it.

To help make ends meet, and to have a little pocket money for his own activities, Grissom would leap out of bed early each morning and make his way across to the downtown bus station, where he would pick up that day's *Indianapolis Star* newspaper for his delivery route. In the evenings he would also collect and deliver copies of the local newspaper, the *Bedford Times*.

As part of Beaver Patrol in Mitchell's Boy Scout Troop 46, Grissom came to love the outdoor hikes and camping and eventually served as leader of the Honor Guard. However, his passion for tying intricate knots with the troop nearly cost him his life when a friend made a hangman's noose and jokingly slipped it over Grissom's head. The boy then threw the other end over a rafter and without thinking hauled his alarmed pal into the air to see if the knot would hold. It did, and his face had turned scarlet before his plight was spotted and he was quickly lowered to the floor.

But young Grissom quickly set aside any animosities, and his outdoor experiences in the Boy Scouts enticed him into his later passions of fishing and hunting.

It truly riled Gus that his short stature precluded him from varsity sports when he entered Mitchell High School in 1940, but his father would prove an enormous encouragement to him to explore areas where he was perhaps more suited. This extended to career talk, and Dennis Grissom actively discouraged his son from following in his railroadman's footsteps. He convinced Grissom to look beyond what he felt were his limitations and find different areas of opportunity. Rather than wallow in disappointment at being too short to make his high school's basketball team, Grissom took up swimming and soon became a fierce competitor in the pool.

While he could not take to the basketball court for his school, he took great pride in being a member of the Boy Scout Honor Guard that presented the American flag before any games. His evident pleasure in this activity during one game soon caught the eye of a fellow student named Betty Lavonne Moore, who played the drum in the school band. She had noticed him before in the school corridors, and when he came and sat down with her during the half-time break she knew that the attraction had been mutual.

It was said of Grissom that he had been interested in engineering even when he was too young to know what it was. Although his attraction for airplanes and flying began moderately for him, by the time he reached sixth grade it began to hold a special fascination, and he loved nothing better than watching newsreel films of pilots on bombing runs. One of his most prized possessions was a gas-engine model airplane given to him by his seventh grade teacher, Joe Bishop. He continued to make model aircraft, and he lost his temper one day when Norman, four years his junior, accidentally sat on one of his treasured model planes and crushed it. But after he had cooled down, he patiently rebuilt the shattered craft.

In the summer months Grissom supplemented his newspaper route income by working in a dry goods store and picking cherries and peaches in the orchards of local growers, who admired his strong work ethic. Some of this money went to model planes and some to excursions to the movies.

By now he and Betty Moore were seeing each other all the time, following an instant and mutual attraction. He later confessed that the first time he saw her he decided she was the girl he was going to marry. "I met Betty Moore when she entered Mitchell High School as a freshman," he recalled, "and that was it—period, exclamation point!"

Soon after, Betty joined Grissom on his visits to the local theater. "I guess that's where most of his money went," she later recalled. "I think we saw every movie they ever made." They were young, but romance blossomed, and after a while they became inseparable. Sometimes his father would allow him to borrow the family car, but such privileges were rare due to wartime gasoline and tire rationing. His father would not have been impressed had he known that Grissom used these occasions to teach Betty to drive out on quiet country roads.

By now flying was definitely the other love of Grissom's life, and he began to put his hard-earned money into flights on barnstorming planes that put down at nearby Bedford airport. He just could not get enough flying time, and he talked animatedly with anyone who would listen about the many thrills of escaping into the skies.

While in high school, Grissom completed a year of precadet training in the Army Air Corps and found this far more enjoyable than studying for exams. He graduated from Mitchell High School in 1944, still with the reputation of being an indifferent student, and on 8 August, Betty's seventeenth birthday, he was inducted into the Army Air Forces at Fort Benjamin Harrison with the expressed goal of becoming a pilot. He was then sent off to Sheppard Air Force Base, a thousand miles away in Wichita Falls, Texas, for five weeks of basic training. Following this he was assigned to Brooks Field in San Antonio, where to his chagrin he spent his days deskbound as a lowly clerk.

Grissom took some short leave and on 6 July 1945, while still in his teens, he and Betty were married in the First Baptist Church in Mitchell. Typically, he had never really proposed. "He never got serious enough for that," Betty said. "He just decided that's what we were going to do, and I went along with it." Before Betty became Mrs. Gus Grissom, her mother took her aside and laid down a little stern advice. She knew that her daughter would lead a lonely and often difficult life as the wife of an air force pilot, and told her bluntly, "I just want you to know that I'm not going to be a baby sitter. I'm not going to raise your kids for you, and if you have any fights, don't come home!" But like most mothers, she did not really mean it.

After the wedding Grissom returned to the air force while Betty remained in Mitchell, continuing to work at the Reliance Manufacturing Company, which made shirts for the navy. Within weeks, and before Grissom could receive his flight training, Japan capitulated and the Second World War was at an end. Now a corporal, he found himself being shunted from one desk job to another and realized that a typewriter was no substitute for an airplane. Keenly disappointed, he decided to leave the service, and his discharge came into effect in November 1945. He then took a temporary job installing doors on school buses at the Carpenter Body Works, but it was the kind of mundane, mind-numbing work that he disliked intensely. Taking his father's advice of setting his goals a little higher, he decided he would become a mechanical engineering student at Purdue University in Indiana. Those indifferent high school grades haunted his admission, but Congress had passed the GI Bill, which made it illegal to refuse a university place to a former serviceman. Forever after, Grissom jokingly thanked his Uncle Sam for making his entry to university possible.

Purdue suited him, and he took to his mechanical engineering studies with vigor. He was in good company at the university—accomplished test pilot Ivan Kincheloe graduated from Purdue in 1949; a quiet ex–naval aviator named Neil Armstrong would graduate in 1955, and the last man to walk on the moon, Gene Cernan, graduated in 1956. A man whose fate would be tragically tied to that of Grissom, Roger Chaffee, was a 1957 graduate.

While Grissom tackled his first semester at Purdue, Betty stayed behind in Mitchell with her parents. He spent those first few months sharing a modest apartment with another male student, traveling back to Mitchell on weekends whenever he could. But when the second semester rolled around and he was studying at the West Lafayette campus, Betty was finally able to join her husband and set up a home of sorts. It was a tough life for the young couple, living in a single ground-floor room and trying to make ends meet on Grissom's GI Bill payments.

Unfortunately the bill did not pay for his entire education, since he was in the service for only one year before entering university. To support himself and Betty and pay for his studies, Grissom worked as a short order cook after classes, while Betty took on a job as a long distance telephone operator to help cover his tuition costs. She deliberately took on the 5 to 11 P.M. shift to keep out of his way while he studied at home. Keen to finish his degree early, Grissom skipped summer vacations—a tactic that paid off.

In February 1950 an ecstatic Grissom graduated from Purdue a full semester early with a bachelor of science degree in mechanical engineering. One of the first tasks he set himself was to find a job immediately, "because I didn't want Betty spending any more of her life at a switchboard," he said. "She had made my degree possible." For a while he contemplated taking a job as a mechanical engineer at a brewery, but his mother was a teetotaler and threw a fit when he told her of his plans. That tantrum helped Grissom decide on the direction he would pursue, as flying was still in his blood. He talked it over with Betty, now pregnant, and they decided he would rejoin the armed forces. It was a close thing, as he was accepted into the last postwar class of cadets to include married men.

A month later he headed to Randolph Air Force Base in Texas for service in the U.S. Air Force as an aviation cadet. He had joined on the understanding that he would be assigned to the Air Materiel Command, the organization for test pilots at that time.

As Betty's mother had warned her, military flying proved enormously taxing on the young couple. While Grissom began his air force training, Betty lived with her sister, Mary Lou Fosbrink, in Seymour, some forty miles from Mitchell. Grissom tried to get to Seymour when he could, but it was quite a distance, and the cost of traveling meant there were long periods when they did not see each other. Things got so bad that when Scott was born on 16 May 1950, his father was engaged in a critical point of his training, and he did not see his baby son until Scott was six months old.

Grissom's career nearly had a major setback. When he flew solo for the first time, his instructor suggested he might like to consider being a navigator rather than a pilot. Grissom was dismayed, but he knew that for some reason he had been having enormous difficulty in trimming the T-6 trainer for proper landing attitude. It had been eating at him, and he could not understand why it was happening. He begged the instructor for another chance, and he was finally given a last opportunity, this time flying with a senior instructor. After takeoff, and to Grissom's great annoyance, the problem persisted through a couple of circuits of the field. At this stage the instructor almost casually asked him why he was not using two small wheels located to the left of the pilot's seat when he wanted to trim the aircraft for landing. Grissom was astonished, as these wheels had not been pointed out to him, and he had no idea what they were for. Just an hour later he was making his landings with ease, and then he went solo.

In September Grissom graduated from basic training and was sent to Williams Air Force Base in Arizona for advanced training. Soon things began to settle down a little on the domestic front. In November Betty and baby Scott were able to join him on base in a small, rented two-bedroom trailer in Wingfoot Gardens, and the young family now tried to live on his meager salary of $105 a month. "By that time," Gus once reflected, "she must have felt that flying equaled poverty!"

Once he completed his training at Williams, Grissom headed off to Luke Air Force Base, also in Arizona, for aerial gunnery training. In March 1951 he graduated as a fighter pilot, received his silver wings, and was commissioned a second lieutenant in the U.S. Air Force. His monthly salary leapt to $400, and he and Betty were finally able to ease the purse strings a little, which came as a considerable relief after years of struggling to make ends meet.

Grissom's first true flight assignment was at Presque Isle Air Force base in Maine, where he served as an F-86 Sabrejet pilot attached to the 75th Fighter Squadron. Then the squadron was sent to Dover, Delaware, for temporary duty. Not long after, in December 1951, he was shipped off to South Korea, where he served with the 334th Fighter Interceptor Squadron of the 4th Fighter Interceptor Wing of the Fifth Air Force, based at Kimpo, just twelve miles from the front line. Once again he had to leave his family behind, so Betty returned to Indiana with young Scott.

Grissom was candid about his first taste of combat: "I was sent to Korea which was excellent training for what came later. I was assigned to remain on duty until I had completed one hundred combat missions—or got knocked out—whichever came first. We chased the MiGs around and the MiGs chased us around and I usually got shot at more than I got to shoot at them. You get used to handling yourself in a situation like this, when death is supposedly at the door, but you learn to take care of yourself."

The 334th Fighter Interceptor Squadron had been shipped to Kimpo in February 1951, and combat patrols soon began operating out of the base. It was quickly discovered that the F-86s held some limitations for the pilots, as they did not have enough range to fly any farther northward than Pyongyang. But they were still exhilarating times for the young airmen. In his usual unconventional way Grissom decided not to name his F-86 Sabre aircraft after a woman, but instead had the name "Scotty" painted on the nose in honor of his baby son back home.

In March 1952, the entire squadron was sent to Suwon. Here the men conducted aerial patrols as far north as the Yalu River border with China. Grissom said later:

*We had a rule in our unit that a pilot had to stand up on an Air Force bus that took us back and forth to the barracks and the flight line until some MiG pilot had shot at him, personally. I got to take a seat after my second mission. I usually flew wing position in combat, to protect the flanks of the other pilots and keep an eye open for any MiGs that might be coming across. Sometimes a bogey would sneak in and start firing at you before you could spot him. There was no time in a spot like that to get scared. You just had enough time to call your flight leader on the radio . . . and tell him in a calm voice that wouldn't rattle him, that it was time to break away fast and get out of there. You also had to remember to tell him which way to break. And you had to make sure to use the correct call sign so you wouldn't get all of the other planes in the way to get back in one piece. It was the kind of situation in which you don't have time to get scared until you're back on the ground or maybe on the way back to the barracks. Then all you can do is have a beer and think it over.*

After spending six months in Korea, Grissom had been promoted to first lieutenant and reached the one hundred–mission mark. He formally requested to fly another twenty-five missions but to his annoyance was turned down. "If you were a shoe salesman," he mused, "you'd want to be where you could sell shoes!" He returned to the United States having earned the Distinguished Flying Cross, awarded after he had broken formation to engage a MiG-15 that was about to jump one of his squadron's reconnaissance aircraft. He had also been awarded the Air Medal with cluster during his tour of duty.

On his return Grissom was transferred to Craig Air Force Base in Alabama to attend Flight Instructor School. After completing that course he was designated a flight instructor at Bryan Air Force Base in Texas, where he found the work more daunting than the combat missions he had flown in Korea. Commenting on his tour of duty there, Gus said: "At least you know what a MiG is going to do. Some of these kids are pretty green and careless sometimes, and you had to think fast and stay cool or they could kill the both of you. I know what I'm going to do when I'm up there, all the time, but I don't know what that student is going to do. You're God to those Cadets, you know. One word from you and they're eliminated. I eliminated only one man, and later even he admitted I did him a favor. It was hard work, but I did a lot of flying in the T-33 jet trainer and it was good experience."

Meanwhile, the Grissom family grew just a little more on 30 December 1954 with the birth of their second son, Mark.

In August 1955 Grissom was admitted to the Air Force Institute of Technology at Wright-Patterson Air Force Base near Dayton, Ohio, to study aeronautical engineering, and Betty dutifully set up home at the base in Fairborn. The following year, he was transferred to Edwards Air Force Base in California to enter the Air Force Test Pilot School, which was (and still is) one of the most demanding courses in the air force. One classmate who would become a close friend was Gordon Cooper. Oddly enough, in his flying life as a combat pilot and later as a test pilot, Grissom had only one serious incident, and that involved Cooper, who would later become a fellow Mercury astronaut. On 23 June 1956 the two men were in a two-seat T-33 that lost power after takeoff from Lowry Field in Denver. The jet crashed back onto the runway, skidded, and burst into flames, but the two men managed to escape without injury. Even though he ascribed no blame to Cooper, from that time on Grissom would always do his own aircraft inspections before takeoff.

After graduating from the Test Pilot Course, Grissom returned to Wright-Patterson in May 1957 with the new rank of captain and duty as a test pilot in the Fighter Branch. It suited him. "This is what I wanted all along," he said, "and after I finished my studies and began the job of testing jet aircraft, well, there wasn't a happier pilot in the Air Force."

For a time things seemed to settle down for Grissom and his family. In 1958, after struggling for years with absences caused by his flying career, the many transfers and resettlements and a postwar shortage in housing, they were thrilled to finally buy a home at 280 Green Valley Drive, on the Indian Mound Estate in Enon, Ohio, just seven miles northeast of their former base home in Fairborn. Enon had the same small-town life that both husband and wife had enjoyed back in Mitchell, and they began settling into a comfortable family life, with Grissom making up for some lost gaps in their lives. The two boys had great fun sledding down a hill near their home—so different to the flat and hot conditions they had known at Edwards. Recreational flying was still a major part of Grissom's life, and he and some air force buddies shared a 1948 Stinson Voyager they bought and kept at a tiny airport just east of New Carlisle, a few minutes' drive from home. On his free days away from base duties he would often take his family up in the Stinson, and they enjoyed these leisurely flights soaring and sightseeing over the local area.

For Betty, domestic life at last seemed to be catching up with her husband. The lawns they had put in were looking better by the day, and the trees they had planted were growing noticeably taller. But just when it looked as if a comfortable family life was theirs, something happened that would change their course forever.

One day, out of the blue, the unit adjutant at Wright-Patterson handed Grissom a top secret Teletype requesting him to report to an address in Washington DC and to wear civilian clothes. There were no other details. As the adjutant handed over the Teletype, he could not help asking, "Gus, what kind of hell have you been raising lately?"

That night Grissom and Betty discussed the mysterious orders. He did not have the faintest notion what it meant, but he knew there was a challenge in there somewhere. Betty was apprehensive but made light of it all. "What are they going to do?" she teased. "Shoot you up in the nose cone of an Atlas?" She was surprisingly close to the mark.

Grissom could not work out what the message meant. "Well, in the Air Force you get some weird orders," he later recalled, "but you obey them, no matter what. On the appointed day, wearing my best civilian suit, and still as baffled as ever, I turned up to the Washington address . . . I was convinced that somehow or another I had wandered right into the middle of a James Bond novel!"

When he walked into the Washington office, his confusion grew even deeper when he found himself surrounded by some similarly baffled fellow test pilots. All of them wondered what they had been summoned for. After a comprehensive and sometimes confusing briefing, Grissom finally learned about Project Mercury and was told that he was one of 110 test pilots whose credentials had earned them an invitation to Washington. Likely candidates had been split into three interview groups, invited to Washington on successive weeks. There were thirty-six test pilots in Grissom's group, and thirty-four decided to volunteer for the new program. The second group yielded much the same result, so it was decided not to even bring in the third group of men.

Grissom started to think seriously about his future:

> It was a big decision for me to make. I figured that I had one of the best jobs in the Air Force, and I was working with fine people. I was stationed at the flight test center at Wright-Patterson, and I was flying a wide range of airplanes and giving them a lot of different tests. It was a job that I thoroughly enjoyed. A lot of people, including me, thought the project sounded a little too much like a stunt than a serious research program. It looked from a distance as if the man they were searching for was only going to be a passenger. I did not want to be just that. I liked flying too much. The more I learned about Project Mercury, however, the more I felt I might be able to help and I figured that I had enough flying experience to handle myself on any kind of shoot-the-chute they wanted to put me on. In fact, I knew darn well I could.

Betty Grissom would later reveal that she fretted more about the effect on her husband if he failed to win selection than on the risks involved in becoming an astronaut. She knew he would take any rejection badly.

Deciding to give Project Mercury a try, Grissom was then subjected to physical and psychological testing. At one point he was nearly disqualified when it was discovered that he suffered from hay fever. He argued that as an astronaut he would be sealed in a pressurized cabin, and no pollen would be sealed in with him. His arguments finally won over the doctors. Beyond this, they could not find any evidence to disqualify him. Grissom was pleased with the results of all of his tests except for the treadmill test. "I was really disappointed in myself and I thought that I could have done better," he said.

Gus had an intense dislike for the psychological testing. It did not make sense to him as a grown man to be asked who he perceived himself to be, or to take inkblot tests. "I tried not to give the headshrinkers anything more than they were asking for. At least, I played it cool and tried not to talk myself into a hole. I did not have the slightest idea what they were trying to prove, but I tried to be honest with them . . . without getting carried away and elaborating too much."

The number of pilots eventually shrank from 110 to 69, then 36. They were invited to undergo further rigorous physical examinations at the Lovelace Clinic in New Mexico. Four men declined, so it was down to just 32.

"I can still back out of it," Grissom had said to Betty when told about the examinations. "They made it clear that any of us could go back to regular duty at any time."

Betty knew her husband all too well by now and realized he would never back away from any kind of challenge. He was just seeking her assurance. "Is it something you really want to do?" she asked him.

"Yes, it is," he replied.

"Then do you even need to ask me?"

Initially NASA was after just six astronauts, but when the quality of the applicants became known the agency squeezed the number to seven. On 13 April 1959, assistant project manager Charles Donlan officially informed Grissom that he had been selected as one of America's Mercury astronauts.

On a sultry afternoon in Washington a crowd of reporters and photographers began to assemble inside an unassuming terra-cotta building known as the Dolley Madison House on Lafayette Square, just a few blocks down from the White House. This was NASA's makeshift headquarters, and excitement was building in what had once been a ballroom on the second floor, but which now served as a temporary press briefing room. It was 9 April 1959, and NASA was about to announce the names of the seven Mercury astronauts, whose identities had been kept a closely guarded secret. The space agency had no desire to elevate these men to hero status, but a stream of media people kept surging into the tiny room, and it became obvious that NASA had somehow underestimated the public's interest in its astronauts. Thoughts of a serious conference dealing with technical issues involving the men were fast dissipating as the press numbers swelled, and jostling became the order of the day.

At the far end of the room television cables snaked in haphazard disarray around tripod clusters of hot lights set up to illuminate the presentation area. Television and movie cameramen scrambled for the best positions, while the nation's reporters were jammed into an inadequately small seating area in front of them. Photographers were gathered at the foot of the curtained stage, nervously checking their watches and equipment as they waited for the curtains to open. Some of the more adventurous types were even perched precariously at the top of ladders at the back of the hall to get a clear view of the presentation area. Several NASA officials stood behind the curtains, while seven nervous test pilots were seated behind name plaques at a felt-covered table dotted with rocket and spacecraft models, listening to the growing din and babble.

As 2:00 P.M. drew near, the buzz of anticipation grew louder, and finally the curtains swept open to reveal NASA's press chief, Walter Bonney. He was standing with a nervous smile in front of seven men seated alphabetically in a line behind a table. A salvo of popping flashbulbs filled the room as cameramen fired off their first photos. After a few minutes Bonney called for silence, and when the excited uproar had died down a little he held up his hands. "Ladies and gentlemen," he pleaded. "May I have your attention please? The rules of this briefing are very simple. In about sixty seconds we will give you the announcement that you have been waiting for—the names of the seven volunteers who will become the Mercury astronaut team! Following the distribution of the kit—and this will be done as speedily as possible—those of you who have P.M. deadline problems had better dash for your phones. We will have about a ten or twelve minute break during which the gentlemen will be available for picture taking."

Confusion reigned once again, then slowly gave way to quiet anticipation. Bonney invited NASA Administrator Keith Glennan to come to center stage and formally introduce the seven men. In the back of the room some NASA assistants began handing out press release folders containing the names and brief biographies of the Mercury astronauts. Immediately several journalists seized these and made a hurried beeline out the door, ready to phone in their stories for the evening edition of their newspaper.

Glennan cleared his throat and spoke up. "Ladies and gentlemen, today we are introducing to you and to the world these seven men who have been selected to begin training for orbital spaceflight. These men, the nation's Project Mercury astronauts, are here after a long and perhaps unprecedented series of evaluations, which told our medical consultants and scientists of their superb adaptability to their upcoming flight. It is my pleasure to introduce to you—and I consider it a very real honor, gentlemen—Malcolm S. Carpenter, Leroy G. Cooper, John H. Glenn Jr., Virgil I. Grissom, Walter M. Schirra Jr., Alan B. Shepard Jr., and Donald K. Slayton. The nation's Mercury astronauts!"

Applause and cheers erupted, and the seven men began to squirm with discomfort from all the attention. If that was not bad enough, the questions they began to field soon after surprised them. The press did not really want to know about test pilot credentials—they asked if their wives supported them, and if they attended church regularly. Grissom was nervous, but like the others he managed to stay calm and say the right words. It was a taste of things to come—they were now hot property, and the world wanted to know all about them. By the following day all seven had become national heroes in their nation's space endeavors without doing anything more valorous than turning up for a press conference.

Grissom knew he could easily handle the jets and astronaut training, but this media attention was a whole new world, and he was really uncomfortable with it. However, he still wanted nothing more than to be an astronaut: "After I had made the grade, I would lie in bed once in a while and think of the capsule and booster and ask myself, 'Now what the hell do you want to get up in that thing for?' I wondered about this especially when I thought about Betty and the boys. But I knew the answer. We all like to be respected in our fields. I happened to be a career officer in the military and, I think, a deeply patriotic one. If my country decided that I was one of the better qualified people for this new mission, then I was proud and happy to help out."

With his new assignment the family was on the move once again, this time to Langley Air Force Base in Virginia where, for a time, the astronauts were based. They set up home in nearby Newport News.

Dr. Robert Voas, one of the men who helped select the astronauts, had defined astronaut characteristics as intelligence without genius, knowledge without inflexibility, a high degree of skill without overtraining, fear but not cowardice, bravery without foolhardiness, self confidence without egotism, physical fitness without being muscle bound, preference for participatory over spectator sports, frankness without blabbermouthing, enjoying life without excess, humor with disproportion, and fast reflexes over panic. Grissom just said he considered himself very fortunate to be participating in such a "weird, wonderful enterprise."

It soon became obvious that Project Mercury was too complex for all seven astronauts to learn about everything there was to know in great detail, so the seven split responsibilities among themselves based on their backgrounds. Grissom took on the Automatic Control System, designed to back up the pilot in case he became incapacitated, or to take over and help control the spacecraft during a rough reentry through the Earth's atmosphere. He also helped with the development of the Attitude Stabilization and Control System, which included sensitive gyro and horizon scanners that kept the spacecraft lined up at the proper angle with respect to the Earth, and twelve hydrogen-peroxide attitude control nozzles.

One of the lesser-liked duties of the Mercury astronauts involved giving speeches, and on one particular occasion Grissom unwittingly created one of those deliciously legendary stories that would always follow him around. He was touring the Convair plant in San Diego with the other six astronauts, all eager to see their Atlas rockets under construction. At one stage the seven were gathered together on a podium in a vast auditorium, where almost every one of the plant's employees and managers had gathered to take a peek at the nation's newest heroes. One of Convair's executives made a short speech, then asked if an astronaut would care to respond. Grissom found himself propelled forward to the microphone, but he had been caught off guard and was unprepared. As the polite applause died down he cleared his throat and suddenly got an acute dose of stage fright. He hesitated, then stammered, "Well . . . do good work!" And then he stepped back into the astronaut line. For just a moment the crowd was silent, then within moments there was wild clapping and cheering. It was as if he had just recited the Gettysburg address, and the workers loved him. "Do good work!" It became their mission, and this undistinguished three-word slogan was stitched onto a huge banner, which was hung above the factory's work bay to serve as an inspiration.

The nineteenth of January, 1961, was a tense day for the seven Mercury astronauts. On this date the project head, Dr. Robert Gilruth, finally broke the news the men had been anticipating, yet dreading. It was the assignment of pilots to the first two manned flights. At that time, the man first on the list would stand a good chance of being history's first spaceman. Gilruth chose his words carefully; after considerable evaluation it had been decided that Alan Shepard would make the first, suborbital flight, Grissom the second, and John Glenn would be the backup pilot to both men.

None of the three chosen would become the first man to fly into space. That distinction would belong to Soviet cosmonaut Yuri Gagarin, who flew a single orbit around the Earth on 12 April 1961. Just three weeks later, on 5 May, a cone-shaped capsule named *Freedom 7* carrying Alan Shepard splashed down in the Atlantic Ocean, and America was back in the Space Race. The pug-nosed astronaut nicknamed "The Cool Cat" had soared 115 miles into space and then hurtled 300 miles down the Atlantic at 5,000 miles an hour in a flight lasting just over fifteen minutes, although he had just spent the past four hours and twenty-seven minutes in the cramped cabin. His first words on reaching safety were, "Boy, what a ride!"

On 21 July 1961 Captain Virgil Grissom became America's second (and the world's third) man in space when he performed a fifteen-minute, thirty-seven-second sub-orbital flight aboard his spacecraft *Liberty Bell 7* on a mission designated Mercury Redstone 4 (MR-4). A familiar routine of technical hitches and holds had delayed the launch by several days, but at 7:20 A.M. that day a Redstone rocket lifted off from a pad at Cape Canaveral and rose in a ballistic arc that would carry *Liberty Bell 7* to an altitude of 118 miles, and 305 miles downrange.

Grissom would go just a little bit farther and faster than Alan Shepard had two months earlier. The Redstone burned for just eight-tenths of a second longer than Shepard's booster, but it was sufficient to propel him thirty miles per hour faster and push him one and a half miles deeper into space. While Shepard was weightless for four minutes and forty-one seconds, Grissom would enjoy weightlessness for thirty-seven seconds longer.

Grissom's spacecraft had some modifications. Instead of the ten-inch porthole through which Shepard tried to make out something of the world below, Grissom had a nineteen-inch window through which he could see land features and a horizon, which he later described as "very smooth as far as I could see . . . a blue band above the Earth, then the dark sky. It is very vivid when you go from the blue to the dark . . . the blue band appears about a quarter of an inch wide."

16. July 1961: Gus Grissom poses with his *Liberty Bell 7* spacecraft.
Behind him backup pilot John Glenn peers into the hatch. (NASA)

At one point as he flew through the pitch-black of space, the normally taciturn Grissom suddenly shouted over the intercom, "I see a star!" But he was wrong. "At least I thought it was a star," he wrote, "and I reported that it was. It seemed about as bright as Polaris. John Glenn had bet me a steak dinner that I would see stars in daytime, and I had bet him I would not. I knew that without atmospheric particles in space to refract the light, we should be able to see stars, at least theoretically. But I did not think I would be able to accommodate my eyes to the darkness fast enough to spot them. as it turned out, John lost his bet. It was Venus that I saw, and Venus is a planet. John had to pay me off after all."

The other major modification to *Liberty Bell 7* was an explosively actuated hatch. Following Shepard's flight the engineers and astronauts had agreed that future spacecraft should have a rapid evacuation capability in the event of an emergency occurring on or below the water, so a small percussion-activated explosive cord was wound around the hatch. It would almost cost Grissom his life.

When *Liberty Bell 7* splashed down, Grissom was surprised that the only sensation was a mild jolt. The spacecraft recovery section went under water as expected, and his window was completely covered with water, although he did say he heard a disconcerting gurgling noise. as the spacecraft slowly righted itself and the recovery section drew clear of the water, Grissom ejected the reserve parachute by actuating the recovery aids switch, and the craft righted itself rapidly. as helicopters made their way to the scene, he completed his final checks. Here is a record of his final minutes in the spacecraft:

*I felt that I was in good condition at this point and started to prepare myself for egress. I had previously opened the faceplate and had disconnected the visor seal while descending on the main parachute. The next moves in order were to disconnect the oxygen outlet hose at the helmet, unfasten the helmet from the suit, release the chest strap, release the lap belt and shoulder harness, release the knee straps, disconnect the biomedical sensors, and roll up the neck dam. The neck dam is a rubber diaphragm that is fastened on the exterior of the suit, below the helmet-attaching ring. After the helmet is disconnected, the neck dam is rolled around the ring and up around the neck, similar to a turtleneck sweater. This left me connected to the spacecraft at two points, the oxygen inlet hose which I needed for cooling and the helmet communications lead.*

*At this time I turned my head to the door. First, I released the restraining wires at both ends and tossed them toward my feet. Then I removed the knife from the door and placed it in the survival pack. The next task was to remove the cover and safety pin from the hatch detonator. I felt at this time that everything had gone nearly perfect and that I would go ahead and mark the switch position chart as had been requested.*

*After about three or four minutes, I instructed the helicopter to come on in and hook onto the spacecraft and confirmed the egress procedures with him. I unhooked my oxygen inlet hose and was lying on the couch, waiting for the helicopter's call to blow the hatch. I was lying flat on my back at this time and I had turned my attention to the knife in the survival pack, wondering if there might be some way I could carry it out with me as a souvenir. I heard the hatch blow—the noise was a dull thud—and looked up to see the blue sky out the hatch and water start to spill in over the doorsill. Just a few minutes before I had gone over egress procedures in my mind and I reacted instinctively. I lifted the helmet from my head and dropped it, reached for the right side of the instrument panel, and pulled myself through the hatch.*

*After I was in the water and away from the spacecraft, I noticed a line from the dye-marker can over my shoulder. The spacecraft was obviously sinking and I was concerned that I might be pulled down with it. I freed myself from the line and noticed that I was floating with my shoulders above water.*

*The helicopter was on top of the spacecraft at this time with all three of its landing gear in the water. I thought the copilot was having difficulty hooking onto the spacecraft and I swam the four or five feet to give him some help. Actually, he had cut the antennae and hooked the spacecraft in record time.*

The helicopter that had secured a steel line to *Liberty Bell 7* made a desperate attempt to save the spacecraft, but the pilot, Lieutenant James Lewis, received a warning signal (later proved erroneous) indicating that the weight it was trying to haul out of the water was too great. The empty capsule weighed some twenty-one hundred pounds, and the landing bag beneath the spacecraft had filled with almost eight thousand pounds of seawater. In addition, a large quantity of water had gushed in through the open hatch. Lewis finally gave up the struggle, and the line was reluctantly severed. *Liberty Bell 7* sank to a resting place on the ocean bed more than three miles down. If that warning light had not illuminated, the spacecraft would probably have been recovered instead of resting for thirty-eight years on the floor of the Atlantic. In 1999 it was retrieved in a remarkable salvage operation guided by Curt Newport, and despite the effects of corrosion it has now been restored to an unexpectedly good condition.

Meanwhile, Grissom was floundering around in the ocean, trying hard to keep himself from sinking, having failed to properly seal the neck dam of his spacesuit. Water was also seeping in through the openings where his oxygen hoses had been attached. While a photographer aboard the second helicopter industriously snapped pictures of the astronaut, Grissom was caught in the rotor wash between the two helicopters and was becoming dangerously exhausted as he struggled to stay afloat. He was frantically signaling for help. When a line with a horse collar was finally lowered he was moments away from sinking, and to make matters worse he was hauled underwater for nearly ten yards before finally being winched upward. His first words on reaching safety inside the helicopter were hardly history making. "Give me something to blow my nose," he growled. "My head is full of sea water!"

Even though the capsule had been lost, NASA was already proclaiming the flight to have been a complete success. Because of all he had endured, Grissom was described as "a bit shaky" when he first stepped onto the deck of the recovery carrier, *Randolph.* He still appeared quite dejected when he took a congratulatory phone call from president Kennedy. He was not only disgusted because the capsule had been lost, but also was also wondering if he would be blamed. A while later he was transported by plane to the Grand Bahamas Islands, where he began an intensive physical and psychological evaluation over the next two days.

Grissom always maintained that he had not blown the hatch of his capsule, either intentionally or accidentally, but the later ignominies and presidential snubs he and his family were alleged to have suffered, as portrayed in the film *The Right Stuff,* were grossly exaggerated. He later admitted he was scared during takeoff, but the film gave the impression of a panicky astronaut who completely lost control after splashdown, which is simply not true.

Paul Haney was NASA's director of Public Affairs at the time, and he said he hates hearing mention of Grissom as "a bad luck astronaut." According to Haney, "Poor old Gus was given a terrible serve by Tom Wolfe and Hollywood. But it is true that he was not accorded the same heroic VIP treatment and flag-waving as Al Shepard a few weeks earlier. James Webb panicked a bit on the whole affair of Gus and the loss of the spacecraft. He decided we would do a hurry-up post-flight press conference in Cocoa Beach, not in Washington as planned several days later. Gus and Betty spent the night in the guest quarters at Patrick Air Force Base, which was about as exciting as a night at Motel 6 near Oklahoma City. Webb made very few PR-type mistakes on his watch, but the MR-4 post-flight happenings was one."

With the spacecraft now resting at the bottom of the sea, there was no sure way of determining what had gone wrong. At a later inquiry into the incident Grissom was cleared of having made any wrong moves, and the premature hatch detonation was put down to an equipment malfunction.

Unfortunately *Liberty Bell 7* carried a great deal of equipment down to the bottom of the Atlantic. All the in-flight films and tape recordings were lost, but most of the crucial data from the flight—including medical information from sensors strapped to the astronaut's body—had been relayed back to base.

With the inquiry completely absolving Grissom of blame for the loss of his spacecraft, he was still one of NASA's and his country's favorite sons. He was further vindicated among his peers following the flights of John Glenn and Wally Schirra. Both suffered nasty bruises to the back of their hands after they depressed the plunger to blow the hatch and exit the spacecraft, but Grissom's postflight records showed that he did not sustain any bruising to his hand, nor any injury to his glove. Wally Schirra was pleased that he had helped his friend prove his innocence in the matter:

> A question had persisted on the blowing of his hatch, and there were those who had maintained that Gus had inadvertently hit the plunger that exploded the bolts. When I was recovered, I remained in my spacecraft until being hoisted aboard the recovery ship. I then blew the hatch on purpose, and the recoil of the plunger injured my hand—it actually caused a cut through a glove that was reinforced by metal. Gus was one of those who flew out to the ship, and I showed him my hand. "How did you cut it," he asked. "I blew the hatch," I replied. Gus smiled, vindicated. It proved he hadn't blown the hatch with a hand, foot, knee or whatever, for he hadn't even suffered a minor bruise.

On 15 July 1962 Grissom was promoted to the rank of major. Four days later he received the General Thomas D. White Trophy as the "Air Force member who has made the most outstanding contribution to the nation's progress in aerospace."

Also in 1962, NASA moved its manned space operations from the temporary quarters at Langley in Virginia to the Manned Spacecraft Center in Houston. Here the Grissom family finally built their first real home, a three-bedroom house in the Timber Cove development near Seabrook. Grissom, tired of the constant public and media attention, took steps to shield his family by insisting that no windows would face the street. He also had a pool installed in the backyard so Betty and the boys could have extra privacy.

That did not mean Grissom ignored the public altogether. Anyone who wrote to him, particularly a child, was always sent a letter and signed photograph, and he made himself available for NASA-sanctioned media events. However, the constant public attention and adulation did sometimes wear him down, and he took to donning disguises. On one occasion he wore a straw hat and sunglasses and asked Deke Slayton what he looked like. Deke's considered reply was, "You look like Gus Grissom." But he was elated when no one noticed him. Noted CBS anchorman Walter Cronkite was well aware of this particular astronaut's hiding habits. "As far as I know he was the only astronaut ever to don a disguise to duck the waiting press. He always considered one of his greatest personal successes his slipping by assembled newsmen in a floppy plantation hat and a pair of dark glasses!"

Following his flight, Grissom acted as CapCom during other Mercury flights but spent most of his time at the McDonnell Aircraft Corporation factory in St. Louis, assisting with the design and construction of the Gemini spacecraft. Slayton later wrote, "Gemini would not fly without a guy at the controls . . . it was laid out the way a pilot likes to have the thing laid out . . . Gus was the guy who did all that."

In time, the Gemini spacecraft became known as the "Gusmobile," although taller astronauts like Ed White and Tom Stafford complained that while it might have been perfect for Grissom's compact five-foot, six-inch frame, their nearly six-foot frames found it a mighty uncomfortable fit.

In 1964 Grissom received his second mission assignment: the command of the first Gemini two-man mission. Alan Shepard was originally scheduled for this flight, but he had fallen victim to a debilitating inner ear problem (later diagnosed as Ménière's disease) and lost his flight status until the problem could be solved. Lieutenant Commander John Young, a thirty-three-year-old test pilot from the second astronaut group, was selected to fly with Grissom on a three-orbit flight scheduled for later that year.

At first the Gemini 3 mission was set for a launch late in December, but two hurricanes and a lightning storm damaged the Cape Kennedy rocket center and forced NASA to postpone the flight. As a result, America did not have a manned spaceflight in 1964. Russia, meanwhile, had been curiously quiet since the dual flight of Valery Bykovsky and Valentina Tereshkova the previous summer.

On 19 January 1965 a robot-piloted Gemini capsule soared 2,126 miles through space over the Atlantic in a precursor flight to the manned mission. The 109-foot-tall Titan 2 rocket hurled the sixty-nine-hundred-pound two-seater spacecraft only twenty-four miles short of its planned landing area. Grissom was jubilant and said the successful space shot left "a clear road ahead" to the flight that would send him and John Young on their four-and-a-half hour, three-orbit flight around the world. "We can't see any problem," he enthused. "I doubt that anyone is happier than John and I."

Early in March the Gemini capsule that would carry Grissom and Young passed a major test at the cape. Controllers conducted a seven-hour countdown, with the astronauts aboard the capsule for about half that time. The test concluded just one minute before launch initiation. Several problems occurred, including a propellant leak in the Titan's second stage, but the mock launch was generally considered a success. Grissom and Young were delighted to hear that plans to launch them in two weeks could proceed.

A massive recovery fleet began to fan out across the Atlantic for the scheduled launch on 23 March. Ships steamed to possible landing areas ranging from the mid-Atlantic to the Canary Islands.

On 17 March NASA received a severe jolt, just under a week from the launch date, when Russia announced it had fired two men into space, and cosmonaut Alexei Leonov had conducted mankind's first walk in space. America had already been stunned a few months before when Russia had launched Voskhod-1 into space, carrying three cosmonauts jammed into one spacecraft. Both flights had obviously been designed to steal the thunder from America's space plans, and Western space experts glumly stated that Russia now held a two-year lead over the United States in manned space flights.

Despite the demoralizing setback of Leonov's space walk, the go-ahead to begin fueling the Titan 2 rocket was given on 22 March. Three days of overcast weather had finally broken up, and hopes had risen dramatically for a launch. Grissom and Young spent the day reviewing critical phases of their flight.

The following day at 9:24 A.M. Florida time the Titan 2 lifted off Pad 19 carrying the two astronauts. The takeoff had been delayed for twenty-four minutes because of a leak in the Titan, but the problem had been rectified with the turn of a wrench. The 150-ton rocket arced into the sky with a thunderous roar from its 430,000-pound thrust engine. Flight controllers reported that everything looked good as the spacecraft approached a speed of 3,000 miles per hour. The first stage of the Titan dropped away, and the 100,000-pound thrust second stage ignited to punch the spacecraft into a 17,500 miles per hour orbital speed. At 9:30, just six minutes after liftoff, Grissom and Young went into orbit 104 miles above Bermuda. The second stage dropped away and the capsule floated free in space. Grissom was ecstatic: "*Molly Brown* says she is happy about 'Go,'" he reported. He had just entered the history books as the first person to make two spaceflights.

Grissom named the Gemini 3 craft *Molly Brown* after the then popular Broadway show *The Unsinkable Molly Brown*. NASA officials demurred after Grissom had suggested calling the spacecraft *Titanic*. As a result, the pilot tradition of naming spacecraft would not be sanctioned again until the Apollo program.

Grissom had carried with him two watches for his sons, Scott and Mark, and for Betty he wore a diamond ring around his neck on a piece of string. An innovative passenger was also aboard—the first computer in space. It weighed fifty pounds and could make seven thousand calculations per second. It was a feature hardly noticed at the time, but its presence on the flight had great long-term significance.

The main objectives of the mission were to test all of the major operating systems and to determine if controlled maneuvering of the spacecraft was possible. With the help of the computer Grissom was able to work out the thrust he needed to change orbit—the first time this had been accomplished by a manned spacecraft. Gemini 3 achieved the significant first of having the orbital path of a spacecraft changed in flight by simulating rendezvous and docking activity. From that time on, astronauts had a genuine ability to fly in space instead of being helplessly carried around the world on a fixed orbital path.

Grissom was thrilled about the spacecraft's performance: "To our intense satisfaction we were able to carry out these maneuvers almost exactly as planned . . . the longer we flew, the more jubilant we felt," he said. "We had a really fine spacecraft, one we could be proud of in every respect."

Scientific experiments were part of the flight, and Grissom botched one to everyone's amusement. "It was pathetically simple," he said. "All I had to do was turn a knob, which would activate a mechanism, which would fertilize some sea urchin eggs to test the effects of weightlessness on living cells. Maybe . . . I had too much adrenaline pumping, but I twisted the handle so hard that I broke it off." Coincidentally, a controller on the ground did exactly the same thing at the same time as Grissom.

Another experiment was to test the new array of packaged space food. As some Gemini flights were to last up to a fortnight, supplying the crews with an adequate diet was essential. Grissom constantly complained about the dehydrated so-called delicacies manufactured by the NASA nutritionists. He was willing to eat the food because there was nothing else available, or so he thought. Before the flight, his backup commander, Wally Schirra, had gone to the popular Wolfie's delicatessen at nearby Cocoa Beach and bought a corned beef sandwich. He gave it to John Young before the flight, and Young zipped it into his space suit. At one point of the flight, when Grissom was complaining again about the unpalatable food on board, Young offered him the sandwich. Grissom was delighted to eat it, until he noticed that crumbs were starting to float around the cabin and the meat's strong smell was quite overpowering.

That smuggled sandwich always seems to come up, even today when Young fields questions about his astronaut career, much to his chagrin. "It was no big deal," he said. "I had this sandwich in my suit pocket. The horizon sensors weren't working right so I gave this sandwich to Gus so he could relax. There was nothing he could do in the dark to make that thing work, until we got back into the daylight." After the flight, Deke Slayton had to explain the stunt to irritated congressmen, and John

Young was given a severe reprimand—not that it had much effect on his career, as he went on to make another five spaceflights and become chief of the Astronaut Office.

James Webb, who had earlier mishandled Grissom's postflight acclamation, was furious when told about the Gemini capsule being named *Molly Brown,* and the corned beef incident proved to be the last straw. He saw to it that neither Grissom nor Young received the customary postflight promotion in rank.

Grissom's comment on the sandwich affair was typical stuff: "After the flight, our superiors at NASA let us know in no uncertain terms that that non-man-rated corn beef sandwiches were out for future space missions. But John's deadpan offer of this strictly non-authorized goodie remains one of the highlights of the flight for me." After listening to complaints about the food from other astronauts, Deke Slayton attempted to eat nothing but space food on the ground for the duration of one flight, and he nearly starved himself to death!

*Molly Brown* splashed down four hours and forty-five minutes after launch, having completed three highly successful orbits and flown 80,000 miles, and was picked up by the prime recovery carrier USS *Intrepid.* To his great annoyance, Grissom became ill while waiting to be picked up, and he would later grumble, "Gemini may be a good spacecraft, but she's a lousy ship!" The spacecraft had come down some sixty miles from the planned splashdown area, but this was later attributed to the failure of the capsule to develop as much lift as expected while Grissom was flying it back to Earth. The two astronauts were ecstatic about their flight. "I do know that if NASA had asked John and me to take *Molly Brown* back into space the day after splashdown, we would have done it with pleasure," Grissom said. "She flew like a queen, did our unsinkable *Molly,* and we were absolutely sure that her sister craft would perform as well."

When the two astronauts arrived back at Cape Kennedy, they outlined the successes and failures of their mission at a press conference. Grissom revealed that the two men got "the biggest surprise of the day" after they came down. "Because of the force of the impact, John and I both hit the windshield!" he said. "It put a big hole in my faceplate. John got a big scratch on his. Then I became seasick. Not being a sailor like John, I had to use one of the seasick bags."

One reporter asked Grissom if he or Young could have emulated the recent Russian feat by walking in space from their Gemini capsule. The question amused Grissom, who replied with a wry smile, "All we had to do was unlock the hatch. But I think we would like some more training to make sure we could get the hatch closed again!"

A triumphant parade and reception followed at Cape Kennedy, and the next day the crew members, accompanied by their families, flew to Washington DC. At a White House ceremony President Lyndon Johnson awarded both men the NASA Distinguished Service Medal. Grissom was thrilled with the experience: "For me personally, the finest reward I received was the opportunity for my wife and sons to meet and shake hands with the president of the United States and with Vice President Humphrey. It was, I know, a moment that Scott and Mark Grissom will remember for the rest of their lives."

Next the crew was honored with a sodden ticker-tape parade in a rain-swept New York City, and then the triumphant parade moved on to other cities around the country. "After all the Russian space spectaculars, the United States was back in the manned space business with probably the most sophisticated spacecraft in the world or out of it," Grissom reflected. "Our reception was the public's way of expressing pride in a national achievement."

Outside the spotlight, Grissom greatly valued being at home with his family, saying, "It sure helped to spend a quiet evening with your wife and children in your own living room." Betty accommodated her husband's schedule by ensuring that all major chores and errands were done during the week so weekends were free for family activities. She rarely asked about his work, and Grissom refused to let job-related problems intrude on his time at home. If he had technical reading to do, he would do it after the boys went to sleep. The family made the most of its limited time together by going skiing in winter, while an annual trip to the Indianapolis 500 race with a side trip to Mitchell to visit relatives was also a highlight. Grissom happily introduced his sons to his two favorite hobbies—fishing and hunting. In spite of his high-profile job, Grissom insisted on a private family life. "Betty and I run our lives as we please," he said. "We don't care anything about fads or frills or the PTA. We don't give a damn about the Joneses."

Not long after Gemini 3, Grissom was promoted to lieutenant colonel in the U.S. Air Force and quietly began to ask his friends in Vietnam if there was a slot for him to do a tour of combat duty there. After they told him that the conflict in Vietnam was nothing like the war he had fought in Korea, he gave the matter no more thought.

His next assignment was as backup commander for Gemini 6, and in March 1966 he was named to command Apollo 1, the first three-man spacecraft specifically designed to take men to the moon. His crew members named at the same time were Ed White as senior pilot and Roger Chaffee, a space rookie, as pilot. The command was not a bad achievement for a man later portrayed in *The Right Stuff* book and film as panicky and snubbed by NASA. The ultimate achievement for any test pilot is to make the first test flight of any prototype craft, and Grissom had now been handed the maiden flights in the Gemini and Apollo programs, so his career was definitely untarnished. In fact, his boss—the grounded Deke Slayton, the king pin in astronaut selections—had apparently told him in private that if Apollo 1 was a success, the rotation system then in place meant he would command the first lunar-landing mission and would possibly become the first man to set foot on the moon.

In an article written for the *World Book Encyclopedia Science Service* in 1966, Grissom talked about his upcoming flight:

*[In* Liberty Bell 7,*] I was a man in a can, just along for the ride.* Molly Brown, *bless her heart, was a machine I could maneuver. And now in Apollo 204, Ed White, Roger Chaffee and I will be in a spacecraft designed to go to the Moon and back. Soon I'll be the first astronaut to make three space flights—one in each of our space programs.*

*My upcoming flight makes* Liberty Bell 7 *look like an early flier. During the past two years, the Gemini program has taught us that we can fly our spacecraft, rendezvous and dock and even perform meaningful tasks outside the spacecraft.*

*My fellow crewmembers and I are finding that our Apollo spacecraft is infinitely more complex than are Gemini or Mercury. And so is the flight plan, even for our own Earth orbiting mission.*

*Our job will be to operate and observe and evaluate all of the spacecraft systems. When necessary, we must come up with suggestions for solutions to any problem we encounter. And this we can only do in actual spaceflight. We may spend anywhere from three to fourteen days in orbit, possibly longer, learning as much as we can about the spacecraft's performance. Even as we fly the mission, people on the ground will be working to make the Apollo lunar spacecraft an even more sophisticated vehicle than ours.*

In spite of Grissom's optimism, the Apollo spacecraft had serious problems. Unlike with the Gemini program, the astronauts inherited a spacecraft that had been designed for them but not with them. Although they did not have a hand in designing the spacecraft, Grissom and his crew were able to exert some influence on Spacecraft 012, which was scheduled for an October 1966 launch. In her book *Starfall,* Betty Grissom wrote, "He and Ed White and Roger Chaffee, along with their supporting staff of engineers and technicians, participated directly in the progressive design and manufacturing reviews and inspections as Spacecraft 012 neared completion. Some of the things Gus saw he did not like."

As pressure mounted, for the first time in his professional career Grissom began to bring his work problems home, as Betty recalls: "When he was at home, he normally did not want to be with the space program. He would rather mess around with the kids. But now he was uptight about it." He had also told Betty if there were going to be a casualty in the program it would be him, as he had been around high performance jets and spacecraft for a long time.

The arrival of Spacecraft 012 at the Kennedy Space Center caused only more problems. It was obvious that many engineering changes needed to be made. The environmental control unit leaked like a dripping tap, and as a result the launch had to be delayed for several months. The Apollo simulator used for training continually broke down and was not in better condition than the spacecraft. Astronaut Walt Cunningham commented, "We knew that the spacecraft was, you know, in poor shape relative to what it ought to be. We felt like we could fly it, but let's face it, it just wasn't as good as it should have been for the job of flying the first Apollo manned mission."

The crew members continued to make do with what they had, and they made hard-won progress for the final preflight tests at the end of January 1967.

Grissom was frustrated and unhappy, but he was also a professional to the core, and he wanted his crew to perform the best possible test flight of this new spacecraft that would one day carry men, including him, to the moon.

§

In June 1965 Edward White made an indelible mark on the world in twenty-one minutes. This highly popular, athletic man became the first American to conduct what we now call an EVA in space. The event was the first time everyday Americans had heard the NASA term EVA, or extravehicular activity, and they tended to shun this acronym in favor of the far more evocative term "space walk." Whatever they called it, history was made on that day, and for those twenty-one minutes Ed White became the most famous man on or off the planet.

A live radio transmission of the space walk made it possible for millions of people around the world to tune in to this historic and dramatic event. These days the public is inured to live television coverage and instant pictures of world events, but back in the early sixties there were no live TV pictures from space, and it was not unusual for mission photographs (and even those of the Apollo moon walks) to be released several days after the crew's return to Earth. When photos of White's space walk were finally made available, they were among the most vivid and astonishing ever released—even to this day. As the decades have passed we have seen dozens of men and women working outside their spacecraft in deep space, but no photographs of this activity will ever have the impact of those first images of White joyously floating in space at the end of a golden tether.

Founded in 1802, the United States Military Academy at West Point stands tall and proud above the Hudson River just fifty miles north of New York City. The USMA has provided America with both military and civilian leaders for all walks of life for nearly two hundred years. A common academy saying is, "At West Point, most of the history we teach was made by people we taught." It certainly is no idle boast, and it complements the academy's incisive motto of "Duty, Honor, Country."

Of the sixty significant battles during the American Civil War, West Point graduates commanded fifty-five of them on each side. The remaining five battles had a graduate commanding one side. Some of the more prominent West Pointers in the Civil War included Ulysses S. Grant, Robert E. Lee, William T. Sherman, Thomas "Stonewall" Jackson, Phil Sheridan, George Meade, Jeb Stuart, and Jefferson Davis, who served as president of the Confederate States.

West Point was a tradition in Ed White's family; its strong academic and leadership programs propelled the White men, especially a certain son, into greatness.

Edward White Sr. was born in Fort Wayne, Indiana, on 22 May 1901 to Alexander and Cecilia Higgins White, members of a prominent Fort Wayne family whose forebears included Midwest pioneers and veterans of colonial wars. It was no coincidence that all three of the Whites' sons joined the armed forces.

James Cecillus White, the eldest son, attended West Point with the Class of 1919 but did not graduate with that class. However, he was commissioned a second lieutenant in the infantry in 1920 and retired as a colonel in 1953. The youngest son, John Alexander White, attended the Naval Academy at Annapolis and graduated as a second lieutenant in the Marine Corps in 1931. He had the misfortune to be stationed in Peking when World War II broke out, was captured, and spent forty-five months in Japanese prisoner-of-war camps. John retired from the Marine Corps with the rank of colonel and wrote a book titled *The United States Marines in North China* before his death in 1992. The middle son, Edward, known as "Eddie," joined the U.S. Army Air Corps after graduating from West Point.

During his time at West Point, Eddie was popular with his classmates and was renowned for his high standards of integrity and loyalty. He was an above average baseball and football player who represented the academy in those sports, but he much preferred to play sports with his company mates. Despite a disciplined study regime, he still had to work hard to achieve academic success, and he graduated 270th in a class of 405.

Following his graduation Eddie was commissioned a second lieutenant in the U.S. Army Air Corps. He underwent pilot training at Brooks and Kelly Fields in Texas and Scott Field in Illinois, gaining his pilot's wings from both Balloon and Airship Schools. On 22 July 1925, he married his hometown sweetheart, Mary Haller.

In 1927, now a first lieutenant, Eddie became the first man to land a dirigible on water, effecting the rescue of a stranded balloonist. Later that year, on 2 November, the Whites' first child, Jeanne, was born. On 15 June the following year, Lieutenants Eddie White and Karl Axtatar were flying in an Air Corps blimp directly over a slow-moving Illinois Central train. They dipped down with great precision and by prearrangement handed a postal clerk a mail satchel, completing the first ever aircraft-to-train transfer.

In 1928 Lieutenant White was ordered back to Brooks Field in Texas to undergo pursuit (or fighter) training. In 1930 he was forced to bail out of a disabled fighter and descended by parachute to a safe landing, thus becoming an honorary member of the aviation fraternity known as the "Caterpillar Club"—airmen whose lives had been saved by hitting the silk. Later that year he and Mary became the proud parents of their second child, a son born on 14 November. He would be christened Edward Higgins White II after his proud father.

The following year the family moved to Wheeler Field on the Hawaiian island of Oahu, where Eddie took over as commander of the 6th Pursuit Squadron. Two very pleasant years passed all too quickly for the young family before they were on the move once again, this time to Washington DC, where Eddie attended the

Army Industrial College. The courses took his career from flying into fiscal matters. To learn more about these areas of responsibility, he spent two years at Harvard University, finally graduating with a master's degree in business administration with honors.

Following the onset of World War II, Lieutenant Colonel White spent most of his time with the expanding Air Material Command, dividing his busy schedule between Wright Field in Dayton, Ohio, and Washington. He was promoted to full colonel in 1942. On 14 March that year a second son was born, and he was christened James Blair White. Eager to be of service to his country, Colonel White requested overseas duty on a regular basis, but he was considered indispensable in his current activities, and to his disappointment his requests were turned down. He did, however, manage to secure a brief special assignment to the China-Burma-India theater in 1945. Two years later the Army Air Corps became the United States Air Force (USAF), and Eddie White, now a brigadier general, was serving as director of the U.S. Air Force Budget Office and was the first acting comptroller of the USAF.

By the time Major General Edward White's career in the air force came to an end with his retirement in 1957, he had amassed over eight thousand hours of flying time in more than one hundred aircraft, and he had twice been awarded the Legion of Merit. He also proudly wore a Distinguished Service Medal and had garnered numerous other medals and commendations. He had been commander of the 1503rd Military Air Service wing out of Tokyo during the Korean War, where his mission had been to transport fresh troops to the combat area and evacuate the wounded, and he carried it out with prodigious distinction.

There was never any question that young Edward White II would follow in his father's footsteps by attending West Point and then joining the air force, but that was still many years away. As he grew up, his parents instilled many fine personal qualities in their son. They taught him the values of self-discipline, persistence, and a single-minded dedication to everything that he did. Through their own lives they also demonstrated to him the importance of balancing a highly focused life with liberal doses of laughter and fun, but never at the expense of others. Ed learned these lessons well and used them successfully throughout his life. It is an outstanding compliment for a career military man if his son follows him into the service: in Eddie White's case, both his sons willingly joined the air force and had highly successful careers of their own.

As a special treat for his twelve-year-old son, White's father took him for a joy ride in a T-6 training aircraft and even allowed him a brief turn at the controls. It was an experience that would help shape the rest of his life. Even though he was barely old enough to strap on a parachute, White remembered taking the controls that day as "the most natural thing in the world to do."

Because his military family moved around the United States on a regular basis, White went to several schools and faced many new situations, but he always made friends wherever he went and was considered an excellent student and athlete.

Fortunately for him, he spent the last three years of high school at Western High School in Washington DC, which had an excellent reputation. Former pupil Iris Coopersmith recalls him being "a very good looking young man with red hair and brown eyes. He was well liked and very good at his studies." While attending Western High White met another young man named Hank West, and they became firm friends. West recalls, "We first met at Western High, probably the best school in the area at the time, where most of the military 'brats' attended regardless of place of residence. Ed lived in Arlington and I lived at Fort Belvoir, Virginia. We shared some classes and were both on the track team where Ed began to blossom early as a hurdler and we were both backup (second string) members of the football team. We were the only two from Western '48 who went on to the Academy that year. My strongest impressions of Ed may well have begun in those years at Western—a thirst for adventure, an unrelenting persistence in all pursuits and a fierce competitiveness."

Another classmate who became a close friend was Bob Glasgow, who added some of his memories: "I knew Ed more as an athlete on the track team. At that time, Ed was all form, but was a little short on speed. He ran the low hurdles. He was a clean-cut guy. It seemed that as Ed progressed through life, he became exceptionally good at whatever he did. One could see him mature, work hard and achieve his goals."

It was around this time that White enlisted in the United States Marine Corps Reserve as a private first class working on aircraft, but this did not prevent him from having a wide range of extracurricular activities at Western. During his final year he was major and battalion commander of the Cadet Regiment, a member of the Rifle Club, construction chairman of the stage crews for the school's theatrical productions, and president of the Hi-Y Club.

As high school graduation drew near, White faced the awkward problem of trying to gain admittance to the United States Military Academy. At the core of his difficulties was a lack of continuous residency in one place, as he needed a congressman to appoint him to the academy. Even though White's father and his Uncle James had attended West Point, there was not (and still is not) a clause that permits sons and daughters of military officers to apply automatically for any of the service academies. To solve the problem, White began to visit Capitol Hill and knock on congressmen's doors in an attempt to get an appointment to West Point.

Qualifications were no problem, as White had obtained some glowing references from the staff at Western, particularly from the principal, Mr. Danowsky, who stated that Ed was "a very good boy who we recommend heartily. He will, if accepted, make a good student at West Point and gives fine promise as a prospective army officer."

White's persistence finally paid off when he received his appointment to West Point from Congressman Ross Rizley of Oklahoma, and he was ordered to report to the academy on 15 July 1948. Hank West was ordered to report at the same time, and he detailed the friends' initiation: "Ed and I were quite pleased with ourselves to have ended up in the small number who missed the first fifteen days of the 60-day ordeal

17. John Smith and Ed White in their West Point
dress uniforms, 1948. Note they have their hats on
back to front. (Courtesy John D. Smith)

of plebe indoctrination at the tender mercies of the First Classmen (Seniors) who made up the 'Beast Detail.' Actually in one sense it was not too bad for us, thanks to the fact that Ed and I had been in the cadet program at Western and so we were proficient at marching up and down, left face, right face, rifle manual of arms, etc. Those without that advantage had an especially hard time at the hands of the 'Detail.'"

Cadet basic training at West Point, better known as "Beast Barracks," is an intensive combination of army recruit drilling and psychological training to ensure the new cadets learn how to take orders before they can give them. Author Bill McWilliams, who graduated from West Point in 1955, described the training for this book:

> For the new cadet who was officially accepted into the Corps of Cadets as a plebe in late August, CBT was much more. He was the raw recruit and officer candidate who was being led and trained by first classmen, men who were putting into practice all they had learned—and all they did not learn—about the principles of leadership during their three prior years as cadets. He learned about taking and following orders before being given the opportunity to lead, he took good and bad orders, just and unjust,

*learned about fair treatment and favoritism, respect and humiliating loss of dignity, because first classmen put their pants on one leg at a time—were young and inexperienced and fallible.*

*The new cadet was also beginning the emotional, intellectual and physical toughening, growth and transformation, that hopefully would make him a far more than capable junior officer four years hence— capable of leading young soldiers and airmen under the most extreme, trying, chaotic, dangerous and fear-inducing circumstances imaginable. Combat on any of the world's battlefields, on the ground and in the skies. Beast Barracks was likewise the beginning of the foundation from which the young commissioned officer could grow into a senior officer, commander, and military leader capable of great responsibility and great statesmanship.*

Another classmate, Owen Holleran, described Beast Barracks and an uncomfortable incident with Ed White:

*My contact with Ed was brief, during Beast Barracks in 1948. Beast Barracks is the training period that new cadets attend during July and August. It is designed to change young civilians into young soldiers and cadets. The training is administered by upper classmen with a great deal of enthusiasm. The new cadets have it impressed on them that they are the lowest of the low, the dregs of the human race and that they are ignorant beyond their wildest imagination. They learn that their life before the Academy is only a memory, one that should be ignored. Whatever they were before, they are now Plebes in the U.S. Corps of Cadets. This has its virtues, of course. It puts all new cadets on the same level, albeit a very low one. It puts a great deal of pressure on the new cadets and weeds out those who are not suited to the life. It is a maelstrom that is one of those experiences you wouldn't take a million for, but you wouldn't take a million to repeat it.*

*Into the crucible came Ed White. Ed and I were in the same company, on the same floor in the barracks. He was handling the pressure very well and having no special difficulties. Then, his father decided to visit. This was not a good thing for two reasons: we weren't supposed to have any visitors during Beast Barracks, and his father was a general in the Air Force. Once his father left, Ed became the target of every upperclassman on the Beast Detail. I have often thought that this may be the real test of Ed White, years before he became a test pilot and an astronaut. The pressures couldn't have been any greater.*

Another cadet, who would become famous two decades later when he flew to the moon, was a young man named Michael Collins. He recalled one particularly unpleasant aspect of his Beast Barracks days:

*I was seventeen and thought I was starving. The West Point food was fine, but the upperclassmen, with their ridiculous dining protocol, didn't let us plebes eat much of it. But if you were on an intercollegiate sports team, the rules were relaxed somewhat. So out to the soccer field I went, along with fifty or so hungry classmates. We were enthusiastic but inept—except for one, a redheaded streak, a raw-boned Pele who seemed to be everywhere on the field at once. That was my introduction to Ed White, a remarkable athlete who was also a member of the championship track relay team.*

*I later discovered that Ed did everything the same way he played sports, with gusto, delight and a cool confidence. His huge lop-sided grin was contagious, and people instinctively felt better when he was around. Ed wanted to be a leader; he worked at it and was very successful at it.*

White, known to many as "Red" because of his copper-colored hair, did make the soccer team as well as the track team and was spared harassment at mealtimes by eating at the team tables. One upperclassman, who would figure prominently in White's astronaut life later on, was Buzz Aldrin. "I met Ed at West Point where he was a year behind me," he recalled. "We sat together at the track table, and for a lanky man, without an ounce of extra fat, Ed White could eat a lot of food." Another teammate was Dick Shea, a former enlisted man with whom Ed became great friends.

It did not take long for White's classmates to take notice of his athletic abilities. One of them, Lloyd Riddlehoover, has a clear memory from that time:

*Each year, as cadets, we had to run the obstacle course, which was in the "Old Gym." Ed was in F-1 and I was in G-1, thus we were in the same "gaggle" that morning for running that ol' obstacle course which was a run against time. For some reason that morning, "the word" went around that Ed was going to try and set a new obstacle course record.*

*Ed got off on the course before I did, so I could watch his progress—he was really smokin'! We made a partial lap on the old elevated running track and then climbed out onto the bars to a shelf stopping down to the gym floor. Well . . . Ed comes dashing on the track, but then did not climb out onto the bars! Oh no . . . he launched himself into space, grabbed the bars and dropped to the floor. The old colonel who was "Master of the Sword" (the head of the Department of Physical Education) was watching—he almost had a heart attack when Ed made this launch. Who knows if anyone else took this chance since "repeats" were immediately forbidden!*

*As I recall, Ed did set a new obstacle course record partially aided by his earlier launch into space that day—not wearing a space suit but "Plebe Skins."*

After the academic year was over, Hank West entered the scene again:

*At the Academy, we were in different regiments with different schedules for academics and other activities so we did not see each other too often. However, during the summer of 1950 the authorities allowed me to switch to the same 30-day leave as Ed's so we could travel together to Japan to visit our parents, who were there as part of the occupation forces. We traveled "space available" on Air Force transports, but the sudden outbreak of the war in Korea immediately diverted all aircraft and we found ourselves "stuck on the beach" in Honolulu. Soon though, a friend of Ed's father came through in his own assigned C-54 aircraft enroute to a new posting in Japan and took us along. I have a photo of Ed in front of a burnt out Japanese tank on Wake Island during a refueling stop.*

*The return trip was a bit more exciting. When we ran out of free rides on Air Force planes in Dayton, Ohio, we were offered a ride to Washington with a civilian contractor in his World War II surplus twin-engine Beechcraft. All went well until he became lost in a rainstorm in eastern Pennsylvania, tried to land on a small airstrip, ran off the runway, hit an embankment, collapsed the landing gear and finally skidded to a stop, thanks to a sturdy barbed-wire fence. No fire, no injuries. Not knowing any better, Ed and I thought it was a great adventure and a good story to take back to school!*

As White progressed through the academy, he began to take on more responsibility for disciplining underclassmen. A member of the Class of '54, Jim Randall, told of a confrontation with White that he would rather forget:

*During the winter of my plebe year, Ed White was my squad leader for a month's time. Since I had an incredible knack for violating regulations, I often ended up on disciplinary calls prior to our breakfast formation. These calls took place in the squad leader's room and consisted of me standing at rigid attention while the squad leader explained in great detail my current faults.*

*Ed had a roommate who raised hamsters or similar small animals. Unfortunately, during my calls to Ed's room, the current pet found me interesting, and would scurry around my feet when I was supposed to be absolutely still. I lived in fear of moving in a way that would cause harm to the animal, for I suspected that even greater harm would come to me.*

*On one call, the little fellow started crawling up the inside of my pant leg. I'm ticklish. I was trying hard not to move, but apparently I was squirming. Ed noticed the movement, and stepped close to me, looking me in the eyes from four inches away. About this time, the animal jumped out of my pant leg and I jumped a bit. Ed had been chewing me out for not standing at attention, but he happened to look down and see the animal scurry away. As Ed took in the situation, he tried very hard to smother a laugh but wasn't quite capable of it. To dismiss me, he should have said "Post!" Instead, to the best of my recollection, he said, "Get the hell out here" in as loud a voice as I ever heard him use. Fortunately, I didn't have to go back to his room on calls after that.*

By the summer of 1951, White had become a first classman. As part of his summer military duties, he was placed on the Beast Barracks detail. One member of the incoming Class of 1955, Jim Drummond, still remembers with great detail the first time he met the future astronaut:

*He was simply the most impressive, self-confident and poised young man I had ever encountered in my eighteen years. Ramrod straight, he carried himself with a natural grace and bearing that seems to be the model of the West Point tradition. He spoke quietly, directly in a no-nonsense manner as he put us into the correct position of soldierly attention. He quickly conveyed to us that our civilian slouch was a thing of the past. In his gray, high-collared dress coat, carrying the two chevrons of a cadet lieutenant, starched white trousers with a razor sharp crease, brilliant spit-polished shoes; he was the epitome of soldierly correctness.*

*Over the next month, we saw much of Ed White, as he was our platoon leader. He led daily morning calisthenics and runs; he instructed dismounted drill and once we were issued rifles, supervised "The School of the Soldier under Arms." He inspected every formation, made on-the-spot corrections of appearance and grooming; inspected our rooms for cleanliness and good order. Two weeks into Beast Barracks, he participated in the "screening" of potential candidates for the Army soccer team of which he was a returning member of the Varsity team.*

*August was his designated month for summer leave and a new chain of command of First Classmen took over responsibility for our training. And I am sure that everyone in my new cadet platoon mentally graded our leadership against the standards set by Ed White. Not one exceeded him in our minds.*

White's final summer vacation from the academy was again spent with Hank West, who recalls this adventure:

*We took off first for a look at Europe, again traveling space available on U.S. Air Force aircraft and on a very tight budget. However, the dollar was extremely strong in Europe in 1951 so we were soon enjoying life in Paris, our first stop. In particular, we quickly became enthusiastic devotees of the delicious and inexpensive French wines, "vin ordinaire" so much that we realized that we should take turns as "Designated Sobriety Person" to keep ourselves out of serious mischief. On one of my evenings as "DSP," Ed's characteristic persistence easily overcame our system. He spotted a large, brass plaque engraved "Folies Bergere" attached to a panel of what turned out to be the stage door of the famous establishment. To Ed's eyes, the perfect trophy/souvenir to take back to West Point where only a handful of cadets in those days had been anywhere near Paris! We were about the same size, but there was no way I could drag him away or otherwise prevent him from securing his prize. Fortunately for us, the gendarmes did not turn up and Ed had logged another "adventure"—one of many to come in future years.*

*After Paris, we made a short trip to London, then spent most of the remaining time in Germany at Wiesbaden and in Bavaria. A hike to the top of the Zugspitz mountain near Garmisch inspired Ed to try and talk a local bartender and part-time alpine guide into taking us on a serious climbing excursion in the nearby Alps complete with ropes, pitons, ice axes, etc. Luckily, the guide thought the better of being on the rope with two complete novices/neophytes so we were spared that particular "adventure." However, first time water-skiing on a mountain lake was a great success despite the attempt by the ex-Waffen ss boat driver to give us a terminal dunking.*

*Our Air Force flight home was by way of Tripoli, Libya, where Ed, as he put it, found some "terrific bargains" in leather wallets, etc, from Arab street peddlers. Back in the U.S., we briefly stayed with Ed's parents in Tuckahoe outside New York City before returning to school. It was long enough for us to go out on a double date where I met my future wife. Ed was best man at the wedding the following year, with his family and soon-to-be wife Pat there.*

White's final return to West Point had an element of sadness to it. In July 1951, eighty-eight cadets were summarily expelled for breaking the Cadet Honor Code, which states, "A Cadet will not lie, steal, or cheat or tolerate anyone who does." It had become evident that there was a covert conspiracy of academic cheating involving perhaps as many as a hundred cadets. Both cadets and graduates treasure the honor code, and violations are dealt with strictly and swiftly. Thirty cadets were from Ed's class and included some of its most promising leaders and scholars. It was a hard time for the institution, as it suddenly endured an intense glare of outside speculation and doubt. Jim Drummond recalls the days that followed:

*At the end of August, the entire Corps of Cadets reassembled and reorganized for the fall academic year. The members of the six new cadet companies were assigned to their regular companies, where they would spend the next four years. I was assigned to Company F, 1st Regiment, where I found that Ed White would be my Cadet Platoon Leader for the next nine months.*

*During the 1951–52 academic year, which ended with his graduation in June 1952, I came to know Ed White much better though at no time were we good friends. The relationships between fourth classmen, plebes and upperclassmen did not allow "friendships" in the conventional sense. During our free time, we would only occasionally pass one another as limits for plebes were much more proscribed than for upperclassmen. I was always, "Mr. Drummond" and he was always "Mr. White, SIR!" In the fall of '51, I ate on the athletic training tables as a member of the plebe football team. Since our dining areas were then together, he often smiled or spoke to me as he passed by saying something such as "You staying out of trouble Mr. Drummond?" (A lowly plebe walks on air from such casual statements of personal interest).*

Lou Tebedo, a former plebe from the Class of 1955, still retains fond memories of a man who had a great influence on his life:

*Ed White was in Company F-1 and I was in D-1. He was a first class-man while I was a plebe, and he was in my Beast Barracks detail. After Beast Barracks when we started the regular academic year, I was having trouble with academics and discipline. Ed befriended me and became my upperclass mentor. Through his kindness and concern for me, I was able to make it through Plebe Year and graduated from the Academy. I later met Ed at Founder's Day (West Point Anniversary) dinner while he was in Michigan during the early part of his astronaut career. Ed had not changed. He was still the great caring person I remembered. I owe the fact that I graduated, in a large part, to Ed White.*

White excelled in soccer, track, handball, and squash. During fall, he played on the army's soccer team and was one of its best players as a halfback and won All-American honors. He was also cocaptain with Dick Shea on the track team, which enjoyed a winning season. Loomis Crandall, Class of '55, has fond memories of those times:

*I was a plebe when Ed was a firstie at West Point. He was co-captain of the track team and I was on the plebe team. We all worked out together although plebes were not allowed to run varsity in those days. Ed was the top quarter-miler on the team, the same event I ran. We worked out together and he never hesitated to give me help and encouragement. His classmate Dick Shea and he would trot around the track together and encourage us, make us feel like we were an important part of the team. I knew back then that they were outstanding leaders, a trait they exhibited a lot on the track field. I feel privileged to have known both of them. Ed*

*was a class act in every way, and had that ability to make even a lowly*
*plebe feel important. And he did it with sincerity.*

Another memory of White on the track team comes from David Patton, another Class of '55 member: "Ed was on the track team—a middle distance runner as I recall. He was a real gentleman and stand-up guy. One of the important West Point traditions is 'Recognition.' This is when an upperclassman shakes a plebe's hand and is from then on first name terms. One day after practice in the field house, Ed just walked up to me and shook my hand and said 'My name's Ed!' For what little remained of the school year before he graduated, I felt we were good friends."

During the track season, White managed to set a West Point record of 53.1 seconds in the four-hundred-meter hurdles, a mark that was still standing in 1967. He also tried out for the 1952 Olympic trials in Berkeley, California, but came fourth in qualifying heats and just missed out on a spot when only the first three runners were selected. It is interesting to speculate where life might have led White had he been selected to represent his country at the Olympics.

Although he participated in the Skeet Shooting Club, the Camera Club, the Ski Club, and the Spanish Club, it was not all studies and athletics for White. At a football game weekend at West Point, he met Patricia Eileen Finegan from Washington DC, a petite blonde who would eventually become Mrs. Edward White II. White also visited with his family frequently. At that time, his father was stationed in New York City and took trips with his wife and son Jim to visit him. Jim Drummond met Jim White and remembers him "as a red headed, fresh faced, handsome young brother about 11 or 12 who obviously idolized his older brother. Ed often took the opportunity to get permission to bring him into the barracks on several occasions."

June Week for the Class of 1952 finally rolled around. Jim Drummond recalls the graduation parade with fondness: "It was Recognition Day, the day of the Graduation Parade, following which the plebes in each company line up and all the company upperclassmen file past, 'introduce' themselves and shake plebe hands. To be able to drop the 'Mr.' title was a significant happening to end Plebe Year. I remember two things about Ed's graduation day. The first was how his little brother Jim stood reveille formation with the company. Second, I remember Ed departing on graduation day following the graduation address by Secretary of the Air Force, Thomas Finletter, dressed in his Air Force officer's uniform and looking as dashing then as the first day I saw him."

Dan Dugan shared a funny recollection from that day: "What I really remember is on the morning following the graduation ball. Standing there in the 'sinks' (showers), as we called them, was Ed White in his fiancée Pat's gown, while Pat was dressed in his cadet dress white uniform. This was at reveille formation, as I recall, and we all got a real kick out of that scene."

White graduated 128th in a class of 523 with a bachelor of science degree and was once again ranked first in the class for physical education. He had always maintained a high degree of physical fitness and coordination that earned him the number one rank in physical education throughout his four years at West Point. That year, together with his photo in the cadet yearbook *Howitzer*, the following description appeared: "An ardent Air Force brat, Ed claims Washington DC as his home . . . He craves excitement and adventure and seldom passes up the chance to do something out of the ordinary. Ed is a strong Air Force file [an A grade in military aptitude] and is sure to reach the top."

Following his decision to join the air force as his career field, and after a two-month graduation leave, White went to Bartow Air Force Base in Florida to begin flight training.

The early fifties were a time of rapid buildup of the armed forces following the onset of the Cold War as well as the hot war in Korea, where a lot of White's West Point army friends ended up. USAF pilot training accelerated rapidly to a level reminiscent of World War II. A dozen or so civilian flying schools sprang up across the southern United States to supplement the small on-base USAF capacity for beginning pilot training. The instructors were all civilians—World War II veterans—with a small cadre of USAF personnel at each school to monitor standardization and serve as check pilots. Most of the airfields were old World War II bases that had been given up by the USAF after the war ended, and many found commercial use beyond just aviation.

At this time flying training programs followed a format radically different from that of earlier years. During World War II, flying students fresh from the streets or farms began with simple, rather slow, fixed landing gear Primary Trainer (PT) aircraft. Those who succeeded then moved on to the Advanced Training (AT) aircraft, which was the AT-6, a much faster and more sophisticated airplane with retractable landing gear. Graduates were then awarded wings and went on to check-out courses in one of the fighters of the time, such as the P-47, P-51, and P-40, followed by assignment to a fighter squadron.

Sometime after the war, a high-level decision was made to simply skip the primary phase and have new students begin immediately with the AT-6, the previous advanced trainer. With that, the "A" was dropped from the AT-6 designation. This was the flight-training program Ed White and Hank West entered in the summer of 1952 along with 120 of their West Point classmates. An equal or larger number of graduates from Annapolis was in the same course. The Air Force Academy did not exist at the time, so about a quarter of the graduates of West Point and Annapolis were permitted to select the USAF as their service of choice.

This phase of training took six months. In February 1953, White married Pat Finegan at Bartow AFB. The next step, advanced training and the awarding of pilot's wings, took place at a USAF Training Command Bases, where students were instructed in either jet training leading to fighter specialization, or in multi-engine courses leading to bomber/transport career paths. White was sent to James Connally AFB in Texas for jet training.

The lead-in aircraft for the jet course was the propeller-driven T-28, a post–World War II trainer with tricycle landing gear, much easier to land than the conventional gear T-6, and with many of the advanced features of prop-driven fighters. For the first time, formation flying was part of the curriculum. The jet qualification course that followed involved a quantum jump to the Lockheed T-33, a jet trainer derived from the F-80 Shooting Star, which had seen extensive service in the Korean War. The F-80 fuselage was stretched to accommodate two ejection seats in tandem, ballast replaced the 50-caliber machine guns, and oversize drop tanks were added to the wingtips, but otherwise it had the same flight characteristics as the F-80.

The jet course included aerobatics, advanced instrument flying (with the student in the rear seat under a hood), two- and four-ship formation, and night flying, but no tactical weapons training. The advanced course added another six months to the total student flying time, which by then was about 250 hours.

It was during this time, on 15 May 1953, that the Whites' son Edward Higgins White III was born. Following the awarding of his wings, White was transferred to Luke AFB in Arizona for Fighter Gunnery School.

His first operational deployment took him to the 22nd Day Fighter Squadron, based at Bitburg in West Germany and isolated in the Eifel Mountains. One of his squadron mates was Buzz Aldrin, with whom he struck up a close friendship. One afternoon in late winter 1958 the two men had been conducting a mock dogfight with some younger fighter pilots, and after landing they were discussing their future ambitions. White revealed that his plan was to get a master's degree in aeronautical engineering at the University of Michigan through the air force program that sent qualified officers to graduate school. Once he had his degree he hoped to gain entry to the one-year test pilot school at Edwards AFB, joining the elite group of military pilots who had experienced the school's rigorous academic and cockpit training. White told Aldrin that when the air force extended its high altitude rocket plane program into spaceflight, he felt he would then be in an excellent position to jockey his way into a cockpit seat, as Aldrin recalls:

> The more we talked the more I realized that the route Ed was taking would suit me a lot better than a career as a line fighter pilot. As much as I liked to fly, my pilot skills would not last forever. But neither of us knew then what the Air Force's moves into space meant. "What do you think they're going to call the guys that finally fly up there?" I asked Ed. "Rocket Pilots?"
> Ed grinned and slung his parachute over his shoulder as we trudged towards the Squadron Ops office. "No," he laughed. "The Air Force is bound to think of a fancier name than that." We'd never heard the word "astronaut."

Hank West, along with his wife and infant daughter, stayed with the Whites while they were on vacation in 1956, and White paid a reciprocal visit to the Wests when his squadron was in Tripoli for aerial gunnery practice. "Ed seemed reasonably content with squadron service at the time," West recalled, "and had received an award for organizing/managing the mobility plan for his unit. However, he was already talking about going back for a Master's in aeronautical engineering after leaving Germany."

While stationed in Germany, White earned a reputation as an accomplished pilot by flying the F-86 and the newer F-100. He also successfully completed the Air Force Survival School in Bad Tolz, West Germany. By this time there had been another significant addition to the White household, a daughter born on 15 September 1956 they named Bonnie Lynn.

The following year White happened to read a newspaper article that would change his life forever. Although it was meant to be a humorous article about future astronauts, it started him thinking. He later said, "Something told me that this is it—this is the type of thing that you are cut out for. From then on, everything I did seemed to be preparing me for space flight."

That September, White entered the School of Engineering at the University of Michigan, sponsored by the air force. One of his classmates who became a close lifelong friend was a fellow air force captain named Jim McDivitt; other classmates included future astronauts Jim Irwin and Ted Freeman. The McDivitts and Whites both lived in Ann Arbor at this time, with the Whites renting a home at 1420 Hatcher Crescent. In 1959 White received his master's degree in aeronautical engineering from the university, passing another of his life's milestones.

By this time NASA had named its first group of astronauts, and all were test pilots. White realized that attending test pilot school would be an absolute necessity for astronaut selection. He had applied for the first group but had been rejected because he was missing this credential. The White family soon moved to Edwards Air Force Base in California, where White attended Class 59C of the USAF Flight Test Pilot School. One of his classmates was his friend Jim McDivitt, while one of his instructors was Captain Tom Stafford, who would also become a NASA astronaut.

After completing test pilot school, White was transferred to Wright-Patterson Air Force Base in Ohio. Hank West wrote, "When I visited Ed and Pat at Wright-Patterson AFB in 1961 he still regretted not getting an assignment to Edwards, the center for most flight testing, after completing his test pilot course, but he was very upbeat about his chance of being selected as an astronaut. The rest, of course, is history."

White had been assigned as an experimental test pilot at Wright-Patterson in the Aeronautic Systems Division. He made flight tests for research and weapon systems development on such aircraft as the C-123, C-131, F-100, F-102, and T-33. He also wrote technical engineering reports and made recommendations for improvements in aircraft design and construction. Another crucial assignment handed to him was flying the aircraft used for weightless training of the Mercury astronauts. Three planes were used to provide the astronauts with brief periods of weightlessness: the Air Force C-131, C-135, and F-100-F. White later said, "I flew the big Air Force cargo planes through weightless maneuvers to test what would happen to a pilot in zero gravity. Two of my passengers were John Glenn and Deke Slayton who were practicing weightless flying for Project Mercury. Two other passengers of mine were chimpanzees Ham and Enos, the first Americans to fly in space. I'm able to kid that I've already gone weightless 1,200 times. This adds up to five hours of weightlessness, enough for about three orbits of the Earth."

In April 1962 NASA began recruiting for the next group of astronauts. The basic requirements applicants needed were a bachelor's degree in engineering or physical sciences, graduation from a test pilot school, extensive experience in jet aircraft, and a recommendation by their employer. The age limit had been reduced from forty to thirty-five, and the maximum height was increased to six feet, much to White's relief. During the Class of 1952's tenth anniversary reunion at West Point, White mentioned to several friends that he was hoping to be selected as an astronaut. His physical skills were still very much in evidence, and during a hilarious limbo contest he outdid everyone and won easily.

In September 1962, having tested around two hundred applicants, NASA announced the names of its newest astronauts. They were Neil Armstrong, Frank Borman, Charles "Pete" Conrad, James Lovell, James McDivitt, Elliot See, Thomas Stafford, John Young, and Ed White. White's dream of selection had come true.

Before the astronauts were introduced to the press, they were ordered to fly anonymously to Houston and check into the Rice Hotel using the manager's name, Max Peck. Eventually, bored with being stuck in their rooms by themselves, the nine men gravitated toward the hotel's bar, where they soon began talking up a storm. While White was reminiscing with navy pilot Jim Lovell about his West Point days, Lovell happened to mention trading cufflinks with a cadet, as a souvenir of the friendship, after an army-navy game. White was quite astonished, and Lovell's jaw dropped open in disbelief when they worked out that Lovell had been the midshipman to whom White had given his cufflink. Lovell had kept it as a memento for all those years.

White moved his family down to Houston, where he and Pat built their dream home in El Lago. One day while White and Jim McDivitt were in Houston finalizing the details of their homes, a group of children asked if they were astronauts. The two answered in the affirmative and were soon surrounded by even more children asking for their autographs. They both expressed surprise, as they had barely been selected and had not done anything of note.

Once the new astronauts had settled in, their seven predecessors quickly sized them up. All members of the second group were judged to be highly skilled pilots, and it was recognized that they had a greater level of formal education than the Mercury group. White stood out in the crowd. When asked an intelligent question, he would answer thoughtfully and to the point, but would rarely volunteer information. The old hands from Mercury picked him as someone to watch.

Already deeply involved in the Gemini program, Gus Grissom was assigned to supervise the new recruits. He gave credit where it was due in his evaluation of the newcomers. "They're all talented," he said. "In fact, when one of them comes up with a new answer for some problem, I think that they are smarter than our group of seven." However, it was made clear to them that as none of them had flown in space or trained for a mission, they were still the new kids on the block and had a lot to learn. In fact, Grissom advised one unnamed astronaut, "Don't feel so smart, you're just an astronaut trainee."

Using the knowledge gained through Project Mercury, NASA adopted a new training program for the astronauts that was much more advanced, refined, and rigorous than previous spaceflight preparations. White and his colleagues soon found themselves participating in a variety of exercises designed to anticipate Project Gemini, the next stage of NASA's manned spaceflight program.

One of the trainees' first excursions was to Cape Canaveral, where they watched the launch of Wally Schirra aboard his *Sigma 7* spacecraft. Training then began by familiarizing the new members of the astronaut corps with details gathered from Project Mercury. They soon gained hands-on experience with the Mercury spacecraft systems and hardware. They learned about flight operations and associated in-flight tasks. They toured the facilities at Cape Canaveral, including the tracking systems and launch areas. Titan, Atlas, Saturn, and Agena soon became part of their vocabulary, as did a large range of acronyms.

Formal classroom training was part of the Gemini program so that astronauts would be able to conduct scientific tasks and speak intelligently with scientists in every field. The astronauts participated in advanced training in meteorology, geology, physics, mathematics, flight mechanics, communications, astronomy, anatomy and physiology, and guidance and navigation, among other fields. The educational component proved taxing, even to a group of men whose IQ averaged approximately 135.

White's assigned area of specialization was in the design and development of spaceflight control systems and related equipment. He enjoyed his work because, in his own words, "It involves the pilot's own touch—the human connection with the spacecraft and the way he maneuvers it. The most important thing is that man—not an automatic machine—is the primary system in spaceflight. A lot of us here on Earth are getting curious about what the Moon's made of and you'll never satisfy man's curiosity unless man goes himself."

Staying in good physical condition was a must for the astronauts. In spite of his training schedule, White still found time to participate in swimming, handball, golf, volleyball, and squash. Rather than drive the three miles to work, he usually preferred to ride his bicycle to the space center. While jogging, he would squeeze a hard rubber ball in his fists to increase the strength in his hands and arms. It was said that he could do fifty push-ups and then roll over and do fifty sit-ups. He also installed a forty-foot rope in his backyard and climbed it regularly. Ed White III recalls that there were pull-up bars in the yard for his father, his sister, and him. His father was widely acknowledged as the fittest of all the astronauts, although his eating habits continually astounded his colleagues. He could eat three main courses and then, with a straight face, ask for dessert. Walt Cunningham once wrote with amusement that Ed White could easily eat his own weight in seafood!

White made ample time for his family during this busy training period. In June 1964, the Whites went to Colorado Springs to see Ed's brother Jim graduate from the United States Air Force Academy, which had opened in 1955. Following graduation, Jim completed a master's degree in political science and economics in seven months and then started his own flight training. He announced that his intention was to follow in his big brother's footsteps and become an astronaut.

After months of comprehensive training, it was announced that Jim McDivitt would command Gemini 4, and Ed White would be the pilot. The selection was a surprise to some space observers who had expected that a Mercury astronaut would command the mission, or that better-known members of the 1962 group would be flying.

Gemini 4's flight plan was a conservative one. The primary objective was to see how the spacecraft and crew would perform during a four-day flight. In addition, thirteen scientific experiments were planned. However, in March 1965 NASA revised the flight plan by adding an attempt to maintain a fixed distance from the second stage of the spacecraft's Titan II launch vehicle, a maneuver that would assist in future rendezvous missions.

On 18 March 1965, Soviet cosmonaut Alexei Leonov became the first man to leave his spacecraft and conduct an EVA, or "space walk." Leonov spent ten minutes on a tether while attached to the Voskhod-2 spacecraft. In light of the Soviet Union's accomplishment, NASA decided to bring forward the EVA originally planned for the Gemini 5 mission. White would now perform an EVA on his flight, even though his suit and propulsion unit were still on the drawing board at the time of the crew's selection. The gear was not certified for use in space until just ten days before Gemini 4's launch, and the EVA was not actually confirmed until a week before the flight. White spent hours in the McDonnell pressure chamber to prepare himself for the space walk. Although a Soviet had been first to walk in space, White was determined to be the first to use jet propulsion and actually maneuver himself in space.

McDivitt and White had planned to call their spacecraft *American Eagle,* but following the displeasure of bureaucrats at NASA Headquarters when Gus Grissom had whimsically named his Gemini capsule *Molly Brown,* the space agency prevented astronauts from naming their spacecraft. Instead, the crew suggested they wear American flags on their space suits, a practice that has continued to this day.

On 3 June 1965, Gemini 4 was launched from the Kennedy Space Center, lifting off at 10:16 A.M. from Pad 19. White, a devout Methodist, had purchased three special items to carry with him during the EVA: a St. Christopher's medal, a gold cross, and a Star of David. "I had great faith in myself and especially in Jim," he later explained, "and also I think that I had a great faith in my God. So the reason I took *these* symbols was that I think that this was the most important thing I had going for me, and I felt while that I couldn't take one for every religion in the country, I could take the three most familiar to me."

Shortly after launch, it became clear that McDivitt's plan to maintain a fixed distance from the jettisoned second stage of the Titan II launch vehicle would have to be abandoned because the stage was tumbling so severely that its orbit had deteriorated from that of the spacecraft. In addition, the new techniques associated with orbital rendezvous mechanics were consuming too much precious fuel. With this objective scrubbed the crew turned its attention to White's EVA, which had been scheduled for the end of the second orbit.

As Gemini 4 slipped into its second orbit, the two astronauts went through the checklist for the EVA equipment. Within the cramped confines of the spacecraft they unpacked White's emergency oxygen pack, his specially designed thermal gloves, and the bulky twenty-five-foot combination primary oxygen umbilical and tether cord. They unstowed and checked the seven-and-a-half-pound maneuvering unit. They assembled the camera equipment that would record White's walk. The crew was meticulous "because it was our first step in space and we wanted to be sure that the procedures were done thoroughly and correctly," White said. As the time for the EVA drew near, the men realized they were rushing through the checklist. McDivitt promptly made a call telling ground controllers it was advisable to delay the EVA until the third orbit to give them sufficient time to properly check and don the equipment.

Finally all was in readiness. Paul Haney, NASA's public affairs officer, was in Gemini Control that day, and as part of the mission commentary he broadcast current events to the public. "Four hours and twenty-four minutes into the mission," he announced. The Hawaii station has just established contact with the pilot, Jim McDivitt, who advises that the cabin has been depressurized. We are standing by for a GO from Hawaii to open the hatch . . . White has opened the door. He has stood up . . ."

Chris Kraft was the flight director in Houston, and through CapCom Grissom he told McDivitt that Houston control was ready for the EVA to begin. McDivitt replied, "He's ready to egress right now."

At this suspenseful point communication with Gemini 4 was lost for a short time as the spacecraft moved beyond the range of the tracking station in Hawaii. Communication was then reestablished through the station at Guaymas in Mexico. Haney told listeners around the world that contact with the spacecraft was back, and McDivitt confirmed that White had left the spacecraft and was looking good.

White tried to balance clinical reporting with the euphoria he was feeling: "The maneuvering unit is good. The only problem I have is that I haven't got enough fuel. I've exhausted the fuel now and I was able to maneuver myself down to the bottom of the spacecraft. I'm looking right down, and it looks like we are coming up on the coast of California, and I'm doing a slow rotation to the right. There is absolutely no disorientation association . . . I don't have the control I had any more . . . there's no difficulty in recontacting the spacecraft . . . particularly in trying to move back. I'm very thankful in having the experience to be first."

At this stage, McDivitt pointed the nose of the spacecraft straight down to the ground, and White continued to report on his experiences: "Okay, now I'm taking a look back at the adaptor . . . the thrusters are clean. The sun in space is not blinding, but it's quite nice. I'm coming back down on the spacecraft. I can sit out here and see the whole California coast."

At one point White was asked how he was feeling, and he replied that he felt "red, white and blue all over." After White reported looking down and seeing Houston, Kraft determined that it was time for the EVA to end, and he told Grissom to get White back into the spacecraft. Grissom tried, but White and McDivitt were rapidly exchanging comments, so he found it hard to break in. Finally McDivitt responded to Grissom's calls, at which point Kraft flipped a switch on his console that allowed him to override the CapCom and talk directly to the spacecraft—an unusual event. He was concerned about the delay in getting White back into the spacecraft, especially since the astronauts would soon be passing into darkness, which would make things even more difficult. He instructed McDivitt in a firm voice to "get him back in!"

McDivitt relayed the message to White: "They want you to come back in now."

White was still experiencing the entrancement of his space walk and the view below. "This is fun!" he responded.

McDivitt sensed that Mission Control did not share his partner's enthusiasm. "Well, get back in," he repeated.

There was a brief pause, then, "I'm coming." As White finally began to lower himself back into the capsule, he remarked, "It's the saddest moment of my life."

White later wrote the following about his space walk:

> It felt just plain normal. From the moment I pulled myself away from Gemini 4, my strongest feeling was doing something that I had been training for. There was absolutely no sensation of falling. The sensation of speed was the same as it was inside the capsule—and that was similar to flying over the Earth in an aircraft at 20,000 feet. There was no feeling at all in being in a hostile environment which space has sometimes been called. It's hard to explain it to anyone, but I felt in perfectly natural surroundings inside the spacecraft and even more so outside it. Part of this may be due to moving around freely after the close quarters of the cabin. Also, the suit was a bit cooler and more comfortable when I got outside.
>
> Naturally, I had a keen awareness of the weightless state and it was most pleasant. After I got back home, my wife Pat asked me for an analogy; she wondered if it compared to swimming under water with an aqualung.

*She came pretty close. In the water, of course, you have something to hold you up; and out there you don't. I'd say the swimming sensation approaches a little more than half of what I expected.*

*The maneuvering gun worked fine, and I knew right away we had something there. By actuating two triggers, I could shoot compressed oxygen out through a system of nozzles and control myself wherever I wanted to go—back and forth or to the left and right or pitch myself upside down. There was a limited amount of air in the tanks, so I used it sparingly.*

*When the supply ran out, I used the tether line to move around. It tended to swing me up top of the spacecraft when I wanted to be out front. I took hold of the tether, pulled myself down on the spacecraft to give myself a little friction and walked around three or four steps until the angle of the tether to the spacecraft got so much that my feet went out from under me.*

*Aside from the technical things I learned, there was very strong personal impression that was the indescribable view around me. It was a sweeping panorama particularly after looking out the small window of the spacecraft. There were the vivid colors of the sky, followed by the clouds, the oceans and the Earth. The greatest view I had was towards the end of the EVA. I had seen Texas and the Gulf States, and then I saw Florida coming into view. At about that time, I rolled over facing down and I could see all the islands of the Caribbean stretching down beneath Florida—the Keys, the Dominican Republic, Cuba, Puerto Rico and so many others. The richness of those colors! The blues of the ocean were so deep and the greens of the shoals and shallow water so clear and light. On the land masses, the foliage and the browns seemed almost truer than if I had been flying at a lower altitude in a conventional aircraft. The visor I wore was coated with gold and it gave me the colors, as you would see them through a pair of sunglasses.*

*Throughout the EVA, my mind was crystal clear and I was pressing to get the most of the limited time. Nevertheless when the order came to go back in, I did feel a certain sadness. There was so much out there that I wanted to learn.*

*I knew it wasn't going to be easy to get back in, because you just don't jump into a spacecraft as you would an automobile. We had to go through in reverse the same things we had done to get outside. I had to dismount the camera that had taken pictures of my walk, stow the cable that had been attached to the camera, take off the umbilical guard and get it out of the way of the hatch, hand the maneuvering gun to Jim, and them climb in backward in my bulky suit and settle down in my seat again.*

*We had quite a struggle closing the hatch again. The normal method was for me to hold onto a canvas strap and turn a large lever to ratchet the hatch back down and seal it. But when I tried it, I discovered the lever was not catching, it was turning free and not ratcheting the hatch down at all. We had trained for this eventuality and knew exactly what to do. While Jim used his strong arms to apply brute force to a lanyard on his side that pulled down the hatch, I used my right hand to engage the gears, then reached forward to operate the handle. Between the two of us, with a lot of pulling and tugging, we finally got the hatch closed. It was a perfect example of teamwork and epitomized to me the vital necessity of having two men in a spacecraft who can literally work as one.*

White's euphoric space walk lasted for twenty-one minutes and the dialogue between the spacecraft and flight control gave credence to the myth that he did not want to return to the spacecraft. The problem was actually an elementary one of communication. White could talk to McDivitt but could not talk to flight control, whereas McDivitt could. So if Chris Kraft had directions for White, they had to be passed through McDivitt. Anyone who had known White for any amount of time knew that he would not disobey an order given to him by his superiors.

Hank West, who by now had retired from the air force and was working for General Dynamics, made the following observation: "Remembering Ed's competitiveness, persistence and love of adventure, I suspect that he must have done everything possible to make sure he was the second man and not the command pilot on that Gemini mission, because he would have known it was the co-pilot who would actually get the choice task of walking in space. The excitement and enthusiasm in his voice and actions during the event, to the extent of almost having to be physically reeled back aboard the spacecraft, clearly showed the Ed I had always known."

Gemini 4 made sixty-two orbits around the Earth, flying a total of 1,609,700 miles before splashdown in the Atlantic Ocean and eventual pickup by the recovery team from the USS *Wasp*. Skeptics had predicted that the astronauts would suffer some horrible side effects from a long duration flight and that the recovery crews would find dead, badly debilitated, or unconscious astronauts once they opened the hatches. However, the recovery helicopter pilot observed an entirely different situation as he hovered overhead. "They were like a couple of kids playing on the beach, splashing in the salt water," he said. White was doing exercises that resembled deep knee bends. Both astronauts were in fine shape, aside from a minor bout of seasickness in White's case.

Astronaut Frank Borman, who was McDivitt's backup for the flight, said that after recovery White astounded everyone, especially the astronauts' doctor, Charles Berry, "by doing a little jig on the flight deck. The next day, White saw a few Marines and midshipmen having a tug of war and joined them. Quite a guy was Edward Higgins White II."

"I felt so good, I didn't know whether to hop, skip, jump or to walk on my hands," White said of his postflight fitness. Later, discussing unsubstantiated reports of the

18. Looking exhausted after their four-day Gemini mission,
Ed White and Jim McDivitt are welcomed aboard
the recovery vessel USS *Wasp*. (NASA)

astronauts' "distinct aroma" after the flight, White quipped, "I thought we smelled fine, it was all those people on the carrier that smelled strange!"

In spite of their obvious delight in the mission, the astronauts had experienced some practical concerns during their flight. They found the work-rest cycles to be inadequate. They worried about running out of water and became overly conservative in their water intake, putting them at risk of dehydration. In addition, White felt that four or five hours after eating, his energy levels were going downhill in a more pronounced manner than they did on Earth. When he enjoyed his next meal he noted that his energy levels bounced up once again. He lost eight pounds during the flight but regained them within days.

Once they had returned home to Houston, the McDivitts held a party to celebrate the astronauts' safe journey and return home. The men and their families were also invited to the White House, where President Lyndon Johnson proclaimed White and McDivitt to be the "Columbuses of the Twentieth Century." He awarded them the NASA Exceptional Service Medal and promoted both to lieutenant colonels in the air force. The president joked that had he seen the EVA pictures beforehand he would have made them full colonels! Johnson also announced that he was sending them and their wives to the Paris Air Show as goodwill ambassadors, where cosmonaut Yuri Gagarin had apparently been showing up the Americans. Once White and McDivitt arrived, enthusiastic French attendees deserted Gagarin and swamped them with requests for autographs.

On their return home the city of Chicago held an enormous ticker-tape parade, and the University of Michigan gave both men honorary doctoral degrees in aeronautical science. Ed joked, "I can hardly get used to people calling me Colonel. I know in a million years I'll never get used to people calling me Doctor!"

During the postflight activities, White found time to visit his alma mater, West Point. The army soccer team was having a winning season, and on this particular day it was playing Seton Hall College. At halftime, and with the army team leading 12–0, White addressed the crowd. According to his old friend Morris Herbert:

> It was an unprecedented scene. Ed stood in front of the stands and spoke to the crowd and both teams. He didn't ask to do it—it was a groundswell of popular demand. His remarks were well chosen, modest, almost humble. After the game, I made a point of coming up to Ed (after speaking to individuals, signing autographs and congratulating the Army team). I thanked him for taking the time to attend the game and agreeing to make a few remarks. In reply, Ed made a strong point. "No Herb," he said, "don't thank me. It was a pleasure and a great privilege to be here." The evening after the soccer game, my oldest son, who was nine at the time, went across the street to ask Ed to autograph a book on space travel my son had. Ed could not have been more gracious. My son, who graduated from West Point in 1979, still has warm and fond memories of Ed White. He was not only an outstanding astronaut—he was an outstanding man in every way. His life exemplified the words of the West Point motto—Duty, Honor, Country.

A future astronaut, Sherwood "Woody" Spring, recalls White's visit as the inspiration of his dream to become an astronaut: "Ed White and Frank Borman came to talk to us at the Point. Ed showed the film from his first space walk and they both took turns describing the processes, events, conditions and activities leading up to his spacewalk (training, launch, cabin conditions). They showed us slides of various events, and spent time discussing the things that kept us fascinated. They also went through a little joke about space water, got a couple of cadets to try some, then announced it was recycled urine!"

Once White returned to NASA duties, he was named backup commander of Gemini 7 with his old West Point classmate Mike Collins as pilot. However, during an early stage of Gemini 10, he told Collins that he had decided he would probably shift over to the Apollo program, which came as no real surprise. "By early 1966, I figured Gemini 10 was mine but now Ed White told me it wasn't going to be his, that he had the word from Deke Slayton that he was moving on to Apollo," Collins wrote. "He was ambivalent about it, wanting to fly another Gemini mission but also wanting to get in on the ground floor of Apollo. Personally, I thought that Apollo made more sense for him at the time, and I thought that he might very well end up first on the Moon, as he had a lot of things going for him. He had projected exactly the right image as the nation's first spacewalker, and why not do the same as the first Moon walker?"

Mike Collins also told the authors that he had always maintained the greatest respect for his friend and colleague: "Ed also had a deep, serious side: he was a proud practicing patriot, and was not ashamed to say so. It is no coincidence that the first American flag to appear on a NASA spacesuit was on his sleeve, nor that he unofficially named his Gemini craft *American Eagle*. A member of the second group of astronauts, Ed was frequently compared by the press to his predecessor John Glenn, mostly on the basis of charisma. It was a comparison that John should be proud of, in all respects."

California-based writer Francis French asked Wally Schirra what he felt Ed White's future might have been. "I think he would have had command of a mission later," Schirra suggested. "Very likely then he would have gone back to the Air Force and had at least three or four stars. I thought he was a real candidate for superstar!" French asked Schirra about the media's tendency to compare White with John Glenn, and Schirra laughed as he replied that White was very much like Glenn, "but more genuine. John craved publicity, Ed was granted it in contrast. A nice choice of words, but I know that's the way it was."

§

Sitting alone on a high, windswept bluff just east of Dayton, Ohio, is a simple thirty-ton tower, fittingly made of pink marble specially freighted over from North Carolina. Nothing surrounds the tower but concentric platforms of stone block and some desultory trees, which occasionally ruffle and sigh in the breeze. One day back in early 1963 the only movement on the hill came from a young naval aviator who was standing in front of the monument. He cast his eyes over the austere but magnificent tower, then his gaze moved upward into the unpredictable blue skies of southwestern Ohio.

Roger Chaffee was filled with admiration and pride, for he was standing at the top of a hill where the Wright brothers had experimented with box kites and gliders, launching themselves into the teeth of winds sixty years earlier. Some soil from Kill Devil Hill in North Carolina, where that first flight by Wilbur and Orville Wright had been made, was even buried inside the monument. as a sudden, skittish wind tousled his dark hair, Chaffee looked down the hill, down to the Huffman Prairie, where modern flight was perfected, and down to where he lived and worked. He could easily make out the broad airstrips, concrete aprons, and clusters of hangars and other buildings that made up the Wright-Patterson Air Force Base.

19. Roger Chaffee. (NASA)

Earlier known as Wright Field, the base had served as the nation's center of military aviation research since 1927. During and after World War II the skies over Wright Field were filled with aircraft performing tests and advancing the state of aeronautical knowledge at a bewildering speed. In 1948 the growing complex of airfields, hangars, and research buildings became one installation under the name of Wright-Patterson Air Force Base.

Twenty-eight-year-old Lieutenant Roger Chaffee was filled that day with the historical significance of the area and felt right at home, for aviation was in his soul. He had enjoyed his first ride in an airplane at the age of seven, when his father, a former barnstorming pilot, had taken the family on a short flight over Lake Michigan. The event had determined the young boy's future. As his love of aviation grew, he would often point out aircraft flying over his Greenville, Michigan, home and say with youthful conviction, "I'll be up there flying in one of those someday."

Always a man of vision and determination, Chaffee had now set his sights even higher—he wanted to be an astronaut. "You'll be flying along some nights with a full Moon," he would say a few years later. "You're up at 45,000 feet. Up there you can see it like you can't see it down here. It's just the big, bright, clear Moon. You look up there and just say to yourself: 'I've got to get up there. I've just got to get one of those flights.'"

Roger Bruce Chaffee was born in Grand Rapids, Michigan, on 15 February 1935, the second child of Donald Lynn and Blanche May (née Mosher) Chaffee. (Mrs. Chaffee preferred to be known as "Mike.") His two-year-old sister was named Donna. The family home was in Greenville, some thirty miles northeast of Grand Rapids.

The Chaffees planned to deliver their son in Greenville, but his father developed scarlet fever a few weeks before the baby was due. Now unable to give birth at the local hospital because the disease was highly contagious, Mike, along with little Donna, quickly packed up and moved to her parents' home in Grand Rapids. It was hard for Don and Mike to be separated, but to their relief the baby was born just two weeks later. However, it would be another ten days before the doctors would finally release Don from his quarantine status so he could see and hold his son for the first time.

As Roger Chaffee grew up, one of his favorite family excursions would be a trip over to Wabasis Creek in Kent County. The two children and their father fished in the clear, cold waters and were often rewarded with a small fish struggling at the end of their line. This and other outings sparked Chaffee's lifelong love of the outdoors.

News of the bombing of Pearl Harbor in December 1941 meant very little to young Roger, but for his father, employed by Army Ordnance, it meant a transfer to Grand Rapids, where he held a new position as chief inspector of Army Ordnance at the Doehler-Jarvis plant. Six months later the family moved to a new home in Grand Rapids, where Chaffee was soon enrolled at Dickinson School.

In 1942 Don Chaffee organized a special surprise for his children, who had both missed a significant part of their summer break when they had fallen ill with measles. On that unforgettable day the whole family took off from Grand Rapids airport, and Don flew westward to Lake Michigan, where he headed about ten miles out over the sparkling water before turning back. Roger was round-eyed with excitement and awe during the entire flight, and a whole new world opened up before him. From that time on, airplanes became a big part of his life. Soon after, Don set up a card table in the house, where he and his son spent many happy hours patiently cutting out and gluing balsa wood model airplanes.

By the time he turned thirteen, Chaffee had discovered the Boy Scout movement and joined up. Soon he began to earn a string of merit badges, and after his first year of scouting he had already achieved his Order of the Arrow, usually reserved for boys fifteen and over. By the time he had completed the eleventh grade at school he had earned just about every merit badge then available to a Boy Scout.

His parents were enormously proud of their son, especially when he became an Eagle Scout later that year. Chaffee loved nothing more than helping other youngsters through scouting, and his Boy Scout leader later said that he should have received his Eagle Scout rating even earlier than the age of sixteen, but he was so busy helping younger children that he did not spend enough time working on his own qualifications. As always, his favorite activities involved hiking, camping, and cooking over a crackling campfire under a star-filled sky.

Around this time Chaffee also developed a deep interest in science and electronics engineering. His parents had just converted the house's heating system from coal to gas, so he asked permission to transform the former coal bin into his own workshop. He cleaned and whitewashed the bin, and from that time on he happily spent hours in his own private laboratory, experimenting with his chemistry set and tinkering with broken radios and other small electrical devices. He still devoted time to building his beloved model airplanes, and when they were finished he worked on tiny propeller-driven engines designed to fit into them.

Chemistry and amateur electronics took a back seat to mechanics and engineering when he started learning to drive at age sixteen. With instruction from his father, Chaffee quickly grasped the fundamentals and was soon clutching that all-important driver's license in his hand. Don allowed his son to borrow the family car from time to time, but like any teenager Chaffee wanted to buy his own vehicle. His parents had taught him how to be thrifty and to save his allowances and paper route money for a day such as this, so he combined his savings with the money he got from selling his bicycle, and he went looking at local car lots. His first automobile was a 1929 Lafayette that he bought for forty-nine dollars, but a few months later he traded it in for a 1934 Ford Sport Coupe. He slaved under the hood of his car, tuning and cleaning until it was his pride and joy.

Despite the attractions that revolve around owning a car, Chaffee did not neglect his studies, and in June 1953 he graduated in the top fifth of his class from Central High School. With a career in the navy in mind, he had earlier taken tests, summarized class grades, and applied for scholarships from the Naval Academy in Annapolis, Rhodes, and the Naval Reserve Officers Training Corps (NROTC). Annapolis sent him an appointment, but he turned it down because it required a promise that he would stay in the navy, and he would not give a promise he might not keep. Rhodes was the next to be eliminated, as it would not accept applicants for engineering fields. A few days before school graduation, Chaffee learned that he had been accepted to NROTC and was to report in September to the Illinois Institute of Technology in Chicago.

Although it almost broke his heart, Chaffee realized he had to sell his car and all his model airplanes, as there would be no time for such things once he entered college. This sad task done, he was ready to face whatever the future might bring.

At the end of September Chaffee wrote from Chicago, telling his parents he had settled in well, was pledging the Phi Kappa Sigma fraternity, and was moving into the fraternity house. His freshman year went well as far as studies were concerned—he scored a B+ average. His name also appeared on the Dean's List of Undergraduate Honor Students. By the time summer vacation came along he had decided he wanted to follow a career in aeronautical engineering.

Chaffee applied to Purdue University in Lafayette, Indiana, which he knew offered a quality aeronautical engineering program. A review board in Washington DC finally sanctioned and approved the request, and Chaffee was accepted to Purdue as a transfer student for the 1954 fall semester.

In the summer of that year, and in accordance with the NROTC program, Chaffee undertook his first summer cruise. First, however, he had to pass some physical tests at the Great Lakes Naval Training Station, and he came perilously close to washing out of an aviation career. At the end of an exhausting day he fronted up for an eye examination, and one eye was found to be so weak that the doctor was going to fail him. Chaffee was alarmed, but fortunately the doctor said he was willing to give him another chance and instructed him to come back fully rested the next day. That night Chaffee strolled along the beach at Lake Michigan, deeply concerned about what would happen if he failed again in the morning. It would certainly mean the end of a military flying career. Somehow he managed to get a good night's sleep, and the next morning, to his immense relief, he passed the eye test to the doctor's satisfaction.

The summer cruise lasted eight weeks aboard the battleship *Wisconsin,* and among other ports of call Chaffee visited England, Scotland, France, and Cuba. Following this he had some time before the start of the next semester, so his father found him some temporary work as a gear cutter. It was hard, tedious, and often dirty work, and at the end of his time there he resolutely said, "I learned one thing on this job—I'm not going to make my living *this* way for the rest of my life!"

Chaffee arrived in Lafayette in the fall of 1954 and was given a warm welcome by his fraternity brothers on Littleton Street. They had been expecting him, and he quickly settled in.

During his junior year at Purdue, Chaffee found his studies in the aeronautics wind tunnel meant he had to commute daily to the airport and back, eight miles away, as well as maintain his campus classes. With some financial assistance from his parents he bought himself a new 1954 Chevrolet sedan. The car helped him to keep to his busy schedule and also drive home every two or three weeks. "as in the past," his father would later say, "he usually was accompanied by a number of friends from school and always by a bundle of washing!"

The flying bug still gripped him, and during one break in 1955 Chaffee drove out to Stair Field in Mulberry, Indiana, with his friend Tommy Keister, who was also keen on learning to fly. Chaffee eventually took four or five lessons with pilot and local flying legend John "Pop" Stair, but he did not have enough money to continue and gain his private license.

In September 1955 Chaffee went on a blind double date with a fraternity friend and was paired off with a pretty young college freshman named Martha Horn from Oklahoma City. Although they enjoyed each other's company that night, Chaffee went away with the impression that his date was "a naïve Southern girl." For her part, Martha had found the young man to be "a handsome but smart-alec upperclassman." But love will always find a way, and despite their first impressions of each other Roger and Martha soon began to date regularly. By Christmas break Roger had asked Martha if she would wear his fraternity pin. To his alarm Martha said she would not give an answer right away, but would think it over during the vacation. She did, and in January the pin was accepted. When Don and Mike Chaffee visited Purdue in the fall to see their son, the romance was in full bloom, and Chaffee told his father, "Dad, I've gone out with a lot of girls, but this is *it*. Someday I'll marry Martha."

At the end of his junior year, Chaffee embarked on his second training cruise, and this time he sailed the North Atlantic aboard the USS *Perry*, visiting Denmark and Sweden.

On 12 October 1956 he took the first giant step in fulfilling the prediction he had given his father: he asked Martha to marry him. This time there was no hesitation— she said yes, and they began making plans for a wedding the following summer.

During his final semester at Purdue, Chaffee undertook flight training as an NROTC air cadet. The aircraft he trained in was a Cessna 172, and his first flight was with his old instructor, "Pop" Stair. In April 1966 Chaffee, then training for his Apollo flight, took time out to answer a letter from "Pop" Stair, and in it he expressed his gratitude:

> *Yes, I am the same Roger Chaffee you taught to fly. I had my first training flight in one of your J-3 Cubs at Stair Field, Mulberry, Indiana. I believe it was in the fall of 1954 or the spring of 1955 that I first came down to your field with Tommy Keister, a fraternity brother of mine, who was also learning to fly. If I remember correctly, I had about four or five flights from you that year and then I decided that I would not have the money to go on and get my private license. Later in the spring of 1957, I again started flying with the NROTC at Purdue and you were my first instructor. You taught me a lot of the fundamentals of flying which I have always carried with me. I still remember how you impressed upon your students to always have an emergency landing field picked out in case of engine failure. One of the first things I do after I take off in a small aircraft is to look for a clearing or field in event of emergency. Of course, with the larger and faster military aircraft I am flying this is not so important because you can only land them on a prepared surface; however, I still look around for that landing site. I will forever be grateful to the excellent instructions that you gave me in basic aircraft and the precepts of safety that you instilled in me.*

Twenty-four days after his first tentative instruction flight at Purdue University Airport, Chaffee finally went solo in the Cessna on 29 March 1957. Following some further work in solo and dual flying he achieved his private pilot's license on 24 May, and his test administrator recommended him for further military flight training.

The following month Chaffee graduated from Purdue with distinction with a bachelor of science degree in aeronautical engineering. To cap his achievement, he also received a key to the National Society of Engineers, which he proudly added to his collection of Phi Kappa Sigma, Tau Beta Pi, and Sigma Gamma Tau fraternity pins. He completed his naval training that August and was commissioned as an ensign in the U.S. Navy. On 24 August, two days after receiving his commission, he married Martha Horn in Oklahoma City.

Following a two-week honeymoon Chaffee was to report aboard the *Lake Champlain* for a six-week cruise, but when he arrived at Norfolk the ship had already sailed. He was then assigned some temporary duty at the base, and Martha was able to join him, albeit for a short time. They found a furnished apartment and set up their first home together, but in November he was ordered to report to Pensacola, Florida, for his military flight training. He first flew the t-34 and then the t-28. He made rapid progress and the following summer was transferred to Kingsville, Texas, where he took on more advanced training in the f9 Cougar jet fighter.

On 17 November 1958 a baby girl named Sheryl became the newest member of the Chaffee family. Sadly, Chaffee had to sail out the following day for carrier training, but he was thankful that he had been home for the birth of their daughter. The training at sea was intense but challenging, and he later declared that "setting that big bird down on the flight deck was like landing on a postage stamp," while night takeoffs could be compared to "getting shot into a bottle of ink."

One of his later involvements was an assignment to vap 62, a heavy photography squadron known as the "Tigers." This meant working with the ra-3b twin-engine jet photoreconnaissance aircraft, and he became one of the youngest pilots ever permitted to fly this particular steed. Early in 1961, with increased concern over events in Cuba, Chaffee was detailed to make dozens of routine reconnaissance flights over the island, sometimes as many as three times a day. Several later biographies would credit him with making u2 spy plane flights over Cuba, but this was just a fanciful misinterpretation. Besides, the u2 was an air force program, and the young naval officer could not have strapped himself into one of its most secret aircraft. This mistake probably came about when Chaffee was later credited with taking some extremely detailed photos that showed the beginning of the Soviet missile buildup in Cuba, which would result in brinkmanship between the two superpowers the following year.

Now one of the navy's brightest young prospects, Chaffee was given as much advanced flight training as he could squeeze in, and one such tour of duty saw him stationed in Africa when his son Stephen was born on 3 July 1961.

By this time, he was taking graduate-level courses in engineering and had his eyes set directly on his nation's space program. He had been intrigued by news of the first satellites, but as humans first set foot out into space his interest intensified. When John Glenn flew his Earth-orbital mission aboard *Friendship 7* in February 1962, Chaffee knew without question what direction he wanted to take. Soon after,

NASA invited applications for its third astronaut group, and that June Chaffee fired off his resume and qualifications. He also told his superiors that he was interested in training as a test pilot for astronaut status.

It was an ideal time for Chaffee to reconsider his career options. He had completed his tours of sea duty and had eighteen hundred hours of flying time packed under his belt. It was therefore opportune when the navy offered him the chance to pursue a master's degree in reliability engineering with the Air Force Institute of Technology at Wright-Patterson AFB. So once again Martha, Sheryl, and Stephen hauled up anchor and moved to a new home in Fairborn, near the base in Dayton, Ohio. At the same time, Chaffee undertook preliminary testing as a NASA astronaut candidate.

The time spent at Wright-Patterson passed quickly, and the number of suitable candidates for NASA's third astronaut intake began to dwindle as the testing intensified. Chaffee knew he had a very good chance, but he became increasingly nervous as the time for notification grew closer. To help himself relax he took off on a hunting trip to Michigan, and when he returned on 14 October there was a message asking him to contact NASA. He had a solemn look on his face as he dialed, trying hard not to seem anxious, but Martha could sense the tension in her husband. Halfway through the conversation his face brightened, and he kept saying "Yes, SIR!" as his smile broadened. She knew what Roger was going to tell her long before he hung up.

Four days later, on 18 October 1963, Lieutenant Chaffee flew to Houston, where he was officially announced as a member of the nation's third group of astronauts.

The abrupt move to Houston meant that once again the Chaffees had to pack their belongings, something they were used to by now, and Chaffee, in his usual systematic way, had everything under control. Until they were able to build their new home, they moved into a small tan duplex in Clear Lake, a suburb southeast of Houston. It was situated quite close to the new Manned Spacecraft Center, which was still undergoing final construction. They located a beautiful building block in a new subdivision, bought it with the windfall money they received from the publication agreement with *Life* magazine, and built a house Chaffee had already designed for them.

That subdivision proved a popular nesting place for the new astronauts and their families. Within a stone's throw were the homes of Mike Collins, Dick Gordon, Jim McDivitt, Al Bean, Buzz Aldrin, and Dave Scott, while Gene Cernan and his family moved in right next door. Chaffee put in the first swimming pool on the new block, while Cernan built a walk-in bar in his family room, so the two houses soon became a focal point for astronaut get-togethers. as a result, the two men and their families would become good friends. Cernan, also a naval aviator, had been a year ahead of Chaffee in the NROTC at Purdue, but they did not really know each other before their selection by NASA. They soon made up for this, however, with hunting trips and other time together. In his 1999 book, *Last Man on the Moon*, Cernan spoke about his friendship with the young lieutenant from Grand Rapids:

*Roger and I had bonded. We shared a dream. We were, in a special way, brothers . . . from the day we reported to NASA, our space careers grew in parallel paths. We shared rental cars, hotel rooms, and often the same airplane . . . On many a Friday night, coming home from a week-long training mission in a T-38 . . . Roger and I would buzz our houses just before turning sharply left, dropping the gear and landing at Ellington Air Force Base. From as far as San Antonio, we would point the needle nose of our plane directly at the driveway separating our houses and roar over Barbuda Lane, shaking the shingles and rattling the dishes at 600 knots. The noisy message let our wives (and neighbors) know that we would be home soon. We would land, jump into our cars, and race down the two-lane Old Galveston Highway, through the single stoplight in the town of Webster at eighty miles per hour and screech up to our houses in less than ten minutes. It was all somewhat illegal, but what the hell, we were astronauts!*

As with the first two astronaut groups, the new astronauts each took on a field of specialization, and Chaffee's was communications. His field involved him in the Deep Space Instrumentation Facility (DSIF), a series of tracking stations around the world, including three powerful installations in Spain, Australia, and more locally in Goldstone, California. The accuracy of the DSIF was of utmost importance to the astronauts, who would be using it to navigate. In *Carrying the Fire*, Michael Collins recalled Chaffee's hard work in establishing a better communications network: "With characteristic energy and enthusiasm, Roger plunged into the arcane world of band widths and Doppler shifts, making sure the complex equipment was going to do all it was advertised to do and that it was simply and sensibly designed from an operator's point of view."

In June 1965 Chaffee served as one of the CapComs on the Gemini 4 mission, together with Chief CapCom Gus Grissom and Gene Cernan. His principal task was to communicate with astronauts Jim McDivitt and Ed White and to relay this information to the director of Flight Crew Operations, Chris Kraft. He would also be paired with Grissom in flying chase planes to take photographs of the launch of an unmanned Saturn 1B rocket.

Chaffee's dedicated expertise and enthusiasm stuck with Grissom, who later said, "Roger is one of the smartest boys I've ever run into. He's just a damned good engineer—there's no other way to explain it. When he starts talking to engineers about their systems, he can just tear those damn guys apart. I've never seen one like him. He's a really great boy."

On 21 March 1966, just days after Neil Armstrong and Dave Scott splashed down following their shortened Gemini 8 mission, NASA announced the names of the six men who would serve as the prime and backup crews on the first Apollo mission.

Chaffee had been in training for more than two and a half years and was ready for any assignment that NASA handed him, but he really coveted a place on the first mission. Chaffee was selected for the primary crew and became the youngest of America's astronauts ever chosen to fly. He was ready to live by the words he had spoken at a press conference two years earlier:

> *I guess when a fellow climbs into a spacecraft, straps himself in and starts waiting for the countdown, he could give what's coming some really serious consideration, but I'm not afraid. I feel a capable pilot should be able to meet the emergencies that may develop. What's more, there's risk to flying an ordinary plane, just as there is to driving a car, walking across a street or going down a stairway.*
>
> *There's an exact, precise job here. When we reach the Moon, studies done there will tell us a great deal about the solar system, and the overall NASA program will produce great benefits for our nation and the world. It already has, in fact.*
>
> *What's more, I'll be doing something for my country, something in which I can take great pride.*

§

It was the accident everyone had dreaded—a fire in a spacecraft. Up on Level 8, where the Apollo 1 craft was located in an area known as the White Room, Pad Leader Donald Babbitt had been standing with James Gleaves and L. D. Reece, ready to isolate spacecraft 012 for the test. Suddenly, at 6:31 P.M., a sharp cry came over the radio from inside the capsule. There was a fire, and Babbitt reacted immediately. "Get them out of there!" he cried.

Next Babbitt yelled out to the elevator technician, instructing him to tell the blockhouse that there was a fire inside the spacecraft. Thick smoke began to billow around the White Room as each of the men grabbed an oxygen mask and then tried to get into the spacecraft. Over in the blockhouse, helpless controllers sat paralyzed with horror as the situation intensified.

Inside the craft the cabin pressure had risen dramatically and the crew was frantically trying to get out. Chaffee had turned up the lights and opened communication links. Ten seconds later he yelled out in despair, "We've got a bad fire—let's get out—let's open her up!"

Emergency escape procedures called for a minimum of ninety seconds to open the hatches and evacuate the spacecraft. In simulations, however, the crew had never accomplished the routines in anywhere close to the minimum times. In these sessions Grissom had to lower White's headrest so that White could reach above and behind his left shoulder to actuate a ratchet-type device that would release the first of a series of latches.

A television camera had been positioned outside the command module to give pictures of the small window in the craft's hatch. The hatch itself was monstrously heavy and opened inward. Those who had been keeping an eye on the test in the control center saw sudden movements of legs and arms on their television monitors. White was seen to reach for the bolts securing the hatch; he suddenly snatched his hands back, then reached out again. Another pair of hands—Grissom's—came into view reaching for the hatch as the flames, which were mostly on his side of the craft, grew in intensity.

According to one source, White had actually made part of a full turn before being overcome by smoke. It is acknowledged that he put in a mighty but ultimately futile effort to open the hatches. The last transmission from the spacecraft was a sharp, unidentified cry of pain.

The pressure within the Apollo craft quickly built up to thirty-six pounds per square inch, until it suddenly ruptured at the right side of the base, below Chaffee's couch. Flames and debris spewed out with a roar into the adjoining White Room. Fire briefly enveloped the outside of the spacecraft. as the cabin oxygen was depleted, the clear flame deepened in color and a thick, dark, and choking smoke quickly developed. Liquid glycol coolant leaked through melted solder joints and continued to feed the fierce flames in the left side of the cabin. A hole was soon burned in the floor.

The heat and intensity of the fire and smoke drove back Babbitt and the other technicians who were desperately attempting to get near the spacecraft. Again and again they plunged into the thick, pungent smoke and heat, hoping to get to the hatch. Others began searching the area for gas masks and fire extinguishers. Choking and gasping in the dense smoke, they continued to run in and out of the White Room, gulping in fresh air before returning. But there was little they could do.

Television pictures now showed an eerie bright glow as the flames continued to rage out of control. There were frantic shouts from the controllers to blow the hatch, even though it could not be opened explosively from either the inside or outside of the spacecraft. In the blockhouse Deke Slayton and astronaut Stu Roosa, who was acting as the spacecraft communicator, watched helplessly as the drama unfolded. Slayton yelled out to two nearby doctors, Fred Kelly and Alan Harter, telling them to get to the spacecraft.

Eventually, five minutes after the alarm had first sounded, the booster cover cap was opened, followed by the inner and outer hatches. At first, no one could see through the smoke, and there were no discernible signs of life. Nearly five minutes later the smoke had cleared sufficiently to reveal the inert bodies of the crew. Chaffee was still strapped in his seat, while White had collapsed across his after several frantic efforts to open the hatch had failed. Even White—said to be among the fittest of the astronauts and as strong as an ox—never really had any chance of opening the hatch. Grissom was found lying on his back on the floor of the spacecraft, where he had apparently crawled in an attempt to escape the fire. All three had their visors closed.

20. The blackened interior of the Apollo 1 spacecraft after the fire. (NASA)

The bodies of Grissom and White were so intertwined below the hatch that it was difficult to tell them apart. Doctors Kelly and Harter conducted a brief examination of the occupants and quickly pronounced what everyone had known they would find—all three men were dead.

Pad 34 was cleared of nonessential personnel, security guards were posted, and official photographers were summoned to record the tragic scene. Throughout that terrible night a team of doctors and technicians labored to remove the bodies of the crew from the gutted spacecraft, while the technicians who had fought so valiantly to open the craft's hatch were attended to by other doctors. In all, twenty-seven men were treated for smoke inhalation, with two admitted to the hospital. Great difficulty was encountered when extricating the bodies of the dead astronauts, because parts of their space suits had fused with molten nylon inside the spacecraft. It was an awkward, filthy, and sickening task that took the team over ninety minutes.

Since the test was thought to have held no particular hazards for anyone involved, safety personnel had not been allocated to the spacecraft. The twenty-seven workers who were located at different parts of the gantry were not truly equipped or trained for emergencies. Even if there had been proper safety equipment and the workers had been trained to use it, they probably still would have been unable to evacuate the crew in time. The only thing that could have saved the lives of the three astronauts would have been a fast-opening hatch.

News of the fire was withheld from the public and media for two hours, during which time the next of kin were informed. Phone lines were cut at the Kennedy and Manned Spacecraft Centers, so even the shocked employees were unable to call and reassure their families they were safe. As a result, the media received several panic-stricken calls from NASA and NAA family members. An initially vague NASA press statement released to the Associated Press stated, "An accidental fire has broken out on the Apollo launch pad, killing at least one person. The space agency says its victim may have been one of the astronauts scheduled to make the trip."

Shortly after, AP released another press bulletin: "One of the three Apollo 1 astronauts has been killed in an explosion or fire on the spacecraft's launch pad at Cape Kennedy. There is no immediate indication as to which of the astronauts was the victim. The three scheduled to make the trip were Virgil Grissom, Edward White and Roger Chaffee. The victim was believed to be a member of the Apollo 1 prime crew. Space Agency officials say that the victim's name is being withheld pending notification of next of kin."

Initial press reports, which hit the news wires soon after, were understandably holocaustic. They spoke of fierce flames and of the spacecraft erupting, all of which was relatively true. Subsequent reports, however, which graphically told of charred and unrecognizable bodies, and chunks of flesh welded to the inside of the hatch, were horrifically overstated. Most people these days recall reading about the deaths of the crew in this exaggerated manner.

White's handprint was indeed etched out in ash on the inside of the hatch as he frantically pushed against it, but his hand was well protected by his space suit glove. There were no "scratches and torn flesh" as was so widely reported. The astronauts were never "incinerated down to the bone"; the fire had been extinguished fairly quickly and the white Apollo suits had provided reasonable protection. This, after all, was what they had been designed to do—to shield the wearer against hostile elements. However, there was some damage to the suits, as the inside temperature of the module at one stage reached more than 1,000 degrees Fahrenheit. About 70 percent of Grissom's space suit had been destroyed, around 25 percent of White's, and about 15 percent of Chaffee's. Grissom had sustained some burns to one of his legs, and Chaffee to his back, but these injuries were entirely survivable.

Gene Kranz, a Mission Control flight director, later stated, "I have never seen a facility or group of people, a group of men so stricken in all their entire lives." The majority of the controllers were fresh out of college and in their early twenties. "Everyone had gone through the agony of listening to this crew over sixteen seconds . . . it was very fresh, very real, and there were many controllers who couldn't cope with the disaster that had occurred," Kranz said.

Elsewhere around the globe the news hit hard, particularly for those closely involved with the Apollo program. Terry Kierans was a supervisor at the Carnarvon Tracking Station in Western Australia when word of the accident came filtering through. "At first we thought the news coming down the communications line from Cape Canaveral was part of the simulation until a teletype explained the awful truth," he said.

At the later memorial services in Seabrook, Texas, Grissom's distraught father, Dennis, asked Wally Schirra about the condition of his son's body. Schirra told him that the space suits had helped protect the bodies, and once the embalming had been done there was little evidence of the burns. The inference was that the coffins could actually have been opened.

Several days after the fire, NASA allowed George Alexander, a reporter from the trade magazine *Aviation Week,* to examine the ruined spacecraft. He compared it to a burnt-out bomber from the Second World War.

Autopsies carried out on the crew revealed that the deaths were caused by carbon monoxide asphyxiation resulting from the inhalation of toxic fumes, with thermal burns as a contributing cause.

Astronaut Michael Collins had been given the grim task of telling Martha Chaffee that her husband was dead, but as usual a support person had been sent straight into the Chaffee house, and this person was Alan Bean's wife, Sue. Somehow Sue managed to maintain her composure as she chatted with Martha, who never had an inkling of the terrible news that awaited her. After all Roger was over at the cape and was not doing any flying that day. Soon after, Collins appeared at the front door, and the look on his face told Martha all she needed to know. "Martha, I'd like to talk to you alone," he said, and she simply said, "Yes." She understood.

In a similar fashion Bill Anders informed Pat White, while Dr. Charles Berry, director of Medical Services at the Manned Spacecraft Center, was the one who gave the devastating news to Betty Grissom. Wally Schirra, who heard the news while flying home to Houston from Cape Kennedy, immediately went next door to the Grissom home to be with Betty and her two children, Scott and Mark.

That day astronaut Frank Borman was on vacation with his family when a State Trooper knocked on his door and relayed a message that Deke Slayton needed to speak with him because an emergency had occurred. As soon as Slayton gave him the news, Borman and his wife, Susan, drove straight to Houston to comfort Pat White. According to Borman, he was livid when he heard what was happening to the new and shocked widow:

> When we got to the White house, some NASA officials had already bugged Pat about funeral plans. Bugged, hell—they had pressured her. Someone in Washington had decided that all three astronauts were to be buried at Arlington National Cemetery and Pat was staging a tearful but losing battle. White's father was also a West Pointer, and Ed had told Pat had anything ever happened, he wanted to be buried at the Academy. "They told me there has to be only one ceremony," she sobbed.
>
> I couldn't believe it; they were worrying about what would make it easier on them than on the victim's families. It was a typical bureaucratic

*reaction and I was angry. "That's nonsense," I told Pat. "We are going to do exactly what you want and I'll take care of it!"*

*I don't remember who I called in Washington except he was damned high on the bureaucratic totem pole. "Ed White's funeral will be at West Point like the family wants," I declared, "so you might as well go ahead and arrange things—that's the way it's going to be!"*

*Ed's death hit me hard, too. We had lost many friends before but never had we lost someone so close, nor had anyone in the space program been killed in a spacecraft. He might as well have been the brother I never had, a man of gentle strength and quiet humor. There was something special about him. He really was the astronaut's astronaut, a handsome, powerfully built man who actually seemed indestructible.*

Ironically, at the time the fire occurred, NASA Administrator Jim Webb was at the White House with other senior managers, astronauts, and the ambassadors of sixty nations, including the Soviet Union. They were celebrating the signing of the Outer Space Treaty, which banned the use of space for military purposes. On hearing of the tragedy, Webb immediately conveyed the horrifying news to President Lyndon Johnson. He was given permission for NASA to investigate the fire—a decision that would later raise the ire of many politicians and journalists. The following morning NASA announced that Dr. Floyd Thompson, head of the space agency's Langley Research Center, would be in charge of a review board given the task of conducting a comprehensive investigation into the fire and its causes. Among the members of this board were astronaut representative Frank Borman and spacecraft designer Max Faget.

News of the tragedy swept like wildfire across the country, and a stunned nation read accounts of the fire in the newspapers and watched as graphic images of the devastation filled their TV screens. President Johnson expressed his grief over the deaths of the astronauts, saying, "Three valiant young men have given their lives in the nation's service. We mourn this great loss and our hearts go out to their families."

Vice President Hubert Humphrey tried that night to reach the astronauts' widows by phone to express his condolences. "It wasn't just another accident," he had told reporters that day. "With Ed White, it was the loss of a great friend."

The visionary engineer who had put America into space, Wernher von Braun, was a shaken man. "All of the astronauts live on a first name basis with death," he stated when pressed for his reaction. "They know the risks and they are willing to take them."

James Webb's reaction was similar. "We've always known something like this would happen sooner or later but it's not going to be permitted to stop the program," he said. "Although everyone realized that some day space pilots would die, who would have thought the first tragedy would be on the ground?"

In spaceflight matters, Tuesday, 31 January 1967, should have been remembered only as the ninth anniversary of the day America's first satellite, Explorer 1, was triumphantly launched into Earth orbit. Instead, four days after the fire, a shocked nation buried three heroes.

On that chill winter morning, Gus Grissom was laid to rest at Arlington National Cemetery. Across America millions of people listened to and watched live broadcasts of the funeral. A volley of rifle shots echoed across the hallowed grounds, and then a bugler sounded the heart-wrenching notes of taps as three jets soared overhead in the missing man formation. Flanking the casket at rigid attention were the six remaining Mercury astronauts in full dress uniforms, bidding farewell the first of their number to fall. President Lyndon Johnson was there, his head bowed in sorrow. At the end of the service he offered Betty Grissom the American flag that had draped her husband's coffin and offered his personal condolences and those of the nation.

Three hours later Roger Chaffee was buried at Grissom's side. Once more the air rang with the sound of gunfire and the mournful sound of a bugle, and three jets roared over Arlington, once again with a gap in their formation to signify a lost pilot.

Even as taps sounded at Arlington, a third ceremony was taking place at Ed White's beloved West Point. The funeral services were held in the Old Cadet Chapel, with Vice President Hubert Humphrey and Lady Bird Johnson in attendance, representing the president, who was at Arlington. White's pastor, the Reverend Conrad Winborn, read the eulogy, and the USMA chaplain Jim Ford read the Cadet Prayer.

The superintendent of the academy, Major General Donald Bennett, led a large contingent of West Point staff, faculty, officers, and cadets to the services and gravesite rites. Astronauts Frank Borman, Neil Armstrong, Pete Conrad, Buzz Aldrin, and Tom Stafford were honorary pallbearers, as were members of White's Class of 1952. Jim McDivitt attended Pat White during the service. White's brother, Jim, escorted Pat White; her children, Edward and Bonnie; and White's parents from the chapel to the gravesite. Many of the mourners, including Lady Bird Johnson, were amazed at Jim's resemblance to his late brother.

A cadet from the Class of 1968, Ron Feher, wrote the following about the funeral:

> Ed White was a hero to those of us who had worn cadet gray during the Sixties. I can remember the impression he made on my fellow cadets and me when he came back to present the Academy with a small American flag he had flown in space with him. I think it was a combination of the awe of seeing a man who had walked in space and the bond that existed between all of us in that long gray line, that this man would be thinking of the Academy and want to bring back another piece of history to reside within the gray-walled womb of his Alma Mater. He had pushed the limit of human experience and courage. He was perhaps what we all wanted to be. Perhaps that's why his death hit so hard.

*I was nothing to Ed White or his family, but I wanted to be at his funeral. It seemed almost inconceivable not to be there, out of respect. I remember walking down Washington Road to the cemetery. I was not alone. In fact, without direction, the Corps and the West Point community assembled spontaneously to say goodbye. I remember so vividly the grief-stricken face of Mrs. White, the black veil, the brown hair, the pain I could not understand but only imagine. We stood at the grave in silence listening to the final words of prayer until the exquisite moment when a formation of Air Force jets swooped by just above the trees and Taps sounded our final solemn tribute. It was the planes that I will always remember: their timing precise, their power speaking more than any of us could say how much we mourned one of our own. I was grateful that our country spoke so eloquently, so simply.*

Bob Stromberg, a member of the Class of 1967, also vividly recalls that sad day:

*I sang in the Protestant Choir and Glee Club while I was a cadet. At the funeral, there was a combined group of Protestant, Catholic and Jewish choirs who sang. You have to remember that we had just escalated our war in Vietnam, and all of us were realizing that the peacetime Army we had joined was not going to stay peaceful for long. We were starting to consider that we would almost certainly graduate to an Army at war. In the midst of this, we are called to sing at the funeral of one of the first astronauts to die. In those days, astronauts were real big heroes to all of America. To be burying one was bad enough, but the moment for me that I will never forget occurred while we were singing the "Alma Mater." We always sang this when we performed, so I had sung it many, many times. However that day was the day I fully realized the significance of the third verse:*

> *And when our work is done,*
> *Our courses on Earth run,*
> *May it be said well done; be thou at peace.*
> *E'er may that line of gray*
> *Increase from day to day,*
> *Live, serve, and die we pray,*
> *West Point for thee.*

*I, and I am sure many other cadets that day had a hard time finishing the words after "die."*

White would have been proud: he was buried next to Major General George Goethals, who had supervised the building of the Panama Canal, and Major General William D. Connor, the thirty-sixth superintendent of the United States Military Academy, West Point.

Following the funerals of the Apollo 1 crew, the investigation into the fire began in earnest. Soon after the bodies had been removed from Pad 34, NASA impounded everything at the launch site, including documents pertaining to the accident. The agency also began to collect and collate eyewitness reports. Journalists had swamped the Kennedy Space Center looking for stories—their theories and innuendos filled America's newspapers for weeks. Many people were looking for quick answers, but it soon became clear that no single cause of the accident could be pinpointed.

Dr. Floyd Thompson set up twenty-one panels to assist the review board in investigating every aspect of the fire. Anticipating the public's demand for explanations and information, NASA requested that Congress hold off its own investigations until the review board had completed its work. One of the first acts carried out was the construction of a clear plastic shield, which was mounted over the gutted spacecraft to avoid the possibility of any crucial evidence being disturbed. Astronaut Frank Borman was the only person allowed in the spacecraft, and he spent hours at a time picking through the blackened interior, desperately trying to isolate the cause of the fire.

Sam Beddington was a seasoned engineer who had once been responsible for the pyrotechnics and recovery systems on the Mercury capsule. Grissom had talked him into joining NASA. "What they assigned me to do was to take the spacecraft apart, and take it apart so carefully that we could determine absolutely what made it blow up. I was so busy with that for six months, that I didn't have time to think about anything else. The first day of the fire, I was supposed to leave my job that night, and on Monday I was supposed to go over to the Program Office. Well, the fire happened at 6:31 P.M. on Friday and I finally got home to change clothes about 9:00 P.M. on Tuesday. That's how busy I was. I lost track of days and nights," Beddington said.

While Beddington's team began its onerous task, spacecraft 014, virtually identical to the Apollo 1 spacecraft, was shipped from California. The review board and its panels had this sister spacecraft similarly dismantled piece by piece for comparison with spacecraft 012. Every piece, every component, was studied and analyzed. While technicians in shifts worked twenty-four hours a day, the review board held daily recorded and transcribed sessions to consider the latest findings or theories.

In a preliminary report to NASA's administrator, Jim Webb, on 14 February, Deputy NASA Administrator Bob Seamans indicated that the fire was indeed a fire, and not an explosion leading to a fire. Physical evidence suggested that the conflagration had passed through more than one stage of intensity before the oxygen inside the cabin had been consumed. By mid-February, the work of tearing down the command module had reached the stage where a two-shift, six-day week could replace around-the-clock operations.

On 21 February, the day that should have seen the scheduled launch of Apollo 1, the board gave a preliminary briefing to George Mueller and other top NASA officials in preparation for a major briefing to Bob Seamans. The following day,

Dr. Thompson informed Seamans that fifteen hundred people were supporting the investigations—six hundred from government, and another nine hundred from industry and various universities. Thompson also stated that the board had planned to complete its report by the end of March. Although the history of the fire after it started had been minutely reconstructed, the specific source of ignition had not been, and might never be, fully determined.

On 25 February, Seamans prepared a memorandum for Jim Webb, listing early recommendations by the board that the administrator could present to Congress:

> "That combustible materials now used be replaced wherever possible with non-flammable materials, that non-metallic materials that are used be arranged to maintain fire breaks, that systems for oxygen or liquid combustibles be made fire resistant and that full flammability tests be conducted with a mock-up of the new configuration."
>
> "That a more rapidly and more easily opened hatch be designed and installed."
>
> "That on-the-pad emergencies be revised to recognize the possibility of a cabin fire."

As it composed its final report, the review board recognized that there had been sloth, ignorance, and carelessness associated with the Apollo 1 craft, but the key word in the detailed information was "oversight." According to the Summary Report of the Board, which was released on 5 April 1967, it seemed no one had realized the extent of fire hazards in an overpressurized, oxygen-filled spacecraft cabin on the ground. The report read, in part:

> *Although the Board was not able to determine conclusively the specific initiator of the Apollo 204 fire, it has identified the conditions which led to the disaster:*
>
> A sealed cabin, pressurized with an oxygen atmosphere,
> An extensive distribution of combustible materials in the cabin,
> Vulnerable wiring carrying spacecraft power,
> Vulnerable plumbing carrying a combustible and corrosive coolant,
> Inadequate provisions for the crew to escape and
> Inadequate provisions for rescue or medical assistance.
>
> *Having identified the conditions that led to the disaster, the Board addressed itself to the question of how these conditions came to exist. Careful consideration of this question leads the Board to the conclusion that in its devotion to the many difficult problems of space travel, the Apollo team failed to give adequate attention to certain mundane but equally vital questions of crew safety.*

*Deficiencies in the design, workmanship, and quality control of the command module were cited, together with the long troubled history of CSM 02 hardware removals and technical difficulties. All elements should be reviewed and the design of joints, wiring, ducting and other issues (such as coolant loop leakage and spillage) addressed. A full vibration test should be conducted and the most effective methods and supplies of equipment for fighting cabin fire investigated.*

*Too many open items were still an issue when the spacecraft was delivered from the prime contractor. Problems with program management and relationships between NASA field centers resulted in confusion and a lack of communication or understanding of responsibility and quality control issues.*

The Thompson Report came to almost three thousand pages and was divided into fourteen booklets. When these booklets were stacked, they created an imposing report some eight inches high. The six appendices were:

The Minutes of the Board's Own Proceedings
Eyewitness Statements and Releases
The Operations Handbook for Spacecraft 012
Final Reports of All Twenty-one Panels
A Brief Summary of Management and Organization
A Schedule of Visible Evidence.

The board also jolted recollections and made NASA spacecraft managers wonder if they had done everything to prevent the fire. During March 1965, Joe Shea and the Crew Systems Division had wrestled with the question of having a one- or two-gas atmosphere of oxygen and nitrogen (similar to what we breathe) in the spacecraft, and the likelihood of fire. Admittedly most of the studies were based on the possibility of fire in space, and it was concluded that creating a pure oxygen environment was safer, lighter in weight, and less complicated. The best way to guard against fire was simply to keep flammable materials out of the cabin—easier said than done, especially with the astronauts' known dependence on the nylon fastener Velcro. Hillard Paige of General Electric had warned Shea against the danger of fires, and only three weeks before the accident Dr. Berry had complained that it was harder to eliminate hazardous materials from the Apollo spacecraft than it had been in the Mercury or Gemini spacecraft.

NASA should have taken a leaf from the combined NASA/NAA X-15 research aircraft. This highly successful, high-altitude aircraft had a two-gas system. When a fire broke out during one X-15 landing, the aircraft was extensively damaged, but pilot Scott Crossfield managed to walk away unharmed as a result of a flight cabin supporting a two-gas system, even though he was not wearing the usual astronaut-style pressure suit and helmet. In its original submission to win the Apollo contract,

NAA had suggested a two-gas system. But such a system would be complicated, with each gas requiring separate regulators and a sensing device to maintain the correct mix.

Spacecraft designer Max Faget favored a pure oxygen environment: "To make sure that you have enough oxygen in the atmosphere, all you do is have to measure pressure. Pressure sensors are very reliable; they're rugged, simple, and mechanical. But a partial-pressure oxygen sensor is a classy little electronic thing. You have to process the signal, calibrate the sensor and have to have backup sensors."

The reasoning behind the use of pure oxygen seemed sound enough. In the vacuum of space the cabin pressure needed to be maintained at less than 6 pounds per square inch (psi). Tests had already proved that any fire at this pressure, even in a pure oxygen environment, could be easily contained and extinguished. During ground tests, however, a sea-level pressure of 14.7 psi would envelop the spacecraft. If the outside pressure exceeded that inside the spacecraft by more than 2 psi, there was a chance that the pressure hull could rupture, so it was impossible to test the spacecraft on the pad using the 5.2 to 5.6 psi that would be standard once the spacecraft had achieved orbit. Instead the engineers cranked up the interior to more than 16 psi to exceed sea-level pressure. It would prove to be a fatal error of reasoning: that easily contained fire in space at less than 6 psi would become an explosive inferno at 16 psi. Any fabric would ignite and burn with uncontrollable intensity, and even aluminum fittings would burn in the oxygen-rich environment.

According to NASA's associate administrator for manned spaceflight, George Mueller, "We spent a great deal of time to find the source of the fire, but it was literally a time bomb just sitting there waiting to go off . . . unfortunately it had to happen then. But we did persevere, and I would say that the good thing that came out of it was we really understood what causes fire on spacecraft. We redid most of the wiring, not that we knew the wiring was at fault, but rather we redid the wiring on Apollo and did it more professionally than the first time around. I think that's probably why the [later] Apollo Program was relatively accident free."

NAA Flight Surgeon Dr. Toby Freedman had argued vehemently against the pure oxygen atmosphere. At Litton Industries, he had witnessed a demonstration in which a piece of cloth was lit in a pure oxygen environment and literally vaporized. However, after many bitter arguments, NASA had settled on the one-gas system.

Once the board's report had been made public, the congressional hearings began. During one session of these hearings, an ambitious Senator (later Vice President) Walter Mondale raised the serious question of negligence by NASA and NAA managers. Mondale had managed to get hold of a copy of the Phillips Report and slammed NASA Administrator Jim Webb over his alleged incompetence.

Fortunately for NASA, Frank Borman was an effective and credible witness, both as a review board member and as an astronaut. In his testimony, Borman reiterated that the cause of the fire was oversight rather than negligence or overconfidence. Fire in all forms of flight had been a matter of concern since the early days of aviation and had been the subject of numerous studies. But the notion that the use of flammable materials and overpressurization of pure oxygen could greatly increase the fire hazard on the ground had never seriously been considered. The following week when Borman, Wally Schirra, Al Shepard, and Jim McDivitt expressed their confidence in NASA's future safety measures, Borman answered a cynical congressman's doubts, saying, "You are asking us do we have confidence in the spacecraft, NASA management, our own training, and . . . our leaders. I am almost embarrassed because our answers appear to be a party line. Everything I said last week has been repeated by the people I see today. The response we have given is the same because it is the truth. . . . We are trying to tell you that we are confident in our management, and in our engineering and in ourselves. I think the question is really: are you confident in us?"

By the time Borman had presented this statement to Congress, both NASA and NAA had responded to the Thompson Report and the criticisms from Congress. Top-level personnel changes were a direct consequence of the charges of mismanagement and negligence. Everett Christensen, the Apollo mission director at NASA Headquarters, resigned, and George Low replaced Joe Shea at the Manned Spacecraft Center in Houston. At NAA, Bill Bergen from the Martin Company replaced Harrison "Stormy" Storms as president of the Space and Information Systems Division. Most NAA officials successfully kept their jobs when they agreed under pressure with the findings and recommendations of the review board, although some privately disagreed that their company should shoulder the entire blame for the fire.

It would be some twenty-two months after the fire that another manned American spacecraft, Apollo 7, was launched into orbit. Barely ten months later Apollo 11, commanded by Neil Armstrong, landed on the moon. Left behind on the lunar surface was an Apollo 1 patch belonging to Scott Grissom, in recognition of the crew members who had given their lives to make a safe program possible.

The aftermath of the Apollo 1 fire had left NASA emphasizing crew safety before everything else, and this remained the policy until the mid-1980s, when NASA was once again inflicted with a spaceflight accident that nearly saw the end of the space agency and all human spaceflight activity by the United States.

Twenty years after the Apollo 1 fire, Lee Atwood, president of North American Aviation from 1948 until 1970, wrote a long and thoughtful recollection of the fire and its causes. His postscript to that recollection gave an important perspective on what it means to be involved in spaceflight and test flying:

> It is, of course, not possible to know, but if the question had been put properly to any of the top Apollo executives (including the writer), e.g., "Did you know that the astronauts are being locked in with all that electrical machinery and the spacecraft is being inflated to 16.7 pounds per square inch with pure oxygen?"—I believe a whistle would have been blown.

*But what about the Congressional investigators' favorite: "You knew or should have known"? "Should" is an interesting word. It lays on an obligation of diligence, perception, action and rectitude with little recip-rocal responsibility. It follows most of us all our lives, but fortunately, it seldom stops the clock.*

*After all organizations are large, and we all take a lot for granted. But "should" is pesky. It seems to skulk around just outside the light of the campfire, and sometimes when the moon is full, its shadowy profile can be seen, along with the misty images of long lost airplanes.*

Three brave men had sacrificed their lives in their nation's quest to reach the moon, but their deaths would soon be overshadowed by the triumphant achievements to follow, during which twelve men would walk on the moon.

For Ed White's family, there would be further grief when his younger brother, Captain James Blair White of the 357th Tactical Fighter Squadron, was listed as missing in action after his aircraft was shot down in 1969. On 24 November that year Captain White was the pilot of an F-105D Thunderchief flying as the number two aircraft assigned to a mission north of the Plain of Jars region of Xianghoang province in northern Laos. He had flown out of his base at Takhli in Thailand and simply never returned to base. Hopes were held that he might have been captured, but at war's end even that faint hope was dashed. A month before he was presumably shot down, Jim White had his photograph taken with some battle damage to his aircraft, and at that time he told the photographer, Jack Gurner, that his ambition was to finish his Vietnam tour and apply to become an astronaut, just like his big brother had been.

Ed White III revealed that his father's ultimate ambition had been to go back into the air force once he had completed his service with NASA, and to be assigned to the Air Force Academy, possibly as commandant of cadets. The air force was, after all, the life he loved.

In the following years there would be many tributes to Gus Grissom, Ed White, and Roger Chaffee. Schools, scholarship funds, planetariums, landmarks, and institutions were named for them. At Purdue University, in memory of two lost graduates, the old Civil Engineering Building was renamed Grissom Hall, while another was renamed Chaffee Hall. In May 1968 Bunker Hill Air Force Base in Peru, Indiana, officially became Grissom Air Force Base. Mitchell celebrated the life of its favorite son by erecting a memorial monument on South Sixth Street, while a Grissom Memorial Museum was erected in nearby Spring Mill State Park.

Thirty years after they died on the launch pad, President Bill Clinton honored the three astronauts at a White House ceremony, when he awarded the Congressional Space Medal of Honor to Ed White and Roger Chaffee. Gus Grissom had already received this prestigious award as the Apollo 1 commander and one of America's most accomplished astronauts. At that time only ten other astronauts had received the medal. President Jimmy Carter had awarded the first six to John Glenn, Neil Armstrong, Alan Shepard, Frank Borman, Pete Conrad, and posthumously to Gus Grissom. President Ronald Reagan presented one to John Young in 1981, President George Bush awarded the medal to Tom Stafford in 1993, and President Bill Clinton presented the medal to Jim Lovell in 1995 and to shuttle astronaut Shannon Lucid in 1996.

The families of Ed White and Roger Chaffee were there at the White House, together with Betty Grissom. Family members were told that the ceremony recognized the nation's significant but unspoken debt of gratitude to the Apollo 1 crew, whose tragic experience led to the establishment of major safety review processes that helped America land safely on the moon and that continue to protect the nation's astronauts today.

For the family of Roger Chaffee it was a doubly satisfying time. A few weeks earlier he had finally been inducted into the Astronaut Hall of Fame after years of denial by the administrators of this private foundation. With their earlier refusal to admit Roger Chaffee, based on the fact that this would have been his maiden flight, Betty Grissom had resigned in protest from the group's board of directors. Eventually the board changed its policy, and Roger Chaffee was finally inducted. Her stand vindicated, Betty Grissom rejoined the board.

Sheryl Chaffee Marshall was delighted that her father was finally gaining some of the recognition he deserved. "My view on being inducted is that it's for some significant contribution you've made," she said at the time. "Flying in space isn't the only contribution. After my father's death, there was so much that NASA figured out and fixed. He believed in the space program. He knew it was dangerous. He gave his life for it and he was willing to do that. He was doing this for the good of the country."

On a tiny area of the moon's surface facing Earth there's a crater named Grissom, and Betty Grissom remains proud of that honor bestowed upon her late husband. "One way or another," she reflected, "I still think old Gus was up there first."

On 27 February 2001 a Titan IV-B booster was launched from Cape Canaveral Air Force Station's Launch Complex 40 carrying the Milstar II F4, a Military Strategic and Tactical Relay System satellite. Traditionally the air force mission managers apply a nickname to each Titan IV-B launch vehicle, and this time in honor of the Apollo 1 crew the rocket had been code-named "Gus." The inspiration behind the tribute was air force captain Reece Stephenson, who had also designed a unique mission patch to commemorate the astronauts who had lost their lives thirty-four years before. The decision had been announced during a special memorial service at Kennedy's Launch Pad 34 a month earlier, and a special collage incorporating the mission patch had been produced for each of the three families.

Michele Tate, who created the artwork for the collage, said, "At first, I thought this project would be a small, behind-the-scenes presentation to the families, but it became a much larger, symbolic gesture on behalf of the Air Force to say to the astronauts' families that we appreciate them, that they're not forgotten. The collage honors the crew of Apollo 1, as well as the men and women in the space program today."

On launch day, the rocket named "Gus" rose majestically into the heavens. Eye-witnesses who knew the significance of the booster's nickname and had cheered the successful launch were soon astonished to see the wind slowly carve the Titan's lingering exhaust contrail into a gigantic number—the number 3.

# 4  By the Light of a Soviet Moon
## Russia's Cosmonauts

*On 20 July 1969, lunar module* Eagle *touched down on the surface of the moon,
carrying astronauts Neil Armstrong and Edwin ("Buzz") Aldrin. It is now known
that the Soviet Union had a program aimed at landing a lone cosmonaut on the
moon before America, but this mission was abandoned because of the success of
the Apollo program and insurmountable technical shortcomings.*

*The names of six Soviet cosmonauts graced the commemorative plaque left on the
moon by the crew of Apollo 15: Yuri Gagarin, Pavel Belyayev, Vladimir Komarov,
Georgy Dobrovolsky, Viktor Patsayev, and Vladislav Volkov. All had flown into
space amid tumultuous publicity, and the latter four had died during the course of
their missions. When David Scott slid the plaque into the lunar soil at the plains
of Hadley, he knew that the names of Russia's cosmonauts might not be complete.*

Since the embryonic days of manned spaceflight, rumors had persisted that unknown cosmonauts had been buried in secret graves. According to the tales, they
had perished during training accidents and, more alarmingly, in actual spaceflight.
A cosmonaut named Alexei Ledovsky was said to have perished in 1957 during a suborbital flight when "transmission was abruptly halted" at a height of two hundred
miles. An explosion at stratospheric altitude in an experimental "space aircraft" is
also said to have taken the life of female cosmonaut Mirija Gromova. In 1960 an
unknown cosmonaut was said to have died when his capsule flew into orbit but
headed off in the wrong direction.

According to a widely spread story at the time, cosmonaut Pyotr Dolgov was
launched into space on 11 October 1960. At that time, Premier Nikita Khrushchev
was visiting the United Nations in New York. He kept extending his stay, and American tracking stations were alerted that there could be a Soviet space feat aimed
at boosting Khrushchev's prestige. After days of waiting and intense speculation,
listening posts in England, Italy, Japan, and Turkey were reported to have finally
homed in on a Soviet launch, and tape recorders began preserving the signals.
Among the signals was the regular beating of a human heart. As the rocket reached
its first staging point the heartbeat pulsed faster as the cosmonaut showed a normal
reaction of fear and excitement at this critical phase. Suddenly, at the moment
the second stage should have ignited, all signals ceased and the tracking devices
lost all contact. Dolgov was allegedly incinerated in a fiery explosion. Lieutenant
Colonel Paul Hickman of the U.S. Army asserted at a National Security Seminar
Conference in Hawaii the following January that there was "good evidence" of two
Soviet cosmonauts dying in unsuccessful attempts to place a manned spacecraft in
orbit. The Pentagon immediately repudiated his remarks.

One would think that the passage of four decades would bring enlightenment, but on the fortieth anniversary of Yuri Gagarin's flight, 12 April 2001, Reuters boldly published a bulletin quoting an Interfax news agency report that three Soviet pilots had died in secret test launches before Gagarin's flight. Interfax quoted Mikhail Rudenko, who worked as an engineer "in one of the main Soviet space centers," as saying that three suborbital flights had been carried out from Kapustin Yar cosmodrome in southern Russia in 1957, 1958, and 1959. Rudenko said that all three flights, in which rockets followed a parabolic trajectory that briefly entered outer space at the highest point, ended in failure and the death of the sole cosmonauts. He even gave their names as Ledovskikh (presumably the previously mentioned Ledovsky), Shiborin, and Mitkov. When asked to comment on the report, Sergei Gorbunov, spokesman for Russia's space and aviation agency Rosaviakosmos, said it was "foolishness, just plain foolishness. I don't think this even deserves comment. It is just an old legend associated with Gagarin's flight."

While Reuters tried to make out that the report was startling news, researchers had known of stories concerning alleged cosmonauts Serenty Shiborin and Andrei Mitkov and their fatal suborbital flights for many years. They could only shake their heads at these fresh and unsubstantiated rumors.

According to the rumor mill, the year 1961, when Yuri Gagarin became the first man to fly into space, was also a bad one for Soviet cosmonauts. Three men named as Belokonev, Grachev, and Kachur were said to have died in precursor Vostok flights in which the sounds of heartbeats were also said to have been monitored.

Then, just one day before Gagarin lifted off on his epic voyage, the British Communist Party newspaper *Daily Worker* carried a dramatic article by a Moscow-based correspondent named Dennis Ogden, reporting on the flight mishap of "cosmonaut" Vladimir Ilyushin. Ogden, who lived in the same building as Ilyushin, had picked up on strong rumors of an impending Soviet spaceflight. Knowing that Ilyushin—a test pilot, and the son of aviation and spacecraft designer Sergei Ilyushin—had been hospitalized after an unexplained accident, he created the story that the Russian had been launched into space in December 1960 and had circled the globe three times. Ogden speculated that the world's first cosmonaut was so badly injured during his flawed ejection landing that the Soviet government considered him unsuitable for presentation as a national hero. Although the Russian space administrators were intensely secretive about their early cosmonauts, it is positively known that Ilyushin was not one of them (and in fact had been gravely injured on 8 June 1960 in an automobile accident).

On 17 May 1961, just weeks after Gagarin's triumphant return from space, two more cosmonauts—a man and a woman—are said to have died in space, uttering feeble calls for help as they orbited into oblivion. A solar flare occurring on 14 October 1961 is said to have dramatically altered the course of a three-man Soviet spacecraft, and it disappeared forever into deep space. The hapless Alexei Belokonev then apparently died a second time after being launched on a flight on 8 November

1962, while an unnamed female cosmonaut met her fate in space on 19 November 1963.

In May 1962 cosmonaut Major Gherman Titov, Gagarin's backup pilot and the man who flew the first one-day mission aboard Vostok-2, was asked about the rumors of cosmonaut fatalities during a television interview in New York. When asked if the Soviet Union had lost a cosmonaut before the successful flight of Yuri Gagarin, Titov responded, "I have heard about that. According to your newspapers, the Soviet Union has lost not one, but five cosmonauts. They even named them. We had no cosmonauts in our country before the first cosmonaut, Yuri Gagarin."

But even in the face of such denials, the rumors would not go away. Early in 1963, as an example of the extent and strength of "dead cosmonaut" stories, the Canadian Press Agency made the startling claim that at least two cosmonauts had died in space. The agency backed up the assertion by saying that the fatalities had been reported in the 31 December 1962 issue of the Soviet government newspaper *Izvestia*. A Russian-speaking correspondent of the *Vancouver Sun,* Arthur Karday, was said to have spotted the reference in a lengthy article about the twin flight in August 1962 of Andrian Nikolayev and Pavel Popovich. In the body of the article, according to Karday, the following appeared: "One of the truly magnificent and awe-inspiring monuments to the human spirit is the self-sacrifice of two other heavenly heroes—Andreyev and Dolgov. One of them, Dolgov, was destined not to return from the stratosphere. He, like the Gorkian eagle, sacrificed his life in order to save hundreds and perhaps thousands of other spacemen through his heroism."

No hint of the circumstances was given in the *Izvestia* article, but it was revealed some years later that Pyotr Dolgov (who was never a cosmonaut) had actually died while engaged in testing an ejector seat to be used in the recovery system for future spacemen. When he exited from a balloon gondola at around ninety-four thousand feet, his helmet visor hit the gondola's hatch and cracked. At that extreme altitude this sudden lack of oxygen, combined with the freezing cold, quickly proved fatal. Although it seems the egress process continued, he was dead when recovery teams reached him.

In the following years other cosmonauts are said to have died in ground and spaceflight accidents, and the world became convinced that some of the rumors about deceased cosmonauts simply had to have some credence. In the early 1960s the rumors about dead cosmonauts almost equalled those concerning the demise of Beatle Paul McCartney later that decade. Soviet space officials still brusquely dismissed the tales but would issue no clarifications when pressed for information, which only served to exacerbate the matter.

Rumors of cosmonaut deaths fed on the obvious reluctance of Russian space officials to discuss anything but their successes. The inherent secrecy of the Russian space program, combined with the Soviets' traditional practice of gross exaggeration, lying, "reinventing" events, and retouching official photos also led space experts around the world to believe that accidents had occurred and been hushed up. Many years later, photographs of men who were obviously cosmonauts began turning up, but official versions of those same photographs had these men airbrushed out. Clumsy, painted-in scenery replaced the images of these mysterious men, while hints of names of some missing Russian cosmonauts began appearing in Soviet books and magazines. It was clear that a huge cover-up had taken place.

Spaceflight writer and investigator James Oberg was at the forefront of those seeking the shrouded truth behind the early Soviet space program. His ground-breaking book *Red Star in Orbit* not only revealed many previously unknown Soviet failures in space but also lifted the lid on Russia's attempts to conceal the identities of several cosmonauts who had either died or been dismissed from the space team. He raised many questions in his book, and most would be answered over the next few years, as the lies and deceits of an earlier era slowly crumbled, and many hidden truths finally came to light.

Oberg and other Western analysts tried for several years to clear up the rumors of Soviet space fatalities, but it was not until 1986 that the Russians finally came clean. In a revealing series of articles published in *Izvestia* to celebrate the twenty-fifth anniversary of Gagarin's flight, leading space journalist Yaroslav Golovanov not only finally gave the names of Russia's first cosmonauts but also reported on the sad deaths of two.

These days scores of researchers have revealed the chronology of Soviet space-flight, although much of this information has been hard won. There was a natural, if rushed, sequence leading up to Gagarin's epic flight. This included precursor flights of Vostok rockets carrying a number of dogs and mannequins to study orbital and ejection processes. In one such exercise, about a month before Gagarin's flight, a group of Russian villagers saw an orange-clad spaceman floating down under a huge parachute after ejecting from his space capsule, which touched down nearby. The cosmonaut then tipped over on landing and remained inert. When anxious villagers reached the site, they found to their relief that the "cosmonaut" (launched under the code name "Ivan Ivanovich") was in fact a space-suited mannequin. The name "Maket" had been prominently painted on his back and helmet—the Russian word for "dummy." Mannequin hero "Ivan" actually made two such ejections after short spaceflights, and in the early 1990s he suffered the ignominy of being sold to the highest bidder at a Sotheby's sale!

The first group of cosmonauts has been fully identified, and none has myste-riously vanished. Injuries and even deaths attributable to spaceflight training have now been revealed, and those involving cosmonauts are well documented. Eminent researchers have meticulously collated lists of every R-7 rocket and spacecraft and payload ever built by the Soviet Union, and each has been accounted for. No matter what alleged "evidence" exists, no one has ever explained how several R-7 launch vehicles could have been produced without appearing somewhere in Soviet records, and launched—particularly with cosmonauts onboard—without being recorded by the Soviets or noted by Western intelligence agencies. This dilemma alone precludes any previously unannounced or "missing" flights: no launch vehicles, no cosmonauts. Rumors and speculation surrounding the Soviet Union's space program, aided by officials' tight-lipped secrecy and overt duplicity, were mostly the results of reporters eager to reveal a huge cover-up.

The patchwork of fabrication still echoes today. In 1998 the now-defunct American spaceflight magazine *Final Frontier* ran a sensational article in which a writer said he had "uncovered" archival material in Moscow, detailing unknown cosmonaut deaths in the early 1960s. James Oberg and dozens of other Western analysts of the Soviet space program could only sigh and reiterate their painstaking and meticulous research. The so-called archival material was already well known and dismissed as a load of rubbish. But once again a new generation of spaceflight enthusiasts was questioning whether cosmonauts had indeed been lost in space.

Returning once again to the facts, twenty military pilots composed the first cosmonaut detachment. They had been interviewed and chosen by 25 February 1960 and reported for training through late April. Of those twenty, only twelve would eventually fly into space. The remaining eight failed to continue in the space program for a number of reasons: three were dismissed for varying acts of insubordination, three were medically disqualified, and two died.

The names of the two cosmonauts who had died, Valentin Bondarenko and Grigori Nelyubov, were not known to the Western world when the Apollo 15 crew prepared its tribute plaque. However, the circumstances of their lives and deaths are now known to us and are revealed in the following condensed accounts. They are told chronologically, in the order of their deaths.

### Valentin Vasilyevich Bondarenko (1937–61)

It was a cold spring morning late in March 1961 when a small funeral procession moved toward a cemetery in the Ukrainian city of Kharkov, in the central Soviet Union. It seemed to be a funeral not unlike tens of thousands before, and like tens of thousands yet to come. A young widow and a small boy were following the coffin, an indication that it was a young man who was about to be buried. And indeed it was. His name was Valentin Bondarenko, and he had turned twenty-four years old the previous month.

Bondarenko had been an air force pilot, and anyone knowing this would have naturally assumed that he had crashed in a jet plane. The monument erected over his grave several months later would also give this impression. Underneath his portrait, name, and dates of birth and death, it said, "With fond memories from your pilot friends."

The grave remained virtually unnoticed and anonymous for a quarter of a century. Then, on the eve of the twenty-fifth anniversary of Yuri Gagarin's historic first manned spaceflight, the Soviet government's newspaper *Izvestia* published a series of articles on the first group of cosmonauts. The articles brought forth many

21. Valentin Vasilyevich Bondarenko (Courtesy Bert Vis)

new and previously hidden facts about these men, who had vigorously competed to make that first flight into space.

Having turned twenty-three only nine days before he was selected for cosmonaut training, Bondarenko was the youngest of the twenty air force pilots who made up the first group. In fact, to this day, no one younger has been selected as an astronaut or cosmonaut.

Valentin Vasilyevich Bondarenko was born in Kharkov on 16 February 1937 and attended the Armavir Higher Air Force School, graduating in 1957. By this time he had married Galina Semyonovna, and they had a son named Alexandr. As a Soviet Air Force fighter pilot, he then served in the Baltic Union Republics for two years. He was one of hundreds of young pilots interviewed by a team of military doctors late in 1959 for a secret new research program, and by February the following year a total of twenty pilots, including Bondarenko, had been selected, notified, and ordered to report for duties as their country's first group of cosmonauts. The delighted Bondarenko might have become world famous, like Yuri Gagarin, Gherman Titov, or Alexei Leonov, had he not made a fatal mistake during one moment of absentmindedness.

In 1960, six out of the group of twenty cosmonauts were chosen for advanced training. They would compete to make the first flights in the Soviet Union's Vostok spacecraft. Bondarenko was not among them; his age was in all probability one of the factors that had kept him out of the group. His turn would come later, he thought.

The fourteen pilots in the second-string group continued the general training and ground experimenting that made up everyday life for the cosmonauts. Among the things they underwent were isolation tests, as Vostok crew members were eventually planned to remain in orbit for several days. This flight time would be spent in a confined space aboard the capsule, and under circumstances that were totally unknown at the time, simply because no one had yet flown into space. Doctors and psychologists constantly monitored the subjects during these tests to assess the way in which isolation might affect them. The main purpose was clear: if the test subject "lost it," he would be deemed unsuitable for spaceflight.

In mid-March 1961 Bondarenko entered a pressure chamber for a ten-day isolation test. The chamber was then filled with a pure oxygen atmosphere at a pressure higher than that outside. But the young cosmonaut trainee had no trouble during his stay—he had done it before and had always managed to finish the tests to everyone's satisfaction. When the test came to an end Bondarenko removed the medical sensors from his body that had helped doctors to monitor his heart rate, respiration, and other functions. He then used a small piece of cotton soaked in alcohol to clean the spots where the sensors had been attached. Without thinking, he threw the cotton wad away. It landed on an electric hot plate used for heating his food, and immediately caught fire. In the oxygen-rich environment the flames grew rapidly, billowing out and setting Bondarenko's training suit alight as he frantically tried to put out the fire. Doctors outside the chamber saw what was happening and tried to open up the chamber and extinguish the intense flames. But to their horror they found it was impossible to open the door until the pressure inside the chamber was equal to that outside. Finally, after several terrifying minutes, they managed to get Bondarenko out of his death trap.

The sight confronting the doctors was a horrifying one. Severe burns covered Bondarenko from head to foot, his training suit had melted, and the skin had been stripped from his body. He was completely hairless, and his eyes had been burned from their sockets. Incredibly enough the young cosmonaut was still alive, and muttering that it was his fault. He was rushed to the hospital but soon went into shock. After eight agonizing hours Bondarenko's tortured body gave up an unwinnable struggle, and he passed away.

The news of the cosmonaut's death was immediately suppressed and became a state top secret. No one would know of Bondarenko's death, other than those who had organized the test, witnessed the accident, treated the dying man, or had professional connections with the cosmonauts. The incident remained secret for the next twenty-five years.

Despite the cover-up, in the early 1980s two intriguing stories began to emerge from Russians who had moved to the West. The stories concerned the death of a young cosmonaut, who had burned to death in an accident around the time of Gagarin's flight in April 1961. The cosmonaut's name was said to be Boyko or Boychenko in one story, and Sergeyev in the other. In the end, both stories proved to be remarkably correct in detail, especially since it was clear that both authors had to rely on their memories in relating the facts that they knew. At the time, however, the Soviets would not confirm any information, and it would take another couple of years before full and graphic details of the accident were published.

It turned out that three weeks after the deadly fire, and almost as if nothing had happened, Yuri Gagarin had boarded his Vostok and flown around the Earth, making him the most famous person on the planet. While Gagarin was being honored and feted all over the Soviet Union, Bondarenko's widow, Galina, and her five-year-old son were still trying to cope with the loss of a loved husband and father.

The twenty-five-year secrecy of Bondarenko's death infuriated many American observers. They felt that if the Soviets had been more open at the time, the fire might have served as a warning to NASA with regard to the dangers of working with a pure oxygen atmosphere on board its spacecraft. The information might, these Americans argued, have even saved the lives of astronauts Grissom, White, and Chaffee.

The revelation of what happened to Bondarenko back in 1961 also resulted in some activity in that cemetery in Kharkov. Once the story was out, the epitaph on his grave was amended. From that time on it read, "With fond memories from your pilot and cosmonaut friends."

Valentin Bondarenko was finally accorded his rightful place in spaceflight history.

### Grigori Grigoryevich Nelyubov (1934–66)

Grigori Nelyubov's life—once so full of zeal and daring—ended in ignominy. Selected in the first cosmonaut detachment in March 1960, he was a young man who might have blazed a trail of glory across the firmament. In fact at one time he was well on line to become the first man in space. But he died in disgrace, under the wheels of a locomotive, spurned by the same nation that might once have embraced him as a colossus of the space age.

Grigori Nelyubov was born in the Crimea on 31 March 1934, and he later attended the Yeisk Higher Air Force School. He brought the skills and daring of his MiG-19 piloting days to the cosmonaut corps, quickly becoming a star pupil and a leading candidate for one of the first flights. He was brash and fiercely competitive and made a point of excelling at all exercises and academic tests laid before him. Apparently Boris Raushenbakh, one of the space program's top officials, was openly advocating Nelyubov as the one who should fly the first space mission. But the young pilot's zeal, and his unconcealed desire to make that pioneering flight, also meant that he soon made a number of potent enemies—many of them in places of influence. Foremost among these was Lieutenant General Nikolai Kamanin, the chief of cosmonaut

22. Grigori Grigoryevich Nelyubov (Courtesy Bert Vis)

training. He did not like Nelyubov's egotistical and outspoken manner, or the way he continually questioned his superiors' decisions. However, he was an outstanding pilot—recognized as perhaps the best in his group—who had worked and studied hard, so Kamanin simply kept a close eye on the young cosmonaut trainee. In July 1960 six of the twenty cosmonauts were selected for concentrated spaceflight training, and it was obvious that Russia's first cosmonaut would come from this elite group. To his undisguised delight, Nelyubov was one of those chosen.

Despite being selected for advanced training, the brash Nelyubov had eventually rubbed the influential Kamanin the wrong way. This meant he lost the chance to be the world's first spaceman when Lieutenant Yuri Gagarin was accorded the great honor. It was further announced to the cosmonauts that Gherman Titov would act as backup pilot for the first Vostok mission. However, Nelyubov did have a role to play in the historic flight, as second backup after Titov. All things being equal, it then followed that he should have served as backup pilot to Titov on the following mission, but again Kamanin's influence was brought to bear. He felt that Nelyubov was unsuited to fly on a solo mission scheduled to last for a full day in space, and replaced him with fellow cosmonaut Andrian Nikolayev.

If Nelyubov felt he would fly on the following mission, involving two cosmonauts flying simultaneously aboard Vostok-3 and 4, he was in for yet another serious disappointment. Kamanin announced that cosmonauts Nikolayev and Popovich would be the pilots, and appointed Nelyubov to the lesser role of ground communicator with the orbiting cosmonauts. Despite these salutary lessons in knowing his place in the system, it is believed Nelyubov was then in line for his first flight. But then his outspoken defiance caused him to be sent spiraling downward from the lofty heights of spaceflight immortality and into the depths of depression and despair.

One evening in May 1963 Nelyubov and fellow cosmonaut trainees Ivan Anikeyev and Valentin Filatyev had been out to dinner on a weekend pass and were returning to the space training center, a walk of almost two miles. They had presumably been drinking, as their loud behavior soon brought them to the notice of a military security patrol on the Chkalovsky railway station. Words were exchanged when the men failed to produce proper credentials for passing through the checkpoint, and a small fracas resulted. The three were subsequently arrested and placed under guard in the office of the duty officer. A check verified that the three men were indeed cosmonauts from the nearby training center.

Nelyubov grew increasingly incensed at their treatment and felt his position in the cosmonaut corps should merit a little more respect. For his part, the duty officer of the security patrol was outraged at the behavior of the overbearing young man, but gave Nelyubov and the others a chance to have the incident pass with little more than a reprimand on the spot. If they apologized for their behavior the charges would be dropped. Anikeyev and Filatyev quickly agreed, but the arrogant Nelyubov declined, suggesting he had friends in high places who would not look kindly on the man if he filed his report. The officer, who had been prepared to let the whole thing pass as a silly drunken episode, had heard enough. He submitted a scathing report of the incident, and it quickly hit the desk of Nikolai Kamanin. To stress the need for strict discipline, and to give a cogent warning to other possible transgressors, Kamanin immediately dismissed the three cosmonauts from the team.

A shattered man, Nelyubov could not come to terms with the fact that he had been sacked and would never fly into space, and had caused his friends to be dismissed from the program. He subsequently returned to flying as part of an interceptor squadron based near Vladivostok.

As his colleagues continued to fly into space, Nelyubov would tell anyone who cared to listen that he had been a cosmonaut, and even a backup to Yuri Gagarin. But by now he had begun drinking heavily. His stories were scoffed at, dismissed as the wishful dreams of a sad loner. A deep depression had also begun to set in, and on 18 February 1966, after another heavy bout of drinking, Grigori Nelyubov walked in front of a train at Ippolitovka, northwest of Vladivostok. It is widely assumed the disgraced cosmonaut took his own life, but the incident has always been officially cited as a "railway accident."

It was not until 1986—a quarter of a century after Yuri Gagarin's pioneering flight—that Grigori Nelyubov was finally revealed as a member of the first group of cosmonauts.

## *Vladimir Mikhailovich Komarov (1927–67)*

Vladimir Komarov's name is in the history books for two distinct reasons—he was not only the first cosmonaut to fly into space twice but also the first space explorer to die during a mission. A member of the first group of cosmonauts, he was held in high esteem by his comrades. Universally well liked, Komarov soon became known to his colleagues as "Volodya"—a playfully affectionate form of his first name. Pavel Popovich, also from that first detachment, said of Komarov, "He was one of the oldest in our group; he was already an engineer when he joined us, but he never looked down on the others. He was warm-hearted, purposeful and industrious. Volodya's prestige was so high that people came to him to discuss all questions: personal as well as questions of our work."

Vladimir Komarov was born in Moscow on 16 March 1927 and passed his childhood in that city. He loved quiet Third Meshchanskaya Street in which he lived, and School No. 235, where he first began his education. On top of an old wardrobe in his bedroom he kept a much-admired collection of model planes he had made himself, while inside the wardrobe were pictures of planes, magazines, and a propeller he had carefully cut out of a tin can. But most of all he liked to climb up the stairs of his house, through a narrow door on the top landing, and cross a dark, silent attic to a dormer window. From here the city of Moscow spread out before him, but it was not the view that fascinated him—it was the airplanes that flew overhead. At a very early age he could identify the different fighters or bombers by the sound of their engines before they came into view. His infatuation with airplanes only grew stronger as he grew older.

At the age of fifteen Komarov enrolled at an air force school, and he officially joined the Red Army in July 1945. This was just a few weeks after the end of World War II, known in the Soviet Union as the "Great Patriotic War."

Komarov married his sweetheart, Valentina Kiselyova, in October 1950, and the following year their son Yevgeny was born. He continued to serve in the air force and in November 1951 was promoted to senior fighter pilot. From 1954 he undertook aviation studies at the Zhukovsky Military Air Academy, graduating in 1959. At one point he was also awarded the title of test pilot third class. In December 1958, while he was studying at the academy, Valentina gave birth to their second child, a daughter they named Irina.

In 1960, Komarov was one of twenty pilots selected as the first group of cosmonauts, but he would have to overcome many difficulties before he finally made it into space. Shortly after his selection he fell ill and was hospitalized for an operation on a ruptured hernia. It took him six months to regain his health, and then he rejoined his colleagues at the spaceflight training center. Despite fears that he had fallen too far behind in the training program, he soon managed to catch up with the others. His diligence and perseverance were rewarded when he was assigned as second backup to Pavel Popovich for Vostok-4. He then moved up to become

23. Vladimir Mikhailovich Komarov (Courtesy Bert Vis)

first backup when the cosmonaut originally holding that position was medically disqualified.

For a while it looked as if Komarov might get the chance to fly a Vostok himself, when an ambitious flight program was devised that would consist of three ships flying in space at the same time. Eventually it was decided that only two spacecraft would be launched, and one would carry the first woman into space, Valentina Tereshkova. Officials felt that this tactic alone would create the desired worldwide sensation.

In February 1964 the Vostok program was terminated, but the chief designer, Sergei Korolev, was given a direct order to convert one of the four remaining one-man Vostok ships into a craft capable of carrying three cosmonauts. The main cause of this direction was the imminent first flight of America's two-seater Gemini spacecraft. Something even more spectacular and audacious was needed, something to convince the Americans that the Soviet Union still held a substantial lead in the Space Race.

The size of this "new" craft, christened Voskhod, caused considerable difficulty for the embattled Korolev, but in the end he managed to squeeze in three seats. This was accomplished at the expense of safety. While the Vostok cosmonauts had used ejection seats to parachute to a safe landing, the Voskhod crew would be forced to remain in the descent capsule until touchdown, which would be far from a comfortable landing. In addition, to save weight and due to a lack of space inside the craft, the planners made a risk-laden decision to dispense with the crew's protective space suits.

A battle started between the various institutions and departments that wanted to have their own representative in the crew. The Vostok program's policy was that seats would be occupied only by qualified air force pilots. Now two additional seats had suddenly become available, and Korolev's design bureau, the Academy of Sciences, and the Ministry of Public Health all wanted their own man onboard. For months bitter discussions dragged on, but in the end a compromise was reached: it was decided that the crew would consist of Komarov as commander; Konstantin Feoktistov, a deputy of Chief Designer Korolev; and Boris Yegorov, a medical doctor.

Voskhod was launched on 12 October 1964 and returned after a flight lasting one day and seventeen minutes. Following a safe landing, the relieved Korolev reportedly said that he could not believe the crew had survived and returned from orbit in one piece, as he simply did not think it was possible to turn a one-man Vostok into a three-man spacecraft.

Although it was lavishly reported that Komarov had been testing spacecraft systems while his two companions conducted medical and geophysical experiments, it became abundantly clear in later years that the real task of the crew was principally to get into space, do a few loops around the Earth, and get back down again. There was precious little room in the spacecraft to do anything else. It was the propaganda factor that mattered—everything else was incidental.

The crew's return was largely overshadowed by other events in the Soviet Union. Following their successful landing, the members were expecting the traditional congratulatory phone call from CPSU General Secretary Nikita Khrushchev, but they waited in vain. On the day they landed Khrushchev had been deposed and replaced by Leonid Brezhnev, who greeted the cosmonauts after their return to Moscow on 19 October.

The flight of Voskhod was followed six months later by that of Voskhod-2. During this twenty-six-hour mission cosmonaut Alexei Leonov managed to steal yet another space "first" from the Americans by conducting the world's first space walk in advance of Ed White's announced attempt of this feat. Although the world now waited for the next stunning Soviet spaceflight achievement, nothing but a curious silence filled the next two years.

On 23 April 1967 the self-imposed silence came to an end when the Soviet press agency reported the successful launch of Soyuz-1, carrying veteran cosmonaut Vladimir Komarov. While most people simply accepted the news, there was mounting excitement for those sleuthing the Soviet space program for clues on the cosmonaut team as well as program and mission plans. It was historically significant that for the first time a cosmonaut was flying a second mission, but what really captured their attention was the name of the spacecraft. The word Soyuz means "union," and although this could have been a simple reference to the USSR, many were convinced that it was also a reference to a planned docking with a second ship. What was also remarkable was that the spaceship was named "Soyuz-1." In the Vostok and Voskhod programs the first ships to be launched had not carried a number designation. Gagarin's spacecraft had simply been called Vostok, and Gherman Titov's Vostok-2. The same applied for Voskhod and Voskhod-2. Observers felt that this number designation had significant implications, and they were right: Soyuz-2 was already on the launch pad.

But then things began to go wrong. Shortly after liftoff Komarov experienced some serious difficulties, and resolving these became his main objective. First, one of the two solar panels intended to supply power to Soyuz-1 failed to deploy shortly after the spacecraft reached orbit. Then, in spite of several attempts, Komarov was unable to manually align his craft after the automatic orientation system failed. The State Commission was advised that the Soyuz-2 launch, set to take place the following day, should be postponed or abandoned. That craft was planned to carry three cosmonauts, two of whom would make a space walk from Soyuz-2 to Komarov's ship after docking, and all three would eventually land in Soyuz-1. Incredibly, the recommendation was ignored, and preparations for the second launch continued. Only hours later, when it became evident that Komarov was unable to rectify the orientation situation, a decision was finally made to cancel the launch of Soyuz-2.

For the best part of twenty-seven hours Komarov worked desperately to gain control over his ship, but his best efforts were all in vain, and he finally received word that Soyuz-1 would be brought back to Earth. A first attempt failed when the craft was not properly aligned for reentry, but a second on the nineteenth orbit was successful, and Soyuz-1 plunged back into the atmosphere.

At this time more things went horribly wrong for Komarov. The main parachute would not deploy due to what was later found to be a design fault in the parachute container. This meant that a smaller drag chute, which opened as planned, was unable to haul out the main parachute. Once the main chute failure occurred a reserve chute was deployed, and this contingency plan would have been successful had it not been for the fact that the small drag chute became inextricably tangled in the reserve parachute. Komarov, sitting anxiously in the plummeting descent module, would have become aware moments later that nothing had happened to retard his fall to Earth. A sudden realization would have swept over him that he was moments away from death. As the Soyuz-1 spacecraft smashed into the ground at high speed, small braking rocket engines, designed to fire moments before a nominal touchdown, exploded. The shattered capsule erupted into flames.

Many years later some remarkable film footage taken shortly after the crash was finally released. It graphically showed the still burning remains of the spacecraft and desperate attempts to extinguish the fire. Later, the recovery crews could do little but extract what they could find of Komarov's charred remains for transportation back to Moscow. The same footage also showed what appeared to be a small provisional grave, covered with an officer's uniform cap. In 1992, the *Moscow News* reported that in the days following the crash Young Pioneers had found more human remains buried at the crash site. However, this report was subsequently refuted with an emphatic statement that the site in question actually marked the place where small remains of the Soyuz-1 descent module itself had been interred.

Komarov's death was a tremendous blow to the Soviet space program, and the whole nation fell into a shocked, collective sadness. His remains were inurned in the Kremlin Wall with full military honors on 26 April. At that time it was not known that Yuri Gagarin had actually been Komarov's backup for the mission. Nor could Gagarin or anyone else have known that less than a year later, another funeral inurnment would take place just a few yards away, this time for the world's first and most famous spaceman.

The usual shroud of secrecy surrounded the flight of Soyuz-1, which brought forth an equally usual string of rumors about Komarov's death. It was said that his wife, Valentina, had been brought to mission control to bid an emotional, tearful farewell to her doomed husband. Prime Minister Alexei Kosygin was said to have talked with Komarov, telling the cosmonaut that his country was proud of him and his forthcoming sacrifice for the space program. During the descent module's reentry American listening stations were reported to have listened to Komarov's pitiful cries while he plummeted to Earth, cursing and renouncing a government that had ordered him to carry out a flight in a trouble-plagued craft that was launched well before it was ready.

Serious observers of the Soviet space program are absolutely certain that these rumors are false. For starters, the program's mission control was situated in Yevpatoriya in the Crimea, while Valentina Komarov would have been at home in Moscow. In addition, mission control would have lost contact with the cosmonaut shortly before the descent module separated from the other two spacecraft modules. This was a perfectly normal occurrence for any returning spacecraft: the ionized air surrounding it causes a radio blackout lasting several minutes. In 1992 the author spoke with an unflown cosmonaut named Alexander Petrushenko, who had literally been the last person in contact with the doomed cosmonaut. During this exchange, Komarov simply reported to Petrushenko that he had carried out the final correction maneuver and was preparing for his return to Earth.

When a successful reentry had been accomplished, Komarov would have felt that any real peril connected with his flight was virtually over. The failure of his parachute system was totally unrelated to the problems he had encountered while in orbit and would have come as a surprise to the descending cosmonaut just seconds from a planned touchdown.

Komarov's early return from space, and his death, probably saved the lives of the three cosmonauts preparing to fly into space aboard Soyuz-2. Two would have perished with him, while investigations subsequently revealed that Soyuz-2's parachute container carried the same design fault as that of Soyuz-1, which would have killed the third cosmonaut.

### Yuri Alexeyevich Gagarin (1934–68)

When Yuri Gagarin was born on 9 March 1934, no one could possibly know that he would become one of the most famous people of the twentieth century. Hundreds of books would be written about his life and deeds, and at the height of the cult that was formed around him, only Lenin would have more statues and busts throughout the Soviet Union. Gagarin's death at the age of thirty-four was considered a national tragedy, and the entire country was in mourning the day his cremated remains were inurned in the Kremlin Wall.

Yuri Alexeyevich Gagarin was born in the small village of Klushino, Smolensk Region, some sixty miles from Moscow. The son of a collective farmer, he entered school in 1941, but his schooling was interrupted by the Nazi invasion. After the war the Gagarin family moved to the town of Gzhatsk, where Yuri continued his studies in secondary school. In 1949, at the age of fifteen, he left school to bring in more money for his parents and became a foundry-shop molder. In 1951 he completed trade school in the town of Lyubertsy, fully qualifying him as a foundryman. He finished an evening school for young workers at the same time.

Next, Gagarin went to an industrial technical school in Saratov on the Volga, finishing with honors in June 1955. While attending this school he took up flight instruction in his spare time at the local flying club, and he decided his future was in the skies. In lieu of seeking foundry employment, Gagarin took part in a summer aviation camp, learning to fly the Yak-18. He then entered the Orenburg Air Force Pilots School as an aviation cadet.

While still at the Orenburg school, Gagarin met his future wife, Valentina Gory-acheva, an attractive nurse trainee. They married on 27 October 1957. The following month he was promoted to lieutenant and graduated the next day, 6 November.

Opting for air force service with the Northern Fleet, Gagarin then took on a two-year basing at Zapolyarny in the Arctic Circle. Once Valentina had completed her nursing course she joined him, and their first child, a daughter they named Yelena, was born on 10 April 1959.

In October 1959, like many other young Soviet air force officers, Gagarin was interviewed by a selection board given the task of assembling a group of pilots who met certain height, medical, and physiological qualifications. As well, they had to have shown extraordinary skill and calmness throughout their flying career. Gagarin, then twenty-five years old, impressed the panel with his talent, record, and candor. In March the following year he was told he had made the cut and would be included in the first selection group of future cosmonaut trainees. He and his family packed their bags and moved to Moscow.

24. Yuri Alexeyevich Gagarin (Courtesy Bert Vis)

As was customary at the time in the Soviet Union, the program was shrouded in secrecy, which meant that the group of twenty cosmonauts trained in complete obscurity at a hidden facility outside of Moscow. Gagarin's colleagues later said that it quickly became evident which of them was best candidate to make the first manned space flight. Apparently Sergei Korolev, the chief designer and man at the helm of the entire Soviet space program, took an instant liking to the young lieutenant with the open, smiling face. As one story goes, when the cosmonauts were first shown the Vostok spacecraft and invited to sit in it, Gagarin, without being told, took off his shoes before climbing inside. Korolev, who had designed the Vostok craft, liked this and other qualities he had noticed in the young pilot. "At decisive moments," he once said, "life itself finds the best person to carry out its plans." On 25 January 1961 Yuri Gagarin passed a final exam and received his full cosmonaut qualification.

Lieutenant Colonel Yevgeny Karpov directed the cosmonaut training and became the first director of the cosmonaut training center. He is quoted as saying that Yuri Gagarin "possessed all the important qualifications: devoted patriotism, complete faith in the success of the flight, excellent health, inexhaustible optimism, a quick and enquiring mind, courage and resolution, self-control, orderliness, industriousness, simplicity, modesty, great human warmth and attentiveness to others."

The Gagarins' second daughter, Galina, was born on 7 March 1961, and later that month the cosmonauts were told what they had already begun to suspect—that Yuri Gagarin was to be the first to fly on Vostok. His backup would be Gherman Titov, with Grigori Nelyubov assigned as second backup.

On 12 April 1961 Lieutenant Yuri Gagarin was launched into space from the Baikonur Cosmodrome in the Soviet Republic of Kazakhstan in Central Asia. During his single orbit around the world he was promoted to major, skipping the rank of captain. It was the first of numerous awards, decorations, and other tokens of admiration he would receive in the years that followed. To the Soviet government, and general secretary of the CPSU Nikita Khrushchev in particular, Gagarin had become the living symbol of the country and its political system as well as the Columbus of the Space Age.

In photographs and films of his arrival back in Moscow after the flight, Gagarin can be seen striding out with one of his shoelaces undone. Ordinarily, such images would have been retouched to delete anything deemed to be unsuitable, but things were left as they were. What better way to show the public that the world's first space traveler was just as human as the rest of us?

More than thirty years later, it became known that his 108-minute flight had not been without serious problems. The return capsule had not properly separated from the service compartment, and it was only the frictional heat of reentry that finally separated the two parts of the spaceship. Since the Vostok capsule was not designed for an acceptably soft landing, Gagarin ejected once he had descended to a safe altitude, and landed by parachute. For three decades the Soviets tried to insist that the cosmonaut had landed in his spacecraft, even though it was quite evident this was untrue. Gagarin, whose identity until this time was unknown to anyone outside his small circle of family, friends, and colleagues, instantly became the most famous person on the planet.

Following his flight, Gagarin was sent on a world tour and turned out to be a public relations dream come true. His friendly, smiling face captured everyone's heart, and the way he addressed and treated people made him immensely popular and feted wherever he went. One story goes that when he was in England attending an official banquet given in his honor by Queen Elizabeth, he looked at the vast array of gleaming eating utensils laid before him and unabashedly told the queen that he was only a simple officer and had no idea about the order in which they should be used. Apparently the queen was quite bemused and very diplomatically stated that though she had been born into royalty, she still was not quite sure herself.

On 25 May 1961 Gagarin was appointed the first commander of the cosmonaut detachment, and two months later was promoted to the rank of lieutenant colonel. He was eventually promoted to full colonel on 6 November 1963, and the following month was appointed deputy director of the training center, under Nikolai Kamanin. But there was a price to pay for his fame and propaganda value: on 11 June 1964 Gagarin was officially grounded, told he was no longer permitted to fly.

Once things had begun to settle down, and as more and more Soviet cosmonauts followed the trail blazed by Gagarin, he began to grow restless and dreamed of going back into space. He submitted an official request for another flight to his commander, General Nikolai Kamanin. The heads of the space program did not want to risk a national hero on another flight, but eventually, albeit reluctantly, they gave in. In October 1966, with the orders grounding him now rescinded, Gagarin was assigned as backup to Vladimir Komarov for the Soyuz-1 and 2 docking mission. This assignment effectively meant he was the prime contender for a follow-up mission, Soyuz-3.

When Komarov was launched in his Soyuz-1 spacecraft, problems immediately developed. The launch of the three-man Soyuz-2, scheduled for the next day, was scrubbed and all efforts were now directed to getting Komarov back safely. Sadly, it would prove futile: Komarov died on impact when his plummeting spacecraft slammed into the Kazakh steppe.

Manned spaceflight in the Soviet Union came to an abrupt halt. Another result of the disaster occurred soon after when Gagarin was once again stood down from flying and told that because of the risks involved in spaceflight, he would never fly in space again. He was too valuable to the government to run the chance of losing his life in the dangerous arena of cosmonautics.

Over the following months Gagarin worked at a desk job, but he was desperately unhappy. He realized his dream of making another trip into the cosmos was rapidly fading, but he kept up his attempts to at least get back to active flying. Finally his management concurred, and on 13 March 1968 the stand-down order was once again rescinded and he was given permission to resume flying jet aircraft. Almost immediately he began flying MiG aircraft, although he was not permitted to fly without an accompanying instructor to gauge his proficiency.

On 27 March Gagarin readied himself for his fifth jet flight, aboard a two-seat MiG-15 with his instructor, Colonel Vladimir Seryogin. Taking off at 10:19 A.M. from the Chkalovsky Air Force Base near the cosmonaut training center, Gagarin and Seryogin soon requested a change of course, which was granted by air traffic controllers. It was the last anyone heard from the MiG.

It was not long before the controllers became concerned. They had lost the fighter's signals from their screens; there was no response to their calls. Search planes were quickly dispatched to look for the missing aircraft, and they soon realized their worst fears. The MiG had come down in a birch wood some thirty miles east of Moscow, near the village of Novoselovo. The two pilots were dead.

Once again the lack of information on the crash released by Soviet officials led to unfounded rumours of a cover-up. Some reports in the West hinted at a technical malfunction bringing the jet down, while others said that a bird hit the MiG. Another report suggested that parts of a weather balloon had been found near the crash site, indicating the aircraft had flown straight into it, bringing both down. There were rumors that the men had received incorrect weather data, in particular the amount of cloud cover, which caused them to believe they were flying at a much higher altitude than was actually the case. At the darker end of the rumor mill were suggestions that the two pilots were actually drunk, and even that the KGB at the order of Leonid Brezhnev had murdered them. At the root of this story was the fact that Gagarin had been a protégé of Nikita Khrushchev, and when Khrushchev had been ousted as leader, Gagarin had reportedly fallen from grace with the Kremlin hierarchy.

Ultimately the official report is the most credible. It stated that the likely cause of the crash was the MiG going into a violent spin after flying into the trailing vortex of another jet fighter. By the time Gagarin and Seryogin managed to control the spin they were too low and probably disoriented in the prevailing thick cloud. Still diving, their aircraft crashed before the pilots could level out and recover some altitude.

Gagarin had turned thirty-four less than three weeks before he died. His death was an enormous blow to the struggling Soviet space program, and the entire country went into mourning. The cosmonaut team was similarly devastated—within less than a year they had lost two of their most liked and respected comrades.

Even today, the mere mention of Gagarin's name is enough to create a warm smile on the face of even the dourest of early cosmonauts. Speaking badly of the man, even more than thirty years after his death, is enough to become an outcast in Star City, where the air force cosmonaut detachment is based. After every spaceflight the crew traditionally lays flowers at the base of a larger-than-life-size statue of Gagarin that looks toward the training center, which was renamed in his honor. In winter, it is the first place in town to be swept clear of snow.

The city closest to Gagarin's place of birth, Gzhatsk, was named after him to reflect his life and achievements. Among other countless national memorials to the world's first spaceman, a Russian spaceflight tracking ship also bears his name.

Yuri Alexeyevich Gagarin will forever be remembered as the first human to fly in space. His successful mission was also a feat of the first magnitude for the Soviet Union as a whole, and its government and the Communist Party in particular. One can only speculate as to what would have happened had he lived. But given that he was removed from the list of active cosmonauts in 1967 and "sentenced" to a desk job, it seems almost certain he would have ended up a general. Also, at the very least, he would have succeeded Lieutenant General Kamanin as head of the cosmonaut training center and the cosmonaut detachment.

As a mark of respect prior to flying into space, every cosmonaut visits Gagarin's office in Zvezdny Gorodok (Star City). On the day he died this office was situated in the training center's administrative building, in a fenced-off area adjacent to the similarly fenced-off and guarded town, outside of Moscow. Following his death, literally everything was removed from his office and taken to the Dom Kosmonavtov, the central building of Zvezdny's living area, which is used for receptions, weddings, and official parties. This area also houses the training center's museum. There, in a room, his office was painstakingly reconstructed. Everything was placed in exactly the same spot and the same way it had been in his real office a few hundred yards away. These visiting cosmonauts each leave a letter on his desk in which they promise to uphold his tradition of valor. They treat Gagarin's office as a shrine, as it reflects the day he walked out for the final time to fly with Vladimir Seryogin. A uniform still hangs from a coatrack, and his flip-over calendar still sits on his desk, opened to 27 March 1968. The clocks in his office are the only truly staged effect. They were set and stopped at the exact time the world's first spaceman died.

### Pavel Ivanovich Belyayev (1925–70)

Among his many achievements, Pavel Belyayev is believed to have been the first cosmonaut to take manual control of a Soviet spacecraft. The autopilot landing system failed in the Voskhod-2 craft he shared with Alexei Leonov, who had just completed the world's first walk in space. Belyayev noticed that the Voskhod's attitude was incorrect for the retro burn and shut it down, sending the craft into an extra orbit while he consulted with Chief Designer Sergei Korolev and ground controllers. He then fired the braking rockets manually, hoping to touch down in the flat steppes of Kazakhstan but ended up missing the intended landing zone by nearly thirteen hundred miles. Voskhod-2 came down in an isolated snowbound forest in the northern Urals and ended up firmly wedged between two large trees, suspended several yards off the ground. The two men spent an anxious, freezing cold day and night in this precarious situation, listening to the howling of hungry packs of wolves. Finally, at dawn, a ski patrol homed in on their signal beacon and located the spacecraft. Two very relieved cosmonauts were then given pairs of skis, and the rescue team guided them through the forest to a waiting helicopter.

Pavel Belyayev was born on 26 June 1925 in the village of Chelishchevo in Vologda Region and spent his early childhood in the village of Minkovo. The son of Ivan Parmenovich Belyayev, a physician's assistant, young Pavel was not interested in pursuing his father's profession and dreamed instead of becoming a hunter or traveler.

In 1937 the family moved to the town of Kamensk-Uralsk, where he became an expert skier, having to ski three miles a day each way to school and back. In his teens he read in the city newspaper a notice of admission to a special air force school in Sverdlovsk and decided to apply. However, his application was rejected because there was no room in the hostel for out-of-town student applicants.

When war began against Germany, Belyayev's elder brothers went off to the front, and he too tried to enlist at the local induction center. He was a year too young to apply and was told to come back when he was old enough. Meanwhile his name was placed on a list of volunteers. A sympathetic neighbor then offered him a job as a lathe operator and he went to work in the Sinarsk pipes factory. He finally received his call-up papers in May 1943 and was assigned to the Third Sarapul military school,

25. Pavel Ivanovich Belyayev (Courtesy Bert Vis)

where he underwent initial naval pilot training. In 1944 he entered the Yeisk Aviation School and graduated as a junior lieutenant on 9 May 1945—the day after war ended with Germany. He was then assigned to the Far East in a unit attached to the Soviet Navy and took part in aerial action against the Japanese, flying Yak, Lavochkin, and MiG fighters. He stayed with his unit in the Far East for a further eleven years. During this period he met and wed Tatyana Filippovna Prikazchikova, and they eventually had two daughters—Irina, born in 1949, and Lyudmila, born in 1955.

In 1956 Belyayev was sent to study at the Red Banner Air Force Academy, and following his graduation three years later was assigned to the Black Sea Fleet as a squadron commander, serving in the Crimea. He came to the cosmonauts' group in 1960, but in August 1961 fractured his leg just above the ankle during a parachute jump. Because of the severity of his injury, few people believed he would be able to continue as a cosmonaut, but his stamina and endurance pulled him through as he exercised continually and underwent remedial therapy. After a year's absence he was deemed fully fit and allowed to recommence his cosmonaut training.

On 18 March 1965 Belyayev realized his dream of spaceflight when he was launched into space as commander of the historic two-man Voskhod-2 mission. During this flight Alexei Leonov became the first man to walk in space, and despite the ignominious end to their flight, it was regarded worldwide as a great triumph.

Belyayev never made another spaceflight, although he was one of the cosmonauts in training for a circumlunar flight scheduled for 1968. This program was canceled following the repeated failure of the N-1 lunar booster, and the continuing success of America's Apollo program.

In December 1969 Belyayev was struck down with an acute illness that it seems he had concealed for some time, not wishing to be removed from flight status. He was hospitalized and diagnosed with a bleeding ulcer. Although it was a relatively simple operation, complications set in following the surgery, and he developed peritonitis. Colonel Pavel Ivanovich Belyayev, the tenth Soviet cosmonaut to fly into space, died in the hospital on 10 January 1970.

But the story does not end there: his death caused something of a quandary for the Soviet government. Should Belyayev be given the honor of burial in the Kremlin Wall? After all, it was argued, he had died of natural causes, and as the tenth cosmonaut to fly into space his achievement was not regarded as significant enough to warrant such eminence. The problem was resolved after a decision was finally made that he deserved to be inurned in the wall. On hearing this his widow flatly refused, saying she wanted him buried in a place where she could visit him, unhindered and whenever she wanted. So Tatyana Belyayev's wishes were eventually realized, and her husband's body was laid to rest in the Novodeviche cemetery in Moscow. Here he was buried alongside many great people from the Soviet Union: politicians, artists, actors, scientists, and others who had stood out in society. A life-size bronze statue of Belyayev wearing a space suit and helmet easily identifies the grave.

### Georgy Timofeyevich Dobrovolsky (1928–71)
### Viktor Ivanovich Patsayev (1933–71)
### Vladislav Nikolayevich Volkov (1935–71)

Maybe it was fate that killed Georgy Dobrovolsky, Vladislav Volkov, and Viktor Patsayev during their record-setting first occupancy of a space station. Or maybe Salyut-1 was just an unlucky ship.

Initially the three cosmonauts had not even been together in one crew. This was an era in the Soviet manned space program when it was common to assign four crews to a flight program. While the first of the four flew, the others trained for upcoming missions, acting as backup and generally moving up one step when each successive prime crew was launched into orbit.

Dobrovolsky had been commander of the fourth crew training for a mission to the Salyut space station, while Volkov and Patsayev were part of the third crew. When the commander of the first crew was dismissed for disciplinary reasons, management at the Gagarin Cosmonaut Training Center moved the commander of the third crew up two places into the first crew. Dobrovolsky was also moved up, becoming commander of the third crew.

26. Georgy Timofeyevich Dobrovolsky (Courtesy Bert Vis)

On 23 April 1971, Soyuz-10 was launched and docked with the Salyut station. A little over five hours later the Soyuz craft unexpectedly disengaged from Salyut and returned to Earth. It was immediately assumed in the West that there had been technical problems that could not be solved. The Soviets emphatically denied this, issuing statements claiming the flight had been a complete success, and it had never been intended for the Soyuz crew to enter the station. Not surprisingly, Western observers did not believe this. Several years later the Soviets finally came clean and belatedly admitted there had indeed been problems with a hatch in the transfer tunnel between Soyuz-10 and the station. Despite the crew members' best efforts, they had been unable to open the balky hatch and were forced to curtail their mission.

Once the problem had been identified and remedied, the backup crew was assigned to fly to Salyut with Soyuz-11 to carry out the mission originally planned for the earlier crew. The commander of Soyuz-11 would be Alexei Leonov, renowned as the first man to walk in space six years earlier. His flight engineer was Valeri Kubasov, another veteran of one mission, and Pyotr Kolodin, who would be making his first spaceflight. The backup crew for this mission was Dobrovolsky, Volkov, and Patsayev.

Preparations for this flight went smoothly, until shortly before the scheduled launch. During a routine medical check Kubasov was diagnosed with a lung ailment.

27. Viktor Ivanovich Patsayev (Courtesy Bert Vis)

Although it later turned out that the affliction was nothing more than an allergic reaction to a pesticide commonly used at the Baikonur Cosmodrome, Kubasov was axed from the prime crew. Astonishingly, just two days before the scheduled launch, the prime crew was replaced in its entirety. The backup crew would now fly Soyuz-11.

The launch, on 6 June 1971, went off without any problems. At 4:55 A.M. the Soyuz-11 spacecraft thundered into orbit atop its rocket. Later that day Soviet newspapers hit the streets with banner headlines announcing this latest feat in the manned space program. Photographs of the three newest cosmonauts covered the front pages. Volkov was already known for his earlier flight aboard Soyuz-7, but the other two men, making their first flights, were new to the public.

Georgy Dobrovolsky was born in the seaside city of Odessa on 1 June 1928. During the latter part of the Second World War he became an enthusiastic member of an underground partisan group but was captured by the Germans in February 1944. Charged with the possession of firearms, Dobrovolsky was sentenced to twenty-five years of hard labor. The following month he managed to break free in company with some other prisoners and saw out the last few months of the war on the run from the Nazis.

28. Vladislav Nikolayevich Volkov (Courtesy Bert Vis)

The first months after the war proved tough for the young Odessite. By day he studied, and by night he unloaded ships in the port. Having grown up with a love for the sea, he applied to enter the Odessa Nautical School, but his anticipation soon turned to dismay when he found out his application had been presented too late, and he had failed to gain admission. Undaunted, he then decided to enroll in the Odessa Air Force school, where young boys were trained for the Soviet Air Force. He graduated in 1946. The next step in Dobrovolsky's military career was the Chuguyev Air Force Pilots School. Graduating from the school in 1950, he then served in fighter regiments and flew a variety of MiG, Yak, and Lavochkin aircraft. He started out as a pilot, then graduated to senior pilot, flight commander, and finally deputy squadron commander. He completed a correspondence course with the Air Force Academy, graduating in 1961. At this time Dobrovolsky became a political worker, while continuing to fly. He also made several parachute jumps, eventually becoming an instructor.

In January 1963 Dobrovolsky joined the Soviet Union's cosmonaut team, reporting for training at the cosmonaut center in Zvezdny Gorodok, outside of Moscow. He had a wife named Lyudmila, a mathematics teacher, and two young daughters.

Viktor Patsayev, born 19 June 1933, was from Aktyubinsk in Kazakhstan. Four years later his family moved to Alga, and in 1948 they settled in Nesterov, in the Kaliningrad region. On completing his secondary school studies (he later described himself as "an average pupil"), Patsayev entered the Penza Polytechnic Institute. After graduating from the institute in 1955 he was sent to work as a design engineer at the Central Aerological Observatory.

From his early boyhood Patsayev had a passion for reading, preferring science fiction novels, but his tastes also ranged from Lermontov to Jack London. As the years passed he developed a keen interest in advanced physics and mathematics. For recreation, he was involved in a variety of sports, including skiing, cycling, fencing, and shooting.

Some time after he started working at the Central Aerological Observatory, Patsayev began publishing scientific articles that caught the attention of his fellow instrumentation specialists. Soon after, and following the first Sputnik launches in 1957, Patsayev left the observatory and began working with precision instruments at the Optyno-Konstruktorskoe Biuro (Research Design Office) headed by Sergei Korolev. There he befriended future cosmonaut Vladislav Volkov, a fellow member of a local flying club. Their friendship deepened when they became members of recovery teams for manned space missions.

Patsayev's decision to become a cosmonaut was apparently gradual, but he was probably spurred on by his friend Volkov's acceptance onto the cosmonaut team in 1966. He finally told Korolev that he would like to experience design work in space and wanted to apply for cosmonaut training. To this end, he began parachute training with other cosmonauts in 1968 and was accepted onto the cosmonaut team in 1969. By this time he and his wife, Vera, a research worker, had a son and daughter.

The story of Vladislav Volkov is similar to that of fellow crew member Viktor Patsayev. Both entered school during the war, and at fourteen both joined the Komsomol. They each studied at technical institutions and worked at OKB Korolev, and together they took lessons at the same flying club and in the same airplane.

Born in Moscow on 23 November 1935, Volkov was tall and good looking, lithe and agile. He always appeared calm and in control, but this facade sometimes hid an impish good humor. He liked to sing and dance and play his guitar, and he spent hours over his sketchbook. Tennis and ice hockey were favorite sporting activities.

Volkov's father, Nikolai, was an aeronautical engineer, while his mother, Olga, worked in aircraft plants for many years. Prior to his first flight, Volkov revealed that his family background had set him on a course to the stars: "I made my choice long ago, as a boy. Partly, probably, because my father and mother worked in the aircraft industry and spent many hours building airplanes. I probably inherited their enthusiasm. I dreamed of becoming a test pilot and testing all the newest planes. I think I was fortunate."

Volkov took his early schooling at Moscow High School, and in 1952 he joined the Moscow Aviation Institute's aeroclub, graduating the following year. He then reenrolled at the institute to gain his engineering degree, but he maintained his flying lessons and also took up parachute jumping. While studying at the institute he met his future wife, Lyudmila Biryukova. They married, and both graduated in 1958. That same year their son Vladimir was born.

Aviation design work soon followed at the okb Korolev, and Volkov was later involved in the construction and testing of the Vostok and Voskhod spacecraft as deputy leading designer. In May 1966 he was selected to join the cosmonaut team.

Volkov's first spaceflight came as flight engineer aboard the three-man Soyuz-7 flight in October 1969. During this flight rendezvous techniques were carried out with two other manned spacecraft, Soyuz-6 and 8. On his return, Volkov was awarded the title of Hero of the Soviet Union.

Soyuz-11 conducted a flawless docking with the Salyut-1 station, and this time the crew transferred with little difficulty. As was common practice, no information on the flight was given, other than the standard announcements that the mission was proceeding smoothly and the crew was fulfilling its scientific research program. The cosmonauts organized their work in shifts around the clock. This work was combined with physical exercises, which included the use of a moving track to simulate the effects of walking and prevent muscles from atrophying in the weightlessness of space.

Two weeks into the mission there was another reason for newspaper headlines— the crew had broken the space endurance record set five years earlier by Gemini astronauts Frank Borman and Jim Lovell. And there was still no indication about how long the Soviet crew might spend aboard Salyut-1.

In later years, it became apparent that the flight was far from trouble-free. While Soviet television showed ghostly pictures of the bearded crew members apparently having the time of their lives, there was no mention of the fact that there were some tensions. Volkov had problems taking a subordinate role to Dobrovolsky, and it took some lengthy discussions with superiors to resolve the matter. Another problem was a small electrical fire in one of the station's systems, causing the complex to fill with acrid smoke. Luckily, the cosmonauts were able to extinguish the fire and continue their work onboard. The fire had been a first in space, and for the Soviet space hierarchy it was not a matter for public release or comment. Like other problems, it was quickly covered up, only to become public many years later.

On 19 June, Viktor Patsayev set his own small "first" in spaceflight history when he became the first person to celebrate a birthday (his thirty-eighth) in space.

Finally, after nearly twenty-four days in orbit, and almost doubling Gemini 7's endurance record, the crew entered its Soyuz craft, undocked from the Salyut station, and prepared to return to Earth. The crew was not wearing protective space suits, a dangerous practice that had somehow gained acceptance in the Soviet manned space program since the flight of the first Voskhod seven years earlier. The suitless cosmonauts had more room and it also saved weight and effort.

As the Soyuz spacecraft plunged into the atmosphere, contact was lost with the ground—a normal event generally lasting around four minutes. Radio waves are unable to pierce the blazing turbulence and ionization associated with reentry. A few minutes later, when radio contact should have been reestablished with the descending spacecraft, Soyuz-11 remained eerily silent. The longer this silence went on, the more ground controllers began to worry. From the time the radio blackout ended until touchdown two thousand miles southeast of Moscow, the crew should have been in touch with flight control.

In the meantime, on the steppes of Kazakhstan, all appeared to be quite normal. The recovery crews reported seeing the descent module gracefully drifting down beneath its massive red and white parachute. Then, as planned, braking rockets automatically fired a fraction of a second before the craft hit the ground, absorbing the shock of impact. Within moments the capsule came to rest on the ground with recovery crews rushing to the scene. With everything appearing to have gone as planned, ground controllers concluded that the spacecraft's radio must have failed in the final phases of the mission.

What happened next would be shrouded in a cloak of official secrecy for many years. The rescuers opened the capsule's hatch, ready to greet an exuberant crew. Instead there was stillness and silence. The three crew members were in an apparent state of repose, as if asleep, and their faces were tranquil. It was quickly established that all three cosmonauts were dead. This news was quickly relayed to Moscow, where government officials could do nothing other than go public with the disastrous news.

With few facts to go on, Westerners were immensely concerned about the deaths. Answers were sought from Soviet space officials, but they remained tight-lipped. Some theorized that the mystery deaths were caused by a complete breakdown of the three cosmonauts' vital organs, made sluggish by protracted weightlessness, under the sudden stress of gravity. The impact of this theory was such that America, and indeed Russia, needed some quick answers.

Twelve days after the tragedy, the Soviets relented but still held back most details. They stated only that the cosmonauts died of "depressurization." What they did not disclose, and would not reveal for some three years, was what had actually caused the tragedy. The culprit had eventually been traced to a small pressure equalization valve that had opened after separation of the descent module from the orbital and service modules. The valve was designed to equalize air pressure within the cabin with the ambient air pressure outside once the Soyuz spacecraft was descending through the denser layers of the atmosphere. However, the valve opened prematurely in the return trajectory, effectively venting the cabin's atmosphere. Because the three cosmonauts were not equipped with pressure suits for launch and reentry, they were totally unprotected from such mishaps. Evidence suggests that they realized there was a leak and tried to locate the source, but all three expired rapidly from asphyxiation. It was later said that something as simple as placing a finger over the leak would have saved the cosmonauts. Tragically, they died only minutes away from the triumphant conclusion of the greatest achievement to that time in the Space Age.

Dobrovolsky, Volkov, and Patsayev did not get the hero's welcome that everyone had envisioned when they undocked from the space station. Instead, the three men received a solemn state funeral, with all three bodies dressed in civilian clothing. Patsayev was the only one to show any sign of injury—he had a large dark bruise high on his right cheek.

The bodies were first laid in state in the Central Home of the Soviet Army Communist Party first secretary, Leonid Brezhnev. Premier Alexei Kosygin, together with President Nikolai Podgorny and other members of the Politburo, stood in the guard of honor at the biers of the three men. Astronaut Tom Stafford was also there; he had flown to Moscow for the funeral as President Nixon's personal envoy. Tens of thousands of Russians silently lined up from early morning to pay their respects, after which a funeral service was held at 2:00 P.M. in Red Square.

Following the service and cremation, the three men's ashes were inurned in Moscow's Kremlin Wall, close to those of Yuri Gagarin and Vladimir Komarov. They were the third, fourth, and fifth cosmonauts to have their ashes consigned there and also the last. With the later demise of the Soviet Union, burials in the wall came to an end.

Many years later the Soviet space program was gradually declassified. Information on its history slowly but surely found its way to the media, and to sleuths in the West who had tried to unearth the program's secrets since the early days. As part of this declassification some amazing film footage was released, shot immediately after the landing of Soyuz-11. It showed the bodies of the three cosmonauts lying on stretchers next to the descent module, while members of the recovery team frantically tried to revive them using CPR. It was a desperate but futile attempt, and in all probability they knew they were too late to save any of the crew.

Halfway around the world in Florida, the crew members of Apollo 15 had been at the Kennedy Space Center in training for their flight when they heard the sad news. At that time they were less than a month from their launch date of 26 July. Dave Scott would later add the names of the three cosmonauts to the small commemorative plaque he was secretly planning to leave on the moon's surface.

The three cosmonauts were posthumously awarded the title of Hero of the Soviet Union, and the Order of Lenin, the Soviet Union's highest honors, given to all returning cosmonauts. In addition, three new tracking ships used to support the space program were named after them.

Salyut-1 was never occupied again, and Soviet missions reverted to crews of two, enabling them to wear space suits during the launch and reentry phases of their flights. Soyuz-12 became a test flight to check out improvements made to the spacecraft. Launched in September 1972, more than a year after the Soyuz-11 disaster, it was not scheduled to dock with the station. By the time a new crew could have flown to Salyut, the station had already been decommissioned.

Superstition is endemic and strong in the Russian manned space program. The failed Soyuz-10 mission, the replacement of the original Soyuz-11 crew, the fire on board the Salyut station, and finally the deaths of Dobrovolsky, Volkov, and Patsayev—cosmonauts quietly spoke of all these things at that time. They all agreed to varying degrees that Salyut-1 was cursed at worst, unlucky at best. There were certainly none that felt sadness for the hapless station when its replacement was finally blasted into orbit. It was, they said, a new beginning.

# 5  A Lonely Stretch of Road
## Major Edward Galen Givens Jr., USAF

*The inescapable irony of Ed Givens's life is that he died in an inauspicious car crash. An accomplished and highly motivated test pilot, he had scorched a path across the skies in some of the most formidable jets around, and then, at the age of thirty-six, had become one of his nation's astronauts. And yet these days his contribution to the space program is virtually overlooked in books about the glory days of Apollo, while his name is conspicuously absent from the index pages of these publications. News of his death made the headlines only in his hometown of Quanah, Texas; elsewhere it was confined to just a few lines on an inner page. Perhaps it was the manner of his death that caused it to be almost disregarded—after all, it involved a road accident on a rainy night, not a spacecraft. Yet, had he not died behind the wheel of his Volkswagen, Givens would almost certainly have become famous as one of the handful of men who flew to the moon.*

It was the evening of 5 June 1967, and Major William ("Bill") Hall, a forty-one-year-old USAF Reserve technician, was in seventh heaven. Just that morning he had been invited to attend a meeting of the Ancient Order of the Quiet Birdmen, a fraternal organization of air force pilots and former officers. Now he found himself talking with some of the best aviators in the country, including a number of elderly pilots who had pioneered flying routes up and down the circuitous South American river systems. Although he had never flown that type of aircraft, Hall had always been fascinated with seaplanes and amphibians, so he was enjoying himself to the hilt as he shot the breeze with these old aviators. As if that were not enough, two astronauts were in attendance, Gordon Cooper and Ed Givens. The latter man was still to make his first spaceflight.

Hall, who hailed from Meadville, Pennsylvania, was in Houston to do some flying in the U-3, a military version of the Cessna 310. It was not a complicated airplane, but there were none back at his base in Youngstown, Ohio, and the pilots who had been assigned there for proficiency flying were soon to be given the U-3 in lieu of the older C-47s currently in use. As the instructor pilot in charge of that program, Hall needed to achieve the necessary flying time and proficiency on a U-3 at Houston's Ellington Air Force Base. Francis ("Fran") Dellorto, forty-five, another air force reservist from Chicago O'Hare, had flown in at the same time for much the same reason.

After half a day of ground school and another half day's flying, the instructor asked Hall and Dellorto if they would like to attend a meeting that night of the Quiet Birdmen, to be held in the Skylane Motel in Pearland. Each year these aviation enthusiasts, pilots, and other special guests would gather to salute fallen comrades and discuss their part in the world of aviation. Hall was familiar with the Birdmen and had always wanted to join the organization, founded by Charles Lindbergh many years before.

Each local area chapter of the Quiet Birdmen held a monthly meeting, and prospective members had to be invited to, and attend, twelve meetings before consideration could be given for full membership. Hall had been to one other meeting, which he had enjoyed a great deal, so he jumped at the opportunity to attend another. He came from a family well entrenched in aviation and the air force. His father, Earl Dewey Hall, had wanted to fly in combat during the Great War, but to his regret had still been gathering experience in flying school at Souther Field in Americus, Georgia, when the war ended. He may have missed his opportunity, but Earl later infused into his three sons a deep love of flying, and all would go on to have long and noteworthy careers in aviation.

Hall and Dellorto's instructor mentioned he would have to go home to change, and then return to the base and pick them up. They would then drive into Pearland, a southeast suburb of Houston located some ten miles west of Ellington airfield. The group arrived at the Skylane Motel after the function had already begun. There were no uniforms, just a group of good-humored men with a common interest in, and love of, aviation. A casual mood prevailed, and the conversations were already flowing. Hall and Dellorto were introduced to several guests, including the two astronauts. Following the usual round of speeches, many of them quite robust and hilarious, Hall sought out Ed Givens for a one-on-one chat, and the two men hit it off well.

Givens was not drinking that night, pointing out that he had an important early morning meeting the next day and would be leaving the function well before it wound up. When Hall mentioned that he and Dellorto were taking some flying instruction early the next day and would also have to leave early, Givens offered them a lift back to their bachelor quarters at Ellington. He said he lived close by the base, and it would save their instructor another long trip. Hall thought this was an excellent idea, as it would give him a further chance to talk with the personable astronaut about NASA's space program.

Around 11:30 Givens found Hall and said he would be leaving shortly, so they rounded up Dellorto and the three men made their farewells. Strolling out, they crossed the motel's parking lot, the asphalt still glistening from a recent shower. Hall was expecting to strap himself into one of the usual astronaut speed machines he had read about, perhaps a racy, red Corvette convertible. He was therefore taken aback when Givens began unlocking his car door. Hall found himself clambering into the backseat of a more sedate, light-colored 1964 Volkswagen Beetle. It happened to be a car very familiar to Hall, as he drove one himself. Dellorto, being the taller of the two passengers, occupied the roomier front seat alongside Givens. The two in front buckled up their lap seat belts; there were no shoulder straps. Givens drove out of the motel's parking lot onto busy Telephone Road. None of them knew that profound tragedy lay in wait just a few miles ahead down the streets of Pearland.

§

Edward Galen Givens Jr. was born on 5 January 1930 to Helen (née Jarrell) and Edward ("Bill") Galen Givens, a bookkeeper in Quanah, Texas. Far away from all the buzz names of Houston, San Antonio, and Dallas, Quanah is situated by U.S. Highway 287, between its more substantial neighbors of Amarillo and Wichita Falls, and just in the bend of the Texas Panhandle. Quanah proclaims itself as much a backwater as any hot, inland place can be.

Young Galen Givens (as his parents always called him) grew up loving the town and its sprawling, surrounding farmland. His younger brother, Donald Jarrell Givens, born two years after him on 26 April 1932, would join him in his adventures, and the two boys spent countless spellbinding hours exploring and playing in and around Quanah. The family home was situated at 904 Shaw Street, and an old, dilapidated, and deserted house a little over a block away provided Givens with endless fun. He loved teasing visiting friends by telling them it was haunted, but for all his ostensible bravado, he too would give the house a wide berth whenever he passed by after dark.

He was quite bright as a student, but otherwise did not seem to stand out from the rest of the student body. "Galen was always recognized as smart," his cousin Barbara Watkins remembered. "He was a good kid who was basically straight forward and much admired [although] he was considered a little snobbish. I do not think he had that many close friends[, but] he was extremely fortunate in having a close family unit. His mom and dad and brother adored and cared for each other."

When Givens reached high school, he began to demonstrate a little added tenacity by taking on extra courses in order to skip a year, and graduated early. As a teenager, he set out to bring to reality his long-held dream of becoming a pilot. To this end he worked in a local grocery store after school and on Saturdays, and he washed cars to raise money for flying lessons. With his hard-won money stuffed deep in his pockets, he hitchhiked the thirty miles west up 287 to Childress Municipal Airport, where he took lessons under the kindly but rigorous instruction of "Red" Emerson, from the Ragsdale Flying Service. At the conclusion of each lesson Givens happily hitchhiked back into Quanah.

Some years later Bill and Helen Givens told a reporter that their son "had never been interested in anything but aviation," and he proved this by getting his student license early in 1946. Then, much to his elation, he made his first solo flight in a Piper Cub the day after he turned sixteen. That flight carried Givens aloft for just fifteen minutes (for which he paid the princely sum of $1.89), but now that he had gone solo there was no holding him back. His future, he knew, was in the skies.

Following his graduation from Quanah High School, Givens spent a semester at Texas A&M University and three semesters at the University of Oklahoma before

29. A young Ed Givens proudly poses in his midshipman's
uniform at the U.S. Naval Academy, Annapolis.
(Courtesy Cathrine Doyle)

receiving an appointment to the U.S. Naval Academy at Annapolis in Maryland as
a member of the Class of 1952. It was a huge upward step in his life, as it meant
his college education was now at hand, and if he graduated he would possess a
bachelor of science degree and an officer's commission in the navy, marine corps,
or the recently formed U.S. Air Force.

In the summer of 1948 Bill and Helen Givens traveled to the East Coast with
their son, and following solemn words of advice deposited him with the marine
guard at the entrance to Annapolis, where he would spend the next four years. They
arranged to see him again later that day before heading back home. His admission
papers showed that he entered Annapolis on 18 June.

The U.S. Naval Academy, founded in 1845, sits on 338 acres between the south
bank of the Severn River and historic Annapolis, the state capital of Maryland.
As he was escorted through the gates, Givens took in the massive, ancient elms,
oaks, and magnolia trees set in vast, perfectly manicured lawns. He marveled at the
French Renaissance, Victorian, and contemporary architecture as well as a spectacular vista of Chesapeake Bay. The grandeur and history of the place were simply
awesome.

The reverie did not last long; he was immediately sent to have his head shaved and pick up his gear and uniform, known as the "white works." He then was assigned to his dormitory room, met his new roommates, and later that day was sworn in as a midshipman fourth class in the 20th Company. Other members of the Class of 1952 were future astronauts Jim Lovell, Tom Stafford, and Donn Eisele. Eisele, with whom he would later be associated on the Apollo 7 mission, would actually be Givens's roommate for two years.

All too soon it was time for Givens to say goodbye to his parents. Bill offered his son a firm handshake and muttered a few words of encouragement, while Helen gave him a fond, tearful kiss before the new group was marched off for its first evening meal. Givens knew it would be some time before he saw his folks again, and he felt a sudden hollowness in his stomach.

As a plebe at the naval academy, Givens had to learn the ropes quickly. The new midshipmen were drilled and marched incessantly, had their swimming proficiency checked, and were taught the basics of sailing. The plebes also had to learn the meticulous skills associated with keeping their rooms in Bancroft Hall spotlessly clean for unheralded and thorough room inspections. Apart from making their beds and stowing all their clothing neatly, they had to wax and polish the floors and wash the showers and windows. If an upperclassmen inspection team found a fault, no matter how minute, demerit points would apply. Every single nook and cranny of the room was carefully probed and tested by their tormentors, using white gloves and black socks.

Despite the plebes' ongoing chore of keeping their room impeccably clean, meal times represented their greatest challenge. Meals were taken in the imposing mess hall, where all midshipmen are served their meals at the same time, three times a day. There would be twelve men at each table—two first classmen on one end, two second classmen at the other, and third and fourth classmen occupying the remaining eight places. The plebes were required to sit bolt upright at the edge of their chair to eat, all the time looking directly ahead. Each forkful of food had to be brought up vertically to the line of the mouth, then inserted in a horizontal motion. If they did not do this to an upperclassman's satisfaction, they had to push their chairs back and squat unsupported in the same position until they either collapsed or were told to resume their seat. If the "square meal" treatment was not enough to endure, the plebes were also bombarded with questions about naval and current affairs topics, which they had to answer correctly.

During that first year, Givens and his new friends could consider themselves to be the lowest of the low at the academy. They had to keep their wits about them or be picked on and shouted at by the upperclassmen, made to do menial chores, or suffer through an unreasonable number of pushups.

As the months passed, and despite missing his family, Givens studied hard. By now the life and customs associated with naval service were becoming second nature to him, while he and the other plebes began to acquire responsibility for

30. Midshipman First Class Edward Givens takes his turn as acting officer of the deck aboard the bridge of destroyer USS *Johnston* during his cruise to Cuba. (Courtesy Cathrine Doyle)

making decisions that could affect hundreds of other midshipmen. Their classroom studies were backed by many hours of practical experience in leadership and naval operations, which included assignments with naval and marine corps units during the summer months.

Among other disciplines on the curriculum, he studied such diverse subjects as history, mathematics, seamanship, navigation, ordnance and gunnery, marine engineering, and electrical engineering. From that first plebe summer until graduation, the Naval Academy's four-year character-development program focused on the attributes of integrity, honor, and mutual respect. Givens knew this, and grew stronger mentally as well as physically.

The midshipmen took overseas training voyages that quickly sorted out those with the weakest stomachs, but the time in foreign ports made it all seem relatively worthwhile. In one group photo in France, Givens and his class, all in full uniform, were photographed standing outside the glorious *Palais de Versailles*. Then, early in 1951, he began his much-anticipated flight training.

The following year Midshipman Givens earned his bachelor of science degree in naval sciences. "Give," as he had become known at the academy, not only impressed his math professors with his proficiency in the subject, but also had taken on certain renown as an adept midfielder in varsity lacrosse.

Just as things seemed to be going so well, a profound tragedy devastated the Givens family. Nineteen-year-old Donald, now a naval aviation cadet, was based at NAS Corpus Christi by the Gulf of Mexico in Texas. At one o'clock in the very early morning of 21 March 1952 he clambered aboard a Consolidated P-4Y2 Privateer, a four-engine maritime patrol aircraft, ready for a routine training flight up to NAS Alameda in California. Accompanying him on the flight were another cadet, four enlisted men, and four officers. A witness later testified that after the aircraft had taken off, he heard the unmistakable sound of an engine or engines misfiring. The pilot apparently fought to gain some altitude, but the Privateer suddenly heeled over to the left and went straight into the water, about a mile offshore near Demit Island. The hull of the aircraft was later found nose down in about ten feet of water, together with the tail section. By the end of that day four bodies had been recovered, with the other six men listed as missing.

Bill and Helen Givens were grief-stricken at the loss of their younger son, and Galen needed some time before he came to grips with the fact that he and his cheeky "baby" brother would never laugh together or discuss flying again. The death was a deeply bitter blow at a time when Givens was just moving into his cherished role of fighter pilot. He applied for some emergency compassionate leave and was granted nine days to be with his family.

After graduating from Annapolis in June, Givens (who now preferred "Ed" over "Galen") chose to enter the air force, receiving a commission as a second lieutenant. He then began his initial six months of flight instruction at Goodfellow Air Force Base in San Angelo, Texas. His first flight with the air force took place on 18 August 1952 in a yellow North American T-6 basic training aircraft. According to his logbooks, he then flew the aircraft nearly every day to build up his proficiency.

He found the T-6, also known as the Texan, to be a very intimidating and awkward plane to master. Many of the pilots joked that it was powered by a washing machine engine rather than the 550 horsepower Pratt and Whitney R-1340 said to be under the cowling. Still, it was flying, and Givens gradually gained confidence in himself and his aircraft.

His final testing flight at Goodfellow took place on 4 February 1953, and he was awarded his wings. Since he was one of the top students, he was awarded the standard privilege of nominating which branch of air force flying he preferred, and he selected fighter training. He was subsequently posted to Chandler, near Phoenix, Arizona, for further flight instruction at Williams AFB. He had heard that the group commander at Williams ruled his students with an iron fist, and that proved to be the case. This commander not only expected them to do well but to excel or get out, and that's exactly what he told the new batch of trainees in his welcoming speech. Those who eventually graduated received the best possible training and went on to become some of the best fighter pilots in America.

At Williams AFB Givens was introduced to the single-prop North American T-28 Trojan, a basic trainer the same size as the Texan but a lot faster at full throttle.

He became proficient at fighter tactics and formation flying, and he learned some simple aerobatics. From 3 June he advanced to the two-seat T-33, a training version of the Shooting Star or T-Bird jet, and his skills improved with every flight. The nimble aircraft was capable of flying parabolic arcs, which meant that the pilots could enjoy brief periods of weightlessness as they came over the top of an arc—Givens's first taste of spaceflight.

His next move was to Perrin AFB in Sherman, Texas, where he continued flying the T-33 from 2 October. Seven weeks later, on 23 November 1953, Givens stepped up yet another notch in his training when he began flying the advanced F-86D, alternating his flight hours between this and the T-33 until 16 December. He loved flying, principally because the F-86D—known to pilots as the "Dog Sabre"—was a powerful, single-seat jet, giving him unchallenged control in the air. The aircraft had been developed as an all-weather interceptor jet aircraft and was the first in the air force to have an all-rocket armament. Because the jet was a single-seater, the pilot had to both fly and operate a radar fire control system, so there was much to learn. The forty-foot aircraft had a single General Electric J-47 turbojet that threw out some 7,650 pounds of thrust, and it could achieve a maximum speed of 715 miles per hour. It was in one of these exhilarating aircraft that Givens later passed through Mach 1 for the first time, exceeding the speed of sound, and a certificate recording this milestone in his aviation career was always a proud feature on his wall.

In 1954, and following a routine promotion to first lieutenant, Givens was assigned to the 35th Fighter Interceptor Group, then on duty in Japan. As a fighter pilot and flight commander on this two-year posting, he began to relish the prospect of one day becoming a test pilot back in the States.

Eventually returning home, he was given a new assignment in January 1956 as an instructor at the Air Force Interceptor Weapons School in Panama City, Florida, where he remained until March 1958. Now bearing the rank of captain, he attended the USAF's Experimental Flight Test Pilot School (TPS) at Edwards AFB in California.

Quite a bit had changed in the organization of the TPS since it had moved over from Wright-Patterson AFB in 1951. When Givens attended the school as a student test pilot, it was under the command of Lt. Col. Herbert V. Leonhardt, who had taken over as commandant in May 1956. Leonhardt was immediately vigorous in acquiring more and better aircraft, facilities, and training resources. He also conducted a complete review of student selection and assignment procedures.

Beneath Commandant Leonhardt was a Training and Operations Branch that implemented training policies through its qualified instructor pilots. This instruction branch of the school had two core elements: Performance, and Stability and Control.

There were now three student classes per year (down from four), with a maximum of sixteen student test pilots in each class, and following Leonhardt's recommendation each course had been lengthened from twenty-eight to thirty-two

31. Test pilot Ed Givens at Edwards Air Force Base. (Courtesy Cathrine Doyle)

weeks. The students honed and broadened their flying skills on such aircraft as the familiar T-33 T-Birds, F-84s, the swept-wing F-86 Sabre, and the NB-57E and studied aerodynamics, engine performance, and a host of other flight-related subjects.

Following the arrival that year of the TF-102A, the school's first delta-winged aircraft, students and instructors could sit side by side in the aircraft's distinctive wide body to train in performance, stability, and control. It was a challenging time for Givens; like other students he found the F-102's flying characteristics markedly different from those of more conventional fighter and bomber aircraft.

The previous year, in keeping with Colonel Leonhardt's policy of staying abreast of aviation and aerospace technology, a revised curriculum was rapidly being set in place, although it would not be fully implemented until the course following Givens's, later that year. The program became roughly equivalent to the final two years of a college-level engineering course.

With these innovations about to be set into place, Givens found himself learning about exciting topics such as rocket engine performance and human factors in spaceflight. He was swept up in the idea that within a handful of years, men would be flying into space. He wanted to be one of them. He studied, trained, and flew hard, and upon graduation on 2 October 1958 he received the A. B. Honts award as the outstanding student of Class 58B. He also picked up the TPS Academic Achievement Award and became one of only a few graduates ever to receive both awards. At the graduation ceremony Col. Paul Ashworth, deputy commander of the Air Force Flight Training Center, presented the awards to Givens. In handing them over he stated that Captain Givens had led his class in "flying ability, academic achievement, attitude and all-around good fellowship." Following his graduation, Givens decided to stay at the test pilot school, now as an instructor in the Stability and Control section.

In 1959 the X-15 rocket plane was already undergoing flight performance testing at Edwards, and it became apparent to some of the instructors that the air force would soon have a need for manned spaceflight operations. Givens, together with his civilian instructor colleague William Schweikhard, took the concept of a full aerospace course to the new commandant of the TPS, Maj. Richard C. Lathrop. He in turn asked his special assistant, Maj. Thomas McElmurry, to help get the project off the ground. When future astronaut Captain Frank Borman joined Group 60C early in 1961, he too became a champion of the aerospace course and helped the men where he could. They tirelessly worked their way through the air force echelon, garnering sufficient interest and support for developing the course.

It took quite a while, but eventually a tentative go-ahead was given, although with limited resources the initial development of the course had to be an in-house effort. On 5 June 1961 the proposal became a reality with an initial class of student aerospace pilots. In the years to come many future NASA astronauts would graduate from the school. On 12 October that year the Experimental Flight Test Pilot School was officially redesignated the USAF Aerospace Research Pilot School.

Unlike his colleagues, Givens did not take part in the initial aerospace course. He had already been returned to the navy on a two-year posting as an exchange project pilot with Air Development Squadron 4, based at Point Mugu Naval Air Station, northwest of Los Angeles. Now he was responsible for conducting and developing procedures and tactics for fleet operations of the F8U-2N Crusader.

From November 1961 to September 1962 Givens was back at Edwards AFB as special assistant to the new commandant of the Aerospace Research Pilots School, Lt. Col. Robert M. Howe, pending a permanent assignment within the staff. He

32. Aerospace Research Pilot's School Class III, photographed in front of an F-104 at Edwards Air Force Base. This group included four future NASA astronauts. *Kneeling from left:* Ed Givens, Tommie Benefield, Charlie Bassett, Greg Neubeck, and Michael Collins. *Standing from left:* Alfred Atwell, Neil Garland, James Roman, Alfred Uhalt, and Joe Engle. (Courtesy AFFTC History Office)

would later become a member of the third ARPS group, or Class III. He was always proud to have played a significant role in getting the aerospace school started.

A few weeks after his return to Edwards he attended a New Year's Eve party to usher in 1962 and caught the eye of an attractive twenty-seven-year-old brunette from Bedford, Massachusetts, named Ada Eva Muuss. She knew Givens's flying colleague Michael Collins and his wife, Pat, and they had talked her into coming along. The attraction was fortunately mutual. Givens and Ada spent the night dancing and talking.

At one point Givens suddenly cried out, "Oh migosh, I forgot—I've got my girlfriend out in my car!" Ada was startled—she just could not believe this about the nice young pilot. So, puzzled, she accompanied him outside to the parking lot. There, in the back of his car, sat a mournful-looking Dalmatian, and Givens solemnly introduced Ada to his "girlfriend," Cleo. The dog was a much-loved family pet for many years to come.

Ada Muuss was a naturalized citizen who had been born in Arnstadt, near Weimar, Germany, on 23 June 1935. Russian soldiers had killed her father during the war, and her mother died of tuberculosis at a very young age, so her Uncle Hans Behling and Aunt Susie, her mother's sister, had raised her. In 1954 they helped her escape from East Germany and the oppressive grip of Russian occupation, and then brought her to America, together with their own four children. Dr. Behling set up a home for his family in Bedford, and Ada lived with them while she attended school to improve her English and further her interest in the science of anesthetics. She became a naturalized American citizen a year after their arrival.

On 24 May 1962, Mercury astronaut Scott Carpenter emulated the spectacular February feat of John Glenn by flying three orbits of the Earth in his spacecraft, *Aurora 7*. Carpenter's daring was not lost on Givens, who was thrilled beyond words to see another American astronaut returning from space, but he now had more pressing matters to attend to—he was getting married three days later.

The new eight-month ARPS course suited Givens admirably. He received space-related training and instruction specifically intended to produce astronaut-qualified pilots, engineers, and program managers for air force spaceflight projects such as the x-20 Dyna-Soar, while still others were already on the drawing boards. He was in good company in this course; his classmates included future astronauts Joe Engle, Michael Collins, and Charlie Bassett. Bassett's wife, Jeannie, was very impressed with Givens and recalled an episode at a party in December 1962:

> The ARPS had their annual Christmas party at a place called the Red Barn. It was the closest spot to Edwards, but as the base was quite isolated it was still quite a drive from our house. All of us were having a wonderful time and Ed, in company with his wonderful new wife Ada, was in rare form. At some point rather late in the evening a woman from the Salvation Army came in with her tambourine seeking contributions. No one paid attention to her except Ed. He said, "Let me have that." And around the room he went, harassing and heckling everyone. By the time he returned the tambourine to the rather stunned woman he'd collected about two hundred dollars! He was quite a guy—as they all were.

Following his graduation from the ARPS in May 1963, Givens became a qualified USAF Group 3 military astronaut-designee, which meant he was now trained and available for selection in any of the air force's proposed manned space programs, or as a NASA astronaut. He was certainly looking at the Dyna-Soar program.

The Dyna-Soar (for "Dynamic Soaring"), or x-20 program, began as the third phase of a hypersonic boost-glide program initiated by the National Advisory Committee for Aeronautics (NACA) and the USAF on 14 February 1957. On 14 October that year all the preliminary studies were incorporated into one proposal and accepted by the USAF as the x-20 Dyna-Soar. Beginning on 1 January 1958, the Boeing and Martin companies began setting down ideas and proposals for a reusable aerodynamic powered space plane. This vehicle would be used in connection with an unspecified weapons system, although it is believed its main purpose was to make a pass over a target with reconnaissance equipment. Boeing was selected on 9 November 1959 as the prime contractor.

Boeing's final design and mock-up of the Dyna-Soar was a small black, delta-winged vehicle forty-five feet long and weighing six tons, with a blunt, rounded nose and twin vertical fins. The Dyna-Soar was designed to be placed in Earth orbit by a booster rocket (later determined to be the Titan III) and brought back to Earth by the firing of retro-rockets, reentering the Earth's atmosphere and landing like a conventional aircraft under the pilot's control. In September 1962, and amid much fanfare, the air force announced the selection of six USAF astronauts to fly the X-20 missions.

Unfortunately for those involved, the enormous cost of the program saw funding gradually whittled away until finally, in December 1963, Project Dyna-Soar was officially canceled. Despite the loss of this program, Givens remained resolute in his ambition to fly into space. After all, he could still apply to NASA for consideration as an astronaut. But then the air force came up with another, more cost-effective space program, this time known as the Manned Orbiting Laboratory, or MOL. This program would rely on a modified Gemini spacecraft mounted atop a long observation platform, and the program was given the official go-ahead by President Lyndon B. Johnson in August 1965.

Suddenly there was renewed activity in the air force to get this innovative but highly classified project underway. Givens, who by now had been promoted to major, was assigned to the Air Force Space Systems Division Office, Detachment 2, as a project officer at the Manned Spacecraft Center in Houston, where he became involved in designing the Astronaut Maneuvering Unit (AMU), which would have been used by the MOL astronauts.

The Missiles and Space Division of LTV Aerospace, a subsidiary of Ling-Temco-Vought, had developed the AMU for the air force. It was designed as a compact strap-on pack, which would virtually convert a space-walking astronaut into an untethered, human satellite. As with the later Manned Maneuvering Unit (MMU), it combined the ability to gently propel astronauts around any axis using a series of hydrogen peroxide fuel jets with a portable life-support system good for an hour's activities outside the spacecraft. An astronaut using the AMU could transfer himself and supplies from one orbiting unit to another and perform intricate or demanding tasks without the need to be tethered to his spacecraft.

Three fully functional units would later be delivered to NASA—one for use on the Gemini 9 mission, and then another on Gemini 12. The first was carried aloft on the redesignated Gemini 9A flight, stowed in the bell-like adaptor section behind the Gemini craft. The plan called for astronaut Gene Cernan to exit the hatch and make his way to the adapter, don the bulky AMU, and then test it out on some purely symbolic maintenance tasks around the spacecraft. But Cernan encountered enormous, unforeseen difficulties in getting around to the adapter. His visor fogged up, making it impossible for him to see what he was doing or where he was going. He

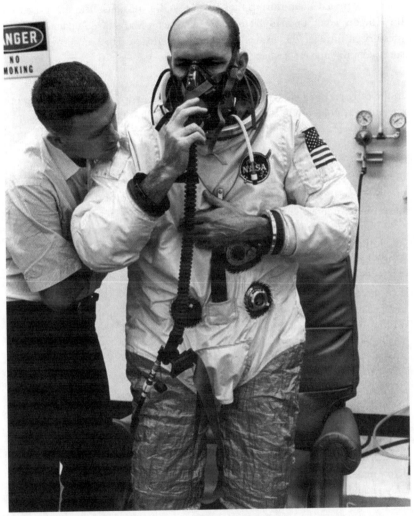

33. Wearing a Gemini EVA space suit fitted with thermal protection material on the legs, Ed Givens prepares to undertake an altitude chamber test. This heavily insulated suit was designed specifically for use with the Astronaut Maneuvering Unit. (NASA)

kept trying to the point of near exhaustion, but in the end was forced to abandon the effort and squeeze himself back into the Gemini craft. The AMU remained untested in actual spaceflight conditions.

Much to the air force's undisguised displeasure, NASA later scrapped plans to carry another AMU on the GT-12 mission. Two modified versions of the AMU would finally make it into space but not for some years later, when the resident astronauts extensively tested them during the Skylab 3 and 4 missions. The units used on these flights would be manufactured by the Martin Marietta Company and used pressurized nitrogen gas in lieu of hydrogen peroxide. The MOL program itself survived until June 1969, when it was canceled.

In the early part of 1964 there was considerable discussion about space programs beyond the Apollo moon landings. NASA was on a roll with the successful completion of Project Mercury and was deep into planning and training for the Gemini program. The Gemini spacecraft would carry two men into orbit on an increasingly ambitious and complicated series of missions. The American public was enamored of the space program, and the astronauts were the nation's newest heroes. Politicians everywhere were tumbling over each other to be seen as advocates of spaceflight as the prospect of lunar and Earth orbital exploration became a national fascination.

With the first planned moon landing still some years away, a preliminary post-Apollo program had already been roughed out in the office of George Mueller, NASA's head of manned spaceflight. Originally known as Apollo X, and later the Apollo Extension System, or AES, this three-pronged series would use Apollo spacecraft in concert with Saturn 1B and V rockets to provide a series of postlanding, manned lunar-orbiting survey flights, extended moon-landing missions, and Earth-orbiting workshop missions. All three types of mission would be flown concurrently. The following year the proposal for the Earth-orbiting flight series would undergo a name change to Apollo Applications Program (AAP).

This development meant that NASA would need to select and train more pilot-astronauts, so Bob Gilruth, in his position as Manned Spacecraft Center director, dispatched Deke Slayton to NASA's headquarters in Washington to put the case before the deputy administrator for manned spaceflight, Dr. George Mueller. Gilruth felt there was a pressing need to swell the pilot-astronaut ranks from the existing thirty, but he knew that Mueller would need to be provided with a convincing argument before making any sort of commitment. Slayton did the job and returned to Houston with a mandate for Gilruth to take onboard as many new astronauts as he felt were needed.

On 10 September 1965 NASA began a recruitment drive for its newest intake of astronauts. As soon as Ed Givens heard about it, he fired in his application. By now he had accumulated more than thirty-five hundred hours of flight time, including twenty-eight hundred in jet aircraft. He sat through several intense interviews and had a thorough physical checkout in the School of Aviation Medicine at Brooks Air Force Base in San Antonio. Another of those interviewed at Brooks, Jack Lousma, remembers it as a day filled with bitter irony. There they were, busting their guts to be selected by NASA, when they heard the shocking news bulletin that Gemini astronauts Elliot See and Charlie Bassett had been killed just hours before in a plane crash in Missouri. It was a sobering piece of news.

By March 1966 Slayton's selection panel, which included astronauts John Young, Mike Collins, Al Bean, and C.C. Williams, had whittled the field of applicants down to thirty-five, and Slayton told them he would take as many of them as were fully qualified. So the panel members put their heads together again and produced a list of nineteen names. Slayton went through the list carefully and, after a short deliberation, took the lot. The new selections gave him a post-Apollo pool of fifty-seven astronauts, although he realistically surmised that several senior astronauts would resign after the initial round of moon landings.

To his delight, Givens was one of those who received the much-anticipated call from Slayton, formally asking if he would like to report to Houston on 1 May to begin training as an astronaut. He quickly accepted, and the names of the Group 5 astronauts were officially announced on 4 April 1966. They came to call themselves the Original Nineteen—a parody on the title of Original Seven bestowed upon the Mercury astronauts. At the announcement of Givens's selection, a reporter asked him if it was a thrill to become an astronaut. He grinned and replied, "That's an understatement!"

By this time Ed and Ada Givens were already living near the space center, on Shadow Creek in El Lago, so there was no resettlement problem associated with his change of career. They had two young children: daughter Cathrine had been born on 11 April 1963, and Edward Galen III on 12 June 1964. The burden on Ada grew immeasurably as her husband threw himself into his NASA training. He worked long hours, flew across the country, and was absent for days on end. When he did arrive home, he was physically and mentally exhausted. But Ada was a strong-willed person, not afraid to tackle any challenge, and she set up a loving home for the children and their faithful dog, Cleo.

The new group's preliminary orientation training was followed in August 1966 by the now-standard one-week desert survival exercise in the Nevada Desert. The men also participated in water survival training at NAS Pensacola and jungle survival techniques in the Panamanian jungle.

NASA was now in the middle of its highly successful Gemini program, but the new astronauts did not train for the two-man missions. Instead, following their initial four months of formal training, they went straight into engineering instruction for the Apollo systems. However, they did perform rendezvous and docking exercises on the Gemini training simulators, using mock-ups of the Agena adapter.

Givens trained hard and downplayed his status a little when asked questions by a fervent media. When one reporter asked him if he saw himself as a modern-day hero, the cigar-smoking Givens just shrugged and said, "I'm no hero. I've just got a job to do, and I try to do it to the best of my ability. This is the pinnacle of my career—it's probably the most interesting and challenging job that I can conceive of. I wouldn't trade it for anything."

One of Givens's tasks crucial to the future success of the Apollo program came his way late summer in 1966. It concerned a facility at MSC called the Space Environment Simulation Laboratory, or SESL, which was essentially a vast chamber capable of simulating the vacuum of space. This was accomplished by placing a subject spacecraft inside the cavernous chamber and pumping out the air, resulting in conditions similar to those encountered at around 140 miles. Other characteristics of spaceflight that could be simulated in the SESL were high temperatures and lighting conditions, both replicated using a battery of powerful carbon-arc lamps. These lamps could bake one side of the spacecraft, while the other side was exposed to extreme cold. A complete Apollo spacecraft, including the service module, spent eighty-three days inside SESL Chamber A, and two tests were carried out—an unmanned test of 92 hours, and a manned test of 163 hours. For the latter, Givens teamed with scientist-astronaut Joe Kerwin and Joe Gagliano, an air force captain assigned to MSC's Flight Crew Support Division. The three men "flew" a simulated six-day mission to the moon inside the Apollo spacecraft, which turned up a number of design flaws and procedural errors that could be remedied in time for the first true manned flight. In conducting this trial, Givens virtually flew the lunar mission he hoped he would one day fly in reality.

Later in their training, around November 1966, the new astronauts were told they would have to make a choice, whether to specialize in the command module or lunar excursion module (LEM), as it was then called. It was emphasized that whatever road they chose, every man would still have a chance of walking on the moon. In the end the split was fairly even, with Givens one of those opting to concentrate on the command module. He knew that specializing in the LEM was certainly a fast-track route to a lunar landing assignment, but his group had been offered a variety of future options. An indefinite number of lunar landings was forecast—certainly more than ten—so Givens probably figured he would fly as a command module pilot (CMP) first, then later take on training as an LEM pilot.

As things stood at that time, planning for NASA's 1967 budget included twenty-six Saturn 1B launches and nineteen Saturn V launches stretching ahead into the mid 1970s. Assuming the first manned lunar landing had taken place by 1969, most schedules envisioned at least two lunar landing missions each year from 1970 to the middle of that decade. There would also be the lunar-orbiting survey missions, planned at one per year, with a crew remaining in lunar orbit for a week. Following the initial series of lunar landing missions, extended surface expeditions were in the pipeline, with crews spending up to two weeks on the moon, supported by shelters and transport vehicles.

With all these forecast missions to anticipate, Givens plunged into his command module training with vigorous exhilaration. Flying the CM to the moon meant he would then have good all-around experience for the Earth-orbiting and lunar programs slated to follow the initial Apollo missions, and he would be one of the more experienced astronauts available for selection—perhaps as a mission commander. Several of his group agreed with him in this thinking, so there was no concerted rush for LEM assignment. Had they been able to see into the future and know there would actually be only six lunar landing missions, the choice of specialization for many might have been different. Most were eventually given their first choice, while others, it seems, were assigned. Some even ended up working in other technical areas. Stu Roosa and Charlie Duke, for instance, found themselves working on issues surrounding the development of the Saturn rocket booster. While this area may have lacked the obvious attraction and advantage of CM and LEM training, it did not seem to matter in the end—both men later flew to the moon, and Duke even walked on its surface.

With the announcement of the first three Apollo crews, Deke Slayton and Jim McDivitt (appointed commander of Apollo 2) felt it was necessary to assign an additional three men to each prime and backup Apollo crew to support them in performing flight-related duties that might otherwise impinge on their valuable training time. The Group 5 astronauts therefore become known as the Apollo support crews. All nine astronauts selected for this role came from the 1966 group, and Givens suddenly found himself with a mission assignment. He was to join Ron Evans and Jack Swigert as the support crew for Apollo 1 (also known at the time as Apollo 204). Their task was to assist the prime and backup crews in engineering details, gathering essential information, and preflight preparations.

Givens had gained a reputation as a solid and dependable worker from the moment he joined the astronaut corps, and his appointment to an early support crew was an affirmation that he was highly regarded by Slayton and the NASA hierarchy. If he did a good job he would be considered for a backup crew position, and then, if all went as planned, for a prime Apollo crew. A further glimmer of his prospects came early in 1967 when Alan Shepard listed Givens to begin helicopter training with Fred Haise, beginning 27 February. It was an early sign that Givens was under consideration for an Apollo mission. His future was looking decidedly bright.

In recent years there had been growing consternation about the Soviet Union's stream of space "firsts." The nation boasted the first satellite, the first living creature sent into orbit, the first man in space, the first woman, the first multimanned spacecraft, and the first person to leave a spacecraft in orbit to conduct what was commonly called a space walk. The Soviets had also been the first to smash a probe into the moon and to photograph its hidden far side. But America had slowly and relentlessly wound in the slack; by the mid 1960s it had not only caught up but had begun eclipsing the Soviet Union's efforts in the big ballgame of manned spaceflight.

After a stuttering start with its manned Mercury program, NASA developed far more sophisticated and reliable hardware and systems. These innovations had begun to outstrip those of the Russians, whose mammoth efforts to create ever more spectacular flights had begun to falter, clearly demonstrating they had reached the limits of their technology. Ten Gemini two-man flights had now taken place, and America held a commanding lead of nearly two thousand hours in orbit—almost four times that of the Soviet Union. At a relatively modest cost of just over a billion and a quarter dollars, and with an impressive list of accomplishments, Gemini had cleared the way for America to go to the moon.

But then the nation's smug complacency had received a massive jolt one Friday evening in January, when a spark created a fire that rapidly engulfed the interior of Apollo spacecraft 012. Within seconds three trapped astronauts lost their lives, and the space program came to a shuddering standstill. Gus Grissom, Ed White, and Roger Chaffee had paid the ultimate price of exploration, and the resultant investigations delayed any further manned flights for the better part of two years.

The loss of the three astronauts hit everyone hard, including the support crew members, who were at the cape when the fire robbed them of three friends and colleagues. Givens called home and spoke to Ada, who was enjoying a visit from her close friend Gratia Lousma. He told her there was a problem at the cape that he could not discuss, and that he would be home quite late. Soon after, the two wives heard the terrible news on Ada's television. Gratia, whose husband, Jack, was on astronaut duties in Huntsville, said she would stay until Givens came home, as neither of them wanted to be alone after hearing the tragic news about men both of them knew well. When Givens walked in well after midnight, the sheer agony of that day was etched deeply into his face.

Despite the loss of the three astronauts, there was some unexpected good news in store for Givens. First, Wally Schirra, Donn Eisele, and Walt Cunningham were now reassigned to the role of prime crew for the first flight, which would become known as Apollo 7. The former Apollo 1 support team members Givens, Evans, and Swigert were advised they would now assist Schirra's prime and backup crews. The second bit of good news, which Givens received on 22 March, was of a far more personal nature; Ada had presented him with another daughter, whom they named Diane Susan Givens.

The training now intensified as everyone knuckled down to the daunting task of getting the Apollo program, and President Kennedy's goal of a manned moon landing, back on track. Having such an overloaded schedule, Givens was actually pleased when he was invited to a rather pleasant diversion one night in June—a meeting of the Quiet Birdmen. He had to be up early the next morning to attend an important meeting, but he was also eager to catch up with a few of his old flying buddies.

It turned out to be an entertaining evening, full of nostalgia and mirth. At some point everyone had to get up and relate what he had been up to, and while several of the guests that night excelled as interesting speakers, many others proved to be outrageously funny. They all had aircraft and aviation in common, and their stories ranged from those of early fighter pilots and flying pioneers to Givens and his fellow astronaut, Mercury pilot Gordon Cooper. It was with genuine regret that Givens told his hosts he had to leave early, but he was nevertheless pleased to have the company of a couple of air force reservists he had met at the gathering. The barracks where he would drop them was not too far from where he lived in Seabrook, so he was not going much out of his way.

Givens cautiously pulled out of the Skylane Motel parking lot and merged into the traffic on the multilane road. The motel was on a corner and there was an unusually large number of cars and trucks shooshing along the rain-slicked road, so he found himself stuck in the right-hand lane at a traffic light where he had intended to make a left turn. He muttered "Nuts!" and told his passengers he had to make a left turn but could do so a little farther down. "You can get up to the freeway on almost every road along here," he assured Fran Dellorto and Bill Hall as he began carefully moving into the left-hand lane.

As the men made their way down Telephone Road, the streetlights on their left grew fewer and fewer in number until eventually there was nothing but a vast blackness. Givens mentioned that Houston airport was somewhere out that way. Hall was not taking a great deal of notice of what was outside; he was leaning forward, his elbows resting on the seats in front so he could talk to his two companions. He was fascinated by the astronaut's thoughts on the Gemini program and NASA's plans to send men to the moon.

After a considerable distance without a cross street, a yellow blinker light came into view at an intersection. "This one ought to go through," Givens said as he took a left turn onto Knapp Road. Hall remembers commenting on the fact that there were no houses or buildings to be seen and how dark it was on that road. Givens agreed, but shrugged it off, lightheartedly suggesting that was the way things were in Texas.

A few minutes later, and traveling below the speed limit at around 55 mph, the three men continued their conversation as they made their way down the dark, straight road. As usual at that time of the year, a little steam was rising from the wet asphalt. At one point Givens slowed as the Volkswagen went over a small rise in the road, and when the headlights dipped back to the road he accelerated once again.

Seconds later, the three men were alarmed to see a dangerous situation looming ahead. Directly in front of them a sturdy guy wire was angling down from a telephone pole on the right side of the road, straight into the middle of the left lane. There had been no indication that the road was about to come to an abrupt end. But Givens was not one to panic; he was a test pilot, and as such he reacted calmly and assuredly, weighing up his options in milliseconds. He stomped down on the brake pedal and, without losing control, deftly steered the small sedan between the pole on the right and the guy wire on the left. However, the road was still wet, and the tires would not grip. Hall, still leaning on the back of the front seats, recalls looking ahead in the beam from the car's headlights and seeing what looked like a relatively smooth field of grass ahead of them. He just had time to think, "That's going to make a pretty good *whooomp* when we run out of road!"

Although not going overly fast, the car skidded along the road for some thirty-three yards before it left the road, heading for what seemed to be a minimally damaging incursion into someone's field. What none of them realized was that beyond where the road curved in a brutally sharp and unmarked left-hand bend was a deep, hidden irrigation ditch. It was 12:02 A.M., and Hall now takes up the narrative:

> The irrigation or drainage ditch was probably three or four feet deep, with a flat bottom and sloping sides. It was wide enough so that as the car left the ground the ditch dropped away under it, the whole car came down flat into it, and slammed into the opposite bank.
>
> Evidently the impact caused me to push the two front seats forward, together with the men in them. The windshield popped out unbroken as a vw was supposed to do. Ed hit the steering wheel and post and was fatally injured right then. His chest was crushed. Fran Dellorto evidently hit the doorpost as the door popped open. It broke his right leg and I think his hip. Seven places as I recall. He hit the dashboard with his chest and broke several ribs and, I seem to recall, separated his sternum. The door frame, I think, put a big gash across his face. I don't remember if his nose was broken or not.
>
> I made out the best. Still with my chin on my hands on the back of the front seats when we hit bottom, the slam down on my fists put a huge bruise on my neck and chin. As the seats leaned forward I slid up them and smashed my face against the mirror and the top of the windshield frame. In the process I broke off three teeth. My head or facial bones were broken at the right brow, temple and cheek. My head was entirely black and blue.
>
> I had been thrown out of the car and found myself laying in the grass and hurting. I laid still and began assessing how badly I had been hurt. I heard some low and some not so low moans from above and behind me, and made a couple of tries to roll over, but everything hurt too badly. At that point I voiced the opinion as loudly as I could that we should lie still, that we were probably hurt badly, and we should wait for help. I received no replies.
>
> I probably passed out, although I remember continuing to explore the inside of my mouth with my tongue, trying to ascertain how many teeth I had lost, and whether they were broken off or knocked out (they were broken off). Then I heard voices and some guy grabbed my head, shoved a flashlight in my eye and pulled up my eyelid. I told him to get that damned light out of my eyes, and he dropped me like a hot potato and said, "This one's okay!" and went to the others. I think there were two or three guys there then.

*The number of people and vehicles kept increasing. Fran was transported first, and they had to call another ambulance for me. I finally figured out that one of us hadn't made it, but I didn't know which one then, and no one would answer my questions.*

*I was in the hospital [Houston's Baptist Memorial Hospital Southeast] about three days, maybe four. Long enough for Fran to recover from surgery enough so that I could talk to him. Gordon Cooper and his wife came in to see me my first day, and to really tell me about Ed. I asked the hospital to get me some pen and paper, and I wrote a letter to Ed's wife to assure her, and anyone from NASA or whatever, that it had not been Ed's fault. Gordon took it to her, and I'm sure NASA made some copies. I never heard from her, and did not expect to.*

*I made arrangements to contact Fran when he would be better. Eventually he was recovering enough to be able to file suit against the city of Pearland. I joined him in the suit, and had to travel to Houston to make a deposition. After the deposition, one of the clerks in the law office took me to the scene on the way back to the field. I was staggered to find that two years later there was still no sign until right at the end of the road, right where we had gone straight ahead, and that sign was hand scribbled with black paint on a deep red background. It was hard to see in broad daylight! The pavement ends, and at the left a little dirt road comes in from that side. The road was covered with skid marks where people had slid. To the left of the dirt road is a house. The night we wrecked, the lady who lives there called the police and the ambulance because there had been so many wrecks there and she knew the numbers by heart. She would not come out to help—she had seen too much mayhem at the end of the road.*

As Hall had suspected, one of them did not make it. Ed Givens, pinned under the steering wheel, had suffered a crushed chest and severe internal injuries. He was alive when police arrived, but died en route to the hospital at 12:40 A.M. A Pearland Police investigator named Jones, who interviewed Hall in the hospital, later noted in his report that Givens had missed turning at either Airport Boulevard or Alameda-Genoa Road to leave Telephone Road en route to Ellington.

More than thirty years after the fatal accident in which Givens died, Hall still has a vivid recollection of that night. He emphatically believes that Givens was driving responsibly:

*I guess the final opinion from here is the one I have had since the accident. Ed Givens was not at fault. He was in full control and driving within the speed limit. If he had any alcohol I neither saw it nor think he could have had much. He displayed no inclination to do anything wrong, even when he could have made the originally intended left turn from the traffic lights outside the meeting place. He assessed the blinking yellow light as a sign of relatively heavy traffic, and he was ready to slow down or brake even when the road merely had a rise that lifted the lights a little. He had the car under control and slowing as rapidly as possible when the road ended, and I don't think he thought there was a ditch there either—it looked like a good field straight ahead.*

*Incidentally, I saw the TV report of the tragedy while in hospital—the road was all covered with multiple skid marks then, many going right off the end of the road.*

Months later, the tragedy claimed two more victims. Fran Dellorto had survived his major injuries and was discharged from the hospital after four weeks. After a period of healing and physiotherapy he had resumed working at O'Hare International Airport. Since he was still physically unable to drive, his wife dutifully took him to work and back each day in their car. One morning they stopped for a red light at a busy intersection, and as the light changed to green they moved off. An impatient driver on their right tried to beat the light, accelerating into the intersection. His car raced through the red light and slammed straight into the passenger side of their automobile. Dellorto and his wife died instantly in the terrible collision.

Ada Givens was informed of her husband's death by astronauts Deke Slayton (then director of Flight Crew Operations) and Stuart Roosa, together with Dr. Charles Berry, the astronauts' physician at MSC. Givens's parents were notified at their Quanah home at 3:10 A.M. Totally distraught by the loss of a second son, they were advised that NASA had already dispatched a Grumman Gulfstream aircraft to transport them to Houston.

On 8 June a solemn forty-minute service was held at the Seabrook Methodist Church, where Ed and Ada Givens had been members. It was located just a few miles down the road from the space center. Barely five months earlier the church had been the site of a memorial service for two of the three Apollo astronauts who had perished in the launch pad fire of 27 January. The three widows were among the three hundred members of the space community, including many astronauts, who now gathered to pay homage to Ed Givens—the seventh from their ranks to die in three years.

Officiating pastor on the day was the Reverend Conrad Winborn, while the Reverend Dallas Lee of Quanah, who had baptized the infant Givens thirty-seven years before in his hometown, conducted the service. He recalled Givens as a boy, and later as a young man "whose life was a dream and a challenge and striding for the other side." He then eulogized the late astronaut as a person of outstanding accomplishments and honors, and as "one of America's finest, one of the world's finest" who "dreamed bigger dreams. He dreamed of the moon. He wanted to go to the moon. We extend our gratitude to him and his lovely little family, and to his parents who have now given two sons to this nation."

Throughout the service Ada Givens, escorted to the church by astronaut Michael Collins, sat quietly dry-eyed beside her husband's grief-stricken parents. Toward the end of Reverend Lee's service, with those at the service singing "A Mighty Fortress Is Our God," four gleaming T-38 jets flown by Givens's fellow astronauts streaked overhead in salute to a fallen comrade. As they roared off into the distance, one peeled away and soared skyward, leaving the symbolic "lost pilot" or "missing man" formation.

Following the service, Givens's body was flown to Quanah in an air force transport aircraft, escorted by astronaut and Annapolis classmate Thomas Stafford. The next day a military funeral service, also conducted by the Reverend Lee, was held at Quanah's First Baptist Church. It had been Ada's decision to bring the body of her husband back to Quanah ("our home," she said at the time) for burial.

The pallbearers at this service were the prime and backup Apollo 7 crew members Wally Schirra, Donn Eisele, Walt Cunningham, John Young, Tom Stafford, and Gene Cernan. Afterward, Givens's body was laid to rest in the old cemetery at Quanah's Memorial Park.

Apart from his grieving widow, the astronaut had left behind a very young family—daughter Cathrine, age four, son Edward, almost three, and baby Diane, just ten weeks old.

On 5 March 1977, Major General Thomas Stafford, commander of the Air Force Flight Test Center at Edwards AFB and a former astronaut who had known Ed Givens well, was on hand to dedicate the Major Edward Galen Givens Space Room in the Hardeman County Museum in Quanah. NASA and the Smithsonian Institution had furnished exhibits for display in the space room.

During the brief dedication ceremony, General Stafford described Givens as an "intrepid pilot, a steady dedicated professional who was completely absorbed in his work." He told the large gathering of family and guests "the citizens of Quanah and Hardeman should take pride . . . in the accomplishments of your native son, Edward Givens, whose efforts were indicative of the true pioneering spirit which is responsible for America's progress as a world leader." He added,

> All of us at some undetermined point in our lifetime entertain visions of contributing to the progress of mankind.
>
> For many, the vision all too often disappears or remains nothing more than the blur of an unfulfilled dream, but there are a select few whose vision have become realities, and whose contributions are responsible for the nation's progress as a world leader. The trials and tribulations of their individual accomplishments have been, and will continue to be, remembered in museum displays all through the country.

*Such a contribution was made by Edward Givens, a Major in the United States Air Force, and one of America's early pioneers in the manned space flight effort.*

More than twenty years after the opening of the library, General Stafford reflected on the life of Ed Givens for this book: "Ed and I go all the way back; we were in the same class in the Naval Academy from 1948 to 1952. I remember him and his wife Ada with very, very fond memories. He was just a top-notch individual, very hard working, very focused, and one of the top men in his group. Ed would certainly have been one of the contenders—one of the first from his group—to fly an early Apollo mission. I'm delighted for Ed's sake, and his family, that his story will finally be told. He was a good man."

Of the nineteen members of Givens's Group 5 astronauts, nine flew to the moon, and three of that number, Charlie Duke, Jim Irwin, and Ed Mitchell, left footprints in the lunar soil. Mitchell remembers very little about Givens, and he told the author that his fellow astronaut's death had simply "happened too soon. Our group had not become very cohesive at that time, and we all had been sent on different technical missions, so that I had little time to interact with Ed and get to know him, except as just another member of our group."

Vance Brand, who flew on the historic Apollo-Soyuz mission in 1975 and later went on to complete two space shuttle missions, was also a member of Group 5. He agreed that there was very little time for this large group to get to know one another particularly well, as he told the author: "I attended astronaut training with Ed Givens, whom I found to be a very likable, energetic and competent Air Force officer. At that time, there were nineteen of us in the fifth class of astronauts going through ocean, desert and jungle training, space science classes, field trips to various NASA centers, and other training for Apollo missions. It was very unfortunate that Ed did not get the chance to participate in Apollo or follow-on missions because of his tragic accident."

Don Lind was another who joined the astronaut program in Givens's selection group, and though he did not get to fly on Apollo, he was the backup pilot for Skylabs 3 and 4 and was the Skylab Rescue Standby pilot. In 1984 he was a Spacelab 3 mission specialist on shuttle mission STS-18. Casting back over more than three decades, he told the author that he and Givens "went through all the initial training together . . . survival training, geology field trips, science classes, visits to the various NASA centers. We grew rather close as a group as we began what we knew would be a great adventure. I found Ed to be very sharp, energetic and enthusiastic about the space program. He was a hard worker. I would have been happy to have flown with him." He described Givens's death as "a real tragedy. He left behind a lovely wife. He would have been proud of his son, who bears his name, and also his little daughters and the beautiful young women that they grew to be."

Among many other tributes paid to Givens, a street at Keesler Air Force Base in Biloxi, Mississippi, was named in his honor.

Ada Givens stayed in Houston after her husband's death. Two years after the accident she and her family moved into another house in El Lago with a much larger yard, which she deemed to be far more suitable for her and the children. Some years later she went on a skiing trip with Gratia Lousma, and on their return Ada was talking to her friend when she remarked, "What in the world am I still doing here in Houston when I could be living somewhere beautiful like the mountains in Colorado?" It was then that she said what had obviously been on her mind for some time. "I'm leaving this place and getting back into life."

Whatever qualities Ada Givens might have lacked, courage and determination were not among them. Prepared to get on with rebuilding her life, she followed her dream and resettled with her family in Colorado. In 1980 she took another plunge and went back to school to be recertified as a nurse anesthetist. Ada then worked at various establishments until she found a position that suited her in Salem, Oregon. Her older daughter, Cathrine, opted to stay in Colorado, while young Ed was already away from home after gaining an appointment in the Air Force Academy. Ada's younger daughter, Diane, was still living with her and went to school in Salem.

A few years later Ada's health began to deteriorate, but she refused to let it slow her down. A diabetic, she was also suffering from a heart disease, but she was otherwise a strong and independent person and never one to complain. Her coworkers had no idea how sick she really was and were not overly concerned when she called in sick on Friday, 7 February 1986. They were more preoccupied with events following the loss of an American space crew, when an explosion had torn apart the space shuttle *Challenger* a few days earlier. The following Monday, 10 February 1986, her colleagues were shocked to learn that Ada Givens had passed away.

Gratia Lousma could not believe that her close friend had gone so suddenly. Ada had phoned from the hospital just that weekend to say she was ill and undergoing treatment but gave the impression it was a passing thing related to her diabetes. Gratia still wonders to this day why Ada did not confide in her about the seriousness of her illness.

These days, Ed and Ada's children lead quiet lives far from Houston and the space program. Cathrine, a labor and delivery nurse, and her husband, Morgan, live in Greensboro, North Carolina, with their five children. Diane, an elementary school teacher, resides in Colorado Springs with her husband, Bill, and their two children.

Like his father, Edward Galen Givens III is better known to his family as Galen. Following for a time in his father's footsteps, he graduated from the Air Force Academy in 1986. He then became an instructor pilot at Enid, Oklahoma, during which time his three sons were born. Galen was then stationed in San Antonio but finally decided to leave the air force and flew F-16 aircraft with the Louisiana Air National Guard. His next move was into commercial aviation, and today he is a pilot with a major domestic American airline. He and his wife, Angie, and their three sons also live in Colorado Springs.

Cathrine reflected on the man she knew ever so briefly, the astronaut father who never came home one night:

> I don't know where to begin to tell you what it was like growing up without my dad. I often felt my family had very high expectations of me because I was Ed Givens' daughter, but other people didn't know that. In looking at stories of the recent crash and death of JFK Jr., I wonder if he would have made it as far as he did without people knowing who his dad was. I've noticed how far he could "ride" his name, but also how strong he was in choosing his own path.
>
> My family knew my dad was incredibly smart and motivated to achievement. I always heard about it through stories, but somehow it seems more real since reading the draft of this chapter. All the bits and pieces that were just parts of memories have now been organized into his life story, and it has helped me learn so much that I never knew before.
>
> The only memory I have of my dad is from when I was three years old. I often remember being at the kitchen table eating dinner when he got home from work—but we could always get up, and he'd pick Galen and I up and swing us high in the air and hug us hello. But that's it. I look at pictures of Galen and I at the beach with him, but don't remember anything in my memory. I do love the beach—it's probably my favorite place to go, so I like to believe my dad must have taught me to love the beach from the beginning.
>
> It was hard not having a father. Nowadays psychologists know girls need their fathers as much as boys do. But years ago I don't think that was recognized. Friends and family really focused on Ed (Galen), trying to help him overcome life without a dad. I've had a lot of emotional issues that I haven't dealt with well. I remember seeing a psychiatrist during a stressful time in nursing school and truly remember that as the first time of crying and being sad about my dad's death. When he died Ed and I weren't even taken to the funeral—I think they were trying to protect us.
>
> My grandma and grandpa—we called them Ma and Pa—told us the most stories. They just about exploded with pride when they talked about him. My mom told me a few stories but I don't think I was old enough to appreciate them. She loved him very much. I believe he was the only man for her—she never dated anyone after he was gone. But she did a great job of being mom and dad—she was stubbornly strong.
>
> And the Lord has given me a wonderful husband too; Morgan has always been interested in my dad and his accomplishments, which has really allowed me to be proud of who I am.

Ed Givens's dreams died with him that tragic night in Pearland. One can only speculate about the feats he might have achieved, the missions he might have flown, and whether he might have ended up renowned as one of the few men who walked on the moon.

In a sense Ed Givens did make it to the moon; his name was among those inscribed on the plaque left on the plains of Hadley by the crew of Apollo 15. However, Givens is the only preshuttle astronaut whose name is not engraved on the Astronaut Memorial Mirror at the Kennedy Space Center. Jerry Carr, who flew on the Skylab 4 mission, was in Givens's astronaut group, and he told the author he was "appalled" that his colleague's name is missing from the memorial: "Just because he was killed on his way home from some function other than work is irrelevant to who he was and what his job was. Once you take on the role of Astronaut you are in the public eye and are forever on duty. Who cares whether you are on the way home from a social function or a spacecraft test? Your life has been committed to the program, and whatever you do you are measured relative to that commitment. No double standards!"

As to the weak peroration that Givens was "off duty" when he died, NASA scientist-astronaut Brian O'Leary recalls his boss Alan Shepard tearing strips off him for attending a friend's wedding in New York without seeking permission. "Remember you're an astronaut now," Shepard warned him. "You're an astronaut twenty-four hours a day, three hundred and sixty-five days a year!"

The argument against his inclusion is poor and still hurtful for his children, and as one of a handful of men who gave their lives in reaching for the moon, Ed Givens deserves far better.

# 6  "Mayday, Mayday!"
## Major Clifton Curtis Williams Jr., USMC

*In many ways, Clifton C. Williams was a giant of a man. Tall, handsome, and muscularly stocky, he was the first bachelor to join the astronaut corps, and only the second marine after John Glenn. From Mobile, Alabama, Williams (known to all as "C.C.") was well liked in the corridors of Houston's Manned Spacecraft Center. He found it easy to make friends with his fellow astronauts, and his round face often split in a wide, affable grin. But that easygoing personality concealed another man—the keen, cool, and sometimes irascible fighter pilot with one driving ambition: to fly to the moon. And yet, in a few terrifying seconds over a Tallahassee pine forest, one of NASA's favored few lost not only his life but also an assured path to enduring spaceflight fame. He professed to have few misconceptions about the slings and arrows of being an astronaut and met life head on, never blinking. Only death deceived him, taking him by surprise. Before his untimely death, Williams had been selected to lope across the lunar surface with Pete Conrad on what would become the second lunar landing, Apollo 12. Instead, he became yet another casualty and grim statistic in America's relentless drive to beat the Russians in putting a man on the moon.*

It was a highly unlikely place to find a bunch of men who might one day fly to the moon. In the sweltering, strength-sapping heat of the Panama jungle a group of astronauts stood in a ragged cluster, trying their hardest to look interested as a Choco Indian demonstrated the best method of turning an ugly reptile into a palatable dinner by broiling it on a skewer. The astronauts looked on with unconcealed bemusement and shook their heads in a shared revulsion, trying not to think what was in store for them in the next few minutes. An unpleasant smell of burning iguana flesh assailed their nostrils and seriously challenged their enthusiasm for the meal they would soon consume.

For once C.C. Williams was relatively subdued, and he was not wearing the usual broad grin across his face. Truth is, he was not much enjoying this jungle survival course, although the company of his astronaut buddies had made it far more endurable. He and "Rusty" Schweickart had been paired off, and the following day each group of two would be transported into the jungle by helicopter for a two-mile hike back to camp. Schweickart rolled his eyes at Williams and grimaced, with a look that suggested a Houston hamburger and malt would go down far better than the charred, scaly iguana.

There was another reason for Williams's discernible lack of enthusiasm—his mind was elsewhere. Just three days before he had embarked on the Panamanian adventure, his longtime sweetheart, Beth Lansche, had flown to Houston from her home in San Francisco. She wanted to be with Williams before he left for the exercise, and to join him in announcing their engagement. Beth was once a water-skiing performer at Florida's Cypress Gardens and was an extremely photogenic and personable young woman. She was also determined and erudite, and not slow to speak up passionately on issues that mattered to her. Despite having a boyfriend in the military, she still proudly marched in anti-Vietnam rallies. Williams would just smile and shake his head. He knew he was marrying a handful in Beth Lansche, but in many ways their differing opinions on matters of great importance only served to strengthen their love. Together, they made a good-looking, obviously happy couple for the eager cameramen.

The day Williams flew out on his jungle course, Beth also departed, heading for her hometown of New Bern, North Carolina, to finalize plans for what was meant to be a small wedding, with just a few immediate family members in attendance. Little wonder that Williams was preoccupied during his survival training—it covered almost the entire period of his engagement. On 1 July, the day after he returned, he and Beth would be married in New Bern. Naturally enough he had received a lot of good-natured ribbing but also many heartfelt congratulations. At least, he joked, it would end a king-size telephone bill between Houston and the West Coast.

When Williams joined NASA he was the astronaut corps's first bachelor, and the press had a field day with the story angle. Being single, he was instantly different from the "standard" astronaut, who seemingly led a rock-solid life with a wife and children firmly by his side. The day he and Beth officially announced their engagement, the press feigned disappointment over the impending loss of the nation's only bachelor astronaut.

Since turning up at Houston in January 1964, the fourteen astronauts of NASA's Group 3 selection had been through the first, or academic phase of their training and were now undertaking the "contingency" part, which included survival training. In the unlikely event that astronauts' spacecraft would have to make an emergency touchdown in a remote corner of the world, NASA required them to learn basic survival techniques in the water, jungle, and desert, where they might be stranded for some time until rescue teams could reach them. Suddenly everyone wanted to know which of his buddies had scouting experience!

During the final phase of the Panama excursion, C.C. Williams just hoped he would not need to scratch all the way through his wedding vows because he was covered with chigger bites. He knew his lower body would look a real treat in the beginning of his married life.

On their last night in Panama, the astronauts all attended a cocktail party thrown by the wing commander of Allbrook AFB. It was held at a grand old hotel where Teddy Roosevelt had stayed when he went to the canal in 1906 to check on its progress—the first president ever to leave the United States. The function, which degenerated into a high-spirited bachelor party for Williams, turned out to be a lot of fun. The men, now showered and shaved, were ready to let their hair down, but instead of heading straight for the bar when they arrived, they first descended upon the trays of canapés. All food items were gone in six minutes flat. Mike Collins described the celebration:

> Perhaps because we were overjoyed to be back at the bar, or perhaps because we all liked C.C. so much and relished his company, or perhaps because we were trying to deaden the nerve conduit between chiggers and brain, I know not the reason, but we did in fact have a real wallbanger of a party. Charlie Bassett was master of ceremonies, and he was a regular William Jennings Bryan, delivering a far-ranging tour de force describing not only the beauty of C.C.'s bride to be, C.C.'s many virtues, the condition of the Panamanian jungles, NASA's approach to flying to the Moon, the economic condition of the country, the moral fiber of the younger generation . . . I think, although my own recollection of it is far from clear, we had to remove him physically from the podium and deposit him, still in good voice, back in his room.

One of the stories Bassett recounted that night concerned Williams and Beth's engagement announcement. Williams, ever the stickler for marine corps correctness and protocol, decided he should write to his senior commanding officer and formally request his permission to be married. Thus a bemused Col. John Glenn, the only other astronaut marine, received Williams's request and was tickled pink to give his wholehearted blessing to the union.

The next morning, all feeling somewhat the worse for wear, the men were crammed aboard a small turboprop aircraft and flown back to Houston. For the astronauts it was back to the lectures, technical meetings, and endless studies, and for Williams a date at the altar. The training days were long and strenuous, but he knew that one day it would all be worth the effort. One day he would be chosen to fly into space.

Clifton Curtis Williams Jr. was born in Mobile, Alabama, on 26 September 1932. He came into the world at the Allen Memorial Home on South Washington to proud parents Curtis and Gertrude (née Medicus) Williams. They were both natives of Mobile, known for its deep bay and harbor area, and widely renowned as "the Azalea City" for its robust profusion of these glorious flowers.

As a new father, Clifton C. Williams (known to his family as Curtis) had initially shied away from having his baby son named after him, and he was pressing for the child to be named James. Gertrude, however, was insistent and unmovable. "I wanted a junior," she told the author, "so we compromised." Her decision prevailed, but the boy soon became known as Jim to his immediate family and friends. The nickname was a simple means of avoiding any confusion between the child's name and that of his father. The youngster eventually began to respond to the nicknames Cliff and C.C.

Young Williams grew up in the family home at 1770 Dauphin Street, situated some four miles west of Mobile's city center. Coincidentally, considering where he would spend his last days, the nearest crossroad was Houston Street. On 29 November 1935 his younger brother, Dick, was born, completing the family.

According to his mother, Williams had "a normal childhood—a public school education—making good grades and having many friends of both sexes." Just like most boys of their age, Williams and his brother enjoyed swimming and playing baseball, but Gertrude does not remember any special interest in aviation—that came later.

Williams took his high school education at Murphy High, located on a sprawling forty-acre campus on South Carlen Street near downtown Mobile. The oldest high school in Alabama, it had originally been named Mobile High School but underwent a name change in 1927. While at Murphy High, Williams pledged to the Delta Sigma fraternity before graduating in 1949. By now the family had relocated elsewhere in Mobile and was living at 115 Mohawk Street.

Over the next two years Williams attended Spring Hill College, where he studied mechanical engineering and served as a member of the U.S. Naval Reserve. The next rung on his scholastic ladder was the Alabama Polytechnic Institute in Auburn. He entered the institute in 1951 to complete his college work on a scholarship through the Naval Reserve, and he quickly settled into college life and NROTC, later becoming a member of the fraternity Sigma Chi; Pi Tau Sigma, the national honorary mechanical society; and Tau Beta Pi, the national engineering society.

On 5 June 1954 Williams graduated with a bachelor's degree in mechanical engineering. His college days now behind him, he enlisted in the Unites States Marine Corps and entered his country's military forces on 9 August 1954, with a service number of 066002 and a commission as a second lieutenant, backdated from 4 June. He was promoted to first lieutenant in December 1954. He then completed Basic School at the Marine Corps School, Quantico, which included fundamental and advanced flight training at the Naval Air Station in Pensacola.

Situated on the Gulf of Mexico, Pensacola was the place where would-be fighter pilots found out if they were truly suited to flying. Many soon washed out, packed their bags, and headed back home to look for a more sedate career. Soon after Williams's group arrived, the young men were assembled in a large auditorium where a few stern-looking officers addressed them. The first stepped up to the lectern and, without any preamble, invited each new recruit to take a look at the men on either side of him. "Be aware," he solemnly declared, "that not all of you will succeed in making it through. By graduation day one of the three of you will no longer be with us." Statistically, the prediction proved to be true for Williams's group. As the months passed a few began to fall by the wayside. Some were eliminated for their inability to cope with classroom studies while others flunked basic flight instruction. Then they moved on to flying single-engine, propeller-driven trainers. More failed aviators got the message and said goodbye.

The training rapidly intensified to include formation and instrument flying, navigation, training in jet aircraft, all-weather flying, and gunnery exercises. By this stage, only the best remained. Then it was time for the tricky stuff, part of which was learning how to land on one of the navy's aircraft carriers. As a prelude to the exercise, the pilots practiced landing on dry ground, touching down on a narrow strip painted onto an airfield. When they were comfortable with their proficiency, and their instructors felt they were ready, it was time for the real thing. On a suitably calm day, with clear skies and very little swell out in the gulf, a carrier was positioned offshore and all was in readiness. The pilots would then take off from the airfield, head out into the gulf, and plant their F-4 jets onto the rock-steady platform of the carrier. With every landing their confidence and skill level grew.

To his immense relief and delight, Williams graduated and was designated a naval aviator on 8 August 1956. Following his detachment from Pensacola he was assigned to VMF-312 and, later, VMF (AW)-531 of Marine Aircraft Group 24, 2nd Marine Aircraft Wing, based at Cherry Point, North Carolina, located in Craven County between New Bern and Morehead City.

It was there in June 1957 that Williams met his future wife, Jane Elizabeth Lansche, the daughter of Judge Bill and Jane Gorham Lansche from New Bern. The Cherry Point Marine Air Corps Station was situated quite near the Lansche home, and Williams had taken an apartment at Atlantic Beach, a favorite vacation spot, with his marine roommate, Chuck Griggs. Beth's girlfriend Ann Hamby was dating Chuck, and it was she who introduced Beth to Williams during one of her trips home from Florida, where she was an aquamaid in a water-skiing troupe at Cypress Gardens.

As time went by, and as the young couple started seeing each other on a regular basis, they would enjoy long walks around New Bern whenever Beth could get time off from her water-skiing duties. They often sat and talked on the grass verge at downtown's Union Park Point, where the Trent and Neuse Rivers converge. Many thousands of years earlier, the Tuscarora Indians had camped and built villages in this same spot. Beth and Williams loved the gentleness and heritage of the area and spent many happy days just enjoying the scenery, a panoply of American history amid tree-lined streets. Whenever he could manage some time off, Williams flew to Florida to be with Beth.

Meanwhile, service life went on for Williams, and he was promoted to captain in December 1958. He also saw temporary duty as staff secretary, Fleet Marine Force, Atlantic, Amphibious Training Group 1–58, at Camp Lejeune, also in North Carolina.

In March 1959, Captain Williams departed for overseas duty with VMF (AW)-531, attached to Marine Aircraft Group 11, 1st Marine Aircraft Wing, serving as flight line officer until July 1960. During this period, he also served aboard the USS Lexington with Fighter Squadron 213 (VF-213), engaged in developing carrier operational capabilities.

In September 1960 Williams entered the U.S. Naval Test Pilot School and upon graduation was assigned to the Naval Air Test Center at Patuxent River, Maryland, where he served as project officer in the Carrier Suitability Branch, Flight Test Division. There, as a test pilot for the next three years, he cut his fighter teeth flying a variety of hot jets onto the pitching decks of aircraft carriers. His work now included land-based and shipboard tests of the F8E, TF8A, F8E (Attack), and A4E aircraft and automatic carrier landing systems. In particular he was project officer for the Chance Vought F8 and McDonnell Douglas A-4 Skyhawk and short airfield tactical support officer.

Late in 1962 Williams played an important role in navy experiments conducted aboard the aircraft carrier USS *Independence*. As project officer on the navy's new supersonic F8U Crusader trainer, Captain Williams became the first pilot to land a two-seater jet on an aircraft carrier while riding in the rear cockpit. It was a considerable feat, given the poor visibility available from that back seat. He and two other test pilots then made four daytime and two night landings as well as twenty-two "touch and go" landings, proving that safe landings could be accomplished from the rear cockpit. One meritorious footnote to this feat was that he had never landed an F8U aboard a carrier before this time, let alone from the rear cockpit. That evening he did it all again—the first time he had ever landed any aircraft at night on a carrier, and again it was from the rear cockpit. The date made the accomplishments even more memorable—it was his thirtieth birthday.

In August 1963 Williams reported to the Marine Corps Intermediate Staff and Command School in Quantico, Virginia, entering the Junior Course. During this assignment he applied for and underwent screening in connection with NASA's astronaut training program. He had actually applied for the second group of astronauts in April 1962 but more in hopeful expectation than anticipation. His application had been stamped as "unqualified." Undaunted by this rejection, and having built up his credits in the meantime, he was eager to try again.

By this time Beth Lansche had left the aquatic squad, and after moving across the country had finally settled into a job she liked as a secretary in San Francisco. It was now a true long-distance courtship, but the two still managed to see each other from time to time.

Quantico was the nation's first Marine Corps Air Station, so Williams was immediately taken with the history and tradition of the place. In 1919 a flying field had been laid out and the land leased to accommodate a squadron returning from action in Europe during the First World War. The present site was selected in 1931, when larger and faster aircraft brought a realization that the original field was exceeding its limitations. In December 1941 the new field was designated a Marine Corps Air Station, as the corps was in desperate need of an East Coast base where officers and enlisted marines could undertake their training. All marine officers began their careers in Quantico and attended professional military education schools at the facility throughout their careers.

34. C.C. Williams clambers into his Crusader jet. He was the first pilot to land on an aircraft carrier while flying solo from the rear cockpit. (Courtesy Beth Williams)

At the time of his selection by NASA in October 1963, Williams was still stationed at Quantico. His promotion to major would be posted following his move to Houston, and he would take with him a total of eighteen hundred hours flying time. Thirteen hundred of those hours had been accumulated piloting jet aircraft. By now he was also an associate member of the Society of Experimental Test Pilots.

Early in October 1963 Williams was given a message to contact NASA at Houston, and he found out he had been selected as an astronaut trainee. He was asked to report to Houston for assignment no later than 15 January 1964.

On the Friday that his selection was announced, Williams phoned his parents in Mobile with the news, revealing that he was in Houston and had known of his selection since the previous Monday. He told his astonished father he had not been allowed to tell anyone until the official announcement was made but promised to stop in and see them briefly on his way back to Quantico. When interviewed by the local press his parents were still getting over the news, and Gertrude said they were "proud, happy and terribly excited" for their son.

Eight days after the announcement, Williams went home for a two-day weekend visit to Mobile and made public appearances at the Greater Gulf States Fair and the Saturday night college football game in Ladd Stadium. In deference to his father's work as Mobile's waterworks superintendent, and his brother, Dick, an engineer with the Alabama Drydocks and Shipbuilding Company in Mobile, Williams also addressed the Alabama-Mississippi section of the American Waterworks Association. The excited residents of Mobile overwhelmed him with their congratulations over news he was still coming to grips with himself. He shook hands everywhere, took dozens of hearty backslaps, and signed hundreds of autographs.

Seven of the new Group 3 astronauts were from the air force, four were navy pilots, two were civilians, and Williams was the sole marine—NASA's first since John Glenn. He would later reveal that he felt one thing might preclude him from becoming an astronaut—his height. So great was his concern that he stayed awake the entire night before his physical, jumping up and down in order to compress his spine and get below the six-foot limit. It worked, and after completing a further battery of tests, examinations, and interviews, he sat back to wait for the all-important phone call, which finally came.

Following the media announcement, Deke Slayton told press reporters that the new astronaut group would carry the space program through the initial manned lunar landings. He added that the space center was even at that time expediting the Gemini phase of the long-range Apollo moon landings. Gemini, he explained, would involve flights of two-man capsules, which would remain in orbit for up to fourteen days. A series of rendezvous flights using unmanned satellites was a key objective, and vital training for the moon shots. At the same time NASA announced that another contingent of astronauts would be selected and named in the fall of 1965. It was envisioned that this group would include some physical scientists, such as experts in geology.

Six months after Williams reported to Houston, in the spring of 1964, he married Beth Lansche one Wednesday evening in St. Paul's Catholic Church in New Bern. More than a hundred close friends and relatives attended the simple ceremony. Beth had been baptized and confirmed in the beautiful and historic church on Middle Street and could never imagine being married elsewhere. Williams was decked out in his pressed dress whites for the military-style ceremony, and his father was there serving as his best man. Beth's one great sadness was that her own father could not be there to witness the marriage and give her away. A recorder's court judge, he had died several years earlier. In his place her brother Bill escorted the bride to the sanctuary. Representing the astronaut corps were Williams's good friends and classmates Ted Freeman and Charlie Bassett. His old marine corps buddies had also heard about the wedding, and they turned up by the carload.

Williams, fresh from the Panamanian jungle, was not expecting Beth to be wearing a traditional wedding gown. She had already renounced this, and he had come to grudgingly accept it. Unbeknown to him, the matron of honor, Beth's good friend Anne Hamby, had talked her into wearing the gown in which she herself had been married. It was certainly worth the change of heart; when Beth walked down the aisle in true bridal fashion, she could see that her fiancé was overwhelmed with happiness. Tears of pride and joy unashamedly filled his eyes.

The press had also attended in droves, and in the days before the wedding had been pestering Beth's and Williams's families for information and interviews. The bride-to-be politely turned them all down, saying she had more important things on her mind. But now, as the happy couple swept out of the church, they walked straight into a maelstrom of cameras, reporters, and well-wishers. Beth recalls that she could not help wondering how the small and normally quiet town of New Bern was coping with such an influx of people. That night her mother entertained the couple at a magnificent reception held in the Governor Tryon Hotel.

Following their honeymoon the newlyweds lived in a house in Dickinson near the Manned Spacecraft Center, and a photo from that time shows a relaxed couple posing happily in front of Williams's bronze Corvette. (He eventually traded in the flashy car for a green Chevrolet pickup and selected a Chevrolet Malibu for Beth.) They also brought a bouncing little puppy into their home, a thoroughbred English bulldog they laughingly named Lord Percy Plushbottom. When not wrapped up in playing with their puppy, Williams loved being in the kitchen, cooking. Beth recalls fondly that he was a good cook, his favorite food being "anything southern."

Throughout his life Williams had been a person of strong religious faith, so when he and Beth moved to Dickinson they began attending services at the local Shrine of the True Cross Roman Catholic Church. He soon formed a great friendship with the assistant pastor, the Reverend Eugene Cargill, and began playfully admonishing him for being out of physical condition. Cargill knew by now that Williams was on a weight-reducing program ordered by NASA's doctors, so he allowed himself to be drawn into joining the astronaut on a fitness campaign, and the two friends regularly played strenuous games of squash in the astronaut gymnasium. The two men enjoyed a spirited rivalry both on and off the squash court. On one occasion Williams and Beth carefully checked the church bulletin to determine which mass the priest would be conducting and then sat quietly in the small white stucco church, listening intently as he spoke. Afterward, Williams took Cargill aside and offered straight-faced criticisms of his sermon. "He would repeat it almost word for word," Father Cargill later recalled. "It was the only thing that ever frightened me about preaching!" But he also spoke with fond remembrance of a devout friend:

> This man had an unbelievable amount of faith. You could not shake it. We had a great deal in common. C.C. was also a very loyal Marine. We celebrated All Saints Day, All Souls Day, Thanksgiving and the Marine Corps birthday, but to him the most important of these was the Marine Corps birthday! This was a command performance for him and he took it very seriously. Beth, myself, and the dog had to begin preparing far in advance for this celebration. On the day, with C.C. dressed up in his full dress white uniform, swords and all, we sang a hymn, drank a toast to the

*Marine Corps, and hollered "Semper Fi!" while the dog barked. Quite a scene!*

*Another aspect of our lives was the fact that we both enjoyed gourmet food and good wine. I can still hear him, as the wine steward would bring the wine for C.C. to test: "You may serve this wine to my friends, and I will take a case of it!" We frequently went to dinner on Friday evenings, after he came back from the Cape in Florida. As he was preparing to land at Ellington Field he would "buzz" the church to let me know that he was home, and to start getting ready. We truly were good friends.*

Nevertheless, the astronaut business was serious stuff. Although it was not all technical books and stupefying lectures, it was likewise not all fun and games—there was some heavy and intense training to be carried out. The men had to condition their bodies to withstand multiple stresses such as those associated with weightlessness and acceleration, vibration, immobilization and disorientation, noise, and heat and cold. They had to become proficient in the use of dozens of training devices and rescue aids, to simulate a number of incidents and learn how to avoid or survive them.

Just as they had undergone contingency training in the Panamanian jungle, the astronauts could not exclude a landing in the ferocious heat and isolation of the desert, so after more classroom studies it was back on the road again. They were transported to a survival-training group near Stead AFB in the dry sagebrush country of western Nevada. Once again they could use only the equipment they would have at hand after an emergency landing as their survival gear.

Apart from survival training, field trips saw the astronauts conveyed to all corners of the country, where they were acquainted with geological compositions similar to those they might encounter on the moon's surface. They descended into the mile-deep grandeur of the Grand Canyon, scouted the Big Bend country of the Rio Grande, visited the Valley of Ten Thousand Smokes in the Katmai Monument in Alaska, and crunched over black lava flows in Arizona's Sunset Crater. Geologists patiently explained to them the forces recorded in layers of stone, and discussed land forms and rock strata at interesting sites such as Slate Hill near Cimarron, and the 137,000-acre Philmont Boy Scouts Ranch, both in northern New Mexico.

During the exercise in the foothills of the Cimarron Mountains, twenty dusty and briar-beaten astronauts spent several hours clambering over ridges and gullies. Covered in scratches, Williams later observed, "I hope we don't have cactus on the Moon!" Using Jeeps instead of the traditional burros, the astronauts spent a full day measuring slopes and dips and following rock layers through the brush country.

The astronauts were sent out individually to find any eye-catching rock samples, which they examined with Dr. E. Dale Jackson, the course leader. They came to learn that the most interesting-looking rocks were not necessarily the most fruitful. That afternoon they sat through a demonstration in rock magnetism and watched tests of seismic instruments. Sensitive receivers were set up to time the echo as small blasts sent sound waves through the underground rock.

Under such expert tutelage the astronauts soon learned to identify samples that would be valued the most to trained geologists. In competition with each other to locate the best samples during such outings, they ventured into rich geological sites where they hacked away at ancient rocks, shale, and basalt. Ice caves, steaming fumaroles, and lava tubes—they studied the lot.

On one such expedition, Mercury astronaut Wally Schirra, part of Williams's geology group, was strolling along collecting rock samples. The irrepressible Schirra, widely known for his wicked humor and "gotchas," was intrigued by Williams's curious comment every time he spotted a particularly interesting specimen. As he stooped over to pick it up, he would loudly announce, "There's another FLR!" Schirra was not eager to display any possible ignorance of geology, so he kept quiet. But after several hours of hearing Williams mutter the same thing again and again, Schirra could no longer suppress his curiosity. Walking over to Williams, he said, "Okay, I give up—just what the heck is an FLR?" Williams grinned, gave Wally a "gotcha" look, and said, "Why that stands for Funny Lookin' Rock!" Schirra groaned, everyone laughed, and from that time on the entire team collected FLRs.

Back in Houston, Al Shepard, chief of the astronaut office, told the new astronauts that they would be given specific areas of responsibility within their workplace. He polled the men about which field they felt they were best qualified for, and in which they would most like to be involved. Williams opted for the areas of range operations and crew safety. Range operations looked at circumstances involving rockets going awry after liftoff. If a rocket did not head east out over the Atlantic as planned, but instead went off course and threatened civilian population areas, the range safety officer would press a button and the errant rocket would be blown to smithereens before it could pose a danger. The same scenario also applied to manned rockets—an onerous consideration. Williams worked closely with the range safety people to ensure every possible precaution was in place. It was one thing to lose colleagues as the result of an accident and another to order the destruction of their rocket.

In his crew safety duties, Williams helped to ensure optimum safety training and evacuation procedures were available to the astronauts, giving them a chance to escape a potentially catastrophic or life-threatening situation. The grave responsibility of his role was made evident to Williams when he sat in on the scheduled launch of Gemini 6 on Sunday, 12 December 1965. Positioned in front of a console that indicated the Titan rocket's fuel and oxidizer tank pressure, he was seated next to booster engineer Charlie Harlan. Between the two men was a red toggle abort switch that either man could press if the Titan's engines shut down or did not develop sufficient thrust immediately after liftoff, creating a potentially catastrophic situation—the rocket would fall back onto the pad. Pressing the abort switch would illuminate a red light in front of the astronauts, and if a verbal "Abort!" command

35. C.C. Williams attacking one of his "funny lookin'
rocks" during a geological expedition. (NASA)

then followed, they would eject horizontally from their capsule. As it happened,
the Titan's rockets did fire, but immediately shut down again—fortunately before
the hold-down clamps had been released. Either of the astronauts onboard could
have hit his own eject button but elected to hold fast and see what happened. In
this way astronauts Wally Schirra and Tom Stafford saved the mission, because an
abortion would probably have damaged their rocket and spacecraft considerably.
Their rendezvous flight with Gemini 7 became one of NASA's finest moments. The
launch shutdown certainly provided Williams with many anxious moments as the
drama unfolded on his console.

Toward the end of 1965 Williams moved a little closer to his first flight, when
Deke Slayton paired him with Al Bean as the tentative backup crew for the last two
Gemini missions. Bean would train with the prime crew as backup commander
and Williams as his pilot. In a sense this was something of a dead-end job, as GT-12
would be the last two-man flight before Project Apollo kicked in, but the assignment
showed that Slayton was preparing the men for bigger things. Had GT-9 flown as
scheduled with Charlie Bassett and Elliot See aboard, Slayton was actually looking
at replacing Bean with See as backup commander for GT-12, and assigning Bean as
chief of the Apollo Applications program—effectively ending his chances of flying
to the moon. Fate, however, would soon play a major role in crew assignments.

With experience came more assignments for the affable marine. On 12 January 1966 he was assigned as CapCom Shift 3 for the Gemini 8 mission. Then, just two days later, he was replaced by Jim Lovell and instead given the vital role of blockhouse communicator for the upcoming AS-204 (Apollo 1) mission.

When Elliot See and Charlie Bassett died in the crash of their T-38 in February 1966, the backup crew of Tom Stafford and Gene Cernan moved into the prime position. Deke Slayton thought about shuffling backup crews for the remaining Gemini missions, but he decided there was no reason to change his prime crews. John Young and Mike Collins had already been selected as the prime crew for GT-10 and were well into their training, and on 21 March it was announced that Pete Conrad and Dick Gordon would be given the GT-11 mission. That same date there was a change for the backup team of Al Bean and C.C. Williams when they were reassigned as the new backup crew for the GT-10 mission, scheduled for the middle of the year. Bean would now be backup for mission commander John Young, and Williams would function as backup pilot for Mike Collins.

As usual, Williams called his parents to tell them about his new assignment. "I just wanted you to know before you read it in the newspapers," he told his father. He had not been home since Christmas due to his work schedule but was in frequent contact by phone. Just two weeks earlier he had called them from Brookley AFB, where he had a few minutes' stopover for refueling en route to the cape for the launch of the Gemini 8 mission. But Curtis Williams had learned from experience that his son was not big on giving details over the phone. "Put your bride on the line," he said. "We get more information from her than we do from you!" Williams chuckled and replied, "I can't. I'm in St. Louis and she's in Houston." He explained that he was in St. Louis to be fitted for a space suit and flight seat at the McDonnell plant.

As backups for the next Gemini mission, Williams and Bean worked and trained with the prime crew of John Young and Mike Collins. This three-day flight was scheduled to rendezvous and dock with their own Agena target rocket, and then with the still-orbiting Agena from the curtailed Gemini 8 mission. Prior to the flight Williams and Bean set up switches and controls within the Gemini spacecraft for the prime crew. Then they flew back to Houston to act as a mission support team at MSC.

There were no last-minute hitches, and the Titan II rocket carrying Gemini 10 lifted off the launch pad on 18 July 1966. Young and Collins successfully docked with their Agena target vehicle and used its propulsion system to rocket them into a higher orbit. For the next two orbits they flew at a record apogee of 474 miles before lowering their orbit to begin the chase for the second Agena. Once again a successful docking was achieved, and Mike Collins performed a tethered space walk over to the Agena, becoming the first person to ever make bodily contact with another orbiting space vehicle. The two astronauts landed after nearly three days in space, having completed forty-three Earth orbits.

The success story that was Gemini continued with an almost flawless Gemini 11 mission two months later. On this occasion astronauts Pete Conrad and Dick Gordon used another Agena's propulsion system to send them to a new record height on an elliptical orbit that saw them reach a maximum altitude of 850 miles, achieved over northwestern Australia. For the first time, astronauts could see the Earth as a true globe. Once again Williams and Bean had assisted in preparations for this flight, and this time the former served as launch CapCom at the Kennedy Space Center. Conrad and Gordon splashed down on 15 September after their three-day flight, landing in the Atlantic a mere one and a half miles from their recovery ship, USS *Guam*.

On 11 November the last flight in the Gemini series took place with the launch of Gemini 12, carrying astronauts Jim Lovell and rookie Buzz Aldrin. Once again their craft successfully rendezvoused and docked with an Agena target vehicle already in orbit, and Aldrin performed an outstanding EVA lasting five and a half hours.

When Lovell and Aldrin splashed down after their four-day mission to end the highly successful Gemini series, George Mueller was so delighted with the results that he decided to accelerate the Apollo program. One of the principal decisions he announced was that of canceling a second manned mission planned to virtually replicate the flight of Apollo 1. He felt the follow-up flight would be a waste of resources and precious time if the first manned mission proved to be a success.

At a news conference called after the splashdown, a jubilant Robert Gilruth declared, "We have done all the things we had to do as a prelude to Apollo."

Late in 1966 Williams was informed that he had been assigned as lunar module pilot to Pete Conrad's crew, which also included Dick Gordon, but their actual flight designation was still pending. Williams was Conrad's second choice for the plum role of LMP—Conrad had argued for his friend and former flight student Al Bean, but Slayton had vetoed the selection. So Conrad chose Williams, whom he had also trained at Patuxent River, to be on his crew. The three men settled into their preliminary training and soon formed a close-knit crew. "He was so thrilled and excited to be flying with Conrad and Gordon," Beth Williams recalled. "He had great respect for both of them and was looking forward to the flight." In November the three men learned that their assignment would be as backup crew for the third manned Apollo mission.

The announcement stated that Jim McDivitt would be the prime crew commander for Apollo 2, the first manned test in space of the lunar landing module. His command module pilot (CMP) would be David Scott, and Rusty Schweickart would be the lunar module pilot (LMP). They would be the first to bear those titles, which were chosen after the first Apollo crew had been named earlier that year and would be in use in all flights after Apollo 1. Their backup crew was comprised of veteran Gemini astronauts Tom Stafford, John Young, and Gene Cernan.

Chosen to command Apollo 3, the first test of the mighty Saturn V moon rocket with a crew aboard, was Frank Borman. Michael Collins was named as CMP and William Anders as LMP. Apollos 2 and 3 were slated for liftoff in 1967, but this schedule depended on the successful completion of other flights. They were the only manned flights penciled in for 1967, but there was the outside possibility of another manned Saturn V shot if everything went well.

On 6 January 1967 Williams and Beth became proud parents of a beautiful baby girl they named Catherine Ann. Everything was going so well, but elsewhere dark clouds of misfortune were beginning to gather. Just three weeks later, on 27 January, NASA would lose three Apollo astronauts in a fire on the launch pad.

Following the AS-204 fire, Deke Slayton had to give some thought to crew reassignments. All scheduled crews had been stood down pending the results of the investigation into the fire. On 24 April 1967 there was a welcome change in the flight designation system, which meant that AS-204 officially (and in concurrence with the expressed wishes of the three widows) became known as Apollo 1. Although it would not be formally acknowledged, it also came to be accepted that the two unmanned Saturn 1-B flights (AS-201 and AS-202), which had already been launched in 1966 carrying Block 1 Apollo capsules, would thereafter be known as Apollos 2 and 3. Apollo 4 would become the first unmanned test flight of the mighty Saturn V rocket—the first in a series of planned launches—before the first manned mission.

Slayton knew that the first Apollo mission could either go to the original AS-204 backup crew of Schirra, Eisele, and Cunningham or the AS-205 prime crew of McDivitt, Scott, and Schweickart. But there was really only one logical solution, as the latter crew members were already well into training for their critical mission flying the first lunar module into Earth orbit (which would ultimately become Apollo 9). Slayton decided to leave them with that assignment and subsequently informed Schirra's crew that it was the new prime crew on the first Apollo flight. Tom Stafford, Gene Cernan, and John Young would serve as backups.

These assignments left McDivitt's flight without a backup crew, so Slayton further announced that Pete Conrad, Dick Gordon, and C.C. Williams would fill this position. Williams could finally allow himself to become excited because he knew only too well NASA's standard operating procedure for crew selections: back up a flight, skip the next two missions, and then become prime crew for the following flight. He realized that if the current timetable held, he would walk on the moon.

As a training LMP, Williams joined other Apollo commanders and backups in becoming proficient at flying helicopters. Following this, they could then start booking time on an ungainly-looking machine called the lunar landing research vehicle (LLRV), designed to simulate a descent to the moon's surface from around fifteen hundred feet, or the last couple of minutes before touchdown. Designed and built by Bell Aerosystems, the free-flying LLRV was then further developed at NASA's Flight

Research Center in California, with three initial units delivered to NASA for astronaut training at Ellington Field.

The LLRV was basically a skeleton framework comprised of tubular aluminum alloy struts and trusses supporting a small, centrally located and vertically mounted General Electric turbofan engine that delivered up to forty-two hundred pounds of thrust. This engine would provide continuous thrust to offset five-sixths of the vehicle's weight, thereby simulating the reduced gravity of the moon. Two hydrogen peroxide lift rockets controlled the LLRV's rate of descent and horizontal movement. Eight pairs of smaller rockets, also fuelled by hydrogen peroxide, allowed the pilot to control the craft's roll, pitch, and yaw.

The astronaut pilot would sit in a special one-man platform extending between two of the vehicle's legs. Although the commander and pilot would be standing in the actual lunar landing module, the LLRV was such a skittish, unforgiving, and even dangerous vehicle to fly, it had to be fitted with an ejection seat. In addition to the pilot's platform there was also an exposed electronics platform, spherical propellant tanks, and plumbing, all supported on four spindly legs. It was such an ugly, preposterous-looking machine that it was soon dubbed "the flying bedstead."

C.C. Williams and the other astronauts chosen to guide the lunar module to the moon's surface flew the LLRV and the later, modified lunar landing training vehicle (LLTV) several times to simulate actual landings. Many of the men would later agree that both vehicles were instrumental in helping them complete successful lunar landings. Using two hand controllers, the pilots would try to balance Earth's gravity as the central engine lifted the highly unstable craft to an altitude of around five hundred feet, then use the smaller thrusters to provide attitude and directional control. They could then hover, rotate, and gimbal their main engine up to six degrees, tilting the vehicle for a better view of their landing site. With all rockets belching out occasional puffs of gas, the sight was a startling one for ground observers. The exercise was only a few minutes' work, but Williams and the others would sometimes return drenched in sweat after the exertions required just to keep the LLRV steady.

As a measure of the craft's instability and flying characteristics, two of the original three LLRVs would later crash to earth and explode due to technical malfunctions, with both pilots barely ejecting in time. One of these hapless aviators was Neil Armstrong, who had earlier helped develop the LLRV and was flying it at Ellington around the same time as Williams. Armstrong managed to eject safely, but the craft was extensively damaged. Despite the dangers associated with flying the LLRVs, Williams and the other astronauts involved in lunar landings were required to perform as many landings in the craft as time permitted.

As a diversion from his grueling training program, Williams sometimes went fishing and hunting, which he enjoyed immensely. Late in September 1967 he teamed up with fellow astronauts Rusty Schweickart and Tom Stafford and took part in the annual One Shot antelope hunt in Lander, Wyoming. This annual event for VIPs was cohosted by the governors of Wyoming and Colorado and was attended by senators,

Hollywood celebrities, and heads of corporations, who competed in teams of three. The special guest that year was comedian Bill Dana of "Jose Jimenez" fame. As Schweikart recalls: "My recollection is that we got two or three 'one-shots,' [which] is getting the antelope with the first (and only) shot. I recall getting mine, but I can't recall which of the other two missed on the first shot. In any event, we didn't win the competition."

It was Thursday, 5 October 1967, and there was a lot going on in C.C. Williams's mind as he wound up his latest assignment at the cape and prepared to fly back to Houston. He had originally been scheduled to spend that day at the Grumman plant in Bethpage, New York, where the lunar module was under construction. Instead he had flown to the Grumman plant a day early, and then made his way to the Florida space center for a meeting of astronauts. This session was eventually canceled, so he decided to fly back to Houston rather than stick around. This fateful decision to depart was also influenced by a personal concern: Williams's father had been recently diagnosed with cancer, so he wanted to visit his parents before flying home to Houston.

News of a far happier nature was also on his mind. Just before he had left Dickinson to fly to the cape, Beth had cornered him in their kitchen and told him they were going to have another baby, due in the spring. Williams was thrilled almost beyond words, and had given Beth a huge hug and a warm kiss. He could hardly believe he was going to be a father again, and he whooped with excitement as he swung his wife around the kitchen. With great reluctance, he finally tore himself away from her and baby Catherine, threw his gear onto the passenger seat of his Chevrolet truck, and clambered in, slamming the door. Beth did not know it as she waved goodbye and blew a kiss, but she would never see her husband again. "My last memory," she told the author, "is the smile on his face as he backed his pickup truck out of the garage."

There was certainly a lot for Williams to consider as he prepared to fly back to Houston. Earlier, and despite his pressure-cooker schedule, he had received permission to make a short flight diversion to Brookley Air Force Base near Mobile, Alabama. There, while his T-38 was being refueled, he could pay a quick visit to his parents. The prognosis on his father was not good, and Williams wanted to see him, however brief that visit might be.

He was flying one of twenty-three dual seat T-38A jet aircraft then in use by the astronauts when he took off from Patrick Air Force Base in Cocoa Beach at 12:52 P.M. His aircraft, NASA 922, was almost brand new, with less than a hundred flying hours on the clock. Two days earlier he and Deke Slayton had flown it from Ellington AFB, and he had logged an inoperative transponder, basically a minor technical problem, but it meant the aircraft was automatically limited to a flight ceiling of 24,000 feet under air traffic regulations. The next day he had flown it from Patrick AFB to the Grumman Aircraft Facility at Peconic River in New York, filing a VFR

36. The week before he died, C.C. Williams enjoyed an antelope hunting expedition with Tom Stafford, Rusty Schweickart, and comedian Bill ("Jose Jimenez") Dana. (Courtesy Beth Williams)

(visual flight rules) flight plan, since the Patrick base radar shop did not stock parts for that particular type of transponder. When he was returning that afternoon he discovered the T-38 had a dead battery. After starting the engines using a jumper battery, he taxied out and took off. Apart from the battery and transponder, there were no problems to log.

For his flight back to Houston, he had once again filed a flight plan indicating a VFR flight at 22,500 feet, with an en route time to Brookley of one hour and twenty-five minutes. Otherwise all procedures and conditions had been normal for takeoff. The weather forecast he had been given was for scattered clouds up to four thousand feet, and twelve miles of visibility, with winds light and variable. It was a typically glorious Florida afternoon with temperatures in the high eighties as he lifted the long, pointed nose of the T-38 into the bright, clear skies and headed north.

Astronauts generally had to do a lot of hackwork, commuting long distances across the country for training or promotional work, but the agile T-38 made life a lot easier for them. Although officially banned from such shenanigans, these young, elite pilots often raced each other to destinations. Supersonic cross-country flights were commonplace, and many tires were burst after touchdown as the astronaut pilots stomped on their brakes to shorten the landing roll and be the first to pull up at the ramp. Frank Borman won a certain notoriety for his "hot refueling" tactics— he topped up his fuel with the J85 engines still running in order to save time at transit points along the way. In-flight, some astronauts were known to shut down one engine to conserve fuel and create new endurance and distance records, at times landing with their fuel tank perilously close to empty.

The T-38 was apparently flying smoothly as Williams raced over Florida, now on a northwest heading. He radioed a position report at 1:03 P.M. over Orlando, advising that he was maintaining a flight level of 22,500 feet. Eleven minutes into the flight everything was progressing normally, and the cities of Ocala and Gainesville passed below as he continued on toward Tallahassee. Next, he was scheduled to perform a turn to the west to pick up his flight track, skirting the Gulf of Mexico shoreline and then flying on to Mobile.

Suddenly, at 1:24 P.M., the aileron control jammed solid. The T-38 immediately pitched over to the left and began spiraling and accelerating downward. As his jet began to spin almost vertically, Williams tried desperately to gain control. As it plummeted down the jet picked up even more speed; soon it was traveling at close to Mach .95. It was later concluded (after exhaustive comparative tests in another T-38) that at around 13,000 feet there would have been an abrupt reduction in the spiraling roll due to Mach effects on the aircraft. Consequently, Williams may have believed he was regaining control and therefore not initiated his ejection procedures. He probably wasted precious seconds in a vain attempt to control the pitch of his T-38 and level it out.

By now the jet had been hurtling toward the ground for some twenty-six to twenty-eight seconds. At this altitude Williams could still have ejected quite safely, but the reduction in his roll rate probably influenced his decision to stay with the jet and eject only if he could not bring it under control. As the ground grew closer, and with no obvious control response, he decided he should radio his intentions to eject as he continued his efforts.

On the T-38 it took around four seconds to channelize the UHF radio when switching to an emergency channel from the frequency used for normal en route communications. Soon after, some FAA ground facilities in the Tallahassee vicinity, and several aircraft in the same area, received his distress call. "Mayday, Mayday!" Williams reported in a rushed but almost businesslike voice as he endeavored to control the aircraft and set up the ejection process. "This is NASA 922, ejecting just off Orlando . . . I mean Tallahassee!" Despite his struggles, Williams still had the presence of mind to correct a transmission error. It is assumed that, thereafter, Williams finally committed himself to ejecting from his plummeting aircraft. The initiation of this move would have chewed up another two precious seconds.

The ejection procedure, from the moment the armrests were raised and the trigger pulled, took one and a half seconds. Tragically, it was all too late. The ejection sequence began as the canopy was blown off at 1,300 to 1,500 feet, with impact now less than one and a half seconds away—fatally close to the ground, and way too low for the slow-opening parachute to deploy and become effective. An instant later the ejection rockets fired and propelled Williams from the cockpit.

Now traveling almost vertically, the T-38 finally shrieked through a plantation of pine trees on the G. W. Humphrey estate near the Georgia border town of Miccosukee, about twenty miles northeast of Tallahassee, and slammed nose-first into a dirt road at the top of a hill. The jet exploded on impact, creating a sandy crater more than thirty feet wide and twelve feet deep. Williams hit the ground right by the aircraft at virtually the same moment, still strapped in his ejection seat.

Responding to the emergency call, members of a helicopter crew from Moody Air Force Base in Valdosta scrambled into their choppers and arrived at the site just ten minutes after the crash. The scene was one of total devastation, but the men began an immediate search for the pilot, hoping he had somehow managed to eject in time. All too soon, however, Williams's remains were found amid the smoking wreckage of the aircraft. A Florida Highway Patrol officer later found a wallet a few yards away, and the pilot's probable identity was known, although still to be confirmed.

A few hours later a salvage team with some heavy equipment arrived from the Moody base to begin the grim task of excavating the crash scene. They closed off the area, as many sightseers had already gathered to examine the smoking heap inside its impact crater. The team reported finding parts of the jet's canopy at the crash site, which originally seemed to indicate that Williams had not ejected from his aircraft. Parts of a parachute were also located and dragged free of the catastrophic mess.

Air force major Joseph Johnson was one of the first military personnel at the scene, and he reported that the pull cord on Williams's parachute was still in place. "The canopy has to have been blown open by the explosion," Johnson explained to reporters. "The plane disintegrated and the body disintegrated with it."

A witness, Brian Thompson of Tallahassee, later reported he was cutting wood with a companion when the air was suddenly filled with an approaching scream of jet engines. "I heard what I thought was a plane breaking the sound barrier," Thompson stated. The two men did not see the crash, but they heard the massive noise of impact as Williams's T-38 slammed into the ground and exploded. Both men rushed to the top of the tall pine and clay hill, where they came across the wreckage. "It looked like it came straight down," Thompson later reported. "It didn't even hit a tree. The plane was almost completely disintegrated. There wasn't even a part big enough to take any effort to pick up. There was no wheel or strut or any other part recognizable." The two men put out a small grass fire before heading off to notify the police.

An air force spokesman from Tyndall Air Force Base near Pensacola later told reporters that he believed Williams might have ridden the jet to his death rather than eject and endanger people living on the outskirts of Tallahassee. However well-meaning his theory might have been, it would prove to be highly unlikely, as Williams had absolutely no control over his aircraft. As an experienced pilot, he would most likely have fought to regain control rather than bail out when he felt he might still be able to recover from the problem.

Further fueling speculation about the cause of the crash, newspapers the following day also began to quote "an informed source" who said that Major Williams never got a chance to eject because it was thought the oxygen system in the plane had failed and he probably blacked out from hypoxia. Although NASA tried unsuccessfully to track down the source of this story, the agency refused to comment on such speculation—later dismissed as highly unlikely by its accident investigation board. Instead, NASA began to broadcast appeals over local radio stations, seeking the help of anyone else who might have witnessed the crash.

Beth Williams was attending a luncheon at the home of neighbors in Dickinson, Texas, when astronaut Jack Lousma and his wife, Gratia, arrived, grim faced and pale. They had been asked to pass on the bad news before Beth happened to hear it on a radio bulletin, or from a reporter, as had Ted Freeman's wife. As soon as Beth saw them heading toward her, she knew they were about to give her the worst news of her life.

Within hours of the crash NASA had appointed an accident Board of Inquiry to try and determine the cause. Those selected were astronaut Alan Shepard as chairman; fellow astronaut Joe Engle; Bud Ream from the Manned Spacecraft Center's Aircraft Operations Office; James Powell, MSC Safety Office; Ralph Keyes, MSC Flight Crew Operations; and Dr. John Zieglschmid, MSC Medical Operations. Astronaut Jerry Carr, like Williams a marine corps major, was appointed summary court officer to assist the bereaved family. The board members flew to the crash site later that evening to begin the onerous job of sifting through the debris and interviewing witnesses.

In his book *The Making of an Ex-Astronaut*, scientist-astronaut Brian O'Leary, who had met Williams in the space center's gym, exemplified the shock that swept through the astronaut community that day when news of the accident hit the space center:

> He was big, very big for an astronaut, and he gave me a friendly, flesh-pressing handshake and said in a loud Alabama voice, "C.C. Williams here. Glad to meetcha." His casual, joking manner and direct approach made me want to know him better.
>
> A week after I had met him in the gym, Williams was headed back to Houston alone in a T-38. At that time a number of us in the astronaut office were organizing a betting pool for the seventh and final game of the World Series between the Boston Red Sox and the St. Louis Cardinals. The game was on television in a conference room and watched by an attentive audience. Early in the game I dashed over to the cafeteria for a bite to eat, hoping I would only miss a half inning. I then returned to the conference room to find nobody there. The same people who just moments ago had been enthusiastically rooting for a team were in their offices with dour expressions. What went wrong, I thought? I asked one girl what the score of the game was. She said she didn't know.

*She then said that C.C. Williams had just been killed in a jet crash.*
*His plane had gone out of control and dove into the ground while rolling*
*at the speed of sound. He didn't have time to eject.*

The news stunned everyone in the astronaut office, and a deep sadness pervaded the hallways. The other astronauts were told to call their wives to reassure them they were okay, because many would soon start hearing over the radio that an unidentified astronaut had been killed in a plane crash. That sort of news spread like wildfire.

Once again a sad ritual began, in which the most obvious reminders of C.C. Williams were quietly removed from the astronaut office. His name tag was taken from his office door and mailbox, and the hundreds of portrait photos he would send out to well-wishers and autograph seekers were packed up and removed. As with earlier astronaut deaths, his colleagues and friends sought to respectfully sweep away any painful reminders that he would never again stride down those polished corridors. They would honor him in their hearts and in their memories.

Clifton and Gert Williams, devastated by the loss of their son, would later say they did not even know he was on his way to see them. "I had no idea," said his distraught father. "I know he made it here as often as possible. I talked to his wife, Beth, last weekend, but he was away on an antelope hunting trip." The Williamses, accompanied by C.C.'s brother, Dick, left immediately for Houston to be with Beth and Catherine.

Williams's body had meanwhile been removed from the crash site and taken to Tallahassee, from where it was transported to Washington National Airport under escort. One of the two men serving as these escorts was fellow Group 3 astronaut Bill Anders.

On 7 October a requiem mass for the life of C.C. Williams was held at 10:00 A.M. in the Shrine of the True Cross Catholic Church in Dickinson, attended by many of the astronauts who had known and liked the gregarious, good-humored marine from Alabama. Beth was escorted to the service by astronaut Jerry Carr and flight nurse to the astronauts, Dee O'Hara. Baby Catherine Ann had been left at home, tended by friends. The Reverend Eugene Cargill, still deeply stunned by the sudden loss of his friend, officiated.

As the service neared its end, four T-38s howled low across the skies above Dickinson, rattling the church's stained-glass windows. One of the jets peeled off, flying straight up into the sun. Then, as Beth Williams left the church with her late husband's parents, the remaining three jets flew over once again in the "missing man" formation as a mark of respect for a lost colleague.

Following the service Williams's body was transported via Moody AFB to Arlington National Cemetery for burial. At 11:00 A.M. on Monday, 9 October, a solemn gravesite service took place after a caisson had borne Williams's coffin to his place of burial, pulled by six white horses and accompanied by an honor guard of two hundred marines. Pallbearers at the service were fellow astronauts Gene Cernan, Richard Gordon, Al Bean, Pete Conrad, Mike Collins, and Jack Lousma. Once again the Reverend Cargill officiated as Williams was laid to rest with full military honors.

In his emotional eulogy, Father Cargill said he had lost a great friend. He described Williams as "truly committed" and "a man of great faith." He went on to say, "When I think of commitment, I think of C.C. Williams. It is a commitment that applied to everything, not just the space program." Father Cargill spoke of how he and Williams would often work out together in the astronauts' gym, and how his friend would compare his astronaut career with that of the churchman: "C.C. felt his own ordination in the space program would be his first flight. He never got to make that flight."

As trusted nurse to the astronauts since 1959, Dee O'Hara had come to know these men and their families particularly well, and she recalled that Williams's funeral was a day of great sadness for her:

> Each death was extremely difficult for me. Some more than others, simply because I may have had a closer relationship with that particular individual. It's the same with any close friend that you lose. We had spent so much time together, and being accepted into their life and being so close to their families, each was quite hard to accept. The job was very stressful just under normal circumstances. A death really caused everyone so much grief, and each one took a piece out of my heart.
>
> Those of us who were privileged enough to work closely with the astronauts got to know them so well, and when the accidents occurred it was just devastating. The one that probably hit me the hardest was C.C. Williams. Beth, his widow, was my best friend and is to this day. I spent so much time with both of them, and through my work at the Aerospace Medical Clinic had known C.C. before they were married. I adored C.C., and the most heartbreaking of all is that his two daughters never knew him. He was so excited when Catherine was born, and then when Beth was pregnant with Jane Dee—he was just so thrilled to be having another baby. Everything was going so well for C.C. and then suddenly I'm at his funeral holding Beth's hand. Life is sometimes so very cruel.

Meanwhile the remains of the T-38 were patiently extracted from the ground at the crash site and removed to Moody AFB, where investigators began the painstaking task of reconstructing the wreckage on a hangar floor to find clues to the cause of the crash. The force of the impact could be measured by the fact that the two engines had to be dragged out of the ground from a depth of eighteen feet through sand and hardpan. Months later, following an exhaustive analysis of all factors involved, and comparative test flights in another T-38 to correlate time sequences and flight profiles, NASA's accident investigation board concluded that the primary cause was a jam in the lateral control system (ailerons) from an unknown source.

Due to the explosively fragmented condition of the wreckage, the board members were unable to pin down exactly what had jammed the controls. The most probable cause, they deduced, was a foreign object in the aileron control system below the rear cockpit. In their conclusions, the men ruled out engine failure, loose baggage in the rear compartment (there had been unsubstantiated talk of a bag sitting in the aft cockpit), pilot incapacitation, and fire as probable causes. They found that the jammed controls caused a sudden and severe roll to the left from level flight, resulting in a steep dive. When Williams had begun the emergency ejection procedure, he was too near the ground and had reached a speed exceeding seven hundred miles per hour.

The accident board members studied records of previous flights in the aircraft but found nothing abnormal apart from the broken transponder and a dead battery the previous day. They recommended that NASA improve its inspection procedures for the T-38 so as to include a mandatory inspection on delivery to NASA. Subsequently, the space agency undertook a thorough periodic inspection of each aircraft's control systems to prevent possible jamming, instructed pilots on the limitations of the ejection systems, and introduced strict new procedures for the safe storage of equipment in all aircraft.

Williams's death caused an immediate shuffling of crew assignments. Most notably, Pete Conrad's original choice for lunar module pilot, Al Bean, was brought into his crew. Had Williams not died, Bean would almost certainly have gone to the Earth-orbiting Apollo Applications Program without ever flying to the moon. Two years later Conrad, Bean, and Richard Gordon, all firm friends (and all navy), enjoyed a highly successful Apollo 12 lunar mission. When the three crew members were asked to design the mission patches they would ultimately wear to the moon in November 1969, they incorporated four stars in the artwork at the suggestion of Bean. One each for themselves and the fourth for "missing man" C.C. Williams, now the fourth member of the Group 3 astronauts to die. As a mark of respect, they also placed Williams's naval aviator's "wings of gold" in the lunar soil.

Today, more than three decades later, the astronauts continue to train and commute across America in the space agency's T-38 jet fleet. Williams was the last NASA astronaut to lose his life flying one of them.

C.C. Williams's father succumbed to his cancer seven months after the accident. He had never gotten over the loss of his older son. Tragically, he died around the same time that Beth went into labor with her second child.

The Williams's daughter Jane Dee Williams was born on 31 May 1968, and the family stayed in their Dickinson home until the two girls were ready to start school. Beth then sold the house and the family moved into the heart of Houston.

After a while, and having toyed with the idea of going into state politics, Beth decided to venture into the business world and earned her real estate license. She sold real estate for the next few years. The family moved again when Catherine was seven and Jane Dee six years old, and the house Beth purchased in Seabrook, Texas, remains her home today. Recently a very proud mother stated that her two daughters had grown into "beautiful young women." Catherine is a graduate of Catholic University in Washington DC. She stayed in DC after graduation and today is a policy analyst. Jane Dee attended Marquette University in Milwaukee, Wisconsin, and now lives and works in Moscow, where she is in charge of operations for TechTrans International. Beth is the founder and president of this Houston-based company.

Comedian Bill Dana, who became known to many as the "Eighth Mercury Astronaut" because of his brilliant Jose Jimenez routines, recently recalled his feelings about the day C.C. Williams died. Dana had been part of the outdoor hunt Williams attended a week before his accident. In part, he said, "I have very clear, bitter-sweet remembrances of the One Shot Antelope Hunt in Lander, Wyoming. My recollection of his passing is enhanced by the fact that my birthday and his deathday are the same. October 5th is also the birthday of Dick Gordon and, of all people, Dr. Robert Goddard, the godfather of modern rocketry."

These days, Beth says her feelings for her late husband remain strong, and she is still bursting with love and pride despite the passage of more than three decades:

> To be real honest with you, I adored that man. I live with his memory every day, along with the girls and his mother, and it's a memory I treasure and keep close to my heart. After all his life is part of our family heritage, and part of me.
>
> After C.C. died I got on with my life, because the whole thing is I had a strong life when I came into the marriage, and it continued on. Can I say this—that we think of him in good humor, my mother-in-law and I, and the girls. It's like he's still there in the periphery as we get on with our lives. I sometimes look up and say "Dammit, C.C. if you want to know what's happening down here you should've stuck around a while. Yes, suck in your breath—I'm gonna do it my way. If you're up there suffering—tough apples, bub!" We're jousting, just like an old married couple.
>
> You know, we weren't married long enough for me to have any bad memories, just three-and-a-half years in all. He and I didn't have fights or any of the bad stuff, but everything that's great in a marriage is what we had. Very simply we met and got married, we had a long romantic honeymoon, I got pregnant and we had our first baby. Of course C.C. was away a lot of the time, running around doing his astronaut business, but our time together was very precious to us. Sure I miss him, but in many ways he's still with me.

Once, responding to a reporter's question about which mission he would like to fly, Williams had answered, "I'd like to go on every flight. Of course, if you said which mission I would most like to have, I'd say the first lunar flight you can make from the standpoint of personal satisfaction and accomplishment." He also said that, in his opinion, "the crews of Apollo would be ninety-nine per cent safe."

"As safe as in an airplane?" the reporter shot back.

Williams did not hesitate: "Really more so."

# Epilogue

*As we reflect on three decades of space science and discovery, it is altogether fitting that we pay tribute to the brave men and women who made the ultimate sacrifice in pursuit of our nation's goals in space. Each of them was dedicated to ensuring America's success in this vitally important program.*

President George H. W. Bush,
the White House, 26 April 1991

Much has been written about the Apollo program and how, ultimately, it evolved into a glorious triumph of human endeavor and technology. What has been largely overlooked is that it took a devastating tragedy to bring it to a successful realization.

America, and NASA in particular, fell into a stunned hiatus after an oxygen-fed fire engulfed the interior of the Apollo 1 spacecraft on Launch Pad 34. Three astronauts died a horrible shared death, trapped in a spacecraft they had often derided for its chronic technical and communications breakdowns. They paid a terrible price for a science program bogged down by contractual tardiness and ineptitude, many poor engineering and design decisions, and an appalling inability to simply sort things out.

The period following the fire was one punctuated by profound reevaluation and investigation. Safety and reliability became the operative words, superseding the previous rush to meet a tight schedule. With many of the key problems soon identified, it was back to square one again, this time with a far more open-door policy. Opinions once denied were now sought, and the astronauts finally had more say in the features and layout of the capsule.

Out of this new spirit of cooperation emerged a series of spacecraft that would carry men to the moon and back many times over. It has been argued that if the fire had not occurred, astronauts may very well have been lost in space, which would have brought the program to an immediate, and possibly even terminal, cessation. It would be some twenty months before NASA's astronauts would once again fly into space, but it was time well spent preparing for the successful missions that followed.

While Projects Mercury and Gemini had objectives related to Earth orbit, this would only be the starting point for Project Apollo. An eventual lunar landing was planned to be accomplished in three phases: first there would be earth orbital missions of up to two weeks' duration to familiarize astronauts with the spacecraft and carry out a series of experiments. Then further Earth-orbital flights would follow, which would enable crews to practice rendezvous and docking techniques with the two-man Lunar Module, and finally a manned lunar landing and return to Earth.

On 26 February 1966 an unmanned Apollo flight was successfully carried out using a Saturn 1B rocket to test the compatibility of the launch vehicle and the

ice in July and August, and then
ly shut down the manned phase
luations continued, however, and
inserted into orbit atop a massive
April 1968. With the first modified
begin America's manned Apollo

: carried astronauts Wally Schirra,
perfect Earth orbit on the Apollo 7
men rendezvoused with the spent
ut docking simulations. They also
e beamed into millions of homes.
on of audacious proportions when
noon. Original plans had called for
it many saw it as simply emulating
her contributing factors, such as a
ut most significantly an unmanned
Soviet Union's Zond probe, which
Administrator Dr. Thomas Paine
the moon on 12 November 1968.
Borman, Jim Lovell, and Bill Anders
ircled the moon, and returned with a
The technical aspect of the mission was
almost eclipsed by its emotional impact. As the three men flew in lunar orbit they
watched in awe as the Earth rose above the moon's surface. Through live television
pictures the world shared with the astronauts this amazing image, as well as the sight
of bleak lunar craters passing below the spacecraft. On Christmas Eve, in another
live transmission, the three astronauts took turns reading passages from the Bible's
book of Genesis. Bill Anders led off, reading the first verse: "In the beginning, God
created the heaven and the Earth. And the Earth was without form, and void; and
darkness was upon the face of the deep." At the conclusion of the reading by all
three men, and with lunar sunset just moments away, Frank Borman wound up
by saying: "And from the crew of Apollo 8, we close with good night, good luck, a
Merry Christmas, and God bless all of you—all of you on the good Earth." That
entire transmission is now regarded as one of the most moving episodes in the
entire spaceflight program.

Apollo 9 lifted off from Launch Pad 39A on 3 March 1969, carrying astronauts
Jim McDivitt, Dave Scott, and Rusty Schweickart into Earth orbit. Their task was
to put the spindly Lunar Module through its paces for the first time. Maneuvering
exercises, rendezvous, and docking were carried out in orbit in a vital test of the
craft that was intended to land men on the moon later that year. The flight was a

complete success. Now just one more mission remained—a final bold test flight, a precursor to the actual moon landing.

Apollo 10 was designated as a full dress rehearsal for the first lunar landing. Its goal was to duplicate every step of the upcoming Apollo 11 flight, with one exception—the astronauts would not touch down on the lunar surface. On 18 May 1969 a Saturn rocket rose slowly off the pad and lifted the Apollo 10 spacecraft into earth orbit at the beginning of its eight-day mission. Once all the systems had been checked, the s-ivb third stage rocket was reignited, and Apollo 10 was propelled away from Earth. Television pictures would later show the transposition and docking of Command Module *Charlie Brown* with Lunar Module *Snoopy*. The combined spacecraft entered lunar orbit on 21 May, following which astronauts Tom Stafford and Gene Cernan floated into the Lunar Module, leaving John Young to fly the Command Module solo around the moon. The two craft undocked, then *Snoopy* descended toward the scarred lunar surface, finally flying just nine miles above the Sea of Tranquility. The descent stage was jettisoned and the ascent stage rose to rendezvous with Young aboard *Charlie Brown*. There were gyration problems, and Stafford had to fly the LM through some difficult maneuvers, but they finally docked, and after the crew had transferred, the LM's ascent stage was jettisoned. The three astronauts completed a final lunar orbit, and then began the long flight home. Apollo 10 had blazed a trail to the moon, and it was confirmed that Apollo 11 would follow as the first lunar landing.

The flight of Apollo 11 stands as one of the greatest achievements in human history and fulfilled the pledge made by President Kennedy back in 1961 to land a man on the moon and return him safely to the Earth. Launched on 16 July 1969, astronauts Neil Armstrong, Buzz Aldrin, and Mike Collins flew to the moon aboard Command Module *Columbia*. Armstrong and Aldrin then transferred to Lunar Module *Eagle* for the final descent to the moon, and on 20 July Neil Armstrong became the first person to ever set foot on another world. Watched by hundreds of millions of people back on Earth, Armstrong planted his booted left foot in the lunar soil and proudly stated, "That's one small step for a man—one giant leap for mankind."

It had cost $24 billion and the lives of eight American astronauts, but the moon race was effectively at an end, while mankind's greatest-ever scientific undertaking had been accomplished ahead of time.

§

In May 1991, three decades after Alan Shepard's suborbital flight first set America on a path to the moon, two thousand people solemnly gathered at the Kennedy Space Center. They were there to dedicate a four-story, polished wall called Space Mirror, a unique combination of science and art, which had been designated a National Memorial by Congress and President George H. W. Bush. Several dozen astronauts and 123 family members of the men whose names were etched into the memorial attended. All wore a red rose in remembrance of lost ones.

Shortly after the *Challenger* tragedy in 1986, a competition was held to design a memorial, which would be sited at the Kennedy Space Center in Florida. A total of 750 entries were received, and in January 1988 a judging panel selected the winning design, created by architects Holt, Hinshaw, Pfau, and Jones of San Francisco.

The Space Mirror stands 42.5 feet high and 50 feet wide, with ninety-three mirror-finished black granite panels, each weighing five hundred pounds. At the time of the monument's dedication, the names of fifteen U.S. astronauts had been carved through the two-inch-thick panels. These names are illuminated from behind by mirrors reflecting the sun's rays through the letters as the monument, constructed on a computer-controlled pedestal, tilts and rotates slowly to track the sun across the sky. The letter spaces are filled with a crystal-clear acrylic minutely roughened on the front side to diffuse the light. At night, and on overcast days, powerful artificial lights illuminate the astronauts' names. The impression one gets is that the names are emblazoned in the heavens.

Facing the Space Mirror is a smaller granite structure into which the following inscription has been cut: "Whenever mankind has sought to conquer new frontiers there have been those who have given their lives for the cause. This Astronauts Memorial, dedicated May 9, 1991 is a tribute to American men and women who have made the ultimate sacrifice believing the conquest of space is worth the risk of life."

Fifteen families were in attendance on that day. They represented seven of the astronauts who died prior to the moon landings, the seven crew members of space shuttle *Challenger*, and Manley "Sonny" Carter, who had flown as a mission specialist on STS-33 and had died the previous month in the crash of a commuter plane.

Vice President Dan Quayle, who at that time headed the National Space Council, declared in his speech that the mirror was "a reminder that these were pioneers who led America into space, and America is there to stay."

Some family members wept, while others struggled to hold back tears as they were summoned one at a time up to the Space Mirror. Many took the opportunity to embrace or shake hands with astronaut Gene Cernan, the last man to walk on the moon. Once there they all stood quietly, holding hands, until the last family member had joined the gathering.

Following this, Dan Quayle placed a wreath at the base of the mirror. Fifteen doves were then released into the Florida skies, and with precise timing four T-38 jets piloted by NASA astronauts scheduled to fly on shuttle mission STS-42 ripped overhead in the "missing man" formation. Sonny Carter had been scheduled to be part of that commemorative formation before he was killed.

Beth Williams was there with daughters Catherine and Jane Dee. Beth had been pregnant at the time her husband was killed, so Jane Dee had never been held in the arms of her astronaut father. When she was asked how she felt after the ceremony, Jane Dee's considered response was, "It brings back a bunch of old baggage, but it's not necessarily bad. It's a little sad—it's happy and it's proud." Nearly a decade later, Jane Dee reflected on the event and her father's memory:

*The day of the dedication of the Astronaut's Memorial was indeed one of the best days I can remember for the Williams family. Most members from Dad's side of the family, some from Mom's side, and extended family were gathered to celebrate and honor my dad. Over the years my mom and grandmother have always taken care to keep his memory an essential part of the family, but this was an occasion to put into perspective his contribution to and sacrifices for the space program. I have always known of his sense of humor, his southern gentility, and his enormous capacity for joy. People who knew him have always been generous with their time and sharing their C.C. anecdotes (of which there is a seemingly limitless supply) to give me this glimpse of the kind of man he was. My sister was a baby and I was not yet born when he died. Certainly, things would have been different had he lived. But to be honest, it is difficult to miss what you never had, and I cannot imagine a better childhood. My mother and her formidable strength saw to that. I would like to think that he is proud of her and the two independent girls she raised.*

Catherine Williams was less than a year old when her father died, but the commemoration day at KSC also meant a lot to her:

*I was elated to be at the memorial dedication. It was a beautiful day and I was sitting next to my mom and paternal grandmother listening to a stream of dignitaries pay homage to my father. I was thinking that although I was only a baby when he died, my father was and is a definite presence in my life. He was such a good role model and lived by a simple philosophy—work hard, be dedicated to your goals, and have a sense of humor. I have dutifully followed this with great success. As the ceremony continued, I began to think about all of the things he missed . . . including my recent college graduation. I could not help but think that my father would be thrilled and beaming with pride over how his little family had survived and excelled. I knew that he would be proud of my academic accomplishments, wry wit, independent nature, and the fact that I look just like him. I also thought he would be pleased that I have a wonderful relationship with my mother, I am considerate of others, I play fair, and I always write thank-you notes. He certainly would love the fact that his wife and daughters adore his mother and have remained close to her. He would undoubtedly rejoice that both of his daughters had grown up to be smart, well adjusted, and, most importantly, happy young women who love and respect him. That glorious day as we honored my father, I was intensely proud . . . both of him and my strong little family.*

Beth Williams is also proud that her husband's name is there for all to see. "I love the memorial," she told me. "I especially appreciated all of the effort and consideration of the people who made it happen."

Ed White III and his sister Bonnie were also there, and Ed reflected on the loss of his father:

> With a tragedy like that there is a sort of denial phase of not wanting to believe it happened. That phase for my family lasted a period of time, maybe five years. My sister would probably say a different period of time. Certainly missing my father was a difficult thing. I was happy that I was old enough to have great memories, that I still have—vivid recollections up to this day. I would talk about them with my sister, and my mother—we had lots of conversations about Dad. Just remembering the good moments. Certainly the Gemini 4 flight, and reliving that as a positive.
>
> The big thing for me that I really felt good about finally facing was that the Apollo 1 disaster was a turning point for the program. The program was moving very fast in the race. Corners were cut here and there, decisions were made for speed versus safety in engineering matters. So the accident allowed time to get back on a timetable that was probably better in the long run for the program. I'm sure everybody would agree on that. It was a turning point. Going to the moon was a tremendous accomplishment in the 1960s, based on the fact that we had to develop the technology to do it.

Scott Grissom was sixteen years old when his father died in the Apollo 1 spacecraft on Launch Pad 34, but for him the years have not diminished the pride he feels for him and his accomplishments, and for what he might have achieved. Here are his thoughts:

> I'm extremely proud that he had already been told that the first lunar landing mission would most likely be his flight . . . He was to be the commander on it, and that's where he should have been. He had been doing a great deal of the work and putting in the effort to get there. He should have had the first ride and been the first person to step on the moon.
>
> I think it has been said best already: "They would never have gotten to the moon without Gus Grissom." I can't remember which book I read this in but I got a big kick out of that because they would have never got there without him. I think that's how it ought to be recorded.

On that Florida day the fifteen names on the memorial read:

> Theodore C. Freeman
> Elliot M. See, Jr.
> Charles A. Bassett II

*Clifton C. Williams, Jr.*
*Virgil "Gus" Grissom*
*Edward H. White II*
*Roger B. Chaffee*
*Francis "Dick" Scobee*
*Michael J. Smith*
*Ellison S. Onizuka*
*Judith A. Resnik*
*Ronald E. McNair*
*S. Christa McAuliffe*
*Gregory B. Jarvis*
*Manley "Sonny" Carter*

Jeannie Bassett recalls being taken aback when she first learned that Charlie's name was to be cut in stone on the monument, as she wasn't quite sure how she would react to the tribute. After more than two decades she felt that such recognition was long overdue, and she was beset with some trepidation. Nevertheless she took her children, Karen and Peter, to the laying of the cornerstone of the Mirror on 11 October 1989, and her concerns were eased. During this ceremony family members representing the astronauts were asked to insert gold stars in a large bronze plaque, which serves as the memorial's cornerstone. Engraved on the plaque are the words, "To those who gave their lives to bring the stars a little closer." The memorial was actually dedicated the day her second husband, Will, who had been diagnosed with leukemia, had his first session of chemotherapy. Despite many colliding emotions, she says the Mirror is a wonderful monument to the fallen astronauts:

> *Karen and Peter went, as did their godparents, Lenene and George Andre. I didn't see it until the addition of Mike Adams—who was a good friend of Charlie's—and Bob Lawrence. I'd often been immensely disappointed that Charlie's many achievements, and even his astronaut career, have never been fully recognized. So many times the only mention of his name in published histories of* NASA *(and even astronaut autobiographies) concerns the fact of his death and the impact it had on the Gemini program. The lack of true recognition by* NASA *and others who failed to acknowledge my husband and the others who died—that's what had really hurt deep down for all those years. However, despite my hesitation my first impression of the Mirror was one of pleasant surprise. From a distance it rather resembles the screen of a drive-in movie theatre, and as I neared it I could actually see the names shining through. Then, as we walked up to the monument some clouds obscured the sun and only patches shone on the Mirror. For that one fleeting moment Charlie's name was beaming through, alone. It took my breath away.*

Karen Bassett says that the Mirror provided her with a very special gift:

*I have glimpses, shadowed memories of Dad's smile, the feel of his arms, his whiskers on my cheek. I have stronger memories of C.C. Williams and the girls, and times with families, neighbors and friends. In the wake of the Apollo 1 fire and C.C.'s accident, it almost seemed that losing a father, young and smart, had a certain inevitability. He was gone. It seemed that a lot of them were. After we moved from Houston, we maintained loose ties to that world, but in time we lost track of many of the "NASA family." Somewhere in all of it, I locked it all away, an eight-year-old's memories of Daddy safely stored.*

*I read about the Space Mirror in an in-flight magazine in 1989. I called to find out if Dad's name would be listed too, and when the woman on the other end of the line said "Oh yes," I was delighted, but speechless. I just hung up. Several months later Mom called to tell me that they were building a memorial at the Cape.*

*We flew out for the groundbreaking ceremony. For the first time since we left Houston, I found myself wrapped in the good company of people who had known Dad. It was like settling into a familiar nest. That feeling only deepened at the dedication. Everyone was there, it seemed, and so many of them had an anecdote—they were eager to share tales of high adventures, hard work and great times. We laughed, and, when alone, cried. It was wonderful and overwhelming. It was the first time in years that I had seen most of them. After the initial flurry of "hellos" and "how are you's?" we settled in to remember and, rather than mourn, to wistfully celebrate all that our fathers and friends had been. I began the slow process of "building" a new understanding of who Dad was—about tradition, and dedication, and courage (and its costs), and humor, and kindness, and compassion, and frustration, and . . . I learned so much from them all. In time, Dad became more whole to me.*

*Since the dedication, I find myself sitting more comfortably with Dad's memory, and memories of Ted and C.C. too. Faith Freeman and I see each other often, and still hold hands when the painful parts of our lives get too close. We were, and are, so lucky. Now we are able to laugh at stories of their fun rather than mourn our loss. The tribute to our fathers makes me proud to have known them all, and especially proud to be Charlie Bassett's daughter. As I said . . . the Mirror provided me with a very special gift: one I didn't expect. One I could never have imagined. But one for which I am grateful beyond words.*

Faith Freeman Hershap was also at the dedication, holding hands most of the time with Karen Bassett for emotional support. Here is how she remembers the event:

*We had gone the night before for a little practice run of the ceremony. The next morning we came back and in a nearby building met Dan Quayle and had our pictures taken with him. When it was time we moved outside and I was absolutely taken back to see hundreds upon hundreds of people in the viewing square, which had been empty the day before. It was breathtaking, and I have to say that my first thought was that all these people were here to thank me, and to thank all of the family members, for the sacrifice we had made for the space program. It was an acknowledgment that the families of these men had also been a vital part of the whole effort. I was just washed with emotion.*

*After we were seated I could see people such as Gene Cernan, Tom Stafford and John Glenn—friends of my family I hadn't seen for years. The warmth of these men towards us that day was just beautiful, and it brought back many strong feelings.*

*I have to say the part that was most special for me personally actually occurred at a reception afterwards. We'd been talking to a few people for a while when Karen Bassett and my husband and I somehow drifted over to the Space Mirror, which was situated behind a little chain barrier to prevent people from getting too close. That's when I decided I just had to touch my father's name—it was a very powerful feeling. So I held Karen's hand and together we climbed over the chain and I was able to touch his name on that beautiful memorial. At that moment I just felt so connected to him; my thoughts were of him and how proud I was of him, and how honored I felt to be acknowledged for his life.*

These days Sheryl Chaffee Marshall remains very close to the nation's space program, as an administrative specialist for NASA at the Kennedy Space Center. Her memories of that eminent and moving occasion are still quite vivid:

*The night before the dedication my husband, two sons, mother, father's parents, a cousin and his family and I attended the dry run of the ceremony and had our first opportunity to view the memorial. At night, the memorial was one of the most beautiful sights I had seen. The lights were shining on it and the whole memorial glowed. The names of the fallen astronauts gleamed on the reflection of the night sky in the granite. The rehearsal was private and only family members and special guests were there. I was so glad to be able to have my first viewing of the memorial without the crowds and the press around. For me this day was long coming and I was so proud to see all the families there, and the support of the community. I was proud of what the Foundation had done to honor our loved ones, and was ready to see these men and women recognized for their contributions and sacrifice to the space program.*

*On the day of the dedication, even with support from my family and other family members, I remember being very nervous about the whole event and also very excited. I had been involved with the Astronaut Memorial Foundation (AMF) almost since its beginning. Because I lived in Florida close to the location of the memorial, the AMF called on me, along with Mr. and Mrs. Jarvis, many times to represent the family members at benefit runs, formal dinners, and ground breakings. I knew what it was like to be interviewed by the press and to be questioned by inquisitive space fans. In the past, I had dealt with these events mostly by myself. This dedication day was different; we were all here together to support each other. We had a common background. We were all familiar with the space program and all had lost someone to the program. Each of our lives had been changed and, on this day, we were once again reminded of our loss.*

*For many years since the Apollo 1 fire I had been trying to find peace in what had happened to my father, and with the fact that I thought these men had been forgotten. This dedication was a beginning for me, a step to my new life. I wanted to be able to remember my father's life and not just his death. After the dedication other events happened to help me find that peace. The thirtieth anniversary of the fire was remembered at a ceremony held in front of the memorial, and then again at Complex 34. The Apollo Saturn V Center at the KSC Visitor Center included the Apollo 1 crew in one of their shows, and the Astronaut Hall of Fame inducted my father into the hall. Finally, I was at peace. People did remember my father's, Gus's and Ed's sacrifice, and they would be remembered whenever someone sees their names glowing on the granite background of the Astronaut Memorial.*

*Since the day of the dedication I have visited the memorial many times. Some changes have been made to the site. In early 2000, the AMF added another granite wall that displays a picture of each of the fallen astronauts and a short biography of their life. This added a personal touch to the memorial and shows to people that these men and women were only human, had families, and were proud of the nation's space program. I am very honored to know that my father's life will be remembered for many years to come.*

As related earlier by Jeannie Bassett, two names were subsequently added to the Space Mirror, bringing the total to seventeen. The more recent additions are X-15 pilot Michael J. Adams and MOL astronaut Robert H. Lawrence. Adams, who had qualified for USAF astronaut status by flying higher than fifty miles in the X-15, was killed on 15 November 1967 during his seventh flight in the space-penetrating research aircraft when it broke apart at high altitude. Lawrence, a USAF Manned Orbiting Laboratory astronaut, and the first African American chosen for spaceflight training, died on 8 December 1967 when his F-104 Starfighter crashed and burned on a runway at Edwards AFB. As recently as 1 February 2003, seven additional names became suddenly and tragically eligible to be immortalized on the memorial. The names of *Columbia* astronauts Rick Husband, William McCool, David Brown, Laurel Clark, Michael Anderson, Kalpana Chawla, and Ilan Ramon will join those of their colleagues who gave their lives in our relentless quest for knowledge and in the name of human exploration.

With names such as Adams, Lawrence, McAuliffe, and Jarvis on the Space Mirror, none of whom were ever NASA astronauts, and Sonny Carter, who was killed off duty in the crash of a commercial aircraft, one would still have to feel a profound sadness at the omission of one man who would have flown to the moon—Major Edward Givens. His three grown children were not invited to the dedication ceremony, and they have to live with the knowledge that their father's many contributions to NASA, and to the history of spaceflight, are not considered valid or valued by the decision makers within the Astronaut Memorial Foundation. Ed Givens died as a NASA astronaut, giving his life for the space program and his country, while his children lost a beloved father. For these reasons alone he deserves to be recognized rather than overlooked.

Whatever problems might exist in suitably recognizing some American astronauts and their achievements, it seems those difficulties pale in relation to the unsatisfactory and even disrespectful way in which some, if not all, of the eight deceased cosmonauts are remembered. Dutch researcher Bert Vis has visited the gravesites of six of the eight cosmonauts to pay his respects, and he is mostly struck by the significant contrast between the last resting places of the heroes in the Kremlin Wall and the nondescript graves of those who did not have the good fortune to fly in space. Vis shares the following observations:

> While Valentin Bondarenko's grave is now identified as that of a cosmonaut after decades of anonymity, few people outside his family, if any, ever visit it. The fact that Grigori Nelyubov was ever a cosmonaut is, in all probability, unknown to anyone who visits the cemetery in Zaporozhe. There's absolutely no reference to it on his tombstone, yet both these men were in the first cosmonaut detachment—the equivalent to America's Mercury 7.
>
> Pavel Belyayev's grave in the famous Novodevichy cemetery in Moscow is still pointed out to tourists as that of a pioneering cosmonaut, but they are usually more interested in the monuments of other famous Russians such as Nikita Khrushchev and Mikhail Gorbachev's wife, Raisa.
>
> As was the case in the Soviet era, the plaque-marked graves of the five cosmonauts in the Kremlin Wall are still shielded from the public by dozens of policemen, and in a way, Yuri Gagarin, Vladimir Komarov, and Vladislav Volkov are less approachable now than they were after they first

37. The crew of Apollo 15 placed a plaque bearing fourteen names of lost space explorers in the lunar soil. A small tin figurine known as *The Fallen Astronaut* has been deliberately toppled in front of the plaque. (NASA)

*flew in space. Although I haven't yet been able to pay my personal respects to Georgy Dobrovolsky and Viktor Patsayev, who are also memorialized in the Kremlin Wall, I am sure the situation is no different. Sometimes a policeman can be persuaded to allow foreigners a brief walk up to the wall, but only after a hefty bribe. I often draw a mental comparison between this situation and the serenity of Arlington Cemetery, the last, respected resting place for most of America's astronauts.*

Despite the tide of euphoria associated with the early days of cosmonauts and space travel, most Russians today are quite indifferent to those past achievements. With endemic poverty, a brutal civil war, and an uncertain future to oppress them, they couldn't care less about what their country is doing in space. Not only that, but they strongly resent the massive costs associated with being a partner in the International Space Station, and they regard sending cosmonauts on missions to this outpost as an unnecessary and wasteful political expediency.

As shadows lengthen across a formerly great nation, those once cast by its revered heroes of the cosmos are rapidly and ineluctably fading.

# References

Aldrin, Buzz, and Malcolm McConnell. *Men from Earth*. New York: Bantam Books, 1989.

Aldrin, Buzz, and Wayne Warga. *Return to Earth*. New York: Random House, 1973.

"America's 6,000-Mile Walk in Space." *National Geographic*, September 1965.

"Apollo: Can Do?" *Newsweek*, 22 May 1967.

"Apollo's Final Seconds." *Newsweek*, 13 January 1967.

"The Apollo Tragedy." *Newsweek*, 6 February 1967.

Armstrong, Neil, Michael Collins, and Edwin Aldrin. *First on the Moon*. Boston: Little Brown, 1970.

Associated Press. *Footprints on the Moon*. Manuscript by John Barbour. New York: The Associated Press, 1969.

"Astronauts Grissom, White, and Chaffee." *Time*, 3 February 1967.

"Astronauts Speak Out on Controversial Contracts." *Newsweek*, 2 November 1963.

Atkinson, Joseph D., Jr., and Jay Shafritz. *The Real Stuff: A History of NASA 's Astronaut Recruitment Policy*. Westport CT: Greenwood Publishing Group, 1985.

Atkinson, Rick. *The Long Gray Line*. Boston: Houghton Mifflin, 1989.

Bassett, Charles A. Letter to Edy Maxim, 17 November 1952. Private collection of Jeannie Bassett.

Beebe, Richard, and Ralph Seabrease. "Lewes Graduate Aims for Moon." *Pirates' Log*. Rehoboth Beach DE: Lewes High School, December 1963.

Benedict, Joy. "Story of Three Wives: Five Years after Apollo Tragedy." *Today Magazine*, 27 January 1972.

Biever, Richard. "Our Gus: Remembering Indiana's Last Astronaut." *Electric Consumer Magazine*, June 1997.

Boos, Rick. "Life without Dad: An Interview with Scott Grissom." *Quest: The History of Spaceflight Quarterly* 5, no. 2 (summer 1996).

Borman, Frank, and Robert J. Serling. *Countdown: An Autobiography*. New York: W. Morrow, 1988.

Boyne, Walter J. *Beyond the Wild Blue: A History of the United States Air Force, 1947–1997*. New York: St. Martin's Press, 1997.

Bulban, Erwin J. "New Astronauts to Pilot Gemini, Apollo." *Aviation Week and Space Technology*, 24 September 1962.

Burgess, Colin. "Altered Courses: Tragedy and Spaceflight History." *Spaceflight*, July 1997.

———. "Fallen Astronaut: The Life and Death of Edward Givens." *Spaceflight*, March 1999.

Burrows, William E. *The Infinite Journey: Eyewitness Accounts of NASA and the Age of Space*. New York: Discovery Books, 2000.

———. *This New Ocean: The Story of the First Space Age*. New York: Random House, 1998.

Cadet Records of Edward H. White II, June 1952. Office of the Dean., U.S. Military Academy, West Point NY.

"The Capsule Fire Flares Up Again." *Life*, 12 September 1971.

Cassutt, Michael. *Who's Who in Space*. New York: Macmillan, 1993.

———. *Who's Who in Space*. New York: Macmillan Library Reference USA, 1999.

———. *Who's Who in Space: The First Twenty-five Years*. Boston: G. K. Hall, 1987.

Catalog of the United States Military Academy, 1950–51. USMA Special Collection, U.S. Military Academy, West Point NY.

Catchpole, John. "The Final Quest for *Liberty Bell 7*." *Spaceflight*, December 1999.

———. "The Quest for *Liberty Bell 7*." *Spaceflight*, September 1999.

Cernan, Eugene, and Don Davis. *The Last Man on the Moon: Astronaut Eugene Cernan and America's Race in Space.* New York: St. Martin's Press, 1999.

Chaffee, Roger B. Letter to John ("Pop") Stair, 4 April 1966. Private collection.

Chaikin, Andrew. *A Man on the Moon: The Voyages of the Apollo Astronauts.* New York: Viking, 1994.

Chappell, Carl. *Seven Minus One: The Story of Gus Grissom.* Mitchell IN: New Frontier Publishing, 1968.

Chrysler, C. Donald, and Don L. Chaffee. *On Course to the Stars: The Roger B. Chaffee Story as Told to Donald C. Chrysler by Don L. Chaffee and Family.* Grand Rapids MI: Kregel Publications, 1968.

Collins, Martin J., and the NASA Division of Space History. *Space Race: The US-USSR Competition to Reach the Moon.* Rohnvert Park Pomegranate, Smithsonian Institution Press, and National Air and Space Museum, 1999.

Collins, Michael. *Carrying the Fire: An Astronaut's Journeys.* New York: Farrar, Straus, and Giroux, 1974.

———. *Liftoff: The Story of America's Adventure in Space.* New York: Grove Press, 1988.

Compton, William David. *Where No Man Has Gone Before: A History of Apollo Lunar Exploration Missions.* Washington DC: National Aeronautics and Space Administration, Office of Management, Scientific and Technical Information Division, 1989.

Cortright, Edgar M., ed. *Apollo Expeditions to the Moon.* Washington DC: Scientific and Technical Information Office, National Aeronautics and Space Administration, 1975.

"Crewmen for the First Apollo Mission." *Aerojet-General Booster*, September 1966.

Cunningham, R. Walter, and Mickey Herskowitz. *The All-American Boys.* New York: Macmillian, 1977.

"Dedication of Edward H. White Avenue of States" (press release). St. Petersburg, FL: St. Petersburg District Council, 14 May 1967.

"Dedication of Space Research Laboratory." Souvenir program. Ann Arbor: University of Michigan, June 1965.

Dethloff, Henry. *Suddenly Tomorrow Came—: A History of the Johnson Space Center.* Washington DC: National Aeronautics and Space Administration; Houston: Lyndon B. Johnson Space Center, 1993.

Dickey, Beth. "Grissom Wins the Battle." *Air and Space Magazine*, August/September 1967.

Doolan, Kate. "We've Got a Fire!" *Electronics Australia*, January 2000.

Dryden, Hugh. "How We Plan to Put Men on the Moon." *National Geographic*, March 1964.

Duke, Charlie, and Dotty Duke. *Moonwalker.* Nashville: Oliver-Nelson Books, 1990.

*Echo Magazines* (Western High School Class of 1948), ed. Iris Coopersmith. Washington DC: Western High School, 1999–2000.

"Elliot See: Kings Point Astronaut." *The Kings Pointer* (U.S. Merchant Marine Academy publication), October 1962.

Endler, James R. *Other Leaders, Other Heroes: West Point's Legacy to America beyond the Field of Battle.* Westport CT: Praegar Publishing, 1998.

Fallaci, Oriana. *If the Sun Dies.* Trans. Pamela Swinglehurst. New York: Antheneum, 1966.

"The Fallen Astronauts." *Life*, 10 February 1967.

"Fireproofing Apollo." *Time*, 1 September 1967.

"First Manned Apollo Launch" (NASA press release). Washington DC: NASA Historical Reference Collection, NASA Headquarters, History Office, 28 October 1966.

Fleming, Glenn B. "No Go: The Dark Side of the Moon." *Spaceflight*, July 1999.

"For the Heroes, Salute and Farewell." *Life*, 10 February 1967.

Furniss, Tim. *One Small Step: The Apollo Missions, the Astronauts, the Aftermath: A Twenty-Year Perspective.* Somerset, England: Haynes Publishing Group, 1989.

———. *Manned Spaceflight Log.* New York: Jane's Publishing, 1983.

"Gemini 4 Extra Vehicular Activity—A Walk in Space" (NASA press release). Washington DC: NASA Historical Reference Collection, NASA Headquarters, History Office, July 1965.

"Gemini 4." NASA Fact Sheet 291-B. Washington DC: NASA Headquarters, History Office, 1965.

Gilruth, Robert R. "The Making of an Astronaut." *National Geographic*, January 1965.

Gordon, Richard. Interview by Francis French. Santa Monica Museum of Flying, California, 4 May 2001. (Interview was incorporated into Francis French. "Apollo—The Best of Times." *Spaceflight*, January 2002.)

Gray, Mike. *Angle of Attack: Harrison Storms and the Race to the Moon*. New York: W. W. Norton, 1992.

Grissom, Betty, and Henry Still. *Starfall*. New York: Crowell, 1974.

Grissom, Gus. "Three Times a Command Pilot." *Indianapolis Star Magazine*, 13 November 1966.

Hall, Al, ed., and the general subject editors of Specialty Publications Division. *Petersen's Book of Man in Space*. 5 vols. Los Angeles: Petersen Publishing Company, 1974.

Hamblin, Dora Jane. "The Fire and Fate Have Left Eight Widows." *Life*, 26 January 1968.

Harland, David Michael. *Exploring the Moon: The Apollo Expeditions*. London and New York: Springer; Chicester, England: Praxis Publishing, 1999.

Hengeveld, Ed. "Apollo: Vacuum Chamber Tests." *Spaceflight*, March and April 2000.

Hooper, Gordon R. *The Soviet Cosmonaut Team: A Comprehensive Guide to the Men and Women of the Soviet Manned Space Programme*. Lowestoft, Suffolk, England: GRH Publications, 1990.

"How Soon the Moon?" *Time*, 14 April 1967.

*Howitzer: Class of 1952*. United States Corps of Cadets Special Collections, U.S. Military Academy, West Point NY.

*Howitzer: Class of 1967*. United States Corps of Cadets Special Collections, U.S. Military Academy, West Point NY.

"Inquest on Apollo." *Time*, 10 February 1967.

Irwin, James B., and William A. Emerson. *To Rule the Night: The Discovery Voyage of Astronaut Jim Irwin*. Boston: G. K. Hall, 1973.

"James Blair White." January 2000. <http://www.pownetwork.org>.

"Jammed Controls Cited in T-38A Crash." *Aviation Week and Space Technology*, 9 September 1968.

Johnson, Lyndon B. Letter to Mrs. Edward H. White II, 31 January 1967. Washington DC: NASA Headquarters, History Office.

Kelly, Fred. *America's Astronauts and Their Indestructible Spirit*. Blue Ridge Summit PA: Aero, 1986.

Kenney, Nathaniel T. "Where Falcons Wear Air Force Blue." *National Geographic*, June 1959.

Kranz, Gene. *Failure Is Not an Option: Mission Control from Mercury to Apollo 13 and Beyond*. New York: Simon and Schuster, 2000.

Lattimer, Dick. *"All We Did Was Fly to the Moon"* [the astronauts' words, as told to Dick Lattimer]. Alachua FL: Whispering Eagle Press, 1983.

Lewis, Richard S. *Appointment on the Moon: The Inside Story of America's Space Venture*. New York: Viking Press, 1968.

"Lost, Found, and Foundered." *Air and Space Magazine*, August/September 1999.

Lovell, Jim, and Jeffrey Kluger. *Lost Moon: The Perilous Voyage of Apollo 13*. Boston: Houghton Mifflin, 1994.

*Lucky Bag: Class of 1952*. U.S. Naval Academy Archives, Annapolis.

Malanowski, Jamie. "Too Many Brave Souls." *Time*, 24 November 1997.

Mansfield, John M. *Man on the Moon*. London: Constable, 1969.

McDivitt, James. "What a Real Thrill It Was to Zap Up." *Life*, 18 June 1965.

"The McDivitt-White Flight." *Time*, 11 June 1965.

"McDivitt, White Named Prime Crew for Second Manned Gemini Flight." *Space News Roundup* (NASA employee newsletter), 5 August 1964.

McLintock, Gordon. Letter to John K. Duckworth, M.D., 11 July 1966. Private collection of Sally See Kneuven.

McWilliams, Bill. *A Return to Glory: The Untold Story of Honor, Dishonor, and Triumph at the United States Military Academy, 1950–53.* Lynchburg VA: Warwick House Publishers, 2000.

Mellberg, William F. *Moon Missions: Man's First Voyages to Another World.* Plymouth MI: Plymouth Press, 1997.

Murray, Charles A., and Catherine Bly Cox. *Apollo: The Race to the Moon.* New York: Simon and Schuster, 1989.

"NASA Training Astronaut Speaks to Regiments." *The Kings Pointer* (U.S. Merchant Marine Academy publication), April 1963.

National Personnel Record Center, St. Louis. Career of Lt. Col. Edward Higgins White II, June 1994.

"The Nation Mourns a Fallen Knight." *Assembly.* United States Military Academy Association of Graduates, winter 1967.

"New Astronaut Candidates." *Aviation Week and Space Technology,* 23 November 1964.

Oberg, James E. "Phantoms of Space." *Space World Magazine,* January 1975.

———. *Red Star in Orbit.* New York: Random House, 1981.

———. *Uncovering Soviet Disasters: Exploring the Limits of Glasnost.* New York: Random House, 1988.

"Obituary, Edward Higgins White II." *Assembly.* United States Military Academy Association of Graduates, summer 1971.

O'Leary, Brian. *The Making of an Ex-Astronaut.* Boston: Houghton Mifflin, 1970.

"The Oxygen Question." *Time,* 10 February 1967.

"The Phillips Report." Washington DC: NASA Historical Reference Collection, NASA Headquarters, History Office, 19 December 1965. <http://www.hq.nasa.gov>.

Portree, David S. F., and Robert C. Trevine. "Walking to Olympus: An EVA Chronology." Washington DC: NASA Historical Reference Collection, NASA Headquarters, History Office, 1997.

"Rendezvous in St. Louis." *Time,* 11 March 1966.

Report of Apollo 204 Review Board. Washington DC: NASA Historical Reference Collection, NASA Headquarters, History Office, 1967.

Schefter, James L. *The Race: The Uncensored Story of How America Beat Russia to the Moon.* New York: Doubleday, 1999.

Schmidt, Robert. "Endless Flights: The Forgotten Astronaut and his Friends." *Kings Pointer Magazine* (U.S. Merchant Marine Academy publication), spring 1999.

Seamans, Robert C., Jr. *Aiming at Targets: The Autobiography of Robert C. Seamans, Jr.* Washington DC: NASA History Office, Office of Policy and Plans, NASA Headquarters, 1996.

See, Elliot, Jr. "How Much Light in Earthshine?" *Life,* 27 September 1963.

"Serving the Nation." U.S. Merchant Marine Academy brochure PK 99–01. Kings Point NY: U.S. Merchant Marine Academy archives.

Shatalov, V. A., and M. F. Rebrov. *Cosmonauts of the USSR: Reader for Senior Forms of Secondary Schools.* Moscow: Prosveshcheniye, 1980.

Shayler, David J. *Disasters and Accidents in Manned Spaceflight.* New York: Springer, 2000.

———. *NASA Astronaut Biographical Data Record Book: Group 3, the Fourteen.* Halesowen, England: Astro Info Service Publications, October 1982.

Shea, Joseph. "Flash Report for the Record" (memo to NASA Headquarters). Washington DC: NASA Headquarters, History Office, 27 January 1967.

Slayton, Donald K. "Deke," and Michael Cassutt. *Deke! U.S. Manned Space: From Mercury to the Shuttle.* New York: Forge, 1994.

Taylor, Maxwell D. "West Point: Its Objectives and Methods." USMA Special Collection, U.S. Military Academy, West Point NY, November 1947.

Thomas, Shirley. *The Apollo Fire and Investigation: Facts Not Considered.* Paris: International Astronautical Federation, 1996.

"Top Flying and Academic Awards." ARDC *Newsreview*, November 1958.

"Twelve Selected for Coming NASA Missions" (NASA press release). Washington DC: NASA Historical Reference Collection, NASA Headquarters, History Office, 21 March 1966.

U.S. Merchant Marine Academy circular 66–5. Kings Point NY: U.S. Merchant Marine Academy archives.

Walker, Howell. "The Making of a West Pointer." *National Geographic*, May 1952.

Wallwork, Jim. "We Follow Those Close Behind You." *Assembly.* United States Military Academy Association of Graduates, July/August 1997.

Weise, Otis L. *The U.S. Astronauts and Their Families.* N.p.: World Book Encyclopedia Science Service, 1965.

"West Pointers in Space." *Assembly.* United States Military Academy Association of Graduates, winter 1969.

White, Edward H., II. "I Felt Red, White, and Blue All Over." *Life*, 18 June 1965.

———. Letter to Mrs. John F. Kennedy, 1963. Private collection.

White, Edward H., III. Interview by Francis French. Santa Monica Museum of Flying, California, 4 May 2001.

Wilford, John Noble. *We Reach the Moon.* New York: Norton, 1969.

Wilhelms, Don. *To a Rocky Moon: A Geologist's History of Lunar Exploration.* Tucson: University of Arizona Press, 1993.

Wolfe, Tom. *The Right Stuff.* New York: Farrar, Straus, and Giroux, 1979.

Yeager, Chuck, and Leo Janos. *Yeager: An Autobiography.* Boston: G. K. Hall, 1985.

Zimmerman, Robert. *Genesis: The Story of Apollo 8: The First Manned Flight to Another World.* New York: Four Walls Eight Windows, 1998.

Zorino, Mary. *Detailed Biographies of the Apollo 204 Crew—Epilogue.* Washington DC: NASA Headquarters, History Office, 8 January 1997. <http://www.hq.nasa.gov>.

## Newspapers

*Ann Arbor News*, 28 January 1967.

*Baltimore Sun*, 2 March 1966.

*Rehoboth Beach Delaware Coast Press*, 31 October 1964.

*Houston Chronicle*, 31 October 1964–6 June 1967.

*Houston Post*, 1 November 1964–9 June 1967.

*Los Angeles Times*, 2 November 1964 and 7 June 1967.

*Mobile Press Register*, 19 October 1963–18 August 1971.

NASA *Roundup* (Houston), 11 November 1964–21 June 1968.

*New York Great Neck Record*, 3 March 1966.

*New York Times*, 19 October 1963–7 October 1967.

*Quanah (Texas) Tribune-Chief*, 6 July 1967–19 November 1998.

*Salisbury (Maryland) Times*, 2 November 1966.

*St. Louis Globe-Democrat*, 1 March 1966.

*St. Louis Post-Dispatch*, 28 February 1966–27 May 1966.

*Tallahassee Democrat*, 6 October 1967–21 July 1999.

*Wilmington Evening Journal*, 17 April 1963 and 2 November 1964.

# Index